Problems and Projects

Nelson Goodman

PROBLEMS
and
PROJECTS

THE BOBBS-MERRILL COMPANY, INC.
Indianapolis and New York

To my mother
Sarah Elizabeth (Woodbury) Goodman
1874–1964

Contents

VIII
Induction

IX
Likeness

X
Puzzle

CONTENTS

Introduction

This book contains most of my previously published papers, excerpts from my three earlier books, and some half-dozen items not before published. These papers have been gathered into chapters according to subject, and a new foreword supplied for each chapter.

The forewords have varying functions: to provide historical notes concerning the papers in the chapter or the problem they deal with; to relate these papers to each other, to other papers in the book, and to the current state of investigation of the problem; and sometimes to correct common misunderstandings or to carry investigation of the problem a step further. Thus while these forewords are primarily instruments of organization, they sometimes suggest new ideas.

Of my published papers omitted here, "The Calculus of Individuals and Its Uses" (with Henry S. Leonard) and several pieces on simplicity have been superseded by *The Structure of Appearance;* and "The Problem of Counterfactual Conditionals" has been used as the first chapter of *Fact, Fiction, and Forecast.* "Sequences" seemed not to fit anywhere, and "Graphs for Linguistics" is unsatisfactory.

On the other hand, I have included "The New Riddle of Induction" from *Fact, Fiction, and Forecast,* "Art and Authenticity" from *Languages of Art,* and—under the title "Talk of Time"— two sections from *Structure of Appearance.* All these deal with topics of rather wide interest and are easily understood apart from the books.

The papers included here vary in difficulty. Only a few, such as V,2, VI,1,2, and VII,1,2,3 call for technical training at the graduate level. All the rest should fall well within the competence of the advanced undergraduate student of philosophy; and at least half of these papers, such as most of those in the first three chapters, should give the elementary student or the serious layman no undue trouble.

Some supplementary readings are suggested at the end of each chapter except the first and last. These lists are partial and arbitrary but, together with references given in text and footnotes, provide some introduction to the bibliography of the topic in question. On some of these topics, such as induction, the literature is vast; on others, such as aboutness and simplicity, most of the literature is covered by the references and reading lists together.

The sources of the several papers making up the book are detailed in a list at the end; and acknowledgement is there made of permissions received. I am grateful to the editors and publishers who have granted such permission, and especially to my collaborators on one or more of these papers: W. V. Quine, Israel Scheffler, and Robert Schwartz. Many of the papers have been corrected or otherwise improved since first published. Graham Roupas did much of the editorial work for the present volume and made many valuable suggestions.

The cross-references in the forewords, text, and footnotes have seemed to me to make a subject index unnecessary, but a name index has been included.

The following abbreviations are often used in referring to my own books: *"SQ"* for *A Study of Qualities* (doctoral dissertation, Harvard University, 1941); *"SA"* for *The Structure of Appearance* (first edition 1951; second edition, The Bobbs-Merrill Co., Inc., Indianapolis, 1966); *"FFF"* for *Fact, Fiction, and Forecast* (first edition, 1955; second edition, Bobbs-Merrill, 1965); *"LA"* for *Languages of Art* (Bobbs-Merrill, 1968). Where there are two editions, reference is always to the second unless otherwise specified. References to parts of these books are italicized—*e.g.*, *"SA IV,3"* to distinguish them from references to the present book—*e.g.*, "IV,3".

The more problems, the more projects; the more projects, the more problems. Yet if there are more beginnings than endings in my work, I hope the reader may now and again have an intimation that not all problems of philosophy are immortal.

Harvard University

Problems and Projects

I

Philosophy

FOREWORD

That most of the items in this chapter are occasional papers is no accident. Except under the stimulus of special circumstance, I have been disinclined to discuss the problem of defining philosophy, its aims, and its methods; for although this is as legitimate a philosophical problem as any other, it has had more than its share of attention in recent times.

What I have written on the problem has usually been retrospective rather than prescriptive. To find out what philosophy is I have usually looked back upon how more specific problems have been attacked—by others and by me. Alone among the papers here, "The Way the World Is" points forward as well as backward, and foreshadows *Languages of Art*.

Statements from two of these papers may appear to contradict one another. In "The Revision of Philosophy", I say "what is wanted is a certain structural correspondence between the world of the system and the world of presystematic language", while in "The Way the World Is" I say "there is no such thing as the structure of the world for any system to conform or fail to conform to". But of course the structure of the world of presystematic language is simply a world-structure under one world-description and not the structure of the world independent of any description; and the correspondence asked for relates two world-descriptions rather than a description to such a world-in-itself.

Occasionally the objection is raised that to speak of descriptions of the world implies that there is such a thing as the world. One might as well point to pictures of Don Quixote to prove that there is one and only one such person. "Picture of Don Quixote" and

3

"description of the world" are one-place predicates and are better replaced by "Don-Quixote-picture" and "world-description" (see further below V,2; also III,4). Rather than there being one and only one Don Quixote, there is none; rather than there being one and only one world, there may be many. This does not mean that all world-descriptions are equally true; but it does raise the question what distinguishes true from false ones (see II,1).

More than once in the present chapter, I urge that isomorphism must replace intensional and even extensional identity as a criterion for constructional definition. In Chapter I of *The Structure of Appearance,* I argue this point more fully and explain in detail the appropriate variety of extensional isomorphism (see also IV,3 below). This reconception of the nature of explicative definition transforms or even resolves some philosophical issues; for an interesting example see the discussion of materialism and the mind-body problem by Lynn Foster.* Other aspects of definition, especially of theoretical terms, are briefly discussed in III,5b below.

In *SA* (Part Two), I do not include under "logic" the calculus of classes or the calculus of individuals, as I do in "Some Reflections on the Theory of Systems". The line between what is logic and what is not, as Quine has insisted, is quite arbitrary. In the book, there were advantages in confining the term "logic" to what is common to all the constructional systems under consideration; in the paper, for a more general audience, I conformed to what seemed to be the more common practice.

The two little talks concluding this chapter are just that. They are unlikely to be fully understood by those who did not know the Second World War and its aftermath. And the defense of analysis and blueberry pie will seem quaint in this age of dogma and drugs.

* Lynn V. Foster, *Constructionalism and the Contemporary Mind-Body Identity Debate,* Doctoral Thesis, Brandeis University, 1971.

1

The Revision of Philosophy

My title refers not to the reworking but more literally to the re-vision of philosophy—a new way of looking at philosophy, a new conception of its nature and objectives, and consequently a new appraisal of its methods and results. I am not concerned with the modification of what has been done by able philosophers from Thales on, but rather with a re-vision, in the sense explained, or a new version, of what has been done and is being done.

Let me hasten to say that this 'new vision' is not original with me, and that it is not even very new. It has been coming into our consciousness slowly over a long period; and it has, I think, been tacitly adopted for sometime past by those who have contributed most to philosophy. But it is often obscured by what even these same people say when they talk *about* philosophy; and it is almost never understood by those whose participation in philosophy consists solely in controversy. Thus I think it may be well to dust off this rather old new vision and hold it up once more to public view.

What follows below constitutes a paper written for a forthcoming volume on Carnap.[1] Although cast in the form of a discussion of the significance of Carnap's *Der Logische Aufbau der Welt*,[2] it deals almost entirely with the more general questions which must be answered before the significance of such a book can be appraised. Thus I am at the same time implicitly defending the point of view of, for example, my own book[3]—which, incidentally, contains an exposition and criticism of a considerable part of the *Aufbau*.

1. Evil Days for the *Aufbau*

The *Aufbau* is a crystallization of much that is widely regarded

1. *The Philosophy of Rudolf Carnap,* edited by Paul Schilpp, in preparation [LaSalle, Illinois: Open Court, 1963]. These sections are published here with Professor Schilpp's permission.

2. Rudolf Carnap, *Der Logische Aufbau der Welt* (Berlin, 1928).

3. *SA.*

5

as the worst in twentieth-century philosophy. It is an anathema to antiempirical metaphysicians and to alogical empiricists, to analytic Oxonians and to antianalytic Bergsonians, to those who would exalt philosophy above the sciences and to those who would abolish philosophy in favor of the sciences. A good part of current polemical writing in philosophical journals is directed against views found in virulent form in the *Aufbau*. The *Aufbau* stands pre-eminent as a horrible example.

My purpose here is to survey and appraise the charges against the *Aufbau*, and to set forth some convictions concerning the significance of the work. This virtually amounts to the unpromising, but welcome, task of defending the *Aufbau* against almost everybody, including Carnap himself—indeed, including a succession of Carnaps who have belittled this early work for different reasons at different times in the twenty-eight years since it was published. But I am more interested in the current atmosphere of opinion concerning the *Aufbau* than in what particular people have said at particular times; and my adversary, except where specifically named, is a composite figure encountered as often in conversation as in the journals.

2. Phenomenalism and the *Aufbau*

In place of the 'impressions' or 'simple ideas' of eighteenth-century British philosophy, Carnap based his system on total moments of experience—the *elementarerlebnisse*—in order to begin as nearly as possible with what he regards as unanalyzed and unprocessed experience. The system is plainly phenomenalistic, and phenomenalism has been under heavy and incessant attack.

The most popular objection is that phenomenalism is *incompletable*. No full and adequate account of the objective and intersubjective world of the sciences can be given, it is contended, upon a purely phenomenalistic basis. Carnap's own first disavowal[4] of the *Aufbau* expressed the conviction that a phenomenalistic system, unlike a physicalistic one, could not be all-embracing for science; and perhaps nothing else he has ever written has found such widespread agreement.

4. In "Die physikalische Sprache als Universalsprache der Wissenschaft", *Erkenntnis*, vol. 2 (1931), pp. 432–465.

The arguments commonly adduced to support the charge of the incompletability of phenomenalism cannot, in the nature of the case, be very cogent by themselves; for the thesis they are designed to prove is not precise enough, and there is available no developed body of theory within which a sound proof might be given. Proof that a complete system cannot be constructed on any phenomenalistic basis prerequires some precise delimitation of the class of phenomenalistic bases, a full statement of admissible methods of construction, and a clear conception of what constitutes completeness of the kind in question; and none of these requirements is easy to meet. Thus, for example, the argument that phenomenalism is incompletable because the infinite world of mathematics and the sciences cannot be accounted for upon a finite basis has at first sight the simple force of the statement that an infinite number of things cannot be made out of a finite number. But if we understand that the question is rather whether we can interpret in terms of statements about a finite number of entities all indispensable statements that *prima facie* refer to an infinite number of entities, the matter cannot be settled so easily.

On the other hand, the thesis that phenomenalism is incompletable hardly needs proof. Surely no complete system will be offered within any foreseeable length of time; and no other means of proving the possibility of completion is in prospect. The task of construction is so formidable, and the tendency to regard it as hopeless is so strong, that the presumption is all against the claim that any phenomenalistic system—or for that matter any system with a very narrow basis—is completable. Even without proof or clarification of the thesis that phenomenalism is incompletable, one is justified in accepting this thesis at least until the opposite is rendered more credible.

But if the thesis—proven or unproven—is accepted, what conclusion can be drawn from it? Usually phenomenalism is taken to be utterly discredited once its incompletability is acknowledged. It is just this step in the argument—a step commonly passed over as obvious—that I want to challenge. I am ready to maintain that the value of efforts to construct a system on a phenomenalistic or any other narrow basis is very little affected by whether or not the system can be completed. Euclid's geometry is not robbed of value by the fact that the circle cannot be squared by Euclidean means. Indeed, acceptance prior to Euclid of the impossibility of squaring the circle with compass and straightedge would not in the least have diminished the importance of developing Euclidean geometry; and it would not, I think, have been ground for turning attention solely to the discussion of the adequacy of various bases or to the development of geometry on a basis broader than Euclid's. Moreover, propositions affirming the Euclidean insolubility of certain problems could hardly have been precisely formulated or have been capable of proof except against the background of elaborated, even if incompletable, mathematical systems. But my point is not just that it was psychologically necessary or helpful to work in this way. What is accomplished in the incompletable system has permanent value when incorporated into a fuller system. Indeed after a system like Euclid's has been developed as far as possible, questions concerning what can be accomplished with even fewer means (*e.g.* without a straightedge or without a given postulate) often still have interest.

The analogy, I take it, is transparent. Incompletability by itself is no decisive objection against the attempt to build a system on a phenomenalistic basis. Only by positive efforts with severely restricted means can we make any progress in construction; only so can we discern the exact limitations of a basis and the exact supplementation needed. And what we achieve may be retained in an expanded system, and will help solve parallel problems in alternative systems. Carnap's suggestion that his single chosen primitive might be enough for a complete system was indeed rash and untenable. But his mistake here was no worse than that of people who thought Euclid's basis enough for a complete plane geometry. The incompletability of the system of the *Aufbau* or of phenomenalism in general is not a very damaging charge.

Incompletability is not the only count urged against phenomenalism. Sometimes the objection is rather that a phenomenalistic system, whether completable or not, is epistemologically false; that it misrepresents the cognitive process. Phenomenal events or qualities, it is held, are not the original elements of knowledge but are products of an artificial and highly sophisticated analysis, so that a phenomenalistic system gives a highly distorted picture of actual cognition.

Any such view rests on the premise that the question "What are the original elements in knowledge?" is a clear and answerable one. And the assumption remains uncontested so long as we are dominated by the tradition that there is a sharp dichotomy between the given and the interpretation put upon it—so long as we picture the knower as a machine that is fed experience in certain lumps and proceeds to grind these up and reunite them in various ways. But I do not think this view of the matter will stand very close scrutiny. For the question "What are the units in which experience is actually given?" seems to amount to the question "What is the real organization of experience before any cognitive organization takes place?" and this, in turn, seems to ask for a description of cognitively unorganized experience. But any description itself effects, so to speak, a cognitive organization; and apart from a description, it is hard to see what organization can be. The search for the original given is sometimes envisaged as an interrogation in which I am first asked what I just saw. I reply, "I saw the worst criminal alive today", but my questioner complains that I am making too many judgments about what I saw; he wants me to tell him exactly what I could see and nothing more. As he continues to press me, I reply successively; "I saw a man", "I saw a human looking animal", "I saw a moving object", "I saw such-and-such a configuration of color patches". But if my questioner is consistent and persistent, none of these replies—or any other I can give him—will satisfy him; for all my answers describe my experience in words and so impose on it some organization or interpretation. What he is covertly demanding is that I describe what I saw without describing it. All my answers may be true descriptions of what I saw, but no description can be a satisfactory answer to the question what I *merely* saw;[5] for the question is a bogus one.

But obviously I cannot discuss the whole question of epistemological priority very thoroughly here. And there is no need. For the value and validity of a constructional system do not depend

5. The snares in the question whether some description describes an experience *just as* it is experienced have been discussed in *SA,* pp. 138–141, and in Wittgenstein's *Philosophical Investigations* (Oxford, Eng.: Basil Blackwell, 1953), pp. 193–214.

upon the epistemological primacy of the elements it starts from, however one may conceive such primacy to be determined. The old idea that philosophy aims at writing the story of the cognitive process had already been abandoned in the *Aufbau*. Carnap warned that his constructions are intended to preserve only the 'logical value' not the 'epistemological value' of the terms defined, and stated expressly that his system is not to be regarded as a portrayal of the process of acquiring knowledge. Nevertheless, he considered the system to be a 'rational reconstruction' of that process, a demonstration of how the ideas dealt with 'could have been' derived from the original given; and for that reason he bases his system on elements that are as close as possible to what he regards as the given. But it becomes almost immediately obvious that if we do not care whether steps in the system picture corresponding steps in cognition, neither do we care whether the system starts from what is originally given. The function of the system is not to portray the genesis—either actual or hypothetical —of ideas, but to exhibit interconnections between them. The consideration relevant in choosing elements for a system is thus not primacy in the cognitive process but serviceability as a basis for an economical, perspicuous, and integrated system.

I shall have more to say on the nature and purpose of constructional systems as we proceed, especially in the following section; but the brief answer to the charge that phenomenalistic systems are false as pictures of the cognitive process is simply that such systems need not be true in this way. Carnap claims a diluted truth of this sort for his system, as he tentatively claims completability for it; but the system is not to be judged in terms of these needless and misleading claims.

A third and more considered line of attack upon phenomenalism is directed toward showing not that phenomenalistic systems are incompletable or false, but that they are disadvantageous—that the important purposes at hand can be better served by starting from a physicalistic basis. It is pointed out that even the most commonplace objects of daily experience are extraordinarily difficult to construct upon a phenomenalistic basis; that the *elementarerlebnisse* or qualities or appearance-events from which a phenomenalistic system proceeds are unfamiliar units of discourse, elusive if not illusive, difficult to catch and identify; and that a system based upon such elements is an ingrown development of technical philosophy, remote from practical concerns or scientific discourse. In contrast, it is held, a physicalistic system begins with familiar and well-understood elements, is able to deal at once with the world of everyday experience, and much more readily yields the objects of the sciences.

This argument, with its appeal to the familiar, the practical, and the scientific, is so overwhelming that those who spend time on phenomenalistic constructions are regarded as stubborn and old-fashioned crackpots who shut their eyes to the facts of life and science. Nevertheless, let us look at the argument more closely.

In the first place, one great advantage claimed for a physicalistic system is that it does not face the difficult and perhaps insoluble problem of constructing physical objects on the basis of phenomena. This is quite true. Likewise, it is true that if you simply use a double compass (a compass with another mounted on one leg) you can trisect any angle. And since a double compass is easy to obtain, and since the goal is to get angles trisected, isn't it impractical and quixotic to deny ourselves use of this instrument? If physical objects are hard to construct in terms of phenomena, why not begin with physical objects? Let's be clear, though, that in both cases we are not solving a problem but evading one. The difference, it will be claimed, is that in the case of geometry the choice is between two equally simple and ordinary bases, while in the shift from a phenomenalistic to a physicalistic system we are dropping an abstruse and elusive basis in favor of a plainly more comprehensible and familiar one. Thus the argument for physicalism here cannot be that it solves a problem that phenomenalism does not, but rather that it begins with a more acceptable basis and frees us of the need for bothering with a difficult and unimportant problem before we come to grips with the realm of everyday life and of science.

The comfortable, homey character of the physicalist's basis lasts only so long as he is arguing for his basis rather than trying to use it. Once he makes any serious beginning toward systematic construction, he quickly finds that ordinary things like tables, desks, and chairs are much too gross, complicated, ill-assorted, and scattered to serve his purpose; and while we are looking the other way, he slips in substitutes. In "Testability and Meaning",[6] for example, Carnap at first speaks of a 'thing-language' in which atomic sentences consist of observable predicates applied to ordinary things.[7] But a few pages later he is speaking of "observable predicates of the thing-language attributed to perceived things of any kind or to space-time points".[8] This last phrase makes a radical addition. Whether the space-time points in question are those of physics or are minimal perceptible regions, they are by no means the familiar things of everyday experience. What the physicalist and the phenomenalist both do is this: they begin informally with ordinary discourse and indicate in terms of it a set of entities that are quite different from ordinary things but possess a uniformity, simplicity, and joint exhaustiveness that make them serviceable as elements for a system. The physicalist does not, any more than the phenomenalist, take the usual objects of daily life as the basic elements of his system.

Moreover, there is a good deal of equivocation about the space-time points taken as elements by the physicalist. When he maintains that he is in a better position to construct the objects of science, the supposition is that his elements are the space-time points of mathematics and physics. But this cannot be the case; for he retains 'observable predicates'. Carnap gives as examples of admissible atomic statements: "This space-time point is warm" and "At this space-time point, is a solid object".[9] Obviously no mathematical space-time point is warm, and at no such point is there any object that is solid or red or that has any other observable quality; observable qualities belong to objects of perceptible size. But if the elements called space-time points are perceptible regions, then we are faced with a good many of the problems—for example, the explication of imperceptible differences—that the physicalist sought to avoid. And his claim that his basis is adequate for con-

6. Rudolf Carnap, "Testability and Meaning", in *Philosophy of Science*, vol. III (1936), pp. 419–471, and vol. IV (1937), pp. 1–40.

7. *Ibid.*, vol. III, p. 466.

8. *Ibid.*, vol. IV, p. 9.

9. *Ibid.*

structing the objects of science no longer looks so plausible. The problem of deriving the objects of physics from such a basis is hardly less formidable than, and is in many ways not very different from, the problem of constructing ordinary objects from a strictly phenomenal basis; and there is no *prima facie* reason to suppose that the one is soluble if the other is not. The physicalist offers the argument that "For every term in the physical language physicists know how to use it on the basis of their observations. Thus every such term is reducible to observable predicates . . .";[10] but the phenomenalist has characteristically argued in exactly parallel fashion that "for every term that is used at all competently, the user knows how to use it on the basis of what appears to him, and thus every term is reducible to phenomenal predicates". If the former argument is good so is the latter; if the latter is bad so is the former. The serviceability of ordinary thing-language for constructing the realm of physics remains a totally unsupported claim.

If the problem of constructing the entities of physics from observable things is so troublesome, one might expect the physicalist to skip it as inessential—as he has already skipped the problem of constructing ordinary objects from phenomena—and to achieve a language adequate for physics by starting from the particles and predicates of physics itself. This would be consistent with the currently popular idea that the goal of all investigation is the prediction and control of nature;[11] but he never quite takes this step, for to do so would be to drop philosophy for physics. The physicalist and other constructionalists are trying to serve some purpose not served by physics and the other sciences; but they cannot formulate the difference very clearly, and often seem unaware of it.

Here a major and delicate question emerges. A good part of the

10. *Ibid.*, vol. III, p. 467.

11. The recent dominance of this idea seems to me to have blocked any clear understanding of either philosophy or the sciences. But some relief is in sight. Psychologists have lately produced experimental evidence that monkeys will exert more effort out of sheer curiosity than for food. Satisfaction of curiosity may in time become almost as respectable a goal as satisfaction of hunger; and then we shall no longer have to justify astrophysics by what it may eventually do for the wheat crop.

dispute over the relative merits of different systematic bases arises from confusion as to pertinent standards. The criteria most often appealed to—such as epistemological primacy, and utility for the sciences—are clearly inappropriate; and just what are the requirements upon an acceptable basis for a philosophical system, as distinguished from a system of psychology or physics, is a neglected, important, and exasperating problem. Luckily, it is beyond the scope of this paper.

In summary, then, the argument that phenomenalism is incompletable has no more weight against the system of the *Aufbau* than the argument that angles cannot be trisected with straightedge and compass has against Euclidean geometry; and the argument that phenomenalism is epistemologically false has no more weight than the argument that Euclid's postulates are not fundamental, self-evident truths. Moreover, the popular arguments for a physicalistic versus a phenomenalistic system involve vacillation as to the physicalistic basis to be used, unsupported claims concerning possible constructions, and tacit appeal to criteria that, applied consistently, would rule out physicalistic as well as phenomenalistic systems and reject all philosophical investigation in favor of the special sciences.

My aim, let me emphasize, is not to advocate phenomenalism as against physicalism, but only to show the weakness of the case against phenomenalism. Systems of both types may well prove to be valuable.

3. Constructionalism and the *Aufbau*

So far, I have considered only the opposition to phenomenalism in particular as distinct from the opposition to constructionalism in general. But there is also active opposition to constructionalism (or 'reductionism' as its enemies call it) of all varieties—not just to a certain choice of basis but to the very program of a systematic logical construction from any set of primitives.

The root of such opposition is, of course, the anti-intellectualism that finds forthright expression in Bergson. The complaint against all definition, analysis, and systematic description is that it employs static, abstract, and Procrustean concepts to construct a bloodless caricature of the rich and pulsating world of experience. Conceptualization, abstraction, symbolization, are instruments of excision and desiccation. This appears to be an attack less against one kind of philosophy than upon philosophy in general as compared with poetry. Or, since poetry uses words and symbols and selects aspects, perhaps the protest is rather against all verbalization as contrasted with nonverbal living. In this extreme form, the position need not much concern us here; for we are considering the *Aufbau* as compared to other philosophical efforts, not as compared to a moonlight walk or a drunken brawl. Yet the basic anti-intellectualistic complaint that philosophy does not duplicate experience is worth noting; for it underlies many another objection to attempts at precision and systematization in philosophy.

The function of a constructional system is not to recreate experience but rather to map it. Though a map is derived from observations of a territory, the map lacks the contours, colors, sounds, smells, and life of the territory, and in size, shape, weight, temperature and most other respects may be about as much unlike what it maps as can well be imagined. It may even be very little like other equally good maps of the same territory. A map is schematic, selective, conventional, condensed, and uniform. And these characteristics are virtues rather than defects. The map not only summarizes, clarifies, and systematizes, it often discloses facts we could hardly learn immediately from our explorations. We may make larger and more complicated maps or even three-dimensional models in order to record more information; but this is not always to the good. For when our map becomes as large and in all other respects the same as the territory mapped—and indeed long before this stage is reached—the purposes of a map are no longer served. There is no such thing as a completely unabridged map; for abridgment is intrinsic to map making.

This, I think, suggests the answer not only to rampant anti-intellectualism but to many another objection against the abstractness, poverty, artificiality, and general unfaithfulness of constructional systems. Let no one complain that the turnpike is not red like the line on the map, that the dotted state boundaries on the map are not visible in the fields, or that the city we arrive at is not a round black dot. Let no one suppose that if a map made according to one scheme of projection is accurate then maps made according to alternative schemes are wrong. And let no one accuse the cartographer of merciless reductionism if his map fails to turn green in the spring.

The anti-intellectualist confronts us with a spurious dilemma. The choice is not between misrepresentation and meticulous reproduction. The relevant question about a system or a map is whether it is serviceable and accurate in the way intended.

Many contemporary philosophers are opposed not to analysis as such but to the use of logic and artificial terminology and to step-by-step construction. A system of formal definitions, the objection runs, raises irrelevant problems, is too rigid and precise, and is too insensitive to the subtle variations of ordinary use. A philosophic problem is considered to arise from lack of care in the use of ordinary language, and the recommended treatment consists simply in explaining in ordinary language the nature of the misuse or misunderstanding of use. The analyses offered as examples of this method are often much needed and highly illuminating. They are like directions that tell us how to go from the post office to the park without taking a wrong turn at the red barn. In general, we need ask such directions only when we are lost or puzzled, since we do most of our daily traveling quite efficiently without them. And good verbal directions, as compared with a map, have obvious virtues: they are in the vernacular, mention recognizable landmarks, and tell us without waste just what we immediately need to know.

But a map has its advantages, too. It is, indeed, in an artificial language, and has to be read and related to the terrain; but it is consistent, comprehensive, and connected. It may needlessly give us a good deal of information we already have well in mind; but it may also reveal unsuspected routes and lead us to rectify misconceptions that might otherwise have gone unquestioned. It gives an organized overall view that no set of verbal directions and no experience in traveling can provide unaided. Verbal directions may often be useful even when we have a map; they may help us interpret the map or save us the trouble. But they do not supplant the map.

There are dangers in maps, of course. A map may be taken too literally or otherwise misread. But the map is not at fault if the user supposes that the numbering of the lines of longitude reflects a scale of metaphysical priority, or if disputes arise over whether a marking off by square miles or by minutes is more in keeping with reality.

We are still, admittedly, in a rather primitive stage of philosophical mapmaking; and no one is to be blamed for an inclination to trust skilled verbal directions as against new and imperfect maps. Nor is the reputation of cartography improved by elaborate maps drawn too hastily on the basis of too little exploration. Yet the opposition to the principles of constructionalism by the practitioners of verbal analysis has always surprised me; for I think there is no irreconcilable conflict of objectives or even of methods. Verbal analysis is a necessary preliminary and accompaniment to systematic construction, and deals with the same sphere of problems. For example, the verbal analyst may well concern himself with explaining the vague locution we use when we say that several things are 'all alike'; and he may well examine the difference between saying that a color is at a given place at a given time and saying that a color is at a given place *and* at a given time. The constructionalist dealing with qualities and particulars will likewise have to be clear on these points. The analyst, treating these as separate problems, may well miss the intriguing relationship between the two, while a systematic treatment shows them to be two cases of a single logical problem.[12] But verbal analysis and logical construction are complementary rather than incompatible. The constructionalist recognizes the anti-intellectualist as an arch enemy, but looks upon the verbal analyst as a valued and respected, if inexplicably hostile, ally.

Apart from entrenched philosophical positions, the opposition to constructionalism degenerates into greeting each proposed definition of a so-and-so as a such-and-such with the naïve protest that a so-and-so is Not Merely a such-and-such but Something More. This betrays a simple failure to grasp what the constructionalist is doing. In defining a so-and-so as a such-and-such, he is not declaring that a so-and-so is nothing but a such-and-such. Carnap dis-

12. For further explanation, see *SA*, pp. 204–214.

claimed any such idea by insisting that his definientia need have only the same extension as his definienda; and as my discussion above suggests, "=df" in a constructional definition is not to be read "is nothing more than" but rather in some such fashion as "is here to be mapped as". But the nature and import of a constructional definition now need to be examined more closely.

4. Extensionalism, Definition, and the *Aufbau*

Some critics of the *Aufbau* take issue primarily neither with its phenomenalistic orientation nor with constructionalism in general but with the particular conception of constructional method that the *Aufbau* sets forth and exemplifies.

The first such objection is against the extensionalism of the *Aufbau*. The only nonformal requirement there placed upon a constructional definition is that the definiendum and the definiens apply to exactly the same things, so that replacement of the one by the other in admissible contexts preserves truth value.[13] Against this, many critics—including the Carnap of today—argue that since such extensional identity does not guarantee sameness of meaning, some more stringent criterion must be adopted.

Let us grant the premise that extensional identity is not a sufficient condition for synonymy. This alone does not settle the main question. For what is at issue here is not a theory of meaning but a theory of constructional definition; and acceptance of a nonextensional criterion for synonymy does not carry with it adoption of a nonextensional criterion for constructional definition.

From what I have said in the preceding section it will be clear why I sharply disagree with contentions that a stronger requirement than extensional identity should be imposed on constructional definitions. This would mistake and defeat the primary function of a constructional system. That function, as I see it, is to exhibit a network of relationships obtaining in the subject-matter; and what is wanted therefore is simply a certain structural

13. The avowed extensionalism of so outstanding a monument of phenomenalism and constructionalism as the *Aufbau* would seem to confute Quine's recent charge (*Mind*, vol. 62 (1953), p. 434) that the notion of analyticity is a "holdover of phenomenalistic reductionism".

correspondence between the world of the system and the world of presystematic language.

Only in this way, as a "structural description"[14] rather than as a book of synonyms or as a full-color portrait of reality, can we understand a system like that of the *Aufbau*. The extensional criterion for constructional definition, far from being too weak, is too strong. To require that the definientia be extensionally identical with the definienda is in effect to claim a literal and exclusive truth for the chosen definitions; for if a quality is in fact identical with a certain class of *elementarerlebnisse,* then it is not identical with a class of some other experiential elements that might be chosen as basic for a different system. Any such claim of exclusive truth is utterly foreign to the spirit and purpose of constructionalism. If we conscientiously try to elicit the criteria we actually employ in discussing and judging the correctness of particular constructions, I think we find that the pertinent requirement is not that each definiens be extensionally identical with its definiendum but rather that the entire system of definientia be *isomorphic,* in a certain specifiable way,[15] to the entire system of definienda. This clears away extraneous and unsatisfiable demands, and leaves room for many different but equally valid alternative systems.

The second common objection against the conception of method embodied in the *Aufbau* is almost the opposite of the first. Carnap himself has taken the lead in maintaining that the restriction to definition as the sole method of construction is much too confining. Not only have we small hope of achieving full definition for all the terms we want to introduce, but there is—he argues—another equally legitimate method of introducing new terms into a system. He claims, indeed, that the introduction of terms through what he calls "reduction sentences" has the advantage of reflecting a common actual procedure of the scientist.

The latter argument is quite beside the point; but the chief trouble is that this supposedly new method of introducing terms adds nothing to the means that were already at our disposal. Reduction

14. Carnap's own term *(Strukturbeschreibung);* see Sec. 12 of the *Aufbau.*

15. See *SA I.*

sentences are merely postulates; and terms introduced through postulates are introduced simply as primitives. The introduction of primitives requires no new method, and there is some danger in concealing it under a new name. For the suggestion that reduction sentences are fundamentally comparable to definitions obscures the fact that each addition of a new and inineliminable primitive (whether by reduction postulate or otherwise) constitutes a sacrifice in the economy of basis and the resultant integration of our system. The difference between frankly adopting a term as primitive and introducing it by reduction sentences is the euphemistic difference between a loss of ground and a strategic retreat.

We may indeed have to add new primitives from time to time in building a system, and we may want to use new syntactical or semantical techniques; but the adoption of new primitives is not a new technique.

The standard criticisms of the *Aufbau's* concept of constructional method, then, seem to me wrong in two ways. First, the extensional criteria for constructional definition need weakening rather than strengthening. Second, the proposed supplementation of the method of definition by the so-called method of 'reduction' adds nothing whatever.

5. Faults of Construction

If we set aside all consideration of general principles and examine in detail the actual constructions in the *Aufbau,* we find a great many faults.[16] A number of these are pointed out in the book itself, for Carnap did not profess to offer more than an imperfect sketch of a system. But there are other difficulties, too; and the cumulative effect is that hardly any construction is free of fault. Moreover, not all these defects are minor slips or mere matters of detail still to be worked out. Some of them are so basic and material that nothing short of rather drastic revision of the whole system is likely to correct them.

Nothing that can be said will explain away these faults or make them less serious; but they should be seen in perspective. They are

16. For a detailed exposition of many of these, see *SA V.*

the faults of an honest and early venture in a new direction. Such troubles can always be avoided by attempting nothing or by keeping cautiously vague; the likelihood of error increases with the earnestness and originality of the effort to attain precision. But the making of errors, the discovery of faults, is the first step toward correcting them. Something has already been accomplished when what is being done and what is being attempted have been clarified far enough to make possible a sound accusation of error. If we compare the *Aufbau* not with what we hope for but with what we had before, we may still not condone its errors—but we can appreciate their significance.

Furthermore, some of the most important errors in the *Aufbau* were not invented by Carnap. They had been made repeatedly and unsuspectingly by generations of earlier philosophers, and are still made today. If Carnap did not correct or even notice them all, the rigorous logical articulation he demanded and began brought them much nearer the surface and made their early discovery inevitable. To take just one example, in discussions of the status of qualities it is often assumed that if we take likeness as the relation obtaining between any two things that have a common quality, then we can define a class of things having a common quality as a class of things that are all alike. But if to say that all are alike is to say merely that each two are alike, this does not guarantee that there is a quality common to all; and in fact no sufficient condition can be given solely in terms of the dyadic likeness of things. This difficulty is customarily camouflaged by the easy locution "all alike". Even Russell has fallen into a similar logical trap.[17] But one can hardly study the *Aufbau* intensively without becoming acutely aware of this problem.

What the opponents of the *Aufbau* usually offer us is not something to replace it, but discussions of methods and programs, arguments for one basis as against another, debates over what can and cannot be done. Altogether too much philosophy these days is, like the present article, merely philosophy about philosophy; the

17. The passages on comprescence and complexes in Bertrand Russell's *An Inquiry into Meaning and Truth* (New York: Norton, 1940, pp. 289–290), and *Human Knowledge* (New York: Simon and Schuster, 1948, p. 294), suffer from a parallel equivocation concerning the comprescence of qualities.

characteristic contemporary philosophical refuge is not metaphysics but metaphilosophy. The admission that the *Aufbau* is full of faults has to be coupled with the observation that the player on the field always gets caught in more mistakes than the player on the bench. And concerning many of the constructional errors in the *Aufbau* we may perhaps say, in summary, that they were serious, unoriginal, and worthwhile.

6. The Significance of the *Aufbau*

I am by no means suggesting, however, that the *Aufbau* is valuable only or primarily for its errors. Once misconceptions and groundless objections have been cleared away, the positive significance of the work becomes very evident.

The *Aufbau* brings to philosophy the powerful techniques of modern logic, along with unprecedented standards of explicitness, coherence, and rigor. It applies to basic philosophical problems the new methods and principles that only a few years before had thrown fresh and brilliant light upon mathematics. The potential importance to philosophy is comparable to the importance of the introduction of Euclidean deductive method into geometry. The *Aufbau,* for all its fragmentary character, and for all its defects, is still one of the fullest examples we have of the logical treatment of problems in nonmathematical philosophy. But its significance in the long run will be measured less by how far it goes than by how far it is superseded.

In stressing the novelty of its contribution, we must not be misled into regarding the *Aufbau* as an aboriginal work, unrelated to the course of thought preceding it. It belongs very much in the main tradition of modern philosophy, and carries forward a little the effort of the British Empiricists of the eighteenth century. Although these philosophers thought of themselves as devoted to a "historical, plain method" of dealing with knowledge, their chief contribution is to the geography rather than the history of our ideas. What were ostensibly inquiries into the question how certain ideas (*e.g.* of qualities) are psychologically derived from certain others (*e.g.* of particulars) were more often than not, I think, simply inquiries into the question how the former ideas may be defined in terms of the latter. And it is just such questions that the *Aufbau* deals with and clarifies. The language may be new but the ancestry of the problems is venerable.

The *Aufbau* cannot yet, however, be relegated to the status of a monument having purely historical interest. Its lessons have not been fully enough learned.

Conclusion

In summary, now, what is the re-vision of philosophy implied in the foregoing discussion? I think its major component is a new and humbler conception of the nature of philosophical truth: a recognition that philosophy aims at describing the world, not at duplicating it, and that analysis, precision, and systematization are thus virtues rather than vices. But along with the permission to be precise, analytic, and systematic goes a heavy responsibility; and the extreme difficulty of achieving these ends, even to a reasonable degree in dealing with even the most limited problems, might well discourage us completely if it were not for another aspect of our new vision of philosophy. And this is simply that we are to apply to philosophy itself the counsel that philosophers are so fond of giving with respect to everything but philosophy: to look upon it *sub specie aeternitatis*.

2

The Way the World Is

1. Introduction

Philosophers sometimes mistake features of discourse for features of the subject of discourse. We seldom conclude that the world consists of words just because a true description of it does, but we sometimes suppose that the structure of the world is the same as the structure of the description. This tendency may even reach the point of linguomorphism when we conceive the world as comprised of atomic objects corresponding to certain proper names, and of atomic facts corresponding to atomic sentences. A *reductio ad absurdum* blossoms when an occasional philosopher maintains that a simple description can be appropriate only if the world is simple; or asserts (and I have heard this said in all seriousness) that a coherent description will be a distortion unless the world happens to be coherent. According to this line of thinking, I suppose that before describing the world in English we ought to determine whether it is written in English, and that we ought to examine very carefully how the world is spelled.

Obviously enough the tongue, the spelling, the typography, the verbosity of a desription reflect no parallel features in the world. Coherence is a characteristic of descriptions, not of the world: the significant question is not whether the world is coherent, but whether our account of it is. And what we call the simplicity of the world is merely the simplicity we are able to achieve in describing it.

But confusion of the sort I am speaking of is relatively transparent at the level of isolated sentences, and so relatively less dangerous than the error of supposing that the structure of a veridical systematic description mirrors forth the structure of the world. Since a system has basic or primitive terms or elements and a graded hierarchy built out of these, we easily come to suppose that the world must consist of corresponding atomic elements put together in similar fashion. No theory advocated in recent years by first-rate philosophers seems more obviously wrong than

24

the picture theory of language. Yet we still find acute philosophers resorting under pressure to a notion of absolutely simple
qualities or particles. And most of those who avoid thinking of
the world as uniquely divisible into absolute elements still commonly suppose that *meanings* do resolve thus uniquely, and so
accept the concealed absolutism involved in maintaining the distinction between analytic and synthetic propositions.

In this paper, however, I am not concerned with any of the
more specific issues I have just touched upon, but with a more
general question. I have been stressing the dangers of mistaking
certain features of discourse for features of the world. This is a
recurrent theme with me, but even this is not my main concern
here. What I want to discuss is an uncomfortable feeling that
comes upon me whenever I warn against the confusion in question. I can hear the anti-intellectualistic, the mystic—my arch
enemy—saying something like this: "Yes, that's just what I've
been telling you all along. All our descriptions are a sorry trav-
esty. Science, language, perception, philosophy—none of these can
ever be utterly faithful to the world as it is. All make abstractions
or conventionalizations of one kind or another, all filter the world
through the mind, through concepts, through the senses, through
language; and all these filtering media in some way distort the
world. It is not just that each gives only a partial truth, but that
each introduces distortion of its own. We never achieve even in
part a really faithful portrayal of the way the world is."

Here speaks the Bergsonian, the obscurantist, seemingly repeating my own words and asking, in effect, "What's the difference between us? Can't we be friends?" Before I am willing to
admit that philosophy must make alliances that strange, I shall
make a determined effort to formulate the difference between
us. But I shall begin by discussing some preliminary, related
questions.

2. The Way the World is Given

Perhaps we can gain some light on the way the world is by
examining the way it is given to us in experience. The question of
the given has a slightly musty sound these days. Even hardened

philosophers have become a little self-conscious about the futility of their debates over the given, and have the grace to rephrase the issue in terms of "ground-elements" or "protocol-sentences". But in one way or another we hear a good deal about getting down to the original, basic, bare elements from which all knowledge is manufactured. Knowing is tacitly conceived as a processing of raw material into a finished product; and an understanding of knowledge is thus supposed to require that we discover just what the raw material is.

Offhand, this seems easy enough. Carnap wanted the ground elements of his system in the *Aufbau* to be as nearly as possible epistemologically primary. In order to arrive at these, he says, we must leave out of ordinary experience all the results of any analysis to which we subject what we initially receive. This means leaving out all divisions along spatial or qualitative boundaries, so that our elements are big lumps, each containing everything in our experience at a given moment. But to say this is to make artificial temporal divisions; and the actual given, Carnap implies, consists not of these big lumps, but of one single stream.

But this way of arriving at the given assumes that the processes of knowing are all processes of analysis. Other philosophers have supposed rather that the processes are all processes of synthesis, and that the given therefore consists of minimal particles that have to be combined with one another in knowing. Still other thinkers hold that both these views are too extreme, and that the world is given in more familiar medium-size pieces, to which both analysis and synthesis are applied. Thus in views of the given we find duplicated the monism, atomism, and the intermediate pluralisms of metaphysics. But which view of the given is right?

Let's look at the question more closely. The several views do not differ about what is contained in the given, or what can be found there. A certain visual presentation, all agree, contains certain colors, places, designs, etc.; it contains the least perceptible particles and it is a whole. The question is not whether the given *is* a single undifferentiated lump or contains many tiny parts; it is a whole comprised of such parts. The issue is not *what* is given but *how* it is given. Is it *given* as a single whole or is it *given as* many small particles? This captures the precise issue—and at the

same time discloses its emptiness. For I do not think any sense
can be made of the phrase *"given as"*. That an experience is given
as several parts surely does not mean that these parts are presented torn asunder; nor can it mean that these parts are parti-
tioned off from one another by perceptible lines of demarcation.
For if such lines of demarcation are there at all, they are there
within the given, for any view of the given. The nearest we could
come to finding any meaning to the question what the world is
given as would be to say that this turns on whether the material in
question is apprehended with a kind of feeling of wholeness or a
feeling of broken-upness. To come that near to finding a meaning
for *"given as"* is not to come near enough to count.

So I am afraid we can get no light on the way the world is by
asking about the way it is given. For the question about the way
it is given evaporates into thin air.

3. The Way the World is to be Seen

Perhaps we shall get further by asking how the world is best
seen. If we can with some confidence grade ways of seeing or
picturing the world according to their degrees of realism, of
absence of distortion, of faithfulness in representing the way the
world is, then surely by reading back from this we can learn a
good deal about the way the world is.

We need consider our everyday ideas about pictures for only
a moment to recognize this as an encouraging approach. For we
rate pictures quite easily according to their approximate degree of
realism. The most realistic picture is the one most like a color-
photograph; and pictures become progressively less realistic, and
more conventionalized or abstract, as they depart from this standard. The way we see the world best, the nearest pictorial approach to the way the world is, is the way the camera sees it. This
version of the whole matter is simple, straightforward, and quite
generally held. But in philosophy as everywhere else, every silver
lining has a big black cloud—and the view described has everything in its favor except that it is, I think, quite wrong.

If I take a photograph of a man with his feet towards me, the
feet may come out as large as his torso. Is this the way I normally

or properly see the man? If so, then why do we call such a photograph distorted? If not, then I can no longer claim to be taking the photographic view of the world as my standard of faithfulness.

The fact of the matter is that this 'distorted' photograph calls our attention to something about seeing that we had ignored. Just in the way that it differs from an ordinary 'realistic' picture, it reveals new facts and possibilities in visual experience. But the 'distorted' photograph is a rather trivial example of something much more general and important. The 'distortion' of the photograph is comparable to the distortion of new or unfamiliar styles of painting. Which is the more faithful portrait of a man—the one by Holbein or the one by Manet or the one by Sharaku or the one by Dürer or the one by Cézanne or the one by Picasso? Each different way of painting represents a different way of seeing; each makes its selection, its emphasis; each uses its own vocabulary of conventionalization. And we need only look hard at the pictures by any such artist to come to see the world in somewhat the same way. For seeing is an activity and the way we perform it depends in large part upon our training. I remember J. B. Neumann saying that once when he happened to see the faces of a movie audience in the reflected glare of the screen he first realized how an African sculptor saw faces. What we regard as the most realistic pictures are merely pictures of the sort that most of us, unfortunately, are brought up on. An African or a Japanese would make a quite different choice when asked to select the pictures that most closely depict what he sees. Indeed our resistance to new or exotic ways of painting stems from our normal lethargic resistance to retraining; and on the other hand the excitement lies in the acquisition of new skill. Thus the discovery of African art thrilled French painters and they learned from it new ways to see and paint. What is less often realized is that the discovery of European art is exciting to the African sculptor for the same reason; it shows him a new way of seeing, and he, too, modifies his work accordingly. Unfortunately, while European absorption of African style often results in an artistic advance, African adoption of European style almost always leads to artistic deterioration. But this is for incidental reasons. The first is that social deterioration of the African is usually simultaneous with the introduction of European art.

The second reason is rather more intriguing: that while the French artist was influenced by the best of African art, the African was fed no doubt on calendar art and pin-up girls. Had he seen Greek and Mediaeval sculpture instead, the results might have been radically different. But I am digressing.

The upshot of all this is that we cannot find out much about the way the world is by asking about the best or most faithful or most realistic way of seeing or picturing it. For the ways of seeing and picturing are many and various; some are strong, effective, useful, intriguing, or sensitive; others are weak, foolish, dull, banal, or blurred. But even if all the latter are excluded, still none of the rest can lay any good claim to be the way of seeing or picturing the world the way it is.

4. The Way the World is to be Described

We come now to a more familiar version of the question of the way the world is. How is the world to be described? Does what we call a true description faithfully depict the world?

Most of us have ringing in our ears Tarski's statement that "it is raining" is true if and only if it is raining, as well as his remark (I think erroneous, but that is beside the point here) that acceptance of this formula constitutes acceptance of a correspondence theory of truth. This way of putting the matter encourages a natural tendency to think of truth in terms of mirroring or faithful reproduction; and we have a slight shock whenever we happen to notice the obvious fact that the sentence "it is raining" is about as different as possible from the rainstorm. This disparity is of the same sort for a true as for a false description. Luckily, therefore, we need not here concern ourselves with the difficult technical matter of the nature of truth; we can confine our attention to admittedly true descriptions. What we must face is the fact that even the truest description comes nowhere near faithfully reproducing the way the world is.

A systematic description of the world, as I noted earlier, is even more vulnerable to this charge; for it has explicit primitives, routes of construction, etc., none of them features of the world described. Some philosophers contend, therefore, that if systematic descriptions introduce an arbitrary artificial order, then we should make our descriptions unsystematic to bring them more into accord with the world. Now the tacit assumption here is that the respects in which a description is unsatisfactory are *just those respects in which it falls short of being a faithful picture;* and the tacit *goal* is to achieve a description that as nearly as possible gives a living likeness. But the goal is a delusive one. For we have seen that even the most realistic way of picturing amounts merely to one kind of conventionalization. In painting, the selection, the emphasis, the conventions are different from but no less peculiar to the vehicle, and no less variable, than those of language. The idea of making verbal descriptions approximate pictorial depiction loses its point when we understand that to turn a description into the most faithful possible picture would amount to nothing more than exchanging some conventions for others.

Thus neither the way the world is given nor any way of seeing or picturing or describing it conveys to us the way the world is.

5. The Way the World Is

We come now to the question: what, then, is the way the world is? Am I still threatened with the friendship of my enemies? It looks very much that way, for I have just reached the mystic's conclusion that there is no representation of the way the world is. But if our accord seems on the surface to have been reinforced, a second look will show how it has been undermined, by what we have been saying.

The complaint that a given true description distorts or is unfaithful to the world has significance in terms of some grading of descriptions according to faithfulness, or in terms of a difference in degree of faithfulness between true descriptions and good pictures. But if we say that all true descriptions and good pictures are equally unfaithful, then in terms of what sample or standard of relative faithfulness are we speaking? We have no longer before us any clear notion of what faithfulness would be. Thus I reject the idea that there is some test of realism or faithfulness in addition to the tests of pictorial goodness and descriptive truth. There are very many different equally true descriptions of the world, and their truth is the only standard of their faithfulness. And when we say of them that they all involve conventionalizations, we are saying that no one of these different descriptions is *exclusively* true, since the others are also true. None of them tells us *the* way the world is, but each of them tells us *a* way the world is.

If I were asked what is *the food* for men, I should have to answer "none". For there are many foods. And if I am asked what is the way the world is, I must likewise answer, "none". For the world is many ways. The mystic holds that there is some way the world is and that this way is not captured by any description. For me, there is no way that is the way the world is; and so of course no description can capture it. But there are many ways the world is, and every true description captures one of them. The difference between my friend and me is, in sum, the enormous difference between absolutism and relativism.

Since the mystic is concerned with the way the world is and finds that the way cannot be expressed, his ultimate response to the question of the way the world is must be, as he recognizes, silence. Since I am concerned rather with the ways the world is, my response must be to construct one or many descriptions. The answer to the question "What is the way the world is? What are the ways the world is?" is not a shush, but a chatter.

6. Postscript

Near the beginning of this paper, I spoke of the obvious falsity of the picture theory of language. I declared rather smugly that a description does not picture what it describes, or even represent the structure of what it describes. The devastating charge against the picture theory of language was that a description cannot represent or mirror forth the world as it is. But we have since observed that a picture doesn't do this either. I began by dropping the picture theory of language and ended by adopting the language theory of pictures. I rejected the picture theory of language on the ground that the structure of a description does not conform to the structure of the world. But I then concluded that there is no such thing as the structure of the world for anything to conform or fail to conform to. You might say that the picture theory of language is as false and as true as the picture theory of pictures; or in other words, that what is false is not the picture theory of language but a certain absolutistic notion concerning both pictures and language. Perhaps eventually I shall learn that what seems most obviously false sometimes isn't.

3

Some Reflections on the Theory of Systems

When I first heard that the general topic of the present session would be "The Philosophical Bearings of Modern Logic", I wondered in exactly what sense the term "bearings" should be taken. Bearings are used in machinery in order to reduce friction and noise; but those of you who have attended these meetings in recent years will agree that the joining of logic and philosophy has accomplished neither purpose. In the course of my remarks, I shall indicate some possible reasons why the application of logic to philosophy tends to make the wheels spin less freely, rather than more so.

By calling my talk "Some Reflections on the Theory of Systems", I have rather put myself on the defensive, because the term "system" is in bad repute in philosophy. It calls to mind the magnificent structures of an earlier day, that were built with more regard to their own grandeur than to the comfort of the facts that had to live in them. In reaction, recent philosophy has tended to emphasize what might be called "spot analysis": the attempt to deal with each separate problem on its own terms as it arises. One danger in this is that we may find ourselves running around in vicious circles—or, what is worse, that we shall run in vicious circles without finding it out. But quite apart from that, we may be overlooking something important in our eagerness to avoid any charge of trimming facts to fit systems. Although a philosophical system does not create fact, any more than a system of coordinates creates motion, still it begins to look more and more as if some facts are *relative* to systems, just as motion is. When we investigate the nature of analytic statements, or try to set up an adequate definition of confirmation, or deal with any of a number of related problems, we repeatedly come upon difficulties that seem to be insoluble except relatively to systems. For instance, an analytic statement is presumably one that follows from the definition of

33

a term. But while it may be quite clear what the definition of a term is *in a given system,* the notion of *the* definition of a term in any absolute sense is as elusive as the notion of an absolutely fixed point. To take another example, when we try to set up explicit standards for confirmation, we are harassed by counter-intuitive results that follow whenever properties of certain troublesome kinds are in question. One remedy, suggested by Professor Carnap, is to restrict ourselves to simple properties and certain specifiable compounds of these. But again it is difficult to see how simplicity of the sort intended can mean anything except with respect to a given system.

A reverence for fact, then, does not call for a renunciation of system. But at the same time, no system is indispensable: none is more true than some alternative system. Yet the fact that there may be a number of systems, each as good as any other, does not mean that there is no point in constructing any particular system. The customer who feels that an automobile of one color is as good as an automobile of any other color, and who recognizes that any automobile he gets will be of some color, does not thereby acquire something to drive. Good philosophical systems are perhaps even a little rarer these days than good automobiles. In both connections, openmindedness is advisable; but in both, the first need is to get something that will run.

For the attempt to construct a philosophical system, modern logic provides us with both a model and a tool. What I want to do here is suggest a few problems, and fewer solutions, that result from the effort to use the tool and profit by the model.

The systems I am concerned with are primarily systems of *definitions,* and one of the first general theoretical problems we face is the question: by what criteria shall we judge whether a given definition is acceptable? A familiar subject of controversy is the adequacy of the criterion of *extensional identity,* by which a definition is judged correct if the definiendum and the definiens denote just the same things. It is often contended that such a standard is too lax, that the definiendum and definiens must not only denote the same things—as might happen in some cases "purely by accident"—but must have the same meaning, the same intension. On the contrary, I believe it can be shown that the cri-

34

terion of extensional identity, far from being too loose, is *too tight;* that it would exclude many definitions we want to admit.

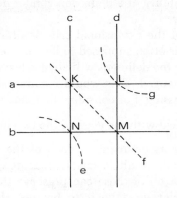

FIGURE 1

Suppose we are concerned with this diagram, in which there are four lines, *a, b, c,* and *d,* and four points of intersection, *K, L, M, N.* Let us assume that the lines are primitive elements of our system, that they comprise the field of our primitive relation, which we need not specify for our present purposes. Now we might define the class of the points *K, L, M, N* as the class of classes of two intersecting lines; in particular, defining *K* as the class of the lines *a* and *c* (or as the corresponding whole). A definition of this sort is quite common and often very useful. To exclude it on the ground of a belief that point *K* 'really is' something different from the class of the lines *a* and *c* would be to misunderstand the purpose of the definition; and would exclude all the many useful definitions reached, for example, by such a means as Whitehead's extensive abstraction. Moreover, if the proposed definition *is* allowed, this can hardly be on the ground of a belief that point *K* 'really is' the class of the lines *a* and *c.* For suppose there are also in the diagram the lines *e, f,* and *g.* Then we might define *K* as the class of the lines *a* and *c,* or the class of *a* and *f,* or the class of *a* and *c* and *f.* Anyone who regards any of these definitions as admissible will hardly deny that the others are equally admissible. Yet the system recognizes that the class of the lines *a* and *c* is not identical with the class of *a* and *f* nor with the class of *a* and *c* and *f*. Since extensional identity of definiendum and definiens can thus obtain in at most one of these admissible definitions, the admissibility of a definition cannot depend upon such extensional identity.

Other versions of the extensional criterion fare no better. The test of a definition is often supposed to be whether replacement of the definiendum by the definiens will always leave the truth-value of a sentence unchanged. This would exclude all the definitions we have been discussing. For consider the following sentence:

s. *K* is identical with the class of the two lines *a* and *c*.

To replace "*K*" by its definiens in each of the three definitions proposed in turn will result in one true sentence and two false ones. Obviously not all of these can preserve the original truth-value of s—whatever we take it to be; yet all are admissible definitions.

What we must do is not merely rephrase the criterion of extensional identity, but drop it in favor of some weaker criterion: for example, some kind of systematic isomorphism. Such definitions as satisfy the criterion of extensional identity will satisfy this criterion also, just as definitions which satisfy a criterion of *intensional* identity presumably also satisfy the weaker criterion of extensional identity; but some definitions which satisfy neither of these stricter criteria will now be admitted. And adoption of a definition will no longer carry with it any commitment as to the extensional or intensional identity or non-identity of the definiendum and definiens.

Besides settling upon what constitutes a satisfactory definition, we have to examine the factors governing the choice of the basic vocabulary in terms of which all the definitions of a given system are to be stated. In addition to the logical apparatus, we shall need one or more extralogical primitives. There is no one best extralogical basis, and the reasons for choosing a given basis at any time will often be very complex. But whatever our other demands may be, we shall always want our basis to be as economical as possible consistently with those demands. It is rather the fashion to decry economy as trivial. We often hear it said that apart from the purely aesthetic consideration of neatness, a basis consisting of only two primitives is no better than a basis consisting of twenty or two hundred primitives of the same sort. But if this position is taken seriously, the system-builder might well take as primitive all the terms or concepts he wants in his entire system, and save himself the trouble of finding definitions. The motives for seeking economy are inseparable from the motives for seeking a system at all.

But granting that economy is wanted, how shall we measure the extent to which it is achieved? The first off-hand answer is, "count the primitives", but this is obviously an unreliable test. For we can ordinarily replace all the primitives of a given system by a single one, of sufficient complexity. Suppose for example that our primitives are "L" meaning "is a line", "F" meaning "is faster than", and "H" meaning "is halfway between in weight", and suppose that each predicate actually applies to at least some elements. The three could then be replaced as primitive by "P" where "$P(x, y, r, s, t, w)$" means "x is a line, and y is faster than r, and s is halfway between t and w in weight". The original predicates "L", "F", and "H" are then readily definable from "P". In measuring economy, then, we have to consider the formal complexity as well as the number of the primitives, but this is not altogether easy. It might seem that all we have to do is to count the number of predicate-places rather than the number of predicates, but this turns out to be unsatisfactory. Working from such elementary principles as that no genuine economy is achieved where replacement is purely automatic, we soon find, for example, that a basis consisting of two two-place predicates is in general simpler than one consisting of one four-place predicate; and that n-place predicates—depending upon their symmetry and other characteristics—may have a complexity-value far greater than n. For example, the complexity-value of a three-place predicate may be as high as 15, and that of a four-place predicate as high as 59. This is not the occasion to go into further details. I wanted only to indicate that here again the use of modern logic leads to new problems and somewhat unexpected results.

The problem of economy of postulates is in some respects parallel to that of the economy of primitives. But whereas we found we could normally reduce all extralogical primitives to one, we find that we can reduce all extralogical postulates to none. Professor Quine and I showed in a paper a few years ago that any finite, consistent set of extralogical postulates can be made deducible theorems of the system—and therefore unnecessary as postulates —merely by constructing the definitions of the system with malice aforethought. For example, suppose that we have as primitive a two-place predicate for the relation of intersection among lines in our diagram, and a postulate to the effect that this relation is symmetrical. We can take as primitive, instead, another word for the same relation, such as the predicate "Crosses", and define "Intersects" as applying to any two lines x and y if and only if x crosses $y,$ and y crosses x. That "intersects" is symmetrical can now be proven from its definition and need no longer be postulated. This procedure can be generalized to eliminate virtually any set of extralogical postulates however complicated. This result is highly paradoxical because it seems to show that we can deduce all extralogical facts—for instance, all scientific truths—without making any extralogical assumptions. The fact that the definitions will be more complex is unimportant, since definitions are by their very nature eliminable from the system. A sufficiently painstaking examination of the matter—such as was undertaken by Professor Langford in his note on our paper, and by Professor Hempel in his review of that note—will remove some of the sting of this paradox. But we are left with the problem how to measure what might be called the assertive economy of a system. Counting postulates, or even counting them and considering their complexity is obviously futile. What we have to do is to develop some method of measuring the basic assertive content of our system. So far as I know, work on this problem has hardly begun.

Finally, before we construct any system, we have to decide what logical apparatus we shall use. It might seem that here efficiency and convenience need be our only considerations, that logic is neutral machinery that cannot affect the philosophical content of a system. But this is quite untenable. In the first place, the line between logic and extralogic is so vague that there is good reason to doubt that it can be drawn at all except by arbitrary enumeration of certain terms as logical. Accordingly, unless we rigorously restrict what we shall acknowledge as logic, we may find ourselves

casually smuggling into our system as logic the means for solving
problems that we find it hard to deal with more constructively.
The most common kind of complaint against modern logic is that
it fails to provide a ready answer to whatever troublesome problem happens to arise. If we find it difficult to explain the meaning
of counterfactual conditionals, someone is sure to suggest that we
just slip into our logic a new so-called "logical" sign for the kind
of sentential connection we need. Obviously this gets us nowhere.
This is one reason why some of us take a puritanical attitude
towards our logical apparatus, and refuse to admit such notions as
intensional implication and the modalities. But even to restrict
ourselves to the familiar extensional logic* may not be severe
enough. For this logic, as Quine has shown, is platonistic; it commits us to acceptance of a vast—indeed infinite—realm of abstract
entities, and it imports these entities into the scope of any system
in which this logic is used. For example, let us suppose that in a
system dealing with our diagram, only lines are recognized as individuals. If we use ordinary classial logic in this system, we are
thereby also recognizing as entities all classes of these lines, all
classes of such classes, and so on; and therefore all sequences and
relations of these lines. Possibly, we may be willing to open our
arms to this multitude; but if so, we must at least be aware that
our logic is responsible for more of our ontology than is the extralogical part of our system. And some of us are *not* willing to countenance such abstract entities at all (if we can help it) either
because we are nominalists or because, for the sake of economy,
we want to commit ourselves to as little as possible. If either nominalism or plain parsimony leads us to insist upon a logic that is
not committed to abstract entities, then we shall have to forego a
large part of the usual modern logic—namely, most of the theory
of classes and relations. This will indeed make the going hard, for
it then becomes very difficult to express even so simple and fundamental a fact as that there are more cats than dogs. The difficulty
of doing without a philosophically objectionable technique is not,
however, any sufficient reason for retaining it.

Perhaps it will appear from what I have said that as soon as we

[* Concerning "logic", see the Foreword to this chapter.]

apply logic to philosophy, or philosophy to logic, we become embroiled in new difficulties and paradoxes, some of which we are
still unable to solve. Indeed I cannot hold the logical philosopher
up to you as a man who has found a magic key to all the riddles
of the universe; rather, he seems to have found a way to cause
himself a good deal of trouble. It is true, as the unlogical philosopher and the unphilosophical logician often point out, that the way
of the logical philosopher is much like that of any transgressor.

4

Review of Urmson's
Philosophical Analysis

J. O. Urmson, *Philosophical Analysis: Its Development between the two World Wars* (New York: Oxford University Press, 1956), pp. x and 200.

This is an objective, historical account of an aspect of the development of philosophy in England over a period of about twenty years. Very briefly, logical atomism sought by means of reductive analysis to describe the world purely in terms of metaphysically simple facts. Difficulties in the idea of language as picturing fact, failures to carry out the wanted reductions, and obscurities in the very notion of simple or atomic facts led to a second phase: logical positivism. Here the goal was rather, still by means of reductive analysis, to show how all knowledge is built out of epistemologically simple experiences (or statements thereof). But this conception also was beset by troubles about the notion of absolute simplicity; and the attempt to identify meaningfulness with verifiability-by-simple-experiences not only resisted satisfactory formulation but also seemed to undermine itself by setting up a requirement it could not meet. This led to a third phase in which philosophy came to be viewed as concerned not with systematic reductive analysis at all but with the interpretation of those aspects and locutions of ordinary language that give rise to puzzlement and confusion. Analysis is directed not to bringing language into clearer accord with fact or to grounding doubtful statements on more certain ones, but to showing in any particular case how trouble can be avoided by recognizing the various different roles played by the sentences concerned.

My summary of Mr. Urmson's story is of course much too brief and crude, and neglects many aspects that he brings out very explicitly. He writes as historian, conscientiously refraining from obtruding criticisms and judgments of his own. Moreover, he is admirably aware of the dangers of schematic history of the kind he is undertaking. He writes, for example, "Neither philosophy nor its history can be studied in paraphrase and précis. . . . The danger . . . is that the impression may be formed that there was a definite school, with an orthodoxy of its own, consciously moving from position to position. . . . Such an impression would, of course, be utterly mistaken"; and later "We have been dealing largely with theories about the nature of philosophy . . . they are usually in part *a priori* theories about what a philosopher should be doing, which may or may not have an effect, not necessarily for the better, on the practice of philosophers. . . . Yet on the whole the best philosophy is little affected by theory; the philosopher sees what needs doing and does it." Nevertheless, a schematic history of this sort can be worthwhile—especially when undertaken by a philosopher so sensitive to its limitations and dangers.

The story he tells, however, is for the most part so well known to English-speaking philosophers that he might well have told it more succinctly. Where terseness and pace might have carried us awake over such familiar ground, we encounter a succession of preliminary and revised formulations, restatements, reviews, and summaries that will tire all but the newest comer to the field. Furthermore, if personal bias is absent from this history so also are novelty and stimulation; the reader is seldom in danger of being diverted by fresh insights or intriguing suggestions. What is worse, Mr. Urmson is not always accurate. Mr. C. G. Hempel calls my attention to the fact that Urmson's mistaken version ("There is something which is both King of France and bald, and only one such thing") of Russell's translation of "The King of France is bald" would be true if there were several Kings of France but only one bald one. Essentially this mistake is made at least three times (pp. 23–24, 29, 32–33).

In the treatment of the first two phases of the development— logical atomism and logical positivism—the author's renunciation of the role of critic is partially compensated for by his presentation of the criticisms that were in fact made both by proponents of these theories and by others. This, if it sheds no new light, at least transmits the old. But he merely describes the third phase— current British analysis—without discussing any of the criticisms that have been made of it. He has available the technically good defense that this third phase did not go beyond its formative stage before the Second World War; and that any criticisms that were made later are not within his chosen scope. But then surely we must question his decision to set the limits of his study as he did, when the inclusion of a few more years would have enabled him to give a much more balanced picture. The reader will wish, indeed, that the author had been more venturesome and allowed himself in his final pages, in place of one more redundant and superfluous postscript entitled "Retrospect", to risk some pages entitled "Prospect". As it is, the most intriguing part of the book is the chapter after the last, which the reader must write for himself. The irony of the objective and unfinished history we find in this book is that it inevitably focuses attention on the question: what are the seeds of destruction that this third phase, too, contains within itself and that will in turn lead to its downfall and replacement?

This is not the place to try to answer that question; but I must say something about it lest the insular reader take it as a sheer impertinence. Philosophy, it is held, is a matter of removing puzzlement and confusion arising from ordinary language. We lay down no general principles, seek no overall theory of knowledge, of the world, or even of language. Rather we are forest wardens watching for fires and rushing to extinguish them wherever they break out. But just what kind of puzzlement and confusion does philosophy set out to correct? Not, I submit, ordinary practical difficulties arising from the ordinary use of ordinary language by ordinary people. The man in the street is not hampered in earning his living by talking as if the mind were a ghost in a machine. It is the philosopher who worries about this. He doesn't understand; he cannot accept this picture; he cannot grasp it or else does not believe that it is a good description of the world. The standards he applies may indeed be hard to elicit and formulate; perhaps they cannot and need not be formulated. But we must not overlook the fact that the philosopher's puzzlement about language is always a puzzlement about interpreting ordinary statements in a philosophically acceptable way. The puzzlement or confusion is a function not only of the language but of our standards or sense of philosophical acceptability. Wittgenstein triumphantly exclaims that his conception of philosophy allows him to stop doing philosophy whenever he pleases. But he can stop doing philosophy, or at least stop needing to do philosophy, only when all philosophical puzzlement and confusion are resolved. And puzzlement and confusion can be resolved only if we either find interpretations of ordinary language that meet our requirements of philosophical acceptability or else relax those requirements enough to take language as it is.

In the second place, the rejection of absolutistic justifications for system-building does not of itself constitute justification for the extremely asystematic character of typical current British analysis. Unwillingness to accept any postulates of geometry as absolute or self-evident truths hardly diminishes the importance of the systematic development of geometries. Unwillingness to take any elements as metaphysical or epistemological ultimates does not make pointless all systematic constructions in philosophy. There are virtues in knowing where we began, where we have gone, and where we are going, even if we fully acknowledge that we might as well have begun somewhere else. Emphasis on spot-analysis is a natural reaction to heavy-handed system-building; but too little regard for system can lead us to run in circles or to overlook important likenesses while we are busy cataloguing subtle distinctions. But I am not arguing a case, I am only suggesting why Mr. Urmson's third phase may some day, even in England, give way to a fourth. There are already signs in the wind.

5

Descartes as Philosopher

Societies dedicated to individual figures of history are often concerned with polishing a reputation that shows a disheartening tendency to tarnish. This is obviously not the case with a Cartesian society. Indeed, Descartes is so widely recognized as the first and one of the greatest modern philosophers that any eulogy I might deliver on this score would only create an unfounded suspicion that I had my misgivings about it. Descartes needs nothing from us. The more interesting question is: what can we learn from Descartes?

When Descartes began intensive philosophical research he was —like so many people today—a soldier returned from the wars. Of course there is a certain difference in that Descartes seems to have chased after wars, while wars today chase after us. But the fact of armed conflict must always undermine complacency. And there is a further similarity between his situation and ours. He was living at a time when the snug world in which men had lived for centuries had been whisked away. It was nearly a hundred years since Copernicus had flung men from a cozy fireside in the center of the universe to the cold outer reaches of space; but Galileo was just confirming the exile so finally that hope of return seemed lost forever. If we—who are accustomed to rapid shifts in scientific theory and to new inventions—feel uncomfortable at the thought that an atomic bomb may blow us off the earth, the mind of a man who was just becoming used to freedom from scholastic stagnation could hardly have been much less disturbed by the intellectual revolution that blew man and the earth together into the far corners of the universe, and wrecked all his comfortable dogmas in the bargain.

How do we react today as we look back on war, and forward to possible annihilation? Being a philosopher, I shall—in order not to disappoint you—permit myself to make what may be a somewhat rash generalization. There are evidences of a widespread feeling that this is a time when philosophy had better devote itself to recovering some faiths, that we have had too much skepticism, too much scientificism, too much emphasis on logical analysis; that men look to philosophy for some solid foothold in the shifting sands and that philosophy had better come up with something fast. We are told that it's time to soft-pedal Cartesian doubt and to pass over Hume; time to rebuild the world and reestablish old values. In short the war and its aftermath are blamed on skepticism and positivism and relativism. We must return to old and cherished principles (even though they have failed us before), because if we question them we may end with nothing. This is the attitude of fear, fear of ourselves and fear of what the truth may be.

Descartes' attitude was very different. War had not left him too tired to do anything but turn back to Aristotle. He did not feel that his intellectual insecurity sprang from a lack of faith or from too critical an examination of authority. Rather he felt that old systems and methods had been found wanting. He was determined to learn the truth if he could, or do without it if he couldn't, but to make no compromise. The preface and the road to truth was the courage and determination to doubt everything that could be doubted.

This is a dangerous proposal—if its danger can be measured by the amount of terror it inspires. I doubt if any board of trustees would be comfortable if the philosophy department of its particular institution were to announce today that skepticism would hereafter be more heavily stressed. But before we all join heads in the sand, let us remind ourselves that political fanaticism, narrow nationalism, class conflict, and racial hatred arise not from an excess of skepticism but from an excess of faith.

There is a second important aspect of Descartes' attitude: his insistence on method. Along with unremitting and purifying doubt went the patient study of the way in which knowledge might be gained. Two of his major philosophical works were entitled *Discourse on the Method of Rightly Conducting the Reason and Seeking for Truth in the Sciences* and *Rules for the Direction of the Mind*.* Rule IV of the latter reads simply, "There is need of

* *Philosophical Works of Descartes*, translated and edited by Elizabeth Haldane and G. K. T. Ross (New York: Dover, 1955), pp. 1–78 and 79–130.

a method of finding out the truth", and Rule IX shows that by
method he does not mean some magic way of acquiring all knowledge in an instant; it reads "We ought to give the whole of our
attention to the most insignificant and most easily mastered facts,
and remain a long time in contemplation of them until we are
accustomed to behold the truth clearly and distinctly."

This seems harmless enough, and perhaps just because attention to method has been so characteristic of modern thought and
so fruitful, it seems rather like a truism. But in the field of contemporary philosophy it is opposed even more violently than is
skepticism. A recent compatriot of Descartes—Bergson—spoke for
one phase of the opposition, holding that the application of any
logical or precise concepts can only result in distorting and in
effect killing actual experience; for Bergson we can attain knowledge only by attuning our intuitions to the vital spirit which constantly manifests itself in the everchanging world. The proposal to
use precise method in philosophy is scorned by some because it
promises too little: because it offers no immediate prospect of a
full and final solution of all the imposing problems of traditional
philosophy. Others oppose it on almost the opposite ground that it
promises too much; they seem to feel that those who attempt to
apply a precise method look upon it as a kind of alchemist's formula which will automatically give us all the answers.

Actually, the insistence upon the formulation and use of method
arises typically, as with Descartes, from a keen consciousness of
the possibility of error, from the realization that truth cannot be
bought quickly or cheaply. It grows out of the recognition that
the universe is so complex and our powers of understanding so
limited that we can achieve knowledge only by painstaking, orderly, step-by-step investigation. And again, attention to method
is evidence of hope; for no one devises and applies a method unless he hopes to progress by it. The counselors of despair are those
who foredoom all precision to failure—who tell us that we can
never expect anything clearer or better-founded than the tenuous
generalizations that have nourished philosophical controversy for
centuries.

This malicious effort to introduce precise method into philosophy is thus in reality an outgrowth of both humility and hope. And

it is the condition of progress. The inspirations of poetical meta-physicians like Bergson will always be as well-grounded as they ever are. But in science and scientific philosophy the great man is one like Galileo or Descartes who provides or reinforces the means by which his own discoveries will be superseded.

In summary, then, Descartes faced his world as a skeptic with a method—in other words, as a courageous, humble and hopeful man. Perhaps our glance back at him may remind us that there can be no security in traditions that failed us; that by patient and systematic use of our best faculties we may advance, but that there is no black market in truth; that the results of wishful and fearful thinking cannot survive encounter with conflicting facts; and—finally—that a belief that will not stand the strictest scrutiny of doubt and reason will not withstand the oratory of the next demagogue.

6

Definition and Dogma

(In the five years since this talk was first delivered [1951], the cause for which it speaks has rapidly lost ground. With the Second World War now twice as far behind us, fading memories of our encounter with frenzy leave us prey to the assaults of unction. Flashes in the desert have already begun to bow the head and close the eyes of the measure of all things. And the sons of the saviors of blueberry pie are seduced by the sounding symbol.)

One of Robert Frost's longer poems ends with the line, "I had a lover's quarrel with the world." The philosopher has a like quarrel with common sense. He is not, as some think, her arch enemy; but rather her devoted admirer, whom she repeatedly betrays.

This has become more strikingly evident in recent years, when many philosophers have turned from the fabrication of magniloquent cosmological conjectures to the minute investigation of humble problems. For as soon as we look very closely at even the most familiar matters, we are beset by paradox and confusion. Let me give a few illustrations. Some of you are doubtless familiar with some of them; but I hope that few of you have yet been troubled by them all.

The first is the best known, and you may remember it if you have been through a course in logic. Obviously no statement can be both true and false; for a statement is true just in case it is not false, and false just in case it is not true. Consider the following statements:

1. College Hall is beautiful.
2. Statement 1 is false.
3. Statement 3 is false.

Now we well know that statement 1 is as false as can be; and that therefore statement 2 is true. But now what about 3? It says that it, itself, is false. Therefore if it truly says this, it must be false; while if it falsely says this, it must be true. In short if it is true, it is false; if it is false, it is true.

49

Now take an example of a quite different kind. Suppose we are investigating the truth of a scientific hypothesis such as that all polar bears are white. Obviously every white polar bear I discover is contributing evidence for—or a confirming instance of—this hypothesis. The general principle involved here seems to be that everything that is both an A and a B stands as a confirming instance for the hypothesis "All A's are B's." Now it clearly must be true that whatever is evidence for a given hypothesis is evidence for any logically equivalent hypothesis; for a logically equivalent hypothesis is merely another way of saying the same thing. Well, the statement "All non-white things are non-polar-bears" and the statement "All polar bears are white" are logically equivalent statements. By our general principle concerning evidence, anything that is not white and not a polar bear—for example, a black shoe—confirms the former statement that all non-white things are non-polar-bears. This black shoe must therefore also be confirming evidence for the equivalent hypothesis that all polar bears are white. Are we to conclude then, that we can confirm the hypothesis that all polar bears are white by assembling black shoes and other such objects? This may be a welcome conclusion to the armchair zoologist who prefers his fireside to Arctic wastes; but it is a highly disconcerting result for the philosopher of science.[1]

A different sort of problem arises with respect to the use of the subjunctive mood, which we handle freely and with confidence in ordinary discourse. Such statements as "If I had arrived two minutes earlier, I would have caught the train" are as common as such statements as "I was just two minutes late." We do not hesitate to say that if Hitler had been Napoleon, he would have had to do without airplanes. But also we do not hesitate to say that if Napoleon had been Hitler, he would have had airplanes. These are cases—like those of Hitler and Napoleon themselves—where a little more hesitation would have been in order. For if Hitler were Napoleon, then certainly Napoleon would be Hitler, and so we are saying with equal assurance that in that case the one individual Hitler-Napoleon would both have had airplanes and not have had them. Or take a slightly different case. Presumably no

---

1. [See further VIII below.]

great man has ever been born in the Aleutian Islands. Shall I say then "If Abraham Lincoln had been born in the Aleutian Islands, he would not have been great", or shall I say "If Abraham Lincoln had been born in the Aleutian Islands, then at least one great man would have been born there"? We begin to question whether we know what we mean by any contrary-to-fact conditional.

I want to go on now to a case very different from all those dealt with so far. Most of us are familiar with the notion of just-noticeable difference in psychology. Let us suppose that we have a set of gray disks differing very slightly from one another in lightness; and let us suppose they are arranged in linear order from lighter to darker as follows:

$$a\ b\ c\ d\ e\ f\ g\ h\ i\ \dots$$

Now for any element here, say d, another element is just-noticeably different from d if it is the nearest element (on either side) that is noticeably different from d. Let us suppose that h is the first such disk to the right of d. Now it may be that e, not noticeably different from d of course, *is* noticeably different from h, and is the first element left of h that is noticeably different from it. Then e and h are just-noticeably different, and d and h, as just seen above, are also just-noticeably different, even though d and h are further apart than e and h. To say that e and h as well as d and h are just-noticeably different is something like saying that although Philadelphia is farther from New York than from Trenton, still Philadelphia is just 100 miles from New York and also just 100 miles from Trenton.

Perhaps, however, our first definition of just-noticeable difference was too hasty. Perhaps we should say that two elements are just-noticeably different if they are nearest noticeably different elements in the sense that nothing between them is noticeably different from either. This makes e and h just-noticeably different but not d and h. But now we get another unwelcome result: although many elements lie to the right of d and are noticeably different from it, not even the first (namely h) is just-noticeably different from it. We find ourselves strongly disinclined to give up saying that h is just-noticeably different from d. But if we change our definition once more, so as to make d and h (but not e and h)

just-noticeably different, we are no better off. For then even though *e* is noticeably different from *h*, and is the first such element left of *h*, still *e* and *h* will not be just-noticeably different by this definition. The only conclusion seems to be that no definition will satisfy what seem like the minimal and simple demands of common sense.[2]

In all these cases, plainly, laborious efforts at careful analysis and precise definition are needed before we can be sure of talking consistently and making sense when we use the terms in question. I have illustrated questions rather than answers in order to show that difficult and important problems arise with respect to very simple and familiar matters of fact.

But the tendency of many philosophers to focus attention upon problems such as these is widely deplored. As the philosopher becomes more scientific in the sense that he becomes more an investigator of problems than an advocate of doctrines, he becomes more and more the object of complaints like those currently raised against the scientist. He is charged with wasting his time on trivial matters of intellectual curiosity rather than on problems of vital and pressing importance to human survival. He is charged with failing to attend to the important problem of establishing a scale of human values. And his skeptical spirit, his critical examination of even the fondest beliefs, and his exposure of the fallacies in even the most elementary and most widely accepted opinion, are held to be responsible for undermining the faith that we need to protect us from the inroads of totalitarian doctrine.

You all hear these charges against the scientist and the scientific philosopher almost daily: the cries of "too much fact, too little value", "too much detail, too little breadth", "too much doubt, too little faith", and so on. The clamor is so loud and constant that there must be many who are persuaded that the only hope of salvation lies in a return to ignorance, witchcraft, and idolatry. But let us look at these complaints more closely.

In the first place, much as we might like to have answers to all the great and grave problems confronting us, can we hope to find sound answers when we are still unable to deal with even the

2. [See further IX,1 below.]

simplest and most familiar matters without becoming embroiled in confusion and contradiction? Can we give answers when we are still unsure of the meaning of the simplest terms in the question? Isn't this like trying to solve equations in higher algebra before we have the laws of arithmetic straight? The appeal to abandon problems of detail and turn to the great issues is an appeal to abandon method and jump to conclusions. There are indeed times of emergency when this must be done. But the making of emergency decisions by conjecture is not the proper business of the scientist or the philosopher. His job is to increase, however slowly, the realm in which he can proceed with clarity and method. If the rulers of Greece had been faced with the problem of building the Brooklyn Bridge, they might have called in the greatest bridge builders of the time; but in the end, the job might have got done sooner if they had called in Euclid.

But let us turn now to the charge that science and analytic philosophy undermine all our faiths and leave us prey to any onset of forceful propaganda. It seems to me that no idea could be more mistaken—that there could be no worse misunderstanding of the dynamics of belief. As a matter of fact, the most promising candidate for apostleship in a new creed is the passionate devotee of an old one, not the skeptic who subjects all proposals to critical scrutiny. There is nothing very surprising about the political fanatic who suddenly becomes a religious zealot. What leaves us open to new dogmas is the habit of uncritical acceptance of beliefs. It is just for this reason that the missionary can win more converts in the jungle than in the laboratory.

Thus I think it is a most dangerous error to suppose that the proper defense against a fanatical creed is faith in a different one. It is like saying that a good way to avoid getting drunk on whiskey is to get drunk on gin, when what we want is to avoid being drunk at all. Getting drunk on one drink is not so different from getting drunk on another as it is from being sober; and the more times one is drunk the more vulnerable he is to getting drunk again. What one needs to stay sober is to learn how to distinguish between various offerings and how to say "no". This is also just what we need to protect ourselves from propaganda.

Let me make it quite clear then that I should like to see a more widespread critical attitude and scientific detachment. Contrary to what is being shouted from the housetops, we need more skepticism rather than more faith. Now this is far from saying that we should regard every opinion as quite as good as every other, that we should refrain from making any judgment. Such nihilism is as much an abandonment of a critical attitude and of intellectual integrity as in zealous faith in a credo. The essence of a skeptical scientific attitude is the use of our fullest powers to make a choice between hypotheses. A hypothesis once chosen may stand as a *conviction* that guides us in action. But it does not become a dogma until we regard it as permanent doctrine and refuse to subject it to repeated scrutiny. I am not proposing that we cease to appraise and compare hypotheses, but rather that we bring our best powers constantly to such comparison and appraisal.

We shall be told that this is against man's nature. It is natural and universal among men, it is said, to believe uncritically in something or someone greater than himself, to trust implicitly in a supernatural power or a great chieftain. All primitive tribes, some say, have some such belief; and all men in time of need, seek the solace of some such unreasoned belief. I need not challenge these facts. It is likewise natural for all men, early in their lives, to crawl on all fours, and to do it later in moments of weakness. But if the natural is what is done in periods of weakness and immaturity, then I suggest that the less natural the rejection of dogmatism and fanaticism is, the better.

But now a really serious question may be raised. Unless we have firm faiths, shall we have the morale to defend ourselves against unquestioning zealots? There is a widespread idea that strength of action varies directly with strength of belief; and that the wild-eyed fanatic is more than a match for any more detached man. I cannot offer any conclusive refutation of this belief, but I should like to make two points. First, if it is true, then we are lost in any case. If the price of victory is sacrifice of intellectual integrity, it is as high as the price of defeat. If we can beat madness only by being mad, we are vanquished before we fight. But this, I realize is cold comfort. I think something more encouraging can be said. For I suspect that the more fanatical a man is, the more actively on the defensive is he with regard to his dogma; that the skeptic rather is the more secure, and thus able to give the better account of himself. Perhaps you remember that during the last war reports came back from investigators who had asked our soldiers what they were fighting for. Everyone was much disturbed by the fact that the consensus was something like this: "We are fighting to get home and eat some blueberry pie." Now although I have enormous respect and deep admiration for blueberry pie, what impressed me about this was the answers that were *not* given. They were not fighting for shibboleths or slogans or grandiose ideals, they were not fighting for an abstract idea or for somebody's system; and the blueberry pie stood for their distrust of such ideals. This seemed to me very encouraging. And in the final test the pie proved itself to be pragmatically, as well as intellectually and somatically, a sturdier inspiration than Manifest Destiny. Perhaps there is hope in this.

Thus, the complaint that science gives us no moral guidance seems to me utterly unjust and obtuse. It is true that science and analytic philosophy do not "establish a scale of values". I don't know what that would mean. But in the development and the practice of scientific method and the scientific attitude, science offers us a pattern of behavior that is incompatible with conflict. Scientists, so long as they behave as scientists, have no battles with one another. It is not doubts that conflict, but beliefs. Bloody wars have been fought for varying beliefs, even for beliefs that call for universal brotherly love; but no one ever fought a man to prove a hypothesis and no one, I suppose, ever fought a duel in defense of Hume's skepticism. It is not what statements we entertain that causes trouble but how we entertain them. What is intelligent as a hypothesis may be vicious as a dogma.

Let no one then delude us into thinking that our only choice is between dogma and dogma. As long as we are free to choose, let us choose definition rather than dogma—hypothesis rather than hysteria. It is time enough for hysteria when hope is lost; and time enough for dogma when it is forced upon us.

I don't know what effect my talk has had upon you. If it has left you quite indifferent, we have both wasted time. If it has annoyed you, I am much encouraged. But if it by any chance appeals to you as a new gospel, it has been a most dismal failure.

II

Origins

FOREWORD

The first of these papers attacks empiricism; the second two attack rationalism. This no more convicts me of nihilism or vacillation than would attacks upon both the geocentric and the heliocentric hypotheses. The philosophical issue is as spurious as the cosmological one; absolute givenness, like absolute fixity, is a phantom; and the answer to the question whether the pristine unprocessed elements of knowledge are delivered to us prenatally or postnatally is that there are none. As pictures of the newborn mind, *tabula rasa* and *tabula inscripta* are both absurd. What I am attacking in all these papers here, as often elsewhere in my work, is epistemological absolutism.

Loss of security—whether as stability, authority, affluence, or certainty—is always painful; and my rejection of certainty is more often decried than applauded. Yet Roderick Firth,[1] after a painstaking study of the whole question, finds himself in substantial agreement with my conclusion. "Sense and Certainty" is not, however, primarily negative. Its major concern is the nature of knowledge, lacking certainty and a 'given'; and a treatment is sketched in terms of initial credibility, maximization of credibility, and signalling. The utility of these notions for dealing with various problems has been explored by several philosophers, especially by Israel Scheffler in the course of *Conditions of Knowledge*[2] and *Science and Subjectivity*.[3] Many remaining leads and

1. "The Anatomy of Certainty", *Philosophical Review,* vol. 76 (1967), pp. 3–27.

2. Glenview, Illinois: Scott, Foresman, 1965. See especially chaps. II and III.

3. Indianapolis: Bobbs-Merrill, 1967. See especially chap. V.

questions here seem to me well worth examining; and my having subsequently done nothing further with them attests only to my interest in too many other problems. Nevertheless, the interest shown here in nonlinguistic reference foreshadows the attention given to the general theory of symbols in *LA*. There, nonlinguistic as well as linguistic symbols may denote, while denotation is contrasted with another mode of reference called "exemplification".

Something more should perhaps be said here on the characteristics of the variety of reference I have called signalling. With a signal, as with an indicator-word, a special spatio-temporal relationship to the concrete symbol often determines the referent or referents: a storm cloud signals impending rain nearby; a quiver of the needle of a seismograph may signal an earthquake half a world away. Furthermore a signal, unlike a musical score, does not merely refer to whatever may comply with it, but has sentential force, saying in effect "a storm is coming", "a deer has just gone by", "an explosion will occur if a flame is brought near", or "stop". A signal may be artificial or natural, linguistic or nonlinguistic; and the replicas, if any, of a signal are seldom coextensive.

While "Sense and Certainty" was read early in my philosophical career as part of a symposium with two distinguished senior philosophers, Hans Reichenbach and my former teacher C. I. Lewis, the other two papers were delivered many years later as parts of symposia on some ideas of the noted linguist and political polemicist Noam Chomsky, one of my former students. Readers who, for lack of familiarity with those ideas, find some difficulty in following my two short papers are perhaps better off that way. The benefits of a cure are hardly sufficient incentive for exposure to the disease.

Yet these two papers are not entirely negative either. For example, Anticus in the dialogue stresses the possible importance that infant proficiency in the use of non-linguistic symbols may have in the acquisition of language. This passage, an outgrowth of my recent studies in the general theory of symbols, has been taken by Jerome Bruner as the text for the last chapter of his latest book.[4] He ventures the bold speculation that the child's

---

4. *Processes of Cognitive Growth* (Clark University Press, 1968).

learning to grasp an object in one hand and operate on it with the other marks the dawning of a distinction between *topic* and *comment* that foreshadows the linguistic distinction between subject and predicate. Whether or not this particular proposal can be carried through, it opens new paths of inquiry.

The discussion of Berkeley's theory of vision reminds us how current in cognitive psychology are some of the issues Berkeley raised.

1

Sense and Certainty

The argument for empirical certainties has two phases. The first is the effort to point out actual statements or kinds of statements that are plainly immune to doubt. The second is the effort to show, quite aside from the question just *what* statements are certain, that on theoretical grounds there must be *some* empirical certainties.

The popular hunting ground for empirical certainty is among statements confined to immediate phenomena. Statements concerning physical objects involve prediction in one way or another, and so may always turn out to be wrong. But, the argument runs, between the presentation of an element in experience and my simultaneous judgment that it is presented, there is no room for error or doubt. We may have trouble formulating these judgments correctly in language, but misuses of language or slips of tongue must not be confused with errors in judgment. If the judgment is immediate and confined to what is fully before me, it cannot be wrong. For how can I be mistaken at a given moment about the sheer content of my experience at that moment?

Despite the forthright appeal of this argument, the fact seems to be that my judgments at a moment about what I immediately apprehend at that moment are often wrong. That is to say, they are often withdrawn for good reason. This is sometimes denied on the ground that, since the momentary experience is instantly gone, the judgment is forever safe from further test. But the judgment I made a few moments ago that a reddish patch occupied the center of my visual field at that moment will be dropped if it conflicts with other judgments having a combined stronger claim to preservation. For example, if I also judged that the patch occupying the same region an instant later was blue, and also that the apparent color was constant over the brief period covering the two instants, I am going to have to drop one of the three judgments; and circumstances may point to the first as well as to either of the others. Indeed judgments concerning immediate phenomena may be rejected in favor of judgments concerning physical objects, as happens when I conclude that it could not have been a reddish patch after all since I was looking at a bluebird in sunlight with my eyes functioning normally. In either sort of case, I cannot reasonably plead a mere slip of the tongue; I am deciding that a judgment was wrong. If a statement may be withdrawn in the interest of compatibility with other statements, it is not certain in any ordinary sense; for certainty consists of immunity to such withdrawal.

Now someone may object that all I have shown is that a judgment concerning phenomena at a given moment may be doubted at some later moment, while what is being claimed is merely that such a judgment is certain *at* the moment in question. This seems to me a confusion. When we talk of certainty we are not—I take it —talking about a feeling of utter conviction; nor are we asking whether a judgment made at a given moment can be withdrawn at that same moment. We are talking of knowledge without possibility of error—or, in practice, of judgment immune to subsequent withdrawal for cause. I cannot be said to be certain about what occurs at a given moment, even at that moment, if I may justifiably change my mind about it at a later moment.

The advocate of empirical certainty, however, is not put off by a failure to find instances or by the problems encountered in arriving at an unexceptionable statement of his thesis. The difficulty of formulating the given must not, Mr. Lewis warns, lead us to suppose that there is no given; for if there were no given there would be no experience as we know it at all. No argument can erase the fact that experience and knowledge are not purely arbitrary, willful inventions. The sheer stubbornness of experience recognized by even the most thoroughgoing idealists is proof enough that there is *something there* in experience, some element not manufactured but given. This cannot be denied whatever may be the difficulties of articulating it.

But this all seems to me to point to, or at least to be compatible with, the conclusion that while something is given, nothing given is true; that while some things may be indubitable, nothing is certain. What we have been urged to grant amounts at most to this: materials for or particles of experience are given, sensory qualities or events or other elements are not created at will but presented, experience has some content even though our description of it may be artificial or wrong and even though the precise differentiation between what is given and what is not given may be virtually impossible. But to such content or materials or particles or elements, the terms "true", "false", and "certain" are quite inapplicable. These elements are simply there or not there. To grant that some are there is not to grant that anything is certain. Such elements may be indubitable in the vacuous sense that doubt is irrelevant to them, as it is to a desk; but they, like the desk, are equally devoid of certainty. They may be before us, but they are neither true nor false. For truth and falsity and certainty pertain to statements or judgments and not to mere particles or materials or elements. Thus, to deny that there are empirical certainties does not imply that experience is a pure fiction, that it is without content, or even that there is no given element.

Some of Mr. Lewis's arguments, however, are aimed directly at showing that there must be some indubitable judgments or statements, not merely that there is something presented. Unless some statements are certain, he argues, none is even probable. Mr. Reichenbach has disputed this argument on mathematical grounds, but perhaps Mr. Lewis intends only to make a somewhat less technical point. It plainly does us no good to know that a statement is probable with respect to certain premises unless we have some confidence in these premises. And we cannot just say that the premises themselves need merely be probable; for this means only that they in turn are probable with respect to other premises, and so on without end. Probability will be genuinely useful in judging the truth of sentences—the argument runs— only if the chain of probability relationships is somewhere moored to certainty. This is closely akin to the argument against a pure coherence theory of truth. Internal coherence is obviously a necessary but not a sufficient condition for the truth of a system; for we need also some means of choosing between equally tight systems that are incompatible with each other. There must be a tie to fact through, it is contended, some immediately certain statements. Otherwise compatibility with a system is not even a probable indication of the truth of any statement.

Now clearly we cannot suppose that statements derive their

credibility from other statements without ever bringing this string of statements to earth. Credibility may be transmitted from one statement to another through deductive or probability connections; but credibility does not spring from these connections by spontaneous generation. Somewhere along the line some statements, whether atomic sense reports or the entire system or something in between, must have initial credibility. So far the argument is sound. To use the term "probability" for this initial credibility is to risk misunderstanding since probability, strictly speaking, is not initial at all but always relative to specified premises. Yet all that is indicated is credibility to some degree, not certainty. To say that some statements must be initially credible if any statement is ever to be credible at all is not to say that any statement is immune to withdrawal. For indeed, as remarked earlier, no matter how strong its initial claim to preservation may be, a statement will be dropped if its retention—along with consequent adjustments in the interest of coherence—results in a system that does not satisfy as well as possible the totality of claims presented by all relevant statements. In the "search for truth" we deal with the clamoring demands of conflicting statements by trying, so to speak, to realize the greatest happiness of the greatest number of them. These demands constitute a different factor from coherence, the wanted means of choosing between different systems, the missing link with fact; yet none is so strong that it may not be denied. That we have probable knowledge, then, implies no certainty but only initial credibility.

Still, I am not satisfied that we have as yet gone to the heart of the matter. Just why is it so important to decide whether or not there is some empirical certainty? Mr. Reichenbach says that Mr. Lewis's view is a vestige of rationalism; but unlike the rationalists, Mr. Lewis obviously is not seeking certainties in order to use them as axioms for a philosophical system. If he could once prove that there are some empirical certainties, I doubt if he would be much disposed to go catch one. Rather he is convinced that such certainties are somehow essential to knowledge as we possess it. And I suspect that both his specific arguments and my counterarguments may leave him, as they leave me, with a feeling that the real issue has not yet been brought into relief. The underlying motivation for Mr. Lewis's whole argument is to be found, I think, in the problem of relating language to what it describes.

Consider the familiar problem faced by a common version of pragmatism. The meaning and truth of a statement are said to lie in its predictive consequences. These consequences are themselves statements; for from statements we can deduce, or even infer with probability, nothing but other statements. But, if the truth of these predictions depends in turn upon the truth of others derived from them, we are lost in an endless regress. The theory rests upon our being able, when a particular moment arrives, to decide with some degree of confidence whether a prediction made concerning that moment is or is not fulfilled. Accordingly, statements describing immediate experience are specifically exempted from the predictive criterion. But what, then, is to be said concerning them? What sort of relationship to experience makes such a statement true or credible? The connection between a statement and the very dissimilar experience it describes is not easy to grasp. Testimony to the rather mysterious character of the relation is found in the oblique way it is referred to in the literature. Mr. Quine wrote recently that a system of statements "impinges at its edges" upon experience; and he has been twitted for waxing so metaphorical. I suspect that the metaphorical term was chosen purposely to intimate that we have here an inadequately understood relationship. Again, Mr. Lewis, choosing simile rather than metaphor, merely likens the relationship to that between an outcry and the fearful apparition that evokes it.

What I am suggesting is that Mr. Lewis is actually more vitally concerned with the directness and immediacy and irreducibility of this relation between sensory experience and sentences describing it than with the certainty of these sentences. For, if this crucial relation seems inexplicable, perhaps—the thought runs—that is just because it is so fundamental and simple as to require no explanation. Learning a language may involve becoming acquainted with this elementary and irreducible relation, of which subsequent cases are instantly recognized. The claim that statements describing bare sense experience are certain then becomes an accidental by-product of the view that their truth is immediately and directly apprehended. And the real challenge that emerges is not to muster arguments showing that there are no empirical certainties, but to point a way of explaining the root relation between language and the nonlinguistic experience it describes.

Plainly we cannot look to resemblance for any help. The English statement "There is a blue patch" and its Chinese equivalent are very unlike, and both are even more unlike the blue patch itself. In no literal sense does language mirror experience. Yet this false start has something in its favor. The explanation in terms of resemblance is very good except for being so wrong. By that I mean that to explain the relation in question is to subsume it under or analyze it into more general relations. Such terms as "describes", "is true", "denotes", and "designates", require explanation insofar as they are idiosyncratic to cases where the first element in question is linguistic. If only words and strings of words denote or are true, our problem is to reduce these linguistic predicates to predicates that have familiar instances in nonlinguistic experience.[1]

A clue to a better starting point than resemblance lies in the fact that a toot may warn of an oncoming train or that a ray of dawn fortell the approach of daylight. Here are nonverbal events standing as *signals* for others. In like fashion two sensory experiences or phenomena are often such that the earlier is a promise or warning or signal of the later. A feeling of warmth may signal the imminent appearance of a fiery red patch in the visual field; an evenly shaded patch may signal a certain tactual experience to come. Of course, the situation is seldom quite so simple. More often, an isolated presentation signals another only conditionally upon certain behavior; that is, the tactual experience ensues only if I reach out my hand in a certain way. But this can be accommodated without difficulty merely by recognizing that a presentation is itself usually a partial, incomplete signal that combines with other presentations (such as those of bodily movements) to con-

---

1. Thus our problem differs from that considered by Tarski in "Der Wahrheitsbegriff in den formalisierten Sprachen", *Studia Philosophica,* vol. 1 (1936) pp. 261–405; English translation in *Logic, Semantics, Metamathematics* (London: Clarendon Press, Oxford U., 1956) in which he defines truth in terms of the linguistic notion of *satisfaction.*

stitute a signal for a subsequent experience. In other words, a signal is often comprised of more than one presentation; but this does not affect the important point that some nonlinguistic experiences function as signals.

If asked for a psychological account of signaling, we might say that the earlier experience arouses an expectation that is fulfilled, or a tension that is released, by the later one. But this and the various questions it inspires are not quite apposite to the present task. Our primary objective is not to explain this relation but to explain certain linguistic predicates in terms of it. So long as we are satisfied that the relation clearly obtains in nonlinguistic experience, we can postpone consideration of its anatomy and genealogy.

If experiences comprised of such presentations as shaded patches can signal, there is no mystery about how an irregular black patch or a brief stretch of sound may function in the same way. And a statement-event,[2] or other string of word-events, is simply some such patch or stretch. Just as a blue patch and some kinaesthetic presentations may signal the coming appearance of a red patch, so also does a statement-event—let us name it "F"— saying in advance that there will be a red patch in the visual field at the time in question, t. Statements are merely more complicated, and hence often more specific, than some other signals. It is clear enough how a signaling system can be elaborated and refined, once even a few signaling relationships are available. Under some circumstances or other, almost anything can be made to serve as a signal for almost any subsequent experience. Differentiation between conditioned and unconditioned signaling is irrelevant to our present purpose.

It may be contended that statements signal by virtue of their meaning, and that their signaling is thus essentially different from that of nonlinguistic elements. On the contrary, I should say rather that statements mean by virtue of their signaling, that meaning derives from—has its roots in—signaling. Yet this is not to say that

2. I use the term "statement-event" at times to emphasize that I think of a statement as an actual utterance or inscription-at-a-moment.

a statement either means or denotes what it signals; the explanation of meaning or denoting in terms of signaling would have to be much more complex than that.

So far, however, only statements like *F* that are in the future tense have been provided for. What are we to do about statements in the present tense? Suppose the statement *P* "There is now a red patch in the visual field" occurs at the time *t* above in question. *P* does not *signal* the simultaneous occurrence of the red patch; for signaling is always forecasting. Nevertheless, we know that *P* is true if and only if *F* is true. Hence *P* is true just in case *F* is a genuine signal. Although *P* does not itself signal the occurrence of the red patch, the truth of *P* is explained in terms of the truth of the earlier statement *F*, which does signal this occurrence. Statements in the past tense can be handled in the same way as those in the present tense; and tenseless statements, depending on whether they occur before, during, or after the time they pertain to, in the same way as statements in, respectively, the future, present, and past tense. A key point of the present proposal lies in its radical departure from the usual attack, which rests the truth of all statements upon that of statements in the present tense and leaves us at a loss to deal with these. After all, a thoroughly predictive theory can be carried through only by basing all truth upon the truth of statement-events concerning later events.

What I have been saying is meant to apply just to rather simple statements, like those illustrated, about phenomena. The relation of other statements to these is not part of my present problem. But even with respect to the simple statements in question, a number of problems must be left untouched. For example, I cannot here discuss the means available for dealing with a statement, in the present tense, such that no correlative statement in the future tense ever happened to occur.

I expect to be told that what I offer is a fragment of a time-worn theory in a somewhat topsy-turvy version. But I make no claim to a complete or unprecedented or pretty theory. Nor am I at all complacent about pragmatic-predictive epistemology in general. What I have tried to do here is to suggest how, in terms of a pragmatism not entirely alien to Mr. Lewis's point of view, the connection between language and what it describes may be given a reasonable explanation. In that case, this relation need no longer be regarded as immediate, mystic, and inexplicable. And this, if I am correct, will remove the last and deepest motivation for the defense of empirical certainty.

2

The Epistemological Argument

(Jason has brought back from the nomads of Outer Cantabridgia something that Anticus suspects is more fleece than golden.)

ANTICUS: Tell me about the resurrection.

JASON: After some centuries, the theory of Innate Ideas has been disinterred, and enthroned as the only adequate explanation for some striking facts concerning human linguistic proficiency.

A: What facts?

J: In the first place, that all natural languages, however diverse in origin and in superficials, have certain remarkable properties in common.

A: But is it remarkable that the elements of any collection have some remarkable properties in common? Surely we can find throughout the random deals of a pack of cards during an evening some very special uniformities; but we do not take them as posing a problem.

J: The claim is of course much stronger: that any language a human being can acquire has the properties in question.

A: I can imagine having a good deal of trouble mastering a language with an alphabet of a million letters and no word less than a million letters long. But does this call for elaborate explanation?

J: The properties in question are more interesting properties of grammatical form and of meaning.

A: Then the claim is indeed material and testable. I suppose these nomads have constructed languages lacking the properties in question, and found that earnest efforts to teach them to human beings fail. This seems to me not only remarkable but incredible; for the human mind strikes me as agile enough to learn, with ap-

This recasting and expansion of the material in my symposium talk "On Some Inimical Ideas" reflects no literary ambitions. The dialogue form offered advantages both in organization and in giving an appropriate tone to discussion of a theory that only my respect for its advocates enables me to take at all seriously.

propriate instruction and explanation, almost any transformation
or distortion of an already familiar language.

J: I have done them an injustice. They hold only that no language lacking the properties in question can be acquired by a
human being as an *initial* language. Once one language is available
and can be used for giving explanation and instruction, the limitations are transcended.

A: That answers my objection; but now I am puzzled as to how
they propose to examine the claim experimentally. Can they
really take an infant at birth, isolate it from all the influences of
our language-bound culture, and attempt to inculcate it with one
of the 'bad' artificial languages?

J: No. They readily admit this cannot be done. They regard
their claim as a hypothesis not subject to such direct experimental
test, but supported by ancillary considerations and evidence.

A: Very well; the claim is that certain statements about the
properties of languages that can be initially acquired are plausible,
and a certain explanation illuminating. But so far we have been
speaking vaguely of 'certain properties' or 'the properties in question'. If we are to judge plausibility, we must surely have a clearer
formulation or illustrations of what these properties are.

J: My informants are not always very explicit about this. They
cite some general grammatical properties now and then; but I
know you would say that each of these has been tailored to fit
the known natural languages and derives rather from the conceptual apparatus we impose upon these languages than from any
remarkable affinities among them. One case that might carry some
weight with you, though, concerns a concocted language called
Grubleen. It differs from ordinary English only in that it contains
the predicates "grue" (for "examined before t and green or not
so examined and blue") and "bleen" (for "examined before t and
blue or not so examined and green") instead of the predicates
"green" and "blue". The claim is that while a user of ordinary
English might be taught to use Grubleen, no human being could
acquire Grubleen as an initial language.

A: Though, as you say, experimental support for this can hardly
be expected. But I have another worry. Let us assume that we
now have before us an example of a language that cannot be

so acquired. Still, what in general is the difference between Grubleen-like and English-like languages? I see by your gesture that you are painfully aware of the difficulties of answering that question. So far we seem to have concluded first that the claim we are discussing cannot be experimentally tested even when we have an acknowledged example of a 'bad' language, and second that the claim has not even been formulated to the extent of citation of a single general property of 'bad' languages.

J: Nevertheless, important conjectures often cannot in the early stages be either precisely stated or actually tested. What you have said does not convince me that the claim ought to be rejected. If it is suggestive or promising enough, we ought rather to help examine and develop it.

A: You are right in principle; but I am not moved to try in this case, since the claim seems to me discredited by antecedent considerations.

J: Such as?

A: What we call a language is a fairly elaborate and sophisticated symbolic system. Don't you think, Jason, that before anyone acquires a language, he has had an abundance of practice in developing and using rudimentary prelinguistic symbolic systems in which gestures and sensory and perceptual occurrences of all sorts function as signs?

J: Yes; but *language*-acquisition is what is at issue.

A: You remember, though, that the real issue is over *initial* acquisition of languages, since once some language is available, acquisition of others is relatively easy.

J: True; but surely you do not call those rudimentary systems languages.

A: No; but I submit that our facility in going from one symbolic system to another is not much affected by whether each or either or neither is called a language; that acquisition of an initial language is acquisition of a secondary symbolic system; and that as we find no interesting limitations upon what we can acquire as a secondary language, we have no ground for believing that there are such limitations upon what we can acquire as a secondary symbolic system. In other words, when initial-language acquisition is seen as secondary-symbolic-system acquisition, the claim

71

that there are rigid limitations upon initial-language acquisition
is deprived of plausibility by the fact that there are no such limitations upon secondary-language acquisition.

J: I am afraid that what you say undermines also a second
claim: that initial-language acquisition is astonishingly fast.

A: Yes. If the language were the first symbolic system acquired,
and the process of acquisition considered to begin with the first
overt use of words, I suppose we might manage to work up some
astonishment. But if acquisition of the first language is merely
passage from a symbolic system already acquired to another that
we are taught, that is a much easier step. On the other hand, if
the process of acquiring the first language is thought of as beginning with the first use of symbols, then it must begin virtually at
birth and takes a long time.

J: Does not all this just move the question back from the nature
of languages that can be initially acquired to the nature of symbolic systems that can be so acquired? I suspect we would find
remarkable uniformities and astonishing speed of acquisition here.

A: We'd certainly have an even harder time doing it. Little of
the unimpressive evidence adduced with respect to languages
would be pertinent here; and obviously we cannot argue back
from uniformity of language to uniformity of prelinguistic system.
We'd have to examine symbols that are not overt and articulate
but rather inaccessible and ill-defined. And since the prelinguistic
systems are likely to be fragmentary as well as rudimentary, we'd
have trouble deciding when a system is acquired. And experimentation under all these difficulties would have to begin with
symbol-using from the moment of birth. But I hardly have to
refute your suspicions. Rather than facts crying for a theory, the
theory is crying for the facts.

J: Your objections are more telling against my inadequate
presentation than against the spirit and substance of what I am
trying to present. All sophistry aside, is there nothing in human
behavior you find striking enough to demand special explanation?

A: I can think of some remarkable behavioral facts that call for
no such explanation as a theory of innate ideas.

J: For example?

A: Well, I learned instantly to fall when dropped, and moreover to fall, no matter where dropped, precisely toward the center of the earth.

J: And for this remarkable fact we do need a theory—the theory of gravitation.

A: A set of laws subsuming this behavior under a very general description; but I am not inclined to attribute knowledge of these laws to the falling objects.

J: But this is mechanical behavior, common to animate and inanimate objects alike. Living things obey more special laws framed in terms of other notions. And human beings, in their cognitive behavior, obey still more special laws that require reference to innate ideas.

A: Your speed there is remarkable enough. Let us take it more slowly. Are you saying that human cognition is explicable only by supposing that the mind is supplied at the start with the interpretation of certain symbols? If that means only that it responds in a fixed way to certain stimuli, this suggests a view of mind we would both reject. What seems to me notable is not the fixity but rather the flexibility of the mind; its ability to adapt, adjust, transform; its way of achieving unity in variety, constancy amid instability, of inventing rather than obeying. The mind does not merely kick when tapped; it gropes. The groping and grasping, the seeking and finding, seem to me more characteristic than any mere program-reading.

J: You Berkeleyans always overstress the groping.

A: And you Leibnizians overstress the predetermination.

J: We go from pettifogging analysis to loose metaphor, and now name-calling! But seriously, I think it is just those capacities of the mind that you praise that can be accounted for only by the instrumentation of innate ideas.

A: We have been paying much less attention to what the theory is than to what it is supposed to explain. Let us now assume that for certain remarkable facts I have no alternative explanation. Of course, that alone does not dictate acceptance of whatever theory may be offered; for that theory might be worse than none. Inability to explain a fact does not condemn me to accept an intrinsically repugnant and incomprehensible theory. Now I gather that the theory here proposed is that certain ideas are implanted in the mind as original equipment.

J: Roughly that.

A: And being ideas, they are in consciousness?

J: No, not necessarily; not even usually.

A: Then they are in the subconscious mind, operating upon cognitive processes, and capable of being brought into full consciousness?

J: Not even that. I may have no direct access to them at all. My only way of discovering them in my own mind may be by the same methods that someone else might use to infer that I have them, or I to infer that he does.

A: Then I am puzzled. You seem to be saying that these innate ideas are neither innate nor ideas.

J: What is innate are not concepts, images, formulae, or pictures, but rather 'inclinations, dispositions, habits, or natural potentialities'.

A: But I thought the ideas were posited to explain the capacities. If all that is claimed is that the mind has certain inclinations and capacities, how can you justify calling these ideas?

J: The justification is historical. Descartes and Leibniz used the term "innate idea" in just this sense. But after all, it is the theory that counts, not the term "innate idea".

A: In that case, why all the effort at historical justification? And why, after admitting the term is controversial and claiming it is unnecessary, do these people go on using it? For a very compelling, but not very good, reason: that until the term "innate idea" is applied, what is advocated is the rather trivial truth that the mind has certain capacities, tendencies, limitations. Once we apply the term, in anything like its normal use, the thesis becomes far from obvious; but unfortunately, it becomes false or meaningless. John Locke made all this acutely clear.

J: Again I am afraid I have not been careful enough. Rather than identify the innate ideas with capacities, etc., I probably should have said that these ideas exist as or are 'innate as' such capacities.

A: A few minutes ago you accused me of sophistry; but I bow

before the subtlety of that last statement. Go again, Jason, and bring back to me all the mysteries of ideas being innate as capacities. Then, if you like, we can talk again about unsubstantiated conjectures that cry for explanation by implausible and untestable hypotheses that hypostatize ideas that are innate in the mind as non-ideas.

3

The Emperor's New Ideas

In brief reply to some of Chomsky's Arguments:

1. I plead not guilty to the charge of ignoring the standard critical evaluation of Locke's argument against innate ideas. What has always shocked me is how badly the commentators miss the central point of Locke's powerful case. Locke had, as I have, a good deal of trouble understanding the so-called theory. He therefore formulated every clear version he could think of and showed each to be either trivially true or obviously false. The remaining versions were too subtle for either him or me to grasp. He did indeed refute the theory only in its cruder—i.e., more intelligible—forms; the rest are forever immune to refutation.

2. On the other hand, I plead guilty to the charge of ignorance of most of current linguistic theory. Linguists are probably justified in taking toward me an attitude like that of Candide's companion toward the playwright ". . . who does not know a word of Arabic and yet the scene is in Arabia; moreover . . . is a man who does not believe in innate ideas; tomorrow I shall bring you twenty articles against him".[1] Such ignorance probably explains why I can never follow the argument that starts from interesting differences in behavior between parallel phrases such as "eager to please" and "easy to please"; that characterizes these differences as matters of 'deep' rather than 'surface' structure; and that moves on to innate ideas.

The extent of my obtuseness will be underlined if I remark that also "cat" and "rat", like "eager" and "easy", are similar in many ways, and that certain parallel longer expressions in which they are embedded behave quite disparately. "Cattle" is plural, "rattle" is singular. There is such a thing as a rattling but not such a thing as a cattling. And while rattles rattle, cattle do not cattle; that is, just as we can 'nominalize' "eager to please" but not "easy to please", so we can 'verbalize' "rattle" but not "cattle". Are all

1. Voltaire, *Candide,* chap. 23.

these peculiarities 'deep' as contrasted with the difference between "cat" and "rat"? I am not denying that the case of "eager" and "easy" may have important features not shared by the case of "cat" and "rat". I am asking for the grounds for the inference from such features, or from any other peculiarities in the behavior of words, to innate ideas.

Use of the term "deep" in these contexts seems to me ill grounded and prejudicial. Mathematicians do indeed use the term "deep", but only—as they use "elegant"—to make quite unofficial and extrasystematic comment. No mathematical argument rests on a distinction between what is deep and what is shallow.

One might argue that the shapes and colors in paintings are in some sense surface (or obvious) features, while the features that identify a picture as by a certain artist or of a certain school or period are in some sense deep (or obscure). Yet we learn with rather few examples to make some of the latter rather subtle distinctions. Must the mind therefore have been endowed at birth with a 'schematism' of artistic styles?

3. The linguist may be forgiven for a vocational myopia that blinds him to all symbol systems other than languages. Anyone else recognizes that gestures, nods of approval and disapproval, pointings, facial expressions, bodily demonstrations, sketches, diagrams, models, play an important role in the acquisition and inculcation of skills of all sorts; and that mastery of symbols of many of these kinds occurs before, and aids enormously, in the acquisition of language.

Chomsky argues that if the symbol systems we acquire prior to the acquisition of a full-fledged language have the characteristics he finds to be essential for a language, then acquisition of the prior systems would be equally remarkable and in need of explanation, while if the prior systems do not have these features, they can be of little help in acquiring a language. The latter part of this argument seems to me quite specious. If a man has made a clock by hand, that is a remarkable accomplishment. I understand it better if he tells me how he first fashioned crude tools, used these to make more refined ones, and eventually made the clock. I do not protest that he could not have made the clock without first having made a timekeeping instrument. The tools used in making the clock are not timekeepers, and from the clock alone we cannot infer back to any specific characterization of the tools made and used at any stage along the way.

4. After arguing that the matter of "grue" and "bleen" is rather irrelevant to the point at issue, Chomsky writes ". . . every language learner (in fact, every mouse, chimpanzee, etc.) uses green rather than grue as a basis for generalization." I am sure that speakers accustomed to projecting "grue" rather than "green" would be equally confident that animals use grue rather than green as a basis for generalization.

5. Chomsky argues that if I am willing to speak of ideas in the mind, I should not find incomprehensible the notion of an idea being in the mind from the start. But from the fact that I know what an embodied idea is—an idea couched in words or other symbols—it does not follow that I know what a disembodied idea is. I know what a horse with spirit is, but not what the spirit is without the horse.

As I use the term "idea" we can reasonably ask whether or not the mind has an idea of one or another characteristic of its behavior. For Chomsky, apparently, such a question is meaningless; for he seems to take such characteristics as themselves ideas. My objection to this is not the violence it does to past or present practice, but the way it encourages an equivocation that gives plausibility to an otherwise preposterous thesis. The innocuous truism that the mind tends to behave in certain ways rather than others is implicitly taken as evidence for the obviously false hypothesis that embodied ideas are in the mind at the start or for the incomprehensible hypothesis that disembodied ideas are.

But just what Chomsky means by "idea" is hard to determine. He rejects most proffered explanations without providing any clear statement of his own. If ideas are not applied symbols, features of structure, dispositions, ways of behaving, mechanisms, what are they? To be told that "idea" is a theoretical term helps very little. He speaks of 'schematisms', but what are these other than systems of linguistic or other symbols used for organizing experience? Perhaps they are *principles* according to which the mind organizes experience, though the mind need not be aware of these principles; they are in the mind only in the sense that they can be inferred from what the mind does. But are these principles anything more than descriptions, by an observer, of the resultant organization? Chomsky's answer may be that what is in question is much more than one among alternative sets of descriptions; it is a theory that by its explanatory and predictive power may vanquish competitors and shine forth as the one and only truth about the mind. Yet even so, the theory need no more be in the minds in question than the theory of gravitation need be in bodies. And since a theory may be embodied in one language or in many languages, but can hardly exist apart from languages, how could it be in the mind prior to language?

Here we may be told that of course the theory is not said to be in the mind described, but rather that the theory ascribes innate ideas to the mind. But what are these ideas? Not applied symbols, dispositions, etc. Are they principles, then? This leads us again around a circuit that is devious enough to make us forget that we are going nowhere.

The theory of innate ideas is by no means crude. It is of exquisite subtlety, like the gossamer golden cloth made for that ancient emperor. But the emperor needs to be told that his wise men, like his tailors, deceive him; that just as the body covered with the miraculous cloth has nothing on it, the mind packed with innate ideas has nothing in it.[2]

2. I am indebted to Robert Schwartz for comments that have led to some revisions of an earlier draft of this paper.

4

Review of Armstrong's
Berkeley's Theory of Vision

D. M. Armstrong, *Berkeley's Theory of Vision: A Critical Examination of Bishop Berkeley's Essay towards a New Theory of Vision* (Melbourne: Melbourne University Press, 1960), pp. xiv, 106.

Berkeley's great small *Essay,* after long neglect, is beginning to receive some of the attention it deserves. The present commentary is serious and respectful; but is not the thorough and balanced study it promises to be at the outset. I should be the last to disagree with Armstrong's insistence upon viewing the *Essay* less as a preface to the *Principles* than as an early monument in the study of what is twice spoken of as 'the structure of appearance'. But Armstrong is almost exclusively concerned with arguing two issues; he gives short shrift to other matters of equal importance, and in his final chapter he leaves Berkeley for Hume.

Much of the book is occupied with the question whether Berkeley is right in maintaining that distance is not immediately seen (or perceived by vision unaided). Armstrong properly rejects many of the usual arguments against this contention. But the argument he ultimately relies upon is a curious one: that the case against immediate perception of distance by touch is even stronger than the case against immediate perception of distance by sight; and that since distance thus cannot be immediately perceived by touch it must be immediately perceived by sight. Surely this is a *nonsequitur*. The natural, and I should suppose standard present-day, conclusion is that perception of distance is the product of cooperation between sight and touch. It is especially surprising that Armstrong overlooks this answer, since he stresses the importance of just such joint operation in arguing for his second major thesis.

This second thesis is that Berkeley is wrong in maintaining that no spatial or other idea is common to any two senses. Here Armstrong makes effective use of the strong arguments available to him: (1) that some facts of perception are understandable only in terms of the integrated operations of more than one sense, and (2) that perception of simultaneity and succession as cutting across, and relating elements from, diverse sense-realms is required for the very process of learning by experience that Berkeley depends upon so heavily.

Of the many other intriguing and significant questions raised by the *Essay*, Armstrong discusses only a few, and in rather cursory fashion. His book is for readers who have first thoroughly studied and long-pondered the *Essay* itself.

Supplementary Readings for Chapter II
secondary to references within text and footnotes

Berkeley, G., "An Essay Towards a New Theory of Vision", *Works on Vision* (C. Turbayne, ed.), Indianapolis: Bobbs-Merrill, 1962.

Lewis, C. I., *Mind and the World Order,* New York: Scribner, 1929, Chap. II.

————., *An Analysis of Knowledge and Valuation,* La Salle, Illinois: Open Court, 1947, Book II, Chaps. VII–IX.

————., "The Given Element in Empirical Knowledge", *Philosophical Review,* Vol. 61 (1952), pp. 168–175.

Locke, J., *An Essay Concerning Human Understanding,* (A. C. Fraser, ed.), New York: Dover, 1959, Books I and IV.

Reichenbach, H., "Are Phenomenal Reports Absolutely Certain?", *Philosophical Review,* Vol. 61 (1952), pp. 147–159.

Russell, B., *An Inquiry into Meaning and Truth,* New York: Norton, 1940, Chaps. IX–XI.

————., *Human Knowledge,* New York: Simon and Schuster, 1948, Part V, Chap. VI.

Scheffler, I., *Conditions of Knowledge,* Glenview, Illinois: Scott, Foresman, 1965, Chaps. II and III.

————., *Science and Subjectivity,* Indianapolis: Bobbs-Merrill, 1967, Chap. V.

III

Art

FOREWORD

The relativism rampant in foregoing chapters reverberates here. In "Art and Authenticity", the popular conviction that there can be no aesthetic difference between two pictures if they cannot be distinguished by merely looking at them is undermined by challenging the very notion of "merely looking". And if, as I have argued above and in the first chapter of *Languages of Art*, there is no one right way of describing or seeing or picturing the world, the availability of equally acceptable alternatives is not a feature that distinguishes science and philosophy from perception and art. To exorcize the myth of absolutism of representation is to breach the barrier separating art from science and open the way to a unified general study of modes of symbolization. "Art and Inquiry" discusses the breakdown of the dichotomy between the arts and the sciences, and suggests a consequent conceptual reorganization of the whole field of knowledge and behavior. "Merit as Means" develops a point that was later summarized in a paragraph of "Art and Inquiry".

The distinction between the autographic and the allographic introduced in "Art and Authenticity" is further refined by the study of notation in the following chapter of *LA;* but one point is not made clear. Where, for example, a composer provides prescriptions in a non-notational system rather than scores, the classes of performances called for do not constitute either autographic or allographic works. They are not autographic; for their identification does not depend on history of production. They are not allographic; for their identification is not independent of history of production. They are non-autographic and non-allographic; for identity of work (true, transitive identity) is not established in this case. The terms "autographic" and "allographic" are mutually exclusive, and they exhaust all cases where work-identity is established at all.

"Some Notes on *Languages of Art*" is my response, in a symposium, to three discussions of the book.[1] In replying to the frequent objection that by taking perfect compliance with the score as the test of a genuine performance of the work I do violence to ordinary usage, I have discussed how the definition of theoretical terms may be controlled by ordinary usage in ways that require neither extensional identity nor, perhaps, even extensional isomorphism.[2] Whether such a criterion for definition of theoretical terms can be consolidated with the isomorphism criterion for constructional definitions deserves further study. "Further Notes" consists of hitherto unpublished replies to selected, as yet unpublished, talks from another symposium; a new note in answer to an intelligent question that has been raised more than once; and published replies to two reviews. Some reviews much abler than these two are listed among the supplementary readings for this chapter.

An unexpected recent development is the detailed and extensive application to musical theory of ideas and formal constructions from *SA,* as well as from *LA,* in Benjamin Boretz's "Meta-Variations: Studies in the Foundations of Musical Thought".[3]

The review of *Art and Illusion* celebrates more than it criticizes an important and illuminating book. Many of the points raised in this review are treated more fully elsewhere in my work: the conventionality of perspective in Chapter I of *Languages of Art;* the nature of schemata and of the distinction between representation and expression in Chapter II of the same book; and the role of schemata in induction in Chapter IV of *Fact, Fiction, and Forecast.*

1. These appear in *Journal of Philosophy,* Vol. 67 (1970), pp. 531–563. They are: "Nelson Goodman's *Languages of Art*", by R. Wollheim, pp. 531–539; "Nelson Goodman's *Languages of Art* from a Musical Point of View", by B. Boretz, pp. 540–552; and "Literature as Performance, Fiction and Art", by Barbara Herrnstein Smith, pp. 553–563.

2. Concerning extensional isomorphism, see the Foreword to Chap. I above, and *SA I.*

3. *Perspectives of New Music,* Vol. 8, no. 1 (Fall 1969), pp. 1–74; and Vol. 8, no. 2 (Spring 1970), pp. 49–111.

1

Art and Authenticity

. . . the most tantalizing question of all: If a fake is so expert that even after the most thorough and trustworthy examination its authenticity is still open to doubt, is it or is it not as satisfactory a work of art as if it were unequivocally genuine?

Aline B. Saarinen*

1. The Perfect Fake

Forgeries of works of art present a nasty practical problem to the collector, the curator, and the art historian, who must often expend taxing amounts of time and energy in determining whether or not particular objects are genuine. But the theoretical problem raised is even more acute. The hardheaded question why there is any aesthetic difference between a deceptive forgery and an original work challenges a basic premiss on which the very functions of collector, museum, and art historian depend. A philosopher of art caught without an answer to this question is at least as badly off as a curator of paintings caught taking a Van Meegeren for a Vermeer.

The question is most strikingly illustrated by the case of a given work and a forgery or copy or repoduction of it. Suppose we have before us, on the left, Rembrandt's original painting *Lucretia* and, on the right, a superlative imitation of it. We know from a fully documented history that the painting on the left is the original; and we know from X-ray photographs and microscopic examination and chemical analysis that the painting on the right is a recent fake. Although there are many differences between the two—e.g., in authorship, age, physical and chemical characteristics, and market value—we cannot see any difference between them; and if they are moved while we sleep, we cannot then tell which is which by merely looking at them. Now we are pressed with the question whether there can be any aesthetic difference between

* *New York Times Book Review,* July 30, 1961, p. 14.

the two pictures; and the questioner's tone often intimates that the answer is plainly *no*, that the only differences here are aesthetically irrelevant.

We must begin by inquiring whether the distinction between what can and what cannot be seen in the pictures by 'merely looking at them' is entirely clear. We are looking at the pictures, but presumably not 'merely looking' at them, when we examine them under a microscope or fluoroscope. Does merely looking, then, mean looking without the use of any instrument? This seems a little unfair to the man who needs glasses to tell a painting from a hippopotamus. But if glasses are permitted at all, how strong may they be, and can we consistently exclude the magnifying glass and the microscope? Again, if incandescent light is permitted, can violet-ray light be ruled out? And even with incandescent light, must it be of medium intensity and from a normal angle, or is a strong raking light permitted? All these cases might be covered by saying that 'merely looking' is looking at the pictures without any use of instruments other than those customarily used in looking at things in general. This will cause trouble when we turn, say, to certain miniature illuminations or Assyrian cylinder seals that we can hardly distinguish from the crudest copies without using a strong glass. Furthermore, even in our case of the two pictures, subtle differences of drawing or painting discoverable only with a magnifying glass may still, quite obviously, be aesthetic differences between the pictures. If a powerful microscope is used instead, this is no longer the case; but just how much magnification is permitted? To specify what is meant by merely looking at the pictures is thus far from easy; but for the sake of argument,[1] let us suppose that all these difficulties have been resolved and the notion of 'merely looking' made clear enough.

Then we must ask who is assumed to be doing the looking. Our questioner does not, I take it, mean to suggest that there is no aesthetic difference between two pictures if at least one person,

---

1. And only for the sake of argument—only in order not to obscure the central issue. All talk of mere looking in what follows is to be understood as occurring within the scope of this temporary concession, not as indicating any acceptance of the notion on my part.

say a cross-eyed wrestler, can see no difference. The more pertinent question is whether there can be any aesthetic difference if
nobody, not even the most skilled expert, can ever tell the pictures
apart by merely looking at them. *But notice now that no one can
ever ascertain by merely looking at the pictures that no one ever
has been or will be able to tell them apart by merely looking at
them.* In other words, the question in its present form concedes
that no one can ascertain by merely looking at the pictures that
there is no aesthetic difference between them. This seems repugnant to our questioner's whole motivation. For if merely looking
can never establish that two pictures are aesthetically the same,
something that is beyond the reach of any given looking is admitted as constituting an aesthetic difference. And in that case,
the reason for not admitting documents and the results of scientific
tests becomes very obscure.

The real issue may be more accurately formulated as the question whether there is any aesthetic difference between the two
pictures *for me* (or for *x*) if I (or *x*) cannot tell them apart by
merely looking at them. But this is not quite right either. For I can
never ascertain merely by looking at the pictures that even I shall
never be able to see any difference between them. And to concede
that something beyond any given looking at the pictures by me
may constitute an aesthetic difference between them *for me* is,
again, quite at odds with the tacit conviction or suspicion that
activates the questioner.

Thus the critical question amounts finally to this: is there any
aesthetic difference between the two pictures for *x* at *t*, where *t* is
a suitable period of time, if *x* cannot tell them apart by merely
looking at them at *t*? Or in other words, can anything that *x* does
not discern by merely looking at the pictures at *t* constitute an
aesthetic difference between them for *x* at *t*?

2. The Answer

In setting out to answer this question, we must bear clearly in
mind that what one can distinguish at any given moment by
merely looking depends not only upon native visual acuity but

upon practice and training.[2] Americans look pretty much alike to a Chinese who has never looked at many of them. Twins may be indistinguishable to all but their closest relatives and acquaintances. Moreover, only through looking at them when someone has named them for us can we learn to tell Joe from Jim upon merely looking at them. Looking at people or things attentively, with the knowledge of certain presently invisible respects in which they differ, increases our ability to discriminate between them—and between other things or other people—upon merely looking at them. Thus pictures that look just alike to the newsboy come to look quite unlike to him by the time he has become a museum director.

Although I see no difference now between the two pictures in question, I may learn to see a difference between them. I cannot determine now by merely looking at them, or in any other way, that I *shall* be able to learn. But the information that they are very different, that the one is the original and the other the forgery, argues against any inference to the conclusion that I *shall not* be able to learn. And the fact that I may later be able to perceive a distinction between the pictures that I cannot perceive now makes the actual differences between them aesthetically important to me now.

Furthermore, to look at the pictures now with the knowledge that the left one is the original and the other the forgery may help develop the ability to tell which is which later by merely looking at them. Thus, with information not derived from the present or any past looking at the pictures, the present looking may have a

2. Germans learning English often cannot, without repeated effort and concentrated attention, hear any differences at all between the vowel sounds in "sup" and "cop". Like effort may sometimes be needed by the native speaker of a language to discern differences in color, etc., that are not marked by his elementary vocabulary. Whether language affects actual sensory discrimination has long been debated among psychologists, anthropologists, and linguists; see the survey of experimentation and controversy in Segall, Campbell, and Herskovits, *The Influence of Culture on Visual Perception* (Indianapolis: Bobbs-Merrill, 1966), pp. 34–48. The issue is unlikely to be resolved without greater clarity in the use of "sensory", "perceptual", and "cognitive", and more care in distinguishing between what a person can do at a given time and what he can learn to do.

quite different bearing upon future lookings from what it would otherwise have. The way the pictures in fact differ constitutes an aesthetic difference between them for me now, because my knowledge of the way they differ bears upon the role of the present looking in training my perceptions to discriminate between these pictures, and between others.

But that is not all. My knowledge of the difference between the two pictures, just because it affects the relationship of the present to future lookings, informs the very character of my present looking. This knowledge instructs me to look at the two pictures differently now, even if what I see is the same. Beyond testifying that I may learn to see a difference, it also indicates to some extent the kind of scrutiny to be applied now, the comparisons and contrasts to be made in imagination, and the relevant associations to be brought to bear. It thereby guides the selection, from my past experience, of items and aspects for use in my present looking. Thus not only later but right now, the unperceived difference between the two pictures is a consideration pertinent to my visual experience with them.

In short, although I cannot tell the pictures apart merely by looking at them now, the fact that the left-hand one is the original and the right-hand one a forgery constitutes an aesthetic difference between them for me now because knowledge of this fact (1) stands as evidence that there may be a difference between them that I can learn to perceive, (2) assigns the present looking a role as training toward such a perceptual discrimination, and (3) makes consequent demands that modify and differentiate my present experience in looking at the two pictures.[3]

Nothing depends here upon my ever actually perceiving or being able to perceive a difference between the two pictures. What

3. In saying that a difference *between the pictures* that is thus relevant to my present experience in looking at them constitutes an aesthetic difference between them, I am of course not saying that everything (e.g., drunkenness, snow blindness, twilight) that may cause my experiences of them to differ constitutes such an aesthetic difference. Not every difference in or arising from how the pictures happen to be looked at counts; only differences in or arising from how they are to be looked at. Concerning the aesthetic, more is said later in this section and in *LA VI,3–6*.

informs the nature and use of my present visual experience is not the fact or the assurance that such a perceptual discrimination is within my reach, but evidence that it may be; and such evidence is provided by the known factual differences between the pictures. Thus the pictures differ aesthetically for me now even if no one will ever be able to tell them apart by merely looking at them.

But suppose it could be *proved* that no one ever will be able to see any difference? This is about as reasonable as asking whether, if it can be proved that the market value and yield of a given U. S. bond and one of a certain nearly bankrupt company will always be the same, there is any financial difference between the two bonds. For what sort of proof could be given? One might suppose that if nobody—not even the most skilled expert—has ever been able to see any difference between the pictures, then the conclusion that I shall never be able to is quite safe; but, as in the case of the Van Meegeren forgeries[4] (of which, more later), distinctions not visible to the expert up to a given time may later become manifest even to the observant layman. Or one might think of some delicate scanning device that compares the color of two pictures at every point and registers the slightest discrepancy. What, though, is meant here by "at every point"? At no mathematical point, of course, is there any color at all; and even some physical particles are too small to have color. The scanning device must thus cover at each instant a region big enough to have color but at least as small as any perceptible region. Just how to manage this is puzzling since "perceptible" in the present context means "discernible by merely looking", and thus the line between perceptible and nonperceptible regions seems to depend on the arbitrary line between a magnifying glass and a microscope. If some such line is drawn, we can never be sure that the delicacy of our instruments is superior to the maximal attainable acuity of unaided perception. Indeed, some experimental psychologists are inclined to conclude that every measurable difference in light can sometimes be

4. For a detailed and fully illustrated account, see P. B. Coremans, *Van Meegeren's Faked Vermeers and De Hooghs,* trans. A. Hardy and C. Hutt (Amsterdam: J. M. Meulenhoff, 1949). The story is outlined in Sepp Schüller, *Forgers, Dealers, Experts,* trans. J. Cleugh (New York: G. P. Putnam's Sons, 1960), pp. 95–105.

detected by the naked eye.[5] And there is a further difficulty. Our scanning device will examine color—that is, reflected light. Since reflected light depends partly upon incident light, illumination of every quality, of every intensity, and from every direction must be tried. And for each case, especially since the paintings do not have a plane surface, a complete scanning must be made from every angle. But of course we cannot cover every variation, or even determine a single absolute correspondence, in even one respect. Thus the search for a proof that I shall never be able to see any difference between the two pictures is futile for more than technological reasons.

Yet suppose we are nevertheless pressed with the question whether, if proof *were* given, there would then be any aesthetic difference for me between the pictures. And suppose we answer this farfetched question in the negative. This will still give our questioner no comfort. For the net result would be that if no difference between the pictures can in fact be perceived, then the existence of an aesthetic difference between them will rest entirely upon what is or is not proved by means other than merely looking at them. This hardly supports the contention that there can be no aesthetic difference without a perceptual difference.

Returning from the realm of the ultra-hypothetical, we may be faced with the protest that the vast aesthetic difference thought to obtain between the Rembrandt and the forgery cannot be accounted for in terms of the search for, or even the discovery of, perceptual differences so slight that they can be made out, if at all, only after much experience and long practice. This objection can be dismissed at once; for minute perceptual differences can bear enormous weight. The clues that tell me whether I have caught the eye of someone across the room are almost indiscernible. The actual differences in sound that distinguish a fine from a mediocre performance can be picked out only by the well-trained ear. Ex-

5. Not surprisingly, since a single quantum of light may excite a retinal receptor. See M. H. Pirenne and F. H. C. Marriott, "The Quantum Theory of Light and the Psycho-Physiology of Vision", in *Psychology,* ed. S. Koch (New York: McGraw-Hill, 1959), Vol. I, p. 290; also Theodore C. Ruch, "Vision", in *Medical Psychology and Biophysics* (Philadelphia: W. B. Saunders, 1960), p. 426.

tremely subtle changes can alter the whole design, feeling, or expression of a painting. Indeed, the slightest perceptual differences sometimes matter the most aesthetically; gross physical damage to a fresco may be less consequential than slight but smug retouching.

All I have attempted to show, of course, is that the two pictures can differ aesthetically, not that the original is better than the forgery. In our example, the original probably is much the better picture, since Rembrandt paintings are in general much better than copies by unknown painters. But a copy of a Lastman by Rembrandt may well be better than the original. We are not called upon here to make such particular comparative judgments or to formulate canons of aesthetic evaluation. We have fully met the demands of our problem by showing that the fact that we cannot tell our two pictures apart merely by looking at them does not imply that they are aesthetically the same—and thus does not force us to conclude that the forgery is as good as the original.

The example we have been using throughout illustrates a special case of a more general question concerning the aesthetic significance of authenticity. Quite aside from the occurrence of forged duplication, does it matter whether an original work is the product of one or another artist or school or period? Suppose that I can easily tell two pictures apart but cannot tell who painted either except by using some device like X-ray photography. Does the fact that the picture is or is not by Rembrandt make any aesthetic difference? What is involved here is the discrimination not of one picture from another but of the class of Rembrandt paintings from the class of other paintings. My chance of learning to make this discrimination correctly—of discovering projectible characteristics that differentiate Rembrandts in general from non-Rembrandts—depends heavily upon the set of examples available as a basis. Thus the fact that the given picture belongs to the one class or the other is important for me to know in learning how to tell Rembrandt paintings from others. In other words, my present (or future) inability to determine the authorship of the given picture without use of scientific apparatus does not imply that the authorship makes no aesthetic difference to me; for knowledge of the authorship, no matter how obtained, can contribute materially toward developing my ability to determine without such apparatus whether or not any picture, including this one on another occasion, is by Rembrandt. Moreover, where information is such as to be important to me when I have it, it is important to me to have, and thus important to me whether I have it or not.

Incidentally, one rather striking puzzle is readily solved in these terms. When Van Meegeren sold his pictures as Vermeers, he deceived most of the best-qualified experts; and only by his confession was the fraud revealed.[6] Nowadays even the fairly knowing layman is astonished that any competent judge could have taken a Van Meegeren for a Vermeer, so obvious are the differences. What has happened? The general level of aesthetic sensibility has hardly risen so fast that the layman of today sees more acutely than the expert of twenty years ago. Rather, the better information now at hand makes the discrimination easier. Presented with a single unfamiliar picture at a time, the expert had to decide whether it was enough like known Vermeers to be by the same artist. And every time a Van Meegeren was added to the corpus of pictures accepted as Vermeers, the criteria for acceptance were modified thereby; and the mistaking of further Van Meegerens for Vermeers became inevitable. Now, however, not only have the Van Meegerens been subtracted from the precedent-class for Vermeer, but also a precedent-class for Van Meegeren has been established. With these two precedent-classes before us, the characteristic differences become so conspicuous that telling other Van Meegerens from Vermeers offers little difficulty. Yesterday's ex-

6. That the forgeries purported to have been painted during a period from which no Vermeers were known made detection more difficult but does not essentially alter the case. Some art historians, on the defensive for their profession, claim that the most perceptive critics suspected the forgeries very early; but actually some of the foremost recognized authorities were completely taken in and for some time even refused to believe Van Meegeren's confession. The reader has a more recent example now before him in the revelation that the famous bronze horse, long exhibited in the Metropolitan Museum and proclaimed as a masterpiece of classical Greek sculpture, is a modern forgery. An official of the museum noticed a seam that apparently neither he nor anyone else had ever seen before, and scientific testing followed. No expert has come forward to claim earlier doubts on aesthetic grounds.

pert might well have avoided his errors if he had had a few known Van Meegerens handy for comparison. And today's layman who so cleverly spots a Van Meegeren may well be caught taking some quite inferior school-piece for a Vermeer.

In answering the questions raised above, I have not attempted the formidable task of defining "aesthetic" in general,[7] but have simply argued that since the exercise, training, and development of our powers of discriminating among works of art are plainly aesthetic activities, the aesthetic properties of a picture include not only those found by looking at it but also those that determine how it is to be looked at. This rather obvious fact would hardly have needed underlining but for the prevalence of the time-honored Tingle-Immersion theory,[8] which tells us that the proper behavior on encountering a work of art is to strip ourselves of all the vestments of knowledge and experience (since they might blunt the immediacy of our enjoyment), then submerge ourselves completely and gauge the aesthetic potency of the work by the intensity and duration of the resulting tingle. The theory is absurd on the face of it and useless for dealing with any of the important problems of aesthetics; but it has become part of the fabric of our common nonsense.

3. The Unfakable

A second problem concerning authenticity is raised by the rather curious fact that in music, unlike painting, there is no such thing as a forgery of a known work. There are, indeed, compositions falsely purporting to be by Haydn as there are paintings falsely purporting to be by Rembrandt; but of the *London Symphony,* unlike the *Lucretia,* there can be no forgeries. Haydn's manuscript is no more genuine an instance of the score than is a printed copy off the press this morning, and last night's performance no less genuine than the premiere. Copies of the score may vary in accuracy, but all accurate copies, even if forgeries of Haydn's

---

7. I deal with that question in *LA VI.*

8. Attributed to Immanuel Tingle and Joseph Immersion (ca. 1800).

manuscript, are equally genuine instances of the score. Performances may vary in correctness and quality and even in 'authenticity' of a more esoteric kind; but all correct performances are equally genuine instances of the work.[9] In contrast, even the most exact copies of the Rembrandt painting are simply imitations or forgeries, not new instances, of the work? Why this difference between the two arts?

Let us speak of a work of art as *autographic* if and only if the distinction between original and forgery of it is significant; or better, if and only if even the most exact duplication of it does not thereby count as genuine.[10] If a work of art is autographic, we may also call that art autographic. Thus painting is autographic, music nonautographic, or *allographic*. These terms are introduced purely for convenience; nothing is implied concerning the relative individuality of expression demanded by or attainable in these arts. Now the problem before us is to account for the fact that some arts but not others are autographic.

One notable difference between painting and music is that the composer's work is done when he has written the score, even though the performances are the end-products, while the painter has to finish the picture. No matter how many studies or revisions are made in either case, painting is in this sense a one-stage and music a two-stage art. Is an art autographic, then, if and only if it is one-stage? Counterexamples come readily to mind. In the first place, literature is not autographic though it is one-stage. There is no such thing as a forgery of Gray's *Elegy*. Any accurate copy of the text of a poem or novel is as much the original work

9. There may indeed be forgeries of performances. Such forgeries are performances that purport to be by a certain musician, etc.; but these, if in accordance with the score, are nevertheless genuine instances of the work. And what concerns me here is a distinction among the arts that depends upon whether there can be forgeries of works, not upon whether there can be forgeries of instances of works. See further what is said below concerning forgeries of editions of literary works and of musical performances.

10. This is to be taken as a preliminary version of a difference we must seek to formulate more precisely. Much of what follows in this chapter has likewise the character of an exploratory introduction to matters calling for fuller and more detailed inquiry in later chapters [of *LA*].

as any other. Yet what the writer produces is ultimate; the text is not merely a means to oral readings as a score is a means to performances in music. An unrecited poem is not so forlorn as an unsung song; and most literary works are never read aloud at all. We might try to make literature into a two-stage art by considering the silent readings to be the end-products, or the instances of a work; but then the lookings at a picture and the listenings to a performance would qualify equally as end-products or instances, so that painting as well as literature would be two-stage and music three-stage. In the second place, printmaking is two-stage and yet autographic. The etcher, for example, makes a plate from which impressions are then taken on paper. These prints are the end-products; and although they may differ appreciably from one another, all are instances of the original work. But even the most exact copy produced otherwise than by printing from that plate counts not as an original but as an imitation or forgery.

So far, our results are negative: not all one-stage arts are autographic and not all autographic arts are one-stage. Furthermore, the example of printmaking refutes the unwary assumption that in every autographic art a particular work exists only as a unique object. The line between an autographic and an allographic art does not coincide with that between a singular and a multiple art. About the only positive conclusion we can draw here is that the autographic arts are those that are singular in the earliest stage; etching is singular in its first stage—the plate is unique—and painting in its only stage. But this hardly helps; for the problem of explaining why some arts are singular is much like the problem of explaining why they are autographic.

4. The Reason

Why, then, can I no more make a forgery of Haydn's symphony or of Gray's poem than I can make an original of Rembrandt's painting or of his etching *Tobit Blind?* Let us suppose that there are various handwritten copies and many editions of a given literary work. Differences between them in style and size of script or type, in color of ink, in kind of paper, in number and layout of pages, in condition, etc., do not matter. All that matters is what may be called *sameness of spelling:* exact correspondence as sequences of letters, spaces, and punctuation marks. Any sequence—even a forgery of the author's manuscript or of a given edition—that so corresponds to a correct copy is itself correct, and nothing is more the original work than is such a correct copy. And since whatever is not an original of the work must fail to meet such an explicit standard of correctness, there can be no deceptive imitation, no forgery, of that work. To verify the spelling or to spell correctly is all that is required to identify an instance of the work or to produce a new instance. In effect, the fact that a literary work is in a definite notation, consisting of certain signs or characters that are to be combined by concatenation, provides the means for distinguishing the properties constitutive of the work from all contingent properties—that is, for fixing the required features and the limits of permissible variation in each. Merely by determining that the copy before us is spelled correctly we can determine that it meets all requirements for the work in question. In painting, on the contrary, with no such alphabet of characters, none of the pictorial properties—none of the properties the picture has as such —is distinguished as constitutive; no such feature can be dismissed as contingent, and no deviation as insignificant. The only way of ascertaining that the *Lucretia* before us is genuine is thus to establish the historical fact that it is the actual object made by Rembrandt. Accordingly, physical identification of the product of the artist's hand, and consequently the conception of forgery of a particular work, assume a significance in painting that they do not have in literature.[11]

What has been said of literary texts obviously applies also to musical scores. The alphabet is different; and the characters in a score, rather than being strung one after the other as in a text, are disposed in a more complex array. Nevertheless, we have a limited set of characters and of positions for them; and correct

11. Such identification does not guarantee that the object possesses the pictorial properties it had originally. Rather, reliance on physical or historical identification is transcended only where we have means of ascertaining that the requisite properties are present.

spelling, in only a slightly expanded sense, is still the sole requirement for a genuine instance of a work. Any false copy is wrongly spelled—has somewhere in place of the right character either another character or an illegible mark that is not a character of the notation in question at all.

But what of performances of music? Music is not autographic in this second stage, either, yet a performance by no means consists of characters from an alphabet. Rather, the constitutive properties demanded of a performance of the symphony are those *prescribed in* the score; and performances that comply with the score may differ appreciably in such musical features as tempo, timbre, phrasing, and expressiveness. To determine compliance requires, indeed, something more than merely knowing the alphabet; it requires the ability to correlate appropriate sounds with the visible signs in the score—to recognize, so to speak, correct pronunciation though without necessarily understanding what is pronounced. The competence required to identify or produce sounds called for by a score increases with the complexity of the composition, but there is nevertheless a theoretically decisive test for compliance; and a performance, whatever its interpretative fidelity and independent merit, has or has not all the constitutive properties of a given work, and is or is not strictly a performance of that work, according as it does or does not pass this test. No historical information concerning the production of the performance can affect the result. Hence deception as to the facts of production is irrelevant, and the notion of a performance that is a forgery of the work is quite empty.

Yet there are forgeries of performances as there are of manuscripts and editions. What makes a performance an instance of a given work is not the same as what makes a performance a premiere, or makes it a performance by a certain musician or upon a Stradivarius violin. Whether a performance has these latter properties is a matter of historical fact; and a performance falsely purporting to have any such property counts as a forgery, not of the musical composition but of a given performance or class of performances.

The comparison between printmaking and music is especially telling. We have already noted that etching, for example, is like

98

music in having two stages and in being multiple in its second stage; but that whereas music is autographic in neither stage, printmaking is autographic in both. Now the situation with respect to the etched plate is clearly the same as with respect to a painting: assurance of genuineness can come only from identification of the actual object produced by the artist. But since the several prints from this plate are all genuine instances of the work, however much they differ in color and amount of ink, quality of impression, kind of paper, etc., one might expect here a full parallel between prints and musical performances. Yet there can be prints that are forgeries of the *Tobit Blind* but not performances that are forgeries of the *London Symphony*. The difference is that in the absence of a notation, not only is there no test of correctness of spelling for a plate but there is no test of compliance with a plate for a print. Comparison of a print with a plate, as of two plates, is no more conclusive than is comparison of two pictures. Minute discrepancies may always go unnoticed; and there is no basis for ruling out any of them as inessential. The only way of ascertaining whether a print is genuine is by finding out whether it was taken from a certain plate.[12] A print falsely purporting to have been so produced is in the full sense a forgery of the work.

Here, as earlier, we must be careful not to confuse genuineness with aesthetic merit. That the distinction between original and forgery is aesthetically important does not, we have seen, imply that the original is superior to the forgery. An original painting may be less rewarding than an inspired copy; a damaged original may have lost most of its former merit; an impression from a badly worn plate may be aesthetically much further removed from an early impression than is a good photographic reproduction. Likewise, an incorrect performance, though therefore not strictly an instance of a given quartet at all, may nevertheless—either because the changes improve what the composer wrote or because of

12. To be original a print must be from a certain plate but need not be printed by the artist. Furthermore, in the case of a woodcut, the artist sometimes only draws upon the block, leaving the cutting to someone else— Holbein's blocks, for example, were usually cut by Lützelberger. Authenticity in an autographic art always depends upon the object's having the requisite, sometimes rather complicated, history of production; but that history does not always include ultimate execution by the original artist.

sensitive interpretation—be better than a correct performance.[13]
Again, several correct performances of about equal merit may
exhibit very different specific aesthetic qualities—power, delicacy, tautness, stodginess, incoherence, etc. Thus even where the
constitutive properties of a work are clearly distinguished by
means of a notation, they cannot be identified with the aesthetic
properties.

Among other arts, sculpture is autographic; cast sculpture is
comparable to printmaking while carved sculpture is comparable
to painting. Architecture and the drama, on the other hand, are
more nearly comparable to music. Any building that conforms
to the plans and specifications, any performance of the text of a
play in accordance with the stage directions, is as original an
instance of the work as any other. But architecture seems to differ
from music in that testing for compliance of a building with the
specifications requires not that these be pronounced, or transcribed into sound, but that their application be understood. This
is true also for the stage directions, as contrasted with the dialogue, of a play. Does this make architecture and the drama less
purely allographic arts? Again, an architect's plans seem a good
deal like a painter's sketches; and painting is an autographic art.
On what grounds can we say that in the one case but not the other
a veritable notation is involved? Such questions cannot be answered until we have carried through some rather painstaking
analysis.

Since an art seems to be allographic just insofar as it is amenable to notation, the case of the dance is especially interesting.
Here we have an art without a traditional notation; and an art
where the ways, and even the possibility, of developing an adequate notation are still matters of controversy. Is the search for
a notation reasonable in the case of the dance but not in the case of
painting? Or, more generally, why is the use of notation appro-

---

13. Of course, I am not saying that a correct(ly spelled) performance is
correct in any of a number of other usual senses. Nevertheless, the composer
or musician is likely to protest indignantly at refusal to accept a performance
with a few wrong notes as an instance of a work; and he surely has ordinary
usage on his side. But ordinary usage here points the way to disaster for
theory (see *LA V,2*).

priate in some arts but not in others? Very briefly and roughly, the answer may be somewhat as follows. Initially, perhaps, all arts are autographic. Where the works are transitory, as in singing and reciting, or require many persons for their production, as in architecture and symphonic music, a notation may be devised in order to transcend the limitations of time and the individual. This involves establishing a distinction between the constitutive and the contingent properties of a work (and in the case of literature, texts have even supplanted oral performances as the primary aesthetic objects). Of course, the notation does not dictate the distinction arbitrarily, but must follow generally—even though it may amend—lines antecedently drawn by the informal classification of performances into works and by practical decisions as to what is prescribed and what is optional. Amenability to notation depends upon a precedent practice that develops only if works of the art in question are commonly either ephemeral or not producible by one person. The dance, like the drama and symphonic and choral music, qualifies on both scores, while painting qualifies on neither.

The general answer to our somewhat slippery second problem of authenticity can be summarized in a few words. A forgery of a work of art is an object falsely purporting to have the history of production requisite for the (or an) original of the work. Where there is a theoretically decisive test for determining that an object has all the constitutive properties of the work in question without determining how or by whom the object was produced, there is no requisite history of production and hence no forgery of any given work. Such a test is provided by a suitable notational system with an articulate set of characters and of relative positions for them. For texts, scores, and perhaps plans, the test is correctness of spelling in this notation; for buildings and performances, the test is compliance with what is correctly spelled. Authority for a notation must be found in an antecedent classification of objects or events into works that cuts across, or admits of a legitimate projection that cuts across, classification by history of production; but definitive identification of works, fully freed from history of production, is achieved only when a notation is established. The allographic art has won its emancipation not by proclamation but by notation.

5. A Task

The two problems of authenticity I have been discussing are rather special and peripheral questions of aesthetics. Answers to them do not amount to an aesthetic theory or even the beginning of one. But failure to answer them can well be the end of one; and their exploration points the way to more basic problems and principles in the general theory of symbols.

Many matters touched upon here need much more careful study. So far, I have only vaguely described, rather than defined, the relations of compliance and of sameness of spelling. I have not examined the features that distinguish notations or notational languages from other languages and from nonlanguages. And I have not discussed the subtle differences between a score, a script, and a sketch. What is wanted now is a fundamental and thoroughgoing inquiry in the nature and function of notation in the arts.

2

Art and Inquiry

A persistent tradition pictures the aesthetic attitude as passive contemplation of the immediately given, direct apprehension of what is presented, uncontaminated by any conceptualization, isolated from all echoes of the past and from all threats and promises of the future, exempt from all enterprise. By purification-rites of disengagement and disinterpretation we are to seek a pristine, unsullied vision of the world. The philosophic faults and aesthetic absurdities of such a view need hardly be recounted until someone seriously goes so far as to maintain that the appropriate aesthetic attitude toward a poem amounts to gazing at the printed page without reading it.

I maintain, on the contrary, that we have to read the painting as well as the poem, and that aesthetic experience is dynamic rather than static. It involves making delicate discriminations and discerning subtle relationships, identifying symbol systems and characters within these systems and what these characters denote and exemplify, interpreting works and reorganizing the world in terms of works and works in terms of the world. Much of our experience and many of our skills are brought to bear and may be transformed by the encounter. The aesthetic 'attitude' is restless, searching, testing—is less attitude than action: creation and re-creation.

What, though, distinguishes such aesthetic activity from other intelligent behavior such as perception, ordinary conduct, and scientific inquiry? One instant answer is that the aesthetic is directed to no practical end, is unconcerned with self-defense or conquest, with acquisition of necessities or luxuries, with prediction and control of nature. But if the aesthetic attitude disowns practical aims, still aimlessness is hardly enough. The aesthetic attitude is inquisitive as contrasted with the acquisitive and self-preservative, but not all non-practical inquiry is aesthetic. To think of science as motivated ultimately by practical goals, as judged or justified by bridges and bombs and the control of nature, is to confuse science with technology. Science seeks knowledge without regard to practical consequences, and is concerned with prediction not as a guide for behavior but as a test of truth. Disinterested inquiry embraces both scientific and aesthetic experience.

Attempts are often made to distinguish the aesthetic in terms of immediate pleasure, but troubles arise and multiply here. Obviously, sheer quantity or intensity of pleasure cannot be the criterion. That a picture or poem provides more pleasure than does a proof is by no means clear; and some human activities unrelated to any of these provide enough more pleasure to render insignificant any differences in amount or degree among various types of inquiry. The claim that aesthetic pleasure is of a different and superior *quality* is by now too transparent a dodge to be taken seriously.

The inevitable next suggestion—that aesthetic experience is distinguished not by pleasure at all but by a special aesthetic emotion—can be dropped on the waste-pile of "dormitive virtue" explanations.

This clears the way for the sophisticated theory that what counts is not pleasure yielded but pleasure 'objectified', pleasure read into  the object as a property thereof. Apart from images of some grotesque process of transfusion, what can this mean? To consider the pleasure as possessed rather than occasioned by the object—to say in effect that the object is pleased—may amount to saying that the object expresses the pleasure. But since some aesthetic objects are sad—express sadness rather than pleasure—this comes nowhere near distinguishing in general between aesthetic and nonaesthetic objects or experience.

Some of these difficulties are diminished and others obscured if we speak of satisfaction rather than pleasure. "Satisfaction" is colorless enough to pass in contexts where "pleasure" is ludicrous, hazy enough to blur counter-instances, and flexible enough to tolerate convenient vacillation in interpretation. Thus we may hope to lessen the temptation to conjure up a special quality or kind of feeling or to indulge in mumbo-jumbo about objectification. Nevertheless, satisfaction pretty plainly fails to distinguish aesthetic from non-aesthetic objects and experiences. Not only does some scientific inquiry yield much satisfaction, but some aesthetic objects and experiences yield none. Music and our listening, pictures and our looking, do not fluctuate between aesthetic and non-aesthetic as the playing or painting varies from exalted to excruciating. Being aesthetic does not exclude being unsatisfactory or being aesthetically bad.

The distinguishing feature, some say, is not satisfaction secured but satisfaction sought: in science, satisfaction is a mere by-product of inquiry; in art, inquiry is a mere means for obtaining satisfaction. The difference is held to be neither in process performed nor in satisfaction enjoyed but in attitude maintained. On this view the scientific *aim* is knowledge, the aesthetic *aim* satisfaction.

But how cleanly can these aims be separated? Does the scholar seek knowledge or the satisfaction of knowing? Obtaining knowledge and satisfying curiosity are so much the same that trying to do either without trying to do the other surely demands a precarious poise. And anyone who does manage to seek the satisfaction without seeking the knowledge will pretty surely get neither, while on the other hand abstention from all anticipation of satisfaction is unlikely to stimulate research. One may indeed be so absorbed in working on a problem as never to think of the satisfaction to be had from solving it; or one may dwell so fondly on the delights of finding a solution as to take no steps toward arriving at one. But if the latter attitude is aesthetic, aesthetic understanding of anything is foredoomed. And I cannot see that these tenuous, ephemeral, and idiosyncratic states of mind mark any significant difference between the aesthetic and the scientific.

Failure to arrive at an acceptable formulation in terms of pleasure or satisfaction, yielded or 'objectified' or anticipated, will hardly dislodge the conviction that the distinction between the scientific and the aesthetic is somehow rooted in the difference between knowing and feeling, between the cognitive and the emotive. This latter deeply entrenched dichotomy is in itself dubious on many grounds, and its application here becomes especially puzzling when aesthetic and scientific experience alike are seen to be fundamentally cognitive in character. But we do not easily part with the idea that art is in some way or other more emotive than is science.

The shift from pleasure or satisfaction to emotion-in-general softens some of the crudities of the hedonistic formulas but leaves us with trouble enough. Paintings and concerts, and the viewing and hearing of them, need not arouse emotion, any more than they need give satisfaction, to be aesthetic; and anticipated emotion is no better criterion than anticipated satisfaction. If the aesthetic is characteristically emotive in some way, we have yet to say in what way.

Any picture of aesthetic experience as a sort of emotional bath or orgy is plainly preposterous. The emotions involved tend to be muted and oblique as compared, for example, with the fear or sorrow or depression or exultation that arises from actual battle or bereavement or defeat or victory, and are not in general keener than the excitement or despair or elation that accompanies scientific exploration and discovery. What the inert spectator feels falls far short of what the characters portrayed on the stage feel, and even of what he himself would feel on witnessing real-life events. And if he leaps on the stage to participate, his response can no longer be called aesthetic. That art is concerned with simulated emotions suggests, as does the copy theory of representation, that art is a poor substitute for reality; that art is imitation, and aesthetic experience a pacifier that only partly compensates for lack of direct acquaintance and contact with the Real.

Often the emotions involved in aesthetic experience are not only somewhat tempered but also reversed in polarity. We welcome some works that arouse emotions we normally shun. Negative emotions of fear, hatred, disgust may become positive when occasioned by a play or painting. The problem of tragedy and the paradox of ugliness are made to order for ancient and modern Freudians, and the opportunity has not been neglected. Tragedy is said to have the effect of purging us of pent-up and hidden negative emotions, or of injecting measured doses of the killed virus to prevent or mitigate the ravages of an actual attack. Art becomes not only palliative but therapeutic, providing both a substitute for good reality and a safeguard against bad reality. Theatres and museums function as adjuncts to Departments of Public Health.

Again, even among works of art and aesthetic experiences of

evident excellence, the emotive component varies widely—from, say, a late Rembrandt to a late Mondrian, or from a Brahms to a Webern quartet. The Mondrian and the Webern are not obviously more emotive than Newton's or Einstein's laws; and a line between emotive and cognitive is less likely to mark off the aesthetic neatly from the scientific than to mark off some aesthetic objects and experiences from others.

All these troubles revive the temptation to posit a special aesthetic emotion or feeling or a special coloration of other emotions occurring in aesthetic experience. This special emotion or coloring may be intense when other emotions are feeble, may be positive when they are negative, and may occur in experience of the most intellectual art and yet be lacking in the most stirring scientific study. All difficulties are resolved—by begging the question. No doubt aesthetic emotions have the property that makes them aesthetic. No doubt things that burn are combustible. The theory of aesthetic phlogiston explains everything and nothing.

Thus two stubborn problems still confront us. First, despite our conviction that aesthetic experience is *some*how emotive rather than cognitive, the failure of formulae in terms of either yielded or anticipated emotions has left us with no way of saying *how*. Second, despite our recognition that emotion in aesthetic experience tends to be denatured and often even inverted, the obvious futility of explanations in terms of a special secretion of the aesthetic glands leaves us without any way of saying *why*. Perhaps the answer to the second question will be found in the answer to the first; perhaps emotion in aesthetic experience behaves as it does because of the role it plays.

Most of the troubles that have been plaguing us can, I have suggested, be blamed on the domineering dichotomy between the cognitive and the emotive. On the one side, we put sensation, perception, inference, conjecture, all nerveless inspection and investigation, fact, and truth; on the other, pleasure, pain, interest, satisfaction, disappointment, all brainless affective response, liking, and loathing. This pretty effectively keeps us from seeing that in aesthetic experience the *emotions function cognitively*. The work of art is apprehended through the feelings as well as through the senses. Emotional numbness disables here as definitely if not as completely as blindness or deafness. Nor are the feelings used exclusively for exploring the emotional content of a work. To some extent, we may feel how a painting looks as we may see how it feels. The actor or dancer—or the spectator—sometimes notes and remembers the feeling of a movement rather than its pattern, insofar as the two can be distinguished at all. Emotion in aesthetic experience is a means of discerning what properties a work has and expresses.

To say this is to invite hot denunciation for cold over-intellectualization; but rather than aesthetic experience being here deprived of emotions, the understanding is being endowed with them. The fact that emotions participate in cognition no more implies that they are not felt than the fact that vision helps us discover properties of objects implies that color-sensations do not occur. Indeed, emotions must be felt—that is, must occur, as sensations must—if they are to be used cognitively. Cognitive use involves discriminating and relating them in order to gauge and grasp the work and integrate it with the rest of our experience and the world. If this is the opposite of passive absorption in sensations and emotions, it by no means amounts to cancelling them. Yet it explains the modifications that emotions may undergo in aesthetic experience.

In the first place, a context of inquiry rather than of indulgence or incitement may result in a characteristic displacement of emotion. The psychological, physiological, and physical setting is different. A dollar earned, a dollar saved, a dollar spent, is still a dollar; affection eventuating in slavery, in frustration, in illumination, is still affection; but in neither case are all three quite the same. Emotions are not so insular as to be untouched by their environment, but cognitive use neither creates new emotions nor imparts to ordinary emotions some magic additive.

Furthermore the frequent disparity between the emotion felt and the emotive content thereby discovered in the object is now readily understood. Pity on the stage may induce pity in the spectator; but greed may arouse disgust, and courage admiration. So may a white house look white at noon, but red at sunset; and a globe looks round from any angle. Sensory and emotive experiences are related in complex ways to the properties of objects.

Also, emotions function cognitively not as separate items but in combination with one another and with other means of knowing. Perception, conception, and feeling intermingle and interact; and an alloy often resists analysis into emotive and non-emotive components. The same pain (or is it the same?) tells of ice or fire. Are anger and indignation different feelings or the same feeling under different circumstances? And does awareness of the overall difference arise from or lead to awareness of the difference in circumstances? The answers do not matter here; for I am not resting anything on the distinction between emotion and other elements in knowing but rather insisting that emotion belongs with them. What does matter is that the comparisons, contrasts, and organization involved in the cognitive process often affect the participating emotions. Some may be intensified, as colors are against a complementary ground, or pointed up by subtle rhyming; others may be softened, as are sounds in a louder context. And some emotions may emerge as properties of the orchestrated whole, belonging like the shape of an eggshell to none of the lesser parts.

Again, negative emotions obviously function cognitively quite as well as positive ones. The horror and revulsion we may feel at *Macbeth* are not lesser means of understanding than the amusement and delight we may find in *Pygmalion*. We are not called upon to suppose that somehow—say by catharsis—the revulsion is transformed into delight, or to explain why the most forbidding portrait is as legitimately aesthetic as the most appealing one; for pleasantness in an emotion is no more a condition for cognitive functioning than is redness in a color-sensation. In aesthetic experience, emotion positive or negative is a mode of sensitivity to a work. The problem of tragedy and the paradox of ugliness evaporate.

Equally plainly, quantity or intensity of emotion is no measure of its cognitive efficacy. A faint emotion may be as informative as an overwhelming one; and finding that a work expresses little or no emotion can be as significant aesthetically as finding that it expresses much. This is overlooked by all attempts to distinguish the aesthetic in terms of amount or degree of emotion.

Although many puzzles are thus resolved and the role of emotion in aesthetic experience clarified, we are still left without a way of distinguishing aesthetic from all other experience. Cognitive employment of the emotions is neither present in every aesthetic, nor absent from every non-aesthetic, experience. We have already noted that some works of art have little or no emotive content, and that even where the emotive content is appreciable, it may sometimes be apprehended by non-emotive means. In daily life, classification of things by feeling is often more vital than classification by other properties: we are likely to be better off if we are skilled in fearing, wanting, braving, or distrusting the right things, animate or inanimate, than if we perceive only their shapes, sizes, weights, etc. And the importance of discernment by feeling does not vanish when the motivation becomes theoretic rather than practical. The zoologist, psychologist, sociologist, even when his aims are purely theoretic, legitimately employs emotion in his investigations. Indeed, in any science, while the requisite objectivity forbids wishful thinking, prejudicial reading of evidence, rejection of unwanted results, avoidance of ominous lines of inquiry, it does not forbid the use of feeling in exploration and discovery, the impetus of inspiration and curiosity, or the cues given by excitement over intriguing problems and promising hypotheses. And the more we discuss these matters, the more we come to realize that emotions are not so clearly differentiated or so sharply separable from other elements in cognition that the distinction can provide a firm basis for answering any moot question.

Repeated failure to find a neat formula for sorting experiences into aesthetic and non-aesthetic, in rough conformity with rough usage, suggests the need for a less simple-minded approach. Perhaps no single, simple, significant feature neatly marks off all arts from all sciences and technologies, or all aesthetic from all scientific and practical experience. In some respects, certain arts may be less like others than like some sciences and technologies; and the traditional classification of objects and activities into the aesthetic and the non-aesthetic may be more harmful than helpful.

Aesthetic and scientific activity alike, I have suggested, consist to a large extent of symbol processing: of inventing, applying, interpreting, transforming, manipulating, symbols and symbol systems. Thus what is called for is a grounded and circumstantial investigation of the most important features of likeness and difference among symbol systems in general, both linguistic and non-linguistic—a study of systems of description, representation, mapping, diagramming, exemplification, expression, and formal notation. Occasional earlier efforts toward a general theory of symbols have been at best fragmentary and at worst infected with serious fallacies and confusions, such as that so-called iconic signs can be distinguished from others on the basis of resemblance to what they stand for, that languages differ from pictures in being more artificial or conventional, and that the difference between analog and digital systems has something to do with analogy and digits.

I cannot now undertake to outline a more systematic investigation into the general theory of symbols, or even to make clear some of its results. I can only try to give you some inkling of what I mean. Some of the features that seem to me to constitute important distinctions among types of symbol system are these:

(1) *Syntactic density,* depending not upon the internal structure of symbols but on the number of symbols and the nature of their ordering in an entire scheme—a feature that distinguishes representational systems from the articulate systems of languages and notations.

(2) *Semantic density,* depending upon the number of reference-classes and the nature of their ordering under a given symbol system—a feature that distinguishes ordinary languages from notational systems such as that of music.

(3) *Exemplification,* reference running not from a label to what it denotes but from a sample to label denoting it—a feature that distinguishes expression from representation and description; and

(4) *Relative syntactic repleteness,* depending on the comprehensiveness of the set of features that are constitutive of the characters of the scheme—a feature that distinguishes pictures from graphic diagrams. I list these without any adequate explanation and without any attempt to justify their choice, merely in order to suggest the kind of characteristics of symbol systems that seems to me relevant.

111

Taken severally, these features are neither necessary nor sufficient for aesthetic experience. Eact cuts across the usual boundary between the aesthetic and the non-aesthetic, and effects some interesting new alliances and alienations. Pictorial representation, for example, is like the symbol system involved in gauging weights or temperatures in being both syntactically and semantically dense; literary expression and geological sampling share the property of being syntactically less replete. Yet while any of the four symptoms may be absent from aesthetic or present in non-aesthetic experience, they probably tend to be present, or present in higher degree, in aesthetic experience. If they are *severally* neither sufficient nor necessary for aesthetic experience, they may be *conjunctively* sufficient and *disjunctively* necessary; perhaps, that is, an experience is aesthetic if it has all these attributes and only if it has at least one of them.

I am not claiming that this proposal conforms faithfully to ordinary usage. Presystematic usage of "aesthetic" and "non-aesthetic" is even less clearly established by practice, and more seriously infected with inept theorizing, than in the case of most terms. Rather I am suggesting that we have here an appropriate use for some badly abused terms. Density, repleteness, and exemplification, then, are earmarks of the aesthetic; articulateness, attenuation, and denotation are earmarks of the non-aesthetic. A vague and yet harsh dichotomy of experiences gives way to a sorting of features, elements, and processes. Classification of a totality as aesthetic or non-aesthetic counts for less than identification of its aesthetic and non-aesthetic aspects. Phases of a decidedly aesthetic compound may be utterly non-aesthetic; for example, a score and its mere reading may be devoid of all aesthetic aspects. On the other hand, aesthetic features may predominate in the delicate qualitative and quantitative discrimination required in testing some scientific hypotheses. Art and science are not altogether alien.

The distinction here drawn between the aesthetic and the non-aesthetic is independent of all considerations of aesthetic value. That is as it should be. An abominable performance of the *London Symphony* is as aesthetic as a superb one; and Piero's *Risen Christ* is no more aesthetic but only better than a hack's. The symptoms of the aesthetic are not marks of merit; and a characterization of the aesthetic neither requires nor provides a definition of aesthetic excellence.

Folklore has it that the good picture is pretty. At the next higher level, "pretty" is replaced by "beautiful", since the best pictures are often obviously not pretty. But again, many of them are in the most obvious sense ugly. If the beautiful excludes the ugly, beauty is no measure of aesthetic merit; but if the beautiful may be ugly, then "beauty" becomes only an alternative and misleading word for aesthetic merit.

Little more light is shed by the dictum that while science is judged by its truth, art is judged by the satisfaction it gives. Many of the objections urged earlier against satisfaction, yielded or anticipated, as a distinguishing feature of the aesthetic weigh also against satisfaction as a criterion of aesthetic merit: satisfaction cannot be identified with pleasure, and positing a special aesthetic feeling begs the question. We are left with the unhelpful formula that what is aesthetically good is aesthetically satisfactory. The question is what makes a work good or satisfactory.

Being satisfactory is in general relative to function and purpose. A good furnace heats the house to the required temperature evenly, economically, quietly, and safely. A good scientific theory accounts for the relevant facts clearly and simply. We have seen that works of art or their instances perform one or more among certain symbol functions: representation, description, exemplification, expression. The question what constitutes effective symbolization of any of these kinds raises in turn the question what purpose such symbolization serves.

An answer sometimes given is that exercise of the symbolic faculties beyond immediate need has the more remote practical purpose of developing our abilities and techniques to cope with future contingencies. Aesthetic experience becomes a gymnasium workout, pictures and symphonies the bar-bells and punching bags we use in strengthening our intellectual muscles. Art equips us for survival, conquest, and gain. And it channels surplus energy away from destructive outlets. It makes the scientist more acute, the merchant more astute, and clears the streets of juvenile delinquents. Art, long derided as the idle amusement of the guilty leisure class, is acclaimed as a universal servant of mankind. This is a comforting view for those who must reconcile aesthetic inclinations with a conviction that all value reduces to practical utility.

More lighthearted and perhaps more simple-minded is the almost opposite answer: that symbolization is an irresponsible propensity of man, that he goes on symbolizing beyond immediate necessity just for the joy of it or because he cannot stop. In aesthetic experience, he is a puppy cavorting or a well-digger who digs doggedly on after finding enough water. Art is not practical but playful or compulsive. Dogs bark because they are canine, men symbolize because they are human; and dogs go on barking and men go on symbolizing when there is no practical need just because they cannot stop and because it is such fun.

A third answer, bypassing the issue over practicality versus fun, points to communication as the purpose of symbolizing. Man is a social animal, communication is a requisite for social intercourse, and symbols are media of communication. Works of art are messages conveying facts, thoughts, and feelings; and their study belongs to the obstreperous and omnivorous new growth called 'communications theory'. Art depends upon and helps sustain society—exists because, and helps insure that, no man is an island.

Each of these explanations—in terms of gymnastics, play, or conversation—distends and distorts a partial truth. Exercise of the symbolizing skills may somewhat improve practical proficiency; the cryptographic character of symbol invention and interpretation does give them the fascination of a game; and symbols are indispensable to communication. But the lawyer or admiral improving his professional competence by hours in museums, the cavorting puppy, the neurotic well-digger, and the woman on the telephone do not, separately or together, give the whole picture. What all three miss is that the drive is curiosity and the aim enlightenment. Use of symbols beyond immediate need is for the sake of understanding, not practice; what compels is the urge to know, what delights is discovery, and communication is secondary to the apprehension and formulation of what is to be communicated. The primary purpose is cognition in and for itself; the practicality, pleasure, compulsion, and communicative utility all depend upon this.

Symbolization, then, is to be judged fundamentally by how well it serves the cognitive purpose: by the delicacy of its discriminations and the aptness of its allusions; by the way it works in grasping, exploring, and informing the world; by how it analyzes, sorts, orders, and organizes; by how it participates in the making, manipulation, retention, and transformation of knowledge. Considerations of simplicity and subtlety, power and precision, scope and selectivity, familiarity and freshness, are all relevant and often contend with one another; their weighting is relative to our interests, our information, and our inquiry.

So much for the cognitive efficacy of symbolization in general, but what of aesthetic excellence in particular? Distinguishing between the aesthetic and the meritorious cuts both ways. If excellence is not required of the aesthetic, neither is the excellence appropriate to aesthetic objects confined to them. Rather, the general excellence just sketched becomes aesthetic when exhibited by aesthetic objects; that is, aesthetic merit is such excellence in any symbolic functioning that, by its particular constellation of attributes, qualifies as aesthetic. This subsumption of aesthetic under cognitive excellence calls for one more reminder that the cognitive, while contrasted with both the practical and the passive, does not exclude the sensory or the emotive, that what we know through art is felt in our bones and nerves and muscles as well as grasped by our minds, that all the sensitivity and responsiveness of the organism participates in the invention and interpretation of symbols.

The problem of ugliness dissolves; for pleasure and prettiness neither define nor measure either the aesthetic experience or the work of art. The pleasantness or unpleasantness of a symbol does not determine its general cognitive efficacy or its specifically aesthetic merit. *Macbeth* and the Goya *Witches' Sabbath* no more call for apology than do *Pygmalion* and the Botticelli *Venus*.

The dynamics of taste, often embarrassing to those who seek inflexible standards of immutable excellence, also become readily understandable. After a time and for a time, the finest painting may pall and the greatest music madden. A work may be successively offensive, fascinating, comfortable, and boring. These are the vicissitudes of the vehicles and instruments of knowledge. We focus upon frontiers; the peak of interest in a symbol tends to occur at the time of revelation, somewhere midway in the passage from the obscure to the obvious. But there is endurance and renewal, too. Discoveries become available knowledge only when preserved in accessible form; the trenchant and laden symbol does not become worthless when it becomes familiar, but is incorporated in the base for further exploration. And where there is density in the symbol system, familiarity is never complete and final; another look may always disclose significant new subtleties. Moreover, what we read from and learn through a symbol varies with what we bring to it. Not only do we discover the world through our symbols but we understand and reappraise our symbols progressively in the light of our growing experience. Both the dynamics and the durability of aesthetic value are natural consequences of its cognitive character.

Like considerations explain the relevance to aesthetic merit of experience remote from the work. What a Manet or Monet or Cézanne does to our subsequent seeing of the world is as pertinent to their appraisal as is any direct confrontation. How our lookings at pictures and our listenings to music inform what we encounter later and elsewhere is integral to them as cognitive. The absurd and awkward myth of the insularity of aesthetic experience can be scrapped.

The role of theme and variation—common in architecture and other arts as well as in music—also becomes intelligible. Establishment and modification of motifs, abstraction and elaboration of patterns, differentiation and interrelation of modes of transformation, all are processes of constructive search; and the measures applicable are not those of passive enjoyment but those of cognitive efficacy: delicacy of discrimination, power of integration, and justice of proportion between recognition and discovery. Indeed, one typical way of advancing knowledge is by progressive variation upon a theme. Among modern composers, theme and variation along with all recognizable pattern is sometimes scorned, and maximum unpredictability is the declared aim; but as C. I. Lewis pointed out, complete irregularity is inconceivable—if no sequence is ever repeated in a given composition, that fact in itself constitutes a notable regularity.

Aesthetic merit, however, is by no means my main concern, and I am somewhat uncomfortable about having arrived at an incipient definition of what is often confusingly called 'beauty'. Excessive concentration on the question of excellence has been responsible, I think, for constriction and distortion of aesthetic inquiry. To say that a work of art is good or even to say how good it is does not after all provide much information, does not tell us whether the work is evocative, robust, vibrant, or exquisitely designed, and still less what are its salient specific qualities of color, shape, or sound. Moreover works of art are not racehorses, and picking a winner is not the primary goal. Conceiving of aesthetic experience as a form of understanding results both in resolving and in devaluing the question of aesthetic value.

In saying that aesthetic experience is cognitive experience distinguished by the dominance of certain symbolic characteristics and judged by standards of cognitive efficacy, have I overlooked the sharpest contrast: that in science, unlike art, the ultimate test is truth? Do not the two domains differ most drastically in that truth means all for the one, nothing for the other?

Despite rife doctrine, truth by itself matters very little in science. We can generate volumes of dependable truths at will so long as we are unconcerned with their importance; the multiplication tables are inexhaustible, and empirical truths abound. Scientific hypotheses, however true, are worthless unless they meet minimal demands of scope or specificity imposed by our inquiry, unless they effect some telling analysis or synthesis, unless they raise or answer significant questions. Truth is not enough; it is at most a necessary condition. But even this concedes too much; the noblest scientific laws are seldom quite true. Minor discrepancies are overridden in the interest of breadth or power or simplicity. Science denies its data as the statesman denies his constituents— within the limits of prudence.

Yet neither is truth one among competing criteria involved in the rating of scientific hypotheses. Given any assemblage of evidence, countless alternative hypotheses conform to it. We cannot choose among them on grounds of truth; for we have no direct access to their truth. Rather we judge them by such features as their simplicity and strength. These criteria are not supplemental to truth but applied hopefully as a means for arriving at the nearest approximation to truth that is compatible with our other interests.

Does this leave us with the cardinal residual difference that truth—though not enough, not necessary, and not a touchstone for choosing among hypotheses—is nevertheless a consideration relevant in science but not in art? Even so meek a formulation suggests too strong a contrast. Truth of a hypothesis after all is a matter of fit—fit with a body of theory, and fit of hypothesis and theory to the data at hand and the facts to be encountered. And as Philipp Frank liked to remind us, goodness of fit takes a two-way adjustment—of theory to facts and of facts to theory—with the double aim of comfort and a new look. But such fitness, such aptness in conforming to and reforming our knowledge and our world, is equally relevant for the aesthetic symbol. Truth and its aesthetic counterpart amount to appropriateness under different names. If we speak of hypotheses but not of works of art as true, that is because we reserve the terms "true" and "false" for symbols in sentential form. I do not say this difference is negligible, but it is specific rather than generic, a difference in field of application rather than in formula, and marks no schism between the scientific and the aesthetic.

None of this is directed toward obliterating the distinction between art and science. Declarations of indissoluble unity—whether of the sciences, the arts, the arts and sciences together, or of mankind—tend anyway to focus attention upon the differences. What I am stressing is that the affinities here are deeper, and the significant differentia other, than is often supposed. The difference between art and science is not that between feeling and fact, intuition and inference, delight and deliberation, synthesis and analysis, sensation and cerebration, concreteness and abstraction, passion and action, mediacy and immediacy, or truth and beauty, but rather a difference in domination of certain specific characteristics of symbols.

The implications of this reconception may go beyond philosophy. We hear a good deal about how the aptitudes and training

118

needed for the arts and for the sciences contrast or even conflict with one another. Earnest and elaborate efforts to devise and test means of finding and fostering aesthetic abilities are always being initiated. But none of this talk or these trials can come to much without an adequate conceptual framework for designing crucial experiments and interpreting their results. Once the arts and sciences are seen to involve working with—inventing, applying, reading, transforming, manipulating—symbol systems that agree and differ in certain specific ways, we can perhaps undertake pointed psychological investigation of how the pertinent skills inhibit or enhance one another; and the outcome might well call for changes in educational technology. Our preliminary study suggests, for example, that some processes requisite for a science are less akin to each other than to some requisite for an art. But let us forego foregone conclusions. Firm and usable results are as far off as badly needed; and the time has come in this field for the false truism and the plangent platitude to give way to the elementary experiment and the hesitant hypothesis.

Whatever consequences might eventually be forthcoming for psychology or education would in any case count as by-products of the theoretical inquiry. The prior aim is to take some steps towards a systematic study of symbols and symbol systems and the ways they function in our perceptions and actions and arts and sciences, and thus in the creation and comprehension of our worlds.

3

Merit as Means

If I ask you to rank according to excellence the Brahms Double Concerto, the Battle of Britain, springtime, *Hamlet* and charity, you may well protest that the question is either ambiguous or meaningless. The ranking will vary with the sort of excellence in question; and if I demand a single overall evaluation, I am either asking you to add elements as alien as apples and asteroids or talking in terms of units so denatured as to lack all significance.

Trouble of the same sort arises, I think, when the items compared are far less heterogeneous—even, for example, when all are works of painting or sculpture. If we are confronted with a Donatello marble, a Goya 'black' painting, a medieval illumination, and a Shang bronze, the question which is best is ridiculous and may be vicious. Works vary in power, subtlety, vibrancy of color, justness of proportion, etc.; but to ask whether a supremely subtle work is better than a supremely powerful one is like asking whether a very tall man is bigger than a very stout one.

What I object to is not merely the oversimplification but the overvaluation of value. Not only is excellence at best multidimensional rather than linear, but also concentration upon questions of excellence diverts attention from more important concerns. It distorts and even inverts the whole task of the philosophy of art, and obscures its relationship to the general theory of knowledge. To understand works of art we must be able to tell power from bluster, subtlety from sophistry, vibrancy from raucousness; and a primary task of aesthetics is to discriminate and interrelate the aspects under which works of art are to be perceived and comprehended. Rather than judgments of specific aesthetic characteristics being mere means toward an ultimate appraisal, judgments of value are often mere means toward discernment of specific characteristics. If a connoisseur tells me that one of two Cycladic figures that seem to me almost indistinguishable is much finer than the other, this inspires me to look for and may help me to find the significant differences between the two. Estimates of excellence are among the minor aids to understanding.

In short, I suspect that the emphasis on excellence in art has been partly to blame for the lack of excellence in aesthetics. Judging the excellence of works of art or the goodness of people is not the best way to understand them. And a criterion of artistic merit is no more the major aim of aesthetics than a criterion of virtue is the major aim of psychology.

4

Some Notes on *Languages of Art*

I am grateful to the three major participants in this symposium for their time and attention, their compliments, and their perceptive criticism. On the whole, there is more agreement than disagreement among us; and perhaps the following remarks will help to resolve some points of difference.

1. Reply to Richard Wollheim

Mr. Wollheim quite correctly suggests that by describing a predicate like "is a unicorn-picture" as an unbreakable one-place predicate, I meant to preclude treating it as a two-place predicate and thus to block the fallacious inference from "*p* is a unicorn-picture" to "there is something that *p* is a picture of". I did not mean to restrict our freedom to treat such predicates as conjunctive; we may, for example, construe "*p* is a unicorn-picture" as elliptical for "*p* is a picture, and *p* is of-a-unicorn". Under that construction, we may logically infer that there is something that is a picture, and also that there is something that is of-a-unicorn, but not that there is anything other than the *p* we started with. We may likewise, as Wollheim has pointed out to me, infer from "*p* is a Pickwick-as-clown picture" that *p* is a clown-picture. Since such predicate-splitting is not prohibited, the epithet "unbreakable"— intended merely to reinforce "one-place"—is misleading and should be omitted.

On the other hand, I do not see the reason for Wollheim's statement: "In order to classify chairs as Louis XIV chairs or Louis XV chairs, we do not have to recognize them as chairs. But in order to classify Louis XIV pictures or Louis XV pictures, we must first recognize them as pictures." It seems to me that a person might easily learn to classify objects in a room as Louis XIV pictures, Louis XV pictures, chairs, and tables without having learned to classify things as pictures or as articles of furniture. It also seems to me that a person might easily learn to classify

things as pictures or as articles of furniture without learning how
to sort these classes into any subclasses. Sometimes we learn first
how to apply general labels and only later how to apply more specific ones; sometimes we learn how to apply specific labels and
only later how to apply more general ones; and this I think is as
true for pictures as for furniture or anything else.

I agree with Wollheim that much of what is said in the book
about representation-as and fictive representation can be applied
to perception. For example, the analysis of representation-as may
well help in clarifying the notion of seeing-as; and rather than say
that someone has been seeing ghosts, we might rather say that he
has been ghost-seeing. On the other hand, I cannot follow Wollheim's discussion of a picture of a sheaf-of-corn that represents
Christ. He says that since we cannot see Christ in the picture, the
picture does not represent Christ as a sheaf of corn. While what
we 'can see in' a picture seems to me far from clear, I should suppose that if we cannot see Christ in a picture of a sheaf of corn,
neither can we see him in a picture of a lamb; yet surely we can
say that Christ is often represented as a lamb.

In his discussion of the relationship between representing a
soandso and being a soandso-picture, Wollheim correctly reports
me as saying, in the early pages (pp. 28, 29) of my book, that if p
is a soandso picture and p denotes a suchandsuch, then p represents a suchandsuch as a soandso. At that stage, I was tentatively
taking representation to be denotation by a picture. Later (especially pp. 41–43 and *V,1*), I point out that denotation by a picture
is not always representation; and this has the retroactive effect of
modifying the formula in question to read: if p is a soandso-
picture and p *represents* a suchandsuch, then p represents a suchandsuch as a soandso. Similar modifications are implied for related passages. None of them seems to affect Wollheim's discussion
appreciably; but the point needs to be understood for the investigation of further questions he raises.

To one of these questions—whether a soandso-picture that represents a suchandsuch is therefore a suchandsuch-as-a-soandso
picture—I think the answer is negative. There is a difference between being a lion-picture representing Churchill and being a
Churchill-as-a-lion-picture, whether or not the latter represents

Churchill. Whether a picture represents a suchandsuch may under some circumstances have some bearing upon, but does not determine, whether it is a suchandsuch-picture.

Wollheim fears that such an answer will leave denotation as the core of only one sense of representation and would endanger "the elegant explanation of the difference between representation and expression, in terms of the 'difference in direction', i.e., denotation *vs.* converse denotation". In saying that denotation is the core of representation, I meant only that denoting is the core of representing. Converse denoting is the core of being a suchandsuch-picture in that the picture is denoted by "suchandsuch-picture". Denoting is thus involved in both cases, but runs from the picture to the object in the first case and from the predicate to the picture in the second. In much the same way, converse denotation is the core of expression.

Being black or small, furthermore, does not—any more than does representing a black or small thing—guarantee that a picture is a black-thing-picture or a small-thing-picture. Representation of Churchill by a black ink drawing, or by a small painting, does not constitute representing Churchill as black, or as small. Rather, Churchill is represented as black by a black-man-picture (which may itself be ochre), or as small by a small-thing-picture (which may itself be large, such as a large baby-picture). Apparently not observing this distinction carefully enough, Wollheim obscures the crucial difference between representing a black horse *by* a white speck and representing the horse *as* a white speck. The white speck that represents a black horse in a photograph is not necessarily or even normally a white-speck-picture or a black-horse-as-white-speck-picture, and does not necessarily or even normally represent the black horse as a white speck or, for that matter, as a black horse.

The main thrust of Wollheim's paper, however, seems to be in his question, "How, or by what (kind of) criteria do we apply predicates in classifying pictures into kinds, or (more succinctly) how do we decide what, in one sense of the term, they represent?" His answer is that we do this according to what we can see in the picture. As I have already indicated, the notion of what we 'can see in' a picture seems to me too unclear to provide any illumination. Mr. Wollheim says further that "what we can see in a picture and [the artist's] intention are linked in that, by and large, an intention to represent x must express itself through the making of a picture in which we can see x". But of course a picture may be a soandso-picture or represent a suchandsuch contrary to the artist's intentions or, as with pictures produced by an automatic camera or by nature, in the absence of any relevant intention. In the setting up of symbol systems, as in the building of bridges, intentions are indeed usually involved; but in both cases, we can study the results independently of the thoughts of the makers.

2. Reply to Benjamin Boretz

Mr. Boretz argues for a phenomenalistic rather than a physicalistic conception of the work of art. In general I regard the choice between a phenomenalistic and a physicalistic system as quite free, but I choose to treat works of art, or their instances, as physical rather than phenomenal in order to discourage what seems to me the mistaken and prevalent identification of the aesthetic with the immediate and uninterpreted. Boretz is not guilty of that error. Rather he envisages, apparently, treating works of art and physical objects as both, though different, constructs from phenomena. I doubt if the net results of this direct route of construction would be very different from those of proceeding from phenomena to physical objects and then to works of art.

"Sounds", Boretz further contends, "are not parts of music. . . . And neither are paint, pigment, or canvas parts of paintings, nor masses of bronze parts of sculptures, nor pages and letters parts of poems." I see nothing wrong in saying that a given bronze object is a sculpture. This is entirely compatible with the object's being something else as well, and by no means implies that to be a bronze object is to be a sculpture. A bronze object is a sculpture insofar as it serves as an aesthetic symbol; it may also serve as a nonaesthetic symbol in other contexts, or function in entirely nonsymbolic ways. It is a hammer by virtue of some of its properties, a sculpture by virtue of others. It is a hammer when pounding a nail, a sculpture when serving as a symbol of a certain kind.

This will not suit Mr. Boretz. What counts, he insists, is not what a work refers to but what it is in itself. I am afraid he overlooks the fact that, according to my treatment, the properties that anything exemplifies or expresses, far from lying outside it, are properties it possesses. Talk about those properties is talk about what the work is. Why not, then, speak simply of properties possessed rather than of properties exemplified and expressed? Because not all the properties the object possesses, but only those it exemplifies or expresses when functioning as a symbol of a certain kind, are relevant to it as a work of art. The capacity for hammering is extraneous to the bronze as a sculpture. Now we may, if we like, take the work of art not to be the concrete object that as an aesthetic symbol exemplifies or expresses certain properties, but to be the abstract complex consisting of the properties it thus symbolizes. The sculpture will then not also be a hammer; rather, the sculpture and the property of being a hammer will be universals that happen to be manifested in one piece of bronze. This version seems to me to have some inconveniences and no compelling advantages, but is in principle interchangeable rather than incompatible with taking the work to be the concrete object—or, as in the case of music or poetry, a class of events or objects.

An ardent formalist, Boretz objects not so much to my theory of expression as to my discussing expression at all. For him, the actual structure of the work is all that matters; the work is fully determined by specifying that structure in detail, and calling the work sad is romantic poppycock. Feelings a work may express, like things or events it may describe, are beside the point. My purpose, of course, was not to advocate or decry formalism or expressionism in music, or realism or abstractionism in painting, or any other artistic doctrine, but merely to explicate the nature of representation, exemplification, expression, and other modes of symbolization.

Nevertheless, I think expression has an importance, even for a formalist, that Boretz overlooks. Admittedly, saying that a musical work is sad—like saying that it is long or rather loud—is pretty vacuous; but this is because sadness, like length and loudness, is a commonplace, obvious, and general property, so that its ascription to a work provides little interesting information. And while sadness—like length and loudness—is indeed a consequence of the detailed make-up of the work, the converse does not hold. Works differing widely in detail may all have the same property of sadness; and the common structural property, the literal correlate of sadness, is not easily specified. To describe a work or passage as muscular, electric, spatial, curvilinear, brittle, or floating may be to describe metaphorically some recondite and highly important structural features. The notion of *the* structure of a work is as specious as the notion of *the* structure of the world. A work, like the world, has as many different structures as there are ways of organizing it, of subsuming it under categorial schemata dependent upon some or other structural affinities with and differences from other works. What seems a definitive structural description may ignore some of the most significant patterns. We may overlook trees for woods, or woods for trees, or groves for either; we may overlook themes for notes; and we may examine every part of a picture without grasping subtle, or even gross, features of composition or design. Understanding a work involves the discovery, the recognition, of unobvious patterns. The requisite breaching of barriers established by habit and literal language often occurs through the importation of schemata from a foreign realm. New likenesses and differences, new relationships and patterns, are thus revealed, and are described by the metaphorical application of these alien terms. Theoretically, these metaphors can be supplanted by complex literal descriptions; but even as metaphors, they are in effect descriptions of structural features. Briefly, the feelings a work expresses are properties it has, not because the work literally has feelings, but because the feeling-terms applied are metaphorical descriptions of structural (or other) properties the work has and exemplifies. Only at the risk of overlooking important structural features of a work can a formalist ignore what the work expresses.

In discussing musical notation, Boretz urges that what is specified in standard scores are not specific pitches but rather certain bands of pitches and that, moreover, the score is intended and used as a design, determining relationships rather than specific pitches or even ranges.

Nothing I have said is at all incompatible with taking note marks as prescribing pitch (and duration) within a range rather than uniquely. Precision or uniqueness is not a requirement for notationality. Indeed, I have pointed out that characters in a notation may have very broad compliance-classes, so long as these classes are differentiated and do not intersect.

Now suppose, going even further, we take the score as prescribing no pitches whatsoever, even within ranges, but only relationships among pitches; that is, as requiring, for example, that the second note should be one range higher than the first, the third two ranges lower than the second, and so on. A score might then be transcribed into numerals as follows:

$$\bullet, 1, -2, 3, 4, -1 \ldots.$$

The performer can now begin with any note he likes, play any note from the next higher range, and so on. Yet we still have a system meeting all the requirements for a notation. Work-preservation in any chain of correct steps between score and performance is assured. And incidentally, my notorious remark that a single deviation from the score disqualifies a performance as a genuine instance of the work will still hold good, though a single error will now consist not in playing a note different from the one specified, but in playing a note not standing in the specified relationship to what precedes it.

Suppose, though, a score is taken rather as a suggestive pattern, prescribing no explicit kind or degree of conformity in a performance. Then, clearly, notationality is lost. Nothing in my theory precludes such an interpretation. I have not been concerned with deciding on the proper interpretation of any vocabulary of symbols but rather with setting forth the conditions under which interpreted systems are notational. Under some interpretations, the standard language of musical scores is notational, and music is allographic; under other interpretations, the language is nonnotational, and music is not allographic. Which interpretation is best is a question I am neither equipped nor required to answer. Nevertheless, since that question is intimately related to the question of the identity of a musical work, and since my saying that the identity of a musical work consists in exact compliance with the score has aroused the ire of many musicians, I should like to point out (in answer to them rather than to Boretz) that the character-

istics that make a performance of a work are not to be confused
with the characteristics that make a good performance unless we
are ready to accept all performances of any work as good performances of it.

3. Reply to Barbara Herrnstein Smith

Mrs. Smith rises as the champion of unwritten literary works. She
complains that according to my view a work never written down,
no matter how often recited, would never exist at all. She feels
I have treated oral utterances, along with silent readings, quite
shabbily.

I plead not guilty. For what seem to me quite sound reasons, I
have indeed treated oral utterances of literary works quite differently from, but no less respectfully than, performances of musical
works. Let me explain.

I have suggested that we have a choice of three ways of construing the relationship between the written and oral versions of a
literary work:

(*a*) to take the oral utterances as compliants of—i.e., as denoted
by—the written inscriptions;

(*b*) to take the written inscriptions as compliants of the oral
utterances;

(*c*) to take utterances and inscriptions both as equally instances of the text—in a broadened sense of "text".

Alternative *a* is analogous to my treatment of music, where the
performances comply with—are denoted by—the score. Why not
choose this course, then? For two reasons: first, that since verbal
as contrasted with musical inscriptions have other compliants such
as objects and events, this would confuse matters by giving verbal
inscriptions two different sets of compliants; second, that since inscriptions and utterances perform the same functions of telling
stories, describing scenes, etc., treating the relation between them
as asymmetrical seems arbitrary and deforming. Both reasons
weigh also against alternative *b* and in favor of *c*—that is, of taking
inscriptions and utterances of words as instances of the same
symbols, with the difference between the written and the oral

counting for no more than differences among fonts of type or among voices of speakers.

Along with this first decision goes another. Obviously, and Mrs. Smith agrees here, a literary work cannot be identified with the objects and events that are denoted by the words. Rather, the work must be identified with the words themselves, written or oral. Thus utterances along with inscriptions are instances of the work. My treatment of literature therefore differs from my treatment of music not in downgrading the verbal utterances but in upgrading the verbal inscriptions. In music, only performances, not inscriptions of the score, count as instances of the work. In literature, on the other hand, the inscriptions and utterances are peers as instances of the work. An unspoken work exists in its inscriptions alone, an unwritten work in its utterances alone; and Mrs. Smith's defense of the unwritten work is unnecessary. Treating poetry and music in the same way, as Mrs. Smith advocates, would not at all affect the status I assign to recitations and performances as instances of a work. Rather, either (1) to the horror of musicians, copies of the score will have to be considered as no less instances of a symphony than are performances, or (2) printed or written copies of a poem will have to be considered not as instances of the poem but as merely prescribing or defining what auditory events are the only instances of the work. Both courses disregard an important difference: that whereas visual characteristics of the score that do not affect performance are irrelevant to a musical work, certain visual characteristics of the text (from simple lineation to the complex layout of some poems by e. e. cummings) are, often, quite apart from any effect upon recitation, integral to a poem.

Silent recitations of a poem or silent performances of a score by a musician might be admitted along with spoken recitations and played performances as instances of works of poetry and music. Still, if a copy of the text exists, a poem that is never recited either silently or aloud has an actual instance, whereas even if a copy of the score exists, a song that is never sung silently or aloud has none.

Mrs. Smith's second complaint is that I count all texts, including grocery slips, as literary works. I do not. To say that all literary works are texts (written or spoken) is not to say that all texts are

literary works. I did not undertake to define the special kinds of
texts that are poems, novels, etc.; and the nearest I came to distinguishing literary works in general from other texts is in suggesting certain 'symptoms of the aesthetic'. These symptoms provide a guide rather than a definition. Mrs. Smith, on the contrary,
seems to propose defining literary works as fictive texts. But
obviously falsity is neither enough nor required to make a text a
literary work. The definition goes wrong both in including all lies
as literary works and in excluding all histories and biographies.
And Franklin's *Autobiography,* while not a literary work if true,
would become one if falsified by inserting "not"s or changing
names and dates.

All that Mrs. Smith really wants to urge, I think, is that what
matters in the case of literary works, fiction or nonfiction, is not
what if anything they denote but what their structure is and
what they evoke or suggest. Early in *LA* (p. 26), I made much the
same point concerning the pictorial arts:

> . . . the world of pictures teems with anonymous fictional persons,
> places, and things. The man in Rembrandt's *Landscape with a
> Huntsman* is presumably no actual person; he is just the man in
> Rembrandt's etching. In other words, the etching represents no
> man but is simply a man-picture, and more particularly a the-
> man-in-Rembrandt's-*Landscape-with-a-Huntsman* picture. And
> even if an actual man be depicted here, his identity matters as
> little as the artist's blood-type. Furthermore, the information
> needed to determine what if anything is denoted by a picture is
> not always accessible. . . .
> But not only where the denotation is null or indeterminate does
> the classification of a picture need to be considered. For the de-
> notation of a picture no more determines its kind than the kind of
> picture determines the denotation. Not every man-picture repre-
> sents a man, and conversely not every picture that represents a
> man is a man-picture. And in the difference between being and
> not being a man-picture lies the difference, among pictures that
> denote a man, between those that do and those that do not repre-
> sent him as a man.

Later (253–254), prominence of what is exemplified or expressed
finds full recognition as a symptom of the aesthetic in general. But
this one feature will not serve by itself to define literary or other
works of art.

As she wants to identify art with fiction, Mrs. Smith wants to identify science with fact. Though granting many of the often overlooked affinities between art and science discussed in my book, she writes: "what we acquire knowledge *of* in a work of art is primarily the work itself" and later "the objects of our aesthetic experiences are artificial worlds, fictive natures, and . . . the consequences of knowing *them* are confused at one's peril with the consequences of knowing nature proper". But if a work of art is artificial, so is a scientific system. What each reveals is a world of its own. The idea that science simply describes nature is no more tenable than the idea that pictures simply mirror it. As I have argued elsewhere,[1] there is no such thing as 'nature proper', no one way the world is, nothing already formulated or framed and waiting to be transcribed. All we ever get is one among the many ways the world is. Furthermore, while I quite agree that knowing a work of art or a scientific system is not for the sake of anything else, still nothing can be known in isolation; for knowing—by sense, emotion, or intellect—involves discriminating, comparing, contrasting, and so relating what is experienced to what lies beyond it.

In science, unlike art, we are indeed usually less concerned with what is exemplified or expressed than with what is asserted. But to say that truth is asked of science but not of art is far too simpleminded a way of drawing the distinction between them. Much else besides—and sometimes even rather than—truth is asked of science. Moreover, when we examine our tests for truth in science we find them far from alien to tests for quality in art.

Mrs. Smith's remark that I almost snub the artist is nicely offset by Mr. Wollheim's remark that I give the artist something like his due.

1. "The Way the World Is", I,2 above.

5

Further Notes

(a) Reply to Morris Weitz [1]

Professor Weitz agrees with my rejection of the various criteria of the aesthetic that have usually been proposed, and seems to agree that the symbolic characteristics I have described are indeed symptoms, or even 'constituent properties' of art. But he rejects my tentative suggestion that these properties may be disjunctively necessary and conjunctively sufficient. And he argues that no properties can have this status because the concept of art of the aesthetic is 'open-ended'.

A symptom, I suppose, is an indication that is neither indispensable nor infallible, but such that its presence or absence may give some degree of probability to the presence or absence of the disease or other condition in question. When Professor Weitz accepts what I have called symptoms as 'constituent properties of art', I must ask him what are the requirements upon a constituent property. Must it be present in every work of art? Is everything that has the property a work of art? If not, what does he mean by constituent property?

I have not suggested that any one of the symbolic properties I list is necessary to the aesthetic—that is, present in every work of art or aesthetic experience, nor on the other hand that any one of them is sufficient—that is such that whatever has the property is aesthetic. My suggestion is that perhaps—and I must insist that I *do* mean "perhaps"—they are disjunctively necessary and conjunctively sufficient. This sounds like a pretty strong statement, but is actually a very weak one. That these properties are disjunctively necessary means that while what is aesthetic need not have any particular one of them, it must have at least some one or another of them. That these properties are conjunctively sufficient

---

1. "Professor Goodman on the Aesthetic", *Journal of Aesthetics and Art Criticism,* forthcoming.

means that while what is nonaesthetic may have one or more of them, whatever has them all is aesthetic. If at least this much is not true for 'constituent properties', what is?

Professor Weitz rejects my conjecture, not on the basis of counterexamples but on the grounds that the concepts of art and of the aesthetic are open-ended and therefore forever immune not only to definitions but to specification in terms of symptomatic characteristics. The implication is, then, that my proposal must be rejected along with all the others I have rejected on the way. To this, I should like to reply:

1. All ordinary concepts are prescientifically open-ended. Under philosophical or scientific enquiry, they are clarified, rectified, systematized; and no concept is immune to such explication or definition, which need no more follow vacillating usage in every detail than a map need show every tree nor turn red in autumn.

2. With a concept as general as that of the aesthetic, considerable disparity between presystematic usage and systematic specification is inevitable. My rejection of a long list of dichotomies proposed for distinguishing the aesthetic from the scientific is not on the ground of such disparity but rather on the ground that many of these dichotomies are untenable in themselves, and that the rest are rather obviously irrelevant.

3. In contrast, I claim that the properties I cite as symptoms of the aesthetic are clearly defined and capture significant features of the presystematic concept. I wrote that "I am not claiming that this proposal conforms faithfully to ordinary usage . . . I am rather suggesting that we have here an appropriate use for some badly abused terms." Still, I am not so much advocating that they be used for reforming this vague ordinary notion of the aesthetic as suggesting that they mark more fruitful and informative distinctions. The line between the aesthetic and the nonaesthetic tends to lose its importance as more consequential bonds and boundaries cutting across it emerge. Critically scrutinizing a traditional conceptual scheme sometimes results in supplementing rather than merely reforming it. The classification of materials according to the proportions of earth, air, fire, and water they contain has yielded to a better system.

(b) Reply to Joseph Margolis[2]

1. Nothing in *Languages of Art* has given more readers the opportunity to throw up their hands in delighted horror than the statement that a performance with a single wrong note does not qualify as a genuine instance of the work in question. This provides many readers with so much self-satisfaction that they ignore what follows in the same paragraph. Let me read into the record the last two sentences of that paragraph: "This is not to say that the exigencies that dictate our technical discourse need govern our everyday speech. I am no more recommending that in ordinary discourse we refuse to say that a pianist who misses a note has performed a Chopin Polonaise than that we refuse to call a whale a fish, the earth spherical, or a grayish-pink human white."

We do not try to define "white"—or "triangle"—so that the term applies to everything we apply it to in daily use. The result would be as useless as the effort is hopeless. The same is true for the definitions I give for "notation", "score", "work", etc. Although they derive from practice, they are idealizations of it seldom actually realized. But the definitions are precise, and useful for measuring actual cases in terms of their approximation to these ideals. The performance with a wrong note is not strictly a performance of the work in question, any more than a man is strictly white, or a diagram on the blackboard strictly a triangle. Indeed, while we may have genuine instances of a musical work (one with all the notes correct), we never see a genuine triangle (consisting of three straight lines without breadth). But in both cases, the definitions adopted, far from being arbitrary or "purely nominal" are controlled by established usage (we would not accept "plane figure with four sides" as defining "triangle"); and they are subject to severe theoretical constraints that emerge when, in geometry or the theory of symbols, we undertake a systematic analysis of our subject-matter.

2. Professor Margolis argues that painting is not irrevocably

---

2. "Numerical Identity and Reference in the Arts", *British Journal of Aesthetics,* Vol. 10 (1970), pp. 138–146.

autographic, that what we now regard as reproductions might come to be as acceptable as the original picture. I have explained some strong reasons why this is unlikely to happen; but I have not maintained that painting is inalterably autographic. For an art to become allographic depends upon establishment of a practice of classifying instances into works in a manner independent of history of production. If and when reproductions of a picture come to be accepted as no less original instances than the initial painting, so that the latter has only the sort of special interest or value that attaches to the manuscript or first edition of a literary work, then indeed the art could become allographic. But it cannot become so by fiat; a practice or tradition must first be established, later to be codified by means of a notation.

Nowadays, especially, there is constant effort to change any characteristic an art may have. I have pointed out that music as conceived by some modern composers is not allographic. And increasing promotion of the 'multiple' or manufactured object moves toward allographic visual art. Nothing in my theory is incompatible with such developments; and I have nowhere argued for fixity.

3. In response to Professor Margolis's objections to my statement that "works of art . . . perform one or more among certain referential functions: representation, description, exemplification, expression", I have no objection to modifying this to read "works of art characteristically function as symbols: representative, exemplificational, or expressive". This allows for example, for fictive representation, and for the fact that a work need not unremittingly function as a symbol, and for the fact that some works, by accident, may not actually so function. Similarly, we might say that a chair characteristically serves the purpose of being sat upon; but few chairs are always sat on, and some remain always vacant. But when a chair functions as a chair, it is sat upon; and when a work of art functions as such, it functions as a symbol. When it does not, it is inert not only as a symbol but as a work of art.

If this modification is all Professor Margolis wants, well and good. It is more or less implicit in what I have written anyway.

But I gather he is claiming more: that a work of art may function as such when it is not functioning as a symbol at all. He disputes my statement that expression is a form of reference. He says that what a picture expresses are those of its properties that are "within a certain range". If this implies that there are properties such that any picture that possesses them expresses them, I cannot agree. Just as not every red piece of cloth exemplifies its redness, so not all metaphorically solid pictures express solidity. One piece of cloth may serve as a sample of its color, another as a sample of its air-filtering properties, while another serves as a pen-wiper exemplifying no property at all. One metaphorically solid picture may exemplify and hence express solidity while another may be metaphorically solid only rather incidentally, without standing as a sample of, and so without exemplifying or expressing, solidity. What matters is not just the property possessed but also whether the referential relationship of exemplification is established between the picture and the property.

The careless remarks that Margolis has added at the end of the published version of his paper hardly call for comment.

(c) A Circle Squared

The question whether similarity, banished as the measure of realism, is covertly reintroduced in the notion of habit as the measure, has been raised in two forms.

How can we explain, except in terms of similarity, the fact that habits develop in certain ways, or along certain routes, rather than others? Similarity is of no use in such an explanation; for no matter along what routes habits developed, they could always be correlated with some similarity or other. Similarity cannot be used to explain why some rather than other similarities correlate with habits.

How can we even distinguish between habitual and nonhabitual behavior except in terms of similarity versus lack of similarity among instances of behavior? The question whether on two occasions we are doing 'the same thing' does indeed depend upon how we classify behavioral events, and habit does consist of doing the 'same' thing under the 'same' circumstances. Without some such classification, "habit" would be meaningless. But to say that the classification depends upon comparative similarities seems to me to explain nothing, unless we stress the fact that any classification would follow some similarities, that the similarities actually followed are those that are more important in that they have attracted our interest and gained prominence through entrenchment, and that the classification can no more truly be said to depend upon than to give rise to such prominence.[3]

(d) Reply to Matthew Lipman[4]

Most of Professor Lipman's review consists in an attack upon a position that he unaccountably attributes to me. His initial mistake, that leads him to consider not what I say but what he thinks I must be saying, is revealed in his statement that given my "assumption that art is non-literal and science is non-metaphorical" I can "hardly escape" the conclusion "that art cannot expect to be taken as seriously as the soberly 'literal' sciences". This seems to him to invalidate my emphatic rejection of any such conclusion.

Now in the first place, I nowhere suggest that the line between art and science coincides with the line between the metaphorical and the literal. Metaphor is involved in expression, but art is not exclusively expressive; and I have (LA, p. 94) explicitly disavowed identification of art with expression or exemplification or representation. Furthermore, use of metaphor is ubiquitous in ordinary discourse and in science. Indeed, I am inclined to think that all measurement is a matter of metaphor.

Furthermore, I have insisted that metaphorical possession of a property is actual possession, and that metaphorical truth is no less genuine, no more arbitrary and capricious, than literal truth. Attempts to explain metaphor (or representation, or natural kinds, etc.) in terms of similarity seem to me utterly futile;[5] but in observing that we cannot explain in general why terms apply

3. On the general unreliability and misuse of similarity, see further IX,2 below.

4. Review of *Languages of Art, Man and World*, August, 1970.

5. In addition to *LA*, see also IX,2 below.

as they do metaphorically, I point out that neither can we explain why they apply as they do literally; i.e. that the general question is as spurious in one case as in the other. This is not to contrast but to assimilate metaphorical and literal application.

Professor Lipman points accusingly at the word "only" in the sentence (*LA*, page 68) "The picture is literally gray but only metaphorically sad." without recognizing that this sentence, at the beginning of a section, is set forth for analysis and interpretation, not as a conclusion, and might well have been in quotation-marks or introduced by some such words as "One says that". Again, he leans heavily on my remark that "a metaphor might be regarded as a calculated category-mistake" without noticing that the "calculated" forestalls and precancels the "mistake". I was here only calling attention to a certain analogy between metaphors and category-mistakes, not by any means saying that metaphors are mistakes. But Professor Lipman's misinterpretation of my views becomes even more glaring when he attributes to me the idea that ". . . when a property belongs to the symbol itself, the exemplification involved is metaphorical". On the contrary, all properties exemplified, whether the exemplification is literal or metaphorical, belong to the symbol itself; that is the very nature of exemplificational reference and what distinguishes it from denotation.

Finally, to show how wrong Professor Lipman is in supposing that I take metaphor, and hence expression, to be "arbitrary", "capricious", "spurious", "specious", or "counterfeit", let me quote a few brief passages from *LA*. Page 68: "Metaphorical possession is indeed not *literal* possession; but possession is actual whether metaphorical or literal. The metaphorical and the literal have to be distinguished within the actual. . . . That is, although a predicate that applies to an object metaphorically does not apply literally, it nevertheless applies. Whether the application is metaphorical or literal depends upon some such feature as its novelty." Page 74: "We may at will apply temperature-predicates to sounds or hues or personalities or to degrees of nearness to a correct answer; but *which* elements in the chosen realm are warm, or are warmer than others, is then very largely determinate." Page 79: "Standards of truth are much the same whether the schema used is transferred [as in metaphor] or not [as in literal truth]."

The views that Professor Lipman disputes are someone else's, not mine.

(e) *Reply to Rudolph Arnheim*

A policy of not replying to reviews is overridden in this case by unwillingness to let obviously false statements stand. In his review (*Science* 9, May 1969, p. 697) of my *Languages of Art*, Rudolph Arnheim writes: "This neatness entices Goodman to assert that a work of music is its score, just as he believes that a work of literature is its text." I quote from page 210 of my book: "Thus in the different arts a work is differently localized. . . . In music, the work is the class of performances compliant with a character. In literature, the work is the character itself."

The quality of the review may be judged from this sample.

6

Review of Gombrich's
Art and Illusion

E. H. Gombrich, *Art and Illusion; a Study of the Psychology of Pictorial Representation.* The A. W. Mellon Lectures in the Fine Arts, 1956, National Gallery of Art, Washington. (New York: Pantheon Books, 1960), xxxi, 466 pp. 319 illus. (Bollingen Series XXXV: 5.)

The philosopher who reads this book is likely to learn a great deal about art and to have some fun. And the more epistemologists read it, the less dismal should be the future literature of the philosophy of perception. This 'study in the psychology of representation' is based on the 1956 A. W. Mellon Lectures in the Fine Arts by Mr. Gombrich, the Director of the Warburg Institute of the University of London. He brings an acute intelligence to bear upon a rich variety of material drawn from long experience with art and from the writings of psychologists, artists, teachers, and critics. He takes what he needs without often being taken in: for example, he judiciously cites relevant findings of Gestalt theory while avoiding its excesses. He does not miss the importance of Berkeley's *New Theory of Vision,* and he has profited from the ideas of Kant and of Popper. The results of his wide learning and hard thinking are set forth in an easy, crisp, and crystalline prose, abundantly illustrated by pictures. The convenience and utility of the book are enhanced by the fact that each picture is placed as close as possible to the relevant text, and by an excellent index.

The future historian of ideas may be struck by finding the familiar duck-rabbit picture occurring in the early pages of books on science, books on philosophy, and books of art, around the middle of the twentieth century. He may conclude that this is less important as evidence of Wittgenstein's influence in these years than as a sign that a community of problems among these fields of inquiry was beginning to be discerned, to the eventual benefit of all three. The duck-rabbit picture on page 5 of Gombrich's book introduces his major concerns: the nature of vision and of repre-

141

sentation, and the problem of reconciling the objectivity of the latter with its conventionality and with the relativity of vision.

That we know what we see is no truer than that we see what we know. Perception depends heavily on conceptual schemata. "There is no innocent eye." The raw material of vision cannot be extracted from the finished product. Our schemata may change and evolve, be revised or replaced, be suggested or informed, by factors of all kinds; but without some schema there is no perception.

Thus representation cannot amount simply to reproducing the world as it is or as it is correctly seen. Differences in style of representation cannot be explained by differences in eyesight or in manual dexterity; for what is to be represented depends upon the schemata in terms of which things are seen. Yet it is still too simple to say that the artist reproduces what he knows rather than what he sees; for representation is never duplication. The painting is flat and static, with a range of color and luminosity much narrower than that in the world. A representation does not duplicate but conveys—describes, so to speak, in a pictorial language. The development of such a language is a long and complex process; and in terms of it, Gombrich proposes to express the evolution of representation.

Our whole edifice of visual schemata and representational vocabulary functions much like a scientific theory, put to the test by the experiment of picture-making. In comparing our pictures with what they represent, we discover inadequacies. This may lead us to revise not only our way of painting but also our way of seeing: not only our representational vocabulary but also our visual schema. We learn to see by looking and to represent by painting; but we also learn to represent by looking and to see by painting. By repeated experimentation and consequent modification of our perception and of our methods of conveying what we perceive, we gradually achieve more and more effective representations.

Gombrich develops these themes in depth and in breadth, documenting them with fascinating evidence gleaned not only from the familiar lore of psychology but also from a study of old drawing-instruction books, of caricatures and cartoons, and—most surprisingly—of the seemly landscapes of Constable. From a Constable lecture comes a principal text:

> Painting is a science and should be pursued as an inquiry . . . of which pictures are but the experiments;

and concerning Cozens's sketches of cloud patterns, which Constable copied, Gombrich writes:

> We know by now what Cozens teaches Constable. Not, indeed, what clouds look like, but a series of possibilities, of schemata, which should increase his awareness through visual classification. It has recently been pointed out how closely Constable's interest in the most elusive phenomena of the visible world comes to that of his countryman and contemporary Luke Howard, to whom we owe the classification of cloud forms into cumulus, cirrus, and stratus. Goethe . . . hailed Howard's effort as . . . "giving form to the indeterminate." Cozens' schemata do the same for the artist who does not merely apply them in his searching study of phenomena but articulates and revises them beyond recognition.

Some further quotations, assembled from various parts of the book, follow:

> Perception is always an active process conditioned by our expectations and adapted to situations. We notice only when we look *for* something, and we look only when our attention is aroused by some disequilibrium. We cannot take in all we see in a room, but we notice if something is changed.

> Without some starting point, some initial schema, we could never get hold of the flux of experience . . . it matters little what these first categories are. . . . The progress of adjustment through trial and error can be compared to the game of 'Twenty Questions' . . . the starting point of a visual record is not knowledge but a guess conditioned by habit and tradition.

> The letterpress of a German woodcut of the sixteenth century informs us that we see here 'the exact counterpart' of a kind of locust that invaded Europe in menacing swarms. But . . . the artist had again used a familiar schema. . . . Perhaps the fact that the German word for a locust is *Heupferd* (hay horse) tempted them to adopt a schema of a horse for the rendering of the insect's prance.

> The layman may wonder whether Giotto could have painted a view of Fiesole in sunshine, but the historian will suspect that, lacking the means, he would not have wanted to, or rather that

he could not have wanted to. We like to assume, somehow, that where there is a will there is also a way, but in matters of art the maxim should read that only where there is a way is there also a will.

... the correct portrait, like the useful map ... is not a faithful record of a visual experience but the faithful construction of a relational model.

Though vision is relative to imposed schemata, and representation further relative to conventions employed, Gombrich nevertheless holds that there are objective standards of representation. Relativism can be overdone, he says; and he speaks repeatedly of testing, correction, adjustment, and even progress in representation—all implying some objectivity. We must recognize that things may be seen in various ways and depicted in terms of different vocabularies; but we must not be forced to conclude that a child's drawing is as accurate a representation of Wivenhoe Park as is Constable's painting, or that the painting is quite as much a representation of a pink elephant as of the Park.

What sort of test, then, do we make when we confront a picture with its subject? From what has already been said, we obviously cannot simply be measuring the degree to which the picture duplicates or resembles the subject. And since visual schemata and representational conventions are themselves being tested, our test must somehow be independent of them. Gombrich answers:

... difference in styles or languages need not stand in the way of correct answers and descriptions. The world may be approached from a different angle and the information given may yet be the same.... To say of a drawing that it is a correct view of Tivoli does not mean, of course, that Tivoli is bounded by wiry lines. It means that those who understand the notion will derive *no false information* from the drawing. ... The complete portrayal might be the one which gives as much correct information about the spot as we would obtain if we looked at it from the very spot where the artist stood ... [but] so complex is the information that reaches us from the visual world that no picture will ever embody it all.

In short, the test is that of degree of sameness of information provided by picture and subject.

This answer does not seem to me very satisfactory. Gombrich

is suggesting in effect that informational content is as independent of visual schemata and of pictorial conventions as it is of languages; that the relation in question is analogous to that between a text and its translation into another language. As he himself warns, the analogy must not be pressed too far. The schemata and conventions are, for instance, much less explicit than the vocabulary and grammar of verbal languages; and translation cannot proceed piecemeal by means of a dictionary. But therefore, I think, the comparison of informational yield must be in terms of serviceability for a given purpose; and I question whether the purpose appropriate in the case of artistic representation can be specified without begging the whole question. Moreover, insofar as the notion of informational equivalence is clear, it will plainly not support the conclusions Gombrich wants. A long verbal description of Tivoli with measurements, etc., can furnish more information than a hasty drawing; yet Gombrich would hardly call the description a better or more complete representation. Upside-down pictures, if we are given the clue, will provide the same information as right-side-up ones; and, indeed, a man can adjust rather quickly to inverting spectacles. Likewise, despite Gombrich's unwillingness to count perspective as conventional (his treatment of this subject is often puzzling), a comparable inversion of perspective can be effected without loss. If we are told truly that in a given picture the nearer persons are represented by the smaller figures, receding railroad tracks by diverging lines, etc., as if drawn in ordinary perspective but *from* rather than *to* the vanishing point, there will be no difference in information-value from that of a usual picture. And in fact, with suitable principles of correlation, Constable's landscape painting could provide an enormous amount of information about a pink elephant.

Thus I think Gombrich fails to resolve a central dilemma. Having exorcised the devil of the correspondence theory of representation, he is adrift on the deep blue sea of the coherence theory; and the informational-equivalence test is not a heavy enough anchor. But it is only fair to observe that the record of the philosopher's encounters with the parallel problem of truth is hardly a triumphant one.

There is much else of interest in the book. One chapter, for example, offers an intriguing explanation of the special character of Greek art. Again, I find food for thought in the similarity between the role of schemata in vision as Gombrich analyzes it and the role of language in prediction as I conceive it. Schemata and projected predicates alike are at first adopted haphazardly and are revised and systematized in the course of experience; and the schemata that survive to become stereotypes inform our perception as profoundly as the predicates that become entrenched inform our predictive thought and behavior. Also, I think that Gombrich's question whether there is really a sharp distinction between representation and expression has long needed asking. He answers that schemata are involved in expression quite as essentially as in representation.

From this, however, he goes on to argue that the hopeless attempt to dispense with all schemata has resulted in the downfall of abstract expressionism. Abstract expressionists will express themselves concretely and vocally on this. The disinterested observer, I think, will doubt whether such a general evaluation of a particular school of painting has any proper place in a book of this kind, and will find that Gombrich's detailed argument, while provocative, fails to prove his case.

That Gombrich seems to me to leave some problems unsolved and to be sometimes wrong is hardly a devastating criticism. The book is a treasure-house of facts and ideas concerning perception and representation, is indispensable to the philosopher and the student of art alike, and is completely absorbing.

Supplementary Readings for Chapter III
secondary to references within text and footnotes

Bach, K., "Part of What a Picture Is", *British Journal of Aesthetics,* Vol. 10 (1970), pp. 119–137.

Beardsley, M., Review of *Languages of Art, Philosophy of Science,* Vol. 37 (1970), pp. 458–463.

Black, M., Review of *Languages of Art, Linguistic Inquiry* (1971, forthcoming).

Brentlinger, A. F., "Nelson Goodman's *Languages of Art*", *Massachusetts Review* (Winter 1970), pp. 202–208.

Cassirer, E., *The Philosophy of Symbolic Forms* (R. Manheim, trans.), New Haven: Yale University Press, 1955.

Dewey, J., *Art as Experience,* New York: Minton, Balch, 1934.

Howard, V. A., "Harvard Project Zero: A Fresh Look at Art Education", *Bulletin* of the American Council for Research in Music Education, No. 21 (Summer 1970), pp. 1–14; revised reprint in *The Journal of Aesthetic Education* (January 1971).

———., "On Musical Expression", *The British Journal of Aesthetics* (1971, forthcoming).

Langer, S., *Philosophy in a New Key,* Cambridge, Mass.: Harvard University Press, 1942.

———., *Feeling and Form,* New York: Scribner, 1953.

Pleydell-Pearce, A. G., Review of *Languages of Art, British Journal of Aesthetics,* Vol. 10 (1970), pp. 191–194.

Presley, C. F., "Review of *Languages of Art*", *Australasian Journal of Philosophy,* Vol. 48 (1970), pp. 373–393.

Smith, C. M., "Symbolic Systems, Cognitive Efficacy, and Aesthetic Education", *Journal of Aesthetic Education* (October 1969), pp. 123–136.

Vuillemin, J., Review of *Languages of Art, Age de la Science,* No. 1 (1970).

Wollheim, R., *Art and Its Objects,* New York: Harper and Row, 1968.

IV

Individuals

FOREWORD

My concern with the theory of individuals and with nominalism began in my undergraduate years and continues through the present. As a student I began exploring the varied ways of organizing the world into units of many different kinds. The first thought of developing some of the basic ideas by use of the (then rather new) techniques of symbolic logic came from my fellow student Henry Leonard, and our collaboration led to "The Calculus of Individuals and its Uses".[1] Simple as it is, the calculus took no little trouble; and innocent as it is, it caused no little trouble, for logic was an unfamiliar and unwelcome intruder into philosophy in those days.

Use of the term "individual" in this context is well established by now; but a good deal of worried discussion preceded its choice. I had at first used the term "unit" and we considered such other possibilities as "hunk" and "chunk". What led us to our reluctant choice among unsuitable alternatives was that there seemed to be some slight precedent for this use in logical contexts, and hope that the misleading associations with continuity, uniformity, sanctity, etc.—most of them shared by any alternatives we could think of—could be dispelled by pointing to the parallel misleading associations that attend extralogical use of the word "class". This hope was hardly fulfilled; and much is still made of the difficulty of thinking of scattered and very heterogeneous elements as parts of one individual. Some such elements, indeed, may not in the popular sense be contained in the same whole, just as some may not in the popular sense belong to the same class. But imaginative

1. *Journal of Symbolic Logic*, Vol. 5 (1940), pp. 44–55.

effort is no more called for in taking any such elements as technically parts of one individual than in taking them as technically members of one class.

Any of a number of primitives will serve for the entire calculus of individuals. In "The Calculus of Individuals", the choice was *discreteness* (" $\rceil$ "); in *SA, overlapping* ("**o**"); and in the following two papers, *part* ("<"). From any of these, definition of the rest and of *identity, sum, product, remainder* or *difference,* and *negate,* is easy.

The calculus of individuals was developed not merely for its own sake but as an instrument for dealing with an infuriating problem—the 'difficulty of imperfect community'[2]—that blocked my search for a way of defining qualities in terms of concrete elements, or concrete elements in terms of qualities. The difficulty can be met by taking as primitive a dyadic predicate of classes rather than of individuals; but that course flouts both the scruples of nominalism and the principle of economy—though the vast increase in complexity of basis could not at that time be accurately measured (see *SA III,8* and *SA VI,7*).

Originally, however, the calculus of individuals was formulated in terms of the calculus of classes, and was thus itself platonistic. Its nominalization was effected in Chapter I of *SA* at no cost beyond replacement of some axioms and definitions by schemata.

Surprisingly this very elementary, familiar, and by now (as logic goes) even old calculus is still raising questions that lead to new discoveries. The core calculus that is part of the general apparatus of many different constructional systems contains no postulate of finitude or infinitude. However, we can easily frame in the calculus a formula (such as that every individual has some proper part) satisfiable only in infinite domains. I used to set my students the problem of either framing a formula satisfiable in all and only finite domains or proving that this cannot be done. Despite a bewildering crop of proposed formulae and an occasional misguided claim that a corollary of the Skolem-Löwenheim theorem settled the matter negatively, the problem went unsolved until a couple of years ago when David Lewis, a former student of

---

2. See further the article cited in footnote 1, pp. 50–54; and *SA V* and *VI*.

mine, and Wilfrid Hodges produced an intricate but convincing proof that no such formula can be found.[3]

As a prelude to this proof, Lewis had pointed out that one formula for infinitiy (viz., that every individual is a proper part of some other) would, if taken as a postulate, make the calculus inconsistent. I then raised the question how we might, if we liked, modify the rest of the calculus to accommodate this axiom. Then Geoffrey Hellman,[4] taking as a guide the Zermelo-Fraenkel device of allowing only relative rather than unrestricted complementation, showed how this might be accomplished if instead of postulating existence of the negate of each individual x that is discrete from any other, we postulate only the existence within any y of the negate of each x that is discrete from some part of y. Hellman went on to argue that the calculus of individuals captures the 'intended' notion of an individual in the sense that every model of the calculus that interprets the identity sign in the normal way is isomorphic to an 'intended' model. This result would have particular interest in the light of adoption of isomorphism as the criterion of constructional definition (see I,1 and I,3 above, and *SA I*). That criterion as it applies to nominalistic systems is here discussed in "A Revision in *The Structure of Appearance*". One sometimes forgotten point emerges clearly along the way: that while a class of individuals is uniquely a class of just those members, a whole made up of individuals may also be made up of quite other parts.

"A World of Individuals" attempts to correct misunderstandings of, and to clarify, both the theory of individuals and the nominalism couched in terms of it. A definitive criterion of nominalism is arrived at by comparing nominalistic and platonistic systems. This paper was delivered as part of a symposium[5] with Father Bochenski and Professor Alonzo Church. When it was republished

3. "Finitude and Infinitude in the Atomic Calculus of Individuals", *Nous*, Vol. 2 (1968), pp. 405–410.

4. "Finitude, Infinitiude, and Isomorphism of Interpretations in some Nominalistic Calculi", *Nous*, Vol. 3 (1969), pp. 413–425.

5. *The Problem of Universals* (Notre Dame, Indiana: University of Notre Dame Press, 1956).

in an anthology on the philosophy of mathematics edited by Benacerraf and Putnam,[6] they suggested in their introduction that a platonist might argue:

> ... that setting up ... a system is more like putting forth a theory to describe ... what is to be found in some remote region of space. ... Consideration of whether the 'generating' relation of the system satisfied nominalistic principles would be strictly irrelevant. We are not generating new entities, we are merely attempting to describe those that there are. And what reason is there to deny that "ϵ" could be employed accurately so to describe?

I had looked upon the nominalist and the platonist, in building constructional systems, as starting from selected basic individuals and as admitting whatever else can be made up of these, but as disagreeing on what can be so made up. Benacerraf and Putnam propose considering the nominalist and the platonist agreeing on what can be made up of the basic individuals, but as disagreeing on the admission of what cannot be so made up. To cover this case, the criterion of nominalism might be somewhat amplified: the nominalist admits only what can be made up of the selected basic individuals, and denies that all classes can be made up of them. The platonist disagrees on one score or the other.

My criterion of nominalism applied only to atomic systems. Two of my former students, M. G. Yoes, Jr.[7] and Richard Schuldenfrei,[8] worked independently on the problem of extending the criterion to non-atomic systems as well. Then Rolf Eberle[9] showed how this can be accomplished. He has furthermore, in a book just received,[10] explored extensively and intensively many problems discussed in *SA*.

Incidentally, all these recent developments along with others

---

6. *Philosophy of Mathematics* (Englewood Cliffs, New Jersey: Prentice-Hall, 1964).

7. "Nominalism and Non-Atomic Systems", *Nous,* Vol. 1 (1967), pp. 193–200.

8. "Eberle on Nominalism in Non-Atomic Systems", *Nous,* Vol. 3 (1969), pp. 427–430.

9. "Non-Atomic Systems of Individuals Revisited", *Nous,* Vol. 3 (1969), pp. 431–434.

10. *Nominalistic Systems* (Dordrecht, Holland: D. Reidel, 1970).

mentioned elsewhere in the present volume (e.g., III Foreword, V, VII, and IX) attest to the longevity of *SA* despite the frequent dismissal of it on one score or another and its death sentence in England for the crime of using logic in philosophy.

"Steps Toward a Constructive Nominalism" resulted from a joint determination to see whether many of the fundamental concepts of mathematics could be developed on a purely nominalistic basis. Quine and I differed in minor details of our conceptions of and attitudes toward nominalism, but not on the program undertaken in this paper or the value of trying to carry it out. Some seemingly rather hopeless problems proved vulnerable. For example, the definition of proof required the ancestral of immediate consequence, and the usual method (Frege's) for defining an ancestral is highly platonistic; but a nominalistic method already devised for defining the ancestral of *matching* (see further IX,1 below and *SA IX* and *X*) was found to serve here also. On the whole, we accomplished more than we expected and about as much as we had hoped—and a good deal more than platonists had anticipated. Indeed, some of my students began to ask what more a platonist would say still needed to be done; and I put the question to Professor Alonzo Church. In a letter of December 1, 1958, he replied as follows:

> In response to the request in your letter of November twentieth for additional tasks that 'nominalistic' (better, finitistic) syntax might be asked to accomplish, the obvious thing to give is just a catalogue of the major results of classical, nonfinitistic syntax. To name a few, there's the deduction theorem—first for propositional calculus, later also for first-order functional (alias 'predicate') calculus—; the proof of the rules of substitution as derived rules—in a formulation of propositional or first-order functional calculus which uses axiom schemata and has no substitution rules—; Post's completeness theorem for the propositional calculus; the metatheorem that every quantifier-free theorem of first-order functional calculus has a quantifier-free proof; the principal results about the Skolem normal form; Gödel's incompleteness theorems—first, say, for the Hilbert (or first-order) arithmetic, but afterwards more generally, for any system satisfying specified conditions—; Gödel's relative consistency proof for the axiom of choice and the generalized continuum hypothesis; the results of Fraenkel, Lindenbaum, and Mostowski concerning the independence of the axiom of choice. It does seem to me that your program requires

you to take these results of classical syntax into account—either to prove them in finitistic syntax, or to prove modified forms of them (with your reasons, if any, for thinking the modification inessential), or to concede that no proof of even a modified form appears to be forth-coming (with your reasons, if any, for thinking the result in question dispensable). In many cases, of course, the difficulty is to state the result in a form that would not make it trivially false in finitistic syntax, or even to find a promising weaker result that could be so stated.

In giving me permission to use this letter, he asks that I call attention to its date, since he would today add many more recent discoveries to this list.

In the first place, I should point out that this letter predated "A World of Individuals", where nominalism is carefully distinguished from finitism. Our position in "Steps" was indeed finitistic as well as nominalistic; but finitism, although a friendly companion of nominalism, is neither identical with nor necessary to it. In the second place, the purpose of "Steps" was not to run the losing race on nominalizing mathematics as fast as it develops, but merely to dislodge some complacent assumptions as to what nominalism cannot do. Not all of mathematics can be instantly dealt with by a nominalistic philosophy, but neither can all the behavior of materials be instantly dealt with by modern chemistry. Finally, are we sure that we want to save everything on Professor Church's list? Admiration for Gödel's incompleteness theorem does not make the result any more welcome. If incompleteness depends essentially upon those aspects of arithmetic or its supposed foundations that are not finitistic or nominalistic, this argues *for* rather than *against* finitism or nominalism. Gödel's result stands as a *reductio ad absurdum* giving notice of an anomaly that calls for correction. Incompleteness is no more to be cherished for the sake of Gödel's theorem than is crime for the sake of detection; banishment of crime and incompleteness to the realm of fiction would hardly be a matter for regret.

1

A World of Individuals

1. Individuals and Classes

For me, as a nominalist, the world is a world of individuals. But this simple statement, I have learned from bitter experience, can be misunderstood in numberless ways. Some misunderstandings have arisen from inadequacies in my own explanations. Other misunderstandings have arisen from inadequate attention to those explanations. Conflicting arguments in bewildering variety have been brought forward to show that nominalism is bad. This paper is one more attempt to make clear what I mean by nominalism and why I think nominalism is good.

A certain amount of trouble can be blamed on emotions attaching to the word "individual". One writer[1] calls it an 'honorific' word; and I am often criticized for applying the term "individual" to something or other that is unworthy of it. Use of a different word, even a coined one, might have been advisable in order to forestall such complaints. Nevertheless, I am prepared to defend the choice of the term "individual" as entirely in accord with a common practice of adapting ordinary language to technical purposes. In some cases, what I take as an individual may indeed lack many characteristics usually associated with the term "individual", and may not count as an individual according to common usage. But the situation with respect to the term "class" is exactly parallel. According to the layman's prelogical usage, children in a schoolroom make up a class, and so do people at a given social level, but Plato and this sheet of paper and the Taj Mahal do not. The term "set" in ordinary usage is perhaps even more restricted than the term "class". Yet by the logician's usage any things whatever make up a class or set. The contention that a genuine whole or individual cannot consist of widely scattered and very unlike parts misses the point as completely as would the contention that

1. Victor Lowe on p. 125 of "Professor Goodman's Concept of an Individual" in the *Philosophical Review*, Vol. 62 (1953), pp. 117–126.

a genuine class cannot consist of widely scattered and very unlike members. In the case of "individuals" as in the case of "class", a technical usage is explicated with the help of a calculus, and the divergence from ordinary usage is expressly noted. A class for Boole need not have social cohesion; and an individual for me need not have personal integration.

Confusion of another kind has resulted from the incautious opening sentence of my joint article[2] with Quine. Although the statement "We do not believe in abstract entities" was intended more as a headline than as final doctrine, and although some reservations concerning it were almost immediately indicated,[3] it has been fair game for critics ever since. Neither of us would write that sentence today, but neither of us would so change it as to affect anything beyond the first paragraph of the article in question. Quine has recently written that he would "now prefer to treat that sentence as a hypothetical statement of conditions for the construction in hand."[4] My own change would be not from the categorical to the hypothetical, but from the vaguely general to the more specific. I do not look upon abstractness as either a necessary or a sufficient test of incomprehensibility; and indeed the line between what is ordinarily called "abstract" and what is ordinarily called "concrete" seems to me vague and capricious. Nominalism for me consists specifically in the refusal to recognize classes.

What has not always been noticed is that essentially this revision is made in my book,[5] published four years later than the joint article. A key principle in this later formulation is that the nominalist rejects classes as incomprehensible, but may take anything whatever as an individual. Some misguided criticism would have been obviated had enough attention been paid to this statement;

2. "Steps Toward a Constructive Nominalism" [IV,2 below].

3. See the third paragraph and the second footnote of the joint article.

4. *From a Logical Point of View*, Harvard University Press, 1953, pp. 173–174.

5. *SA*, see especially p. 39. Incidentally (as explained in the book and later in the present article) since any nominalistic system is readily translated into a platonistic one, acceptance of most of the book by no means depends upon an acceptance of nominalism. This has been explicitly acknowledged by most of my critics.

but I suspect that some of my critics feel they do me a kindness by not taking it seriously. Further explanation may help.

Nominalism as I conceive it (and I am not here speaking for Quine) does not involve excluding abstract entities, spirits, intimations of immortality, or anything of the sort; but requires only that whatever is admitted as an entity at all be construed as an individual. A given philosopher, nominalist or not, may impose very stringent requirements upon what he will admit as an entity; but these requirements, however sound they may be and however intimately associated with traditional nominalism, are quite independent of nominalism in my sense. The nominalism I have described demands only that all entities admitted, no matter what they are, be treated as individuals. Just what this means, I shall explain in the following sections; but for the moment we may suppose that to treat entities as individuals for a system is to take them as values of the variables of lowest type in the system.

Incidentally, several of my critics have confused themselves by lumping together, without due attention to context, passages from different parts of *Structure of Appearance*. In Chapter *VI*, I discuss the choice of elements for a certain constructional system; but this does not turn upon the propriety of construing certain entities as individuals. Whatever we are willing to recognize as an entity at all may be construed as an individual. But in building a system, we must consider carefully what entities we are willing to recognize at all—or better, what terms we are willing to interpret as denoting and what terms we want to interpret syncategorematically. Important as the question is, nominalism does not decide it. I have never suggested that nominalism is enough to make a system acceptable. I have suggested only that platonism is enough to make it inacceptable. But more of this later.

Now, however, is nominalism consequential at all? If the nominalist is free to construe anything he pleases as an individual, can't he even construe a class as an individual?

Whatever can be construed as a class can indeed be construed as an individual, and yet a class cannot be construed as an individual. If this seems paradoxical, it can perhaps be clarified by means of an analogy. Suppose that in a certain game a player is to begin by dealing each card from his hand onto the table at either his left or his right; he may put any card on either side and may move a card from side to side if he likes. Then while it is quite true that he is free to put any card on either side, he can never get a left-hand card on the right-hand side; for a card is a left-hand card or a right-hand card according as it lies on his left or his right. Similarly, a table is an individual, or the class of its legs and top, or the class of its molecule-classes of atoms, according to the way it is construed in a system. And whether the Great Dipper is an individual or a class of stars depends upon the system we are using. We can construe anything as an individual (and aside from nominalistic scruples we can construe anything as a class); but we can no more construe a class as an individual than we can get a left-hand card on the right-hand side.

2. The Principle of Nominalism

In brief, while the nominalist may construe anything as an individual, he refuses to construe anything as a class. But just what is the principle of this refusal? In *SA* I said that, roughly speaking, the nominalist balks at a distinction of entities without a distinction of content; and some of my critics have overlooked the more explicit formulation that soon followed. The nominalist denies that two different entities can be made up of the same entities. Let us suppose, for example, that a nominalist and a platonist start with the same minimal, atomic elements[6] for their systems; merely for comparative purposes take the number of these atoms as 5. The nominalist admits also all wholes or individual sums comprised of these, and so has a universe of $2^5 - 1$, or 31, entities. He cannot concoct any more; for whatever individuals among the 31 are added together, the result is another individual among those 31. Our platonist, we may suppose, admits no sums of atoms but admits all classes of them. This, not counting the null and unit classes, gives him also 31 entities. But he further admits all classes of classes of atoms; and by this single step he welcomes into his universe $2^{31} - 1$, or over two billion, additional entities. And he has

---

6. An atomic element—or atom—of a system is simply an element of the system that contains no lesser elements for the system. Depending on the system, an electron or a molecule or a planet might be taken as an atom.

no thought of stopping there. He also admits all classes of classes of classes of atoms, and so on *ad infinitum,* climbing up through an explosively expanding universe towards a prodigiously teeming Platonic Heaven. He gets all these extra entities out of his original five by a magical process that enables him to make two or more distinct entities from exactly the same entities. And it is just here that the nominalist draws the line.

In the nominalist's world, if we start from any two distinct entities and break each of them down as far as we like (by taking parts, parts of parts, and so on), we always arrive at some entity that is contained in one but not the other of our two original entities. In the platonist's world, on the contrary, there are at least two different entities that we can so break down (by taking members, members of members, and so on) as to arrive at exactly the same entities. For instance, suppose K has two members: the class of a and b, and the class of c and d; and suppose L has two members: the class of a and c, and the class of b and d. Then although K and L are different classes, they alike break down into a, b, c, and d. Again K breaks down into the same entities as does the class having K and L as its members. These are clear cases of what the nominalist objects to as a distinction of entities without distinction of content.

This discloses the relationship between nominalism and extensionalism, which springs from a common aversion to the unwonted multiplication of entities. Extensionalism precludes the composition of more than one entity out of exactly the same entities by membership; nominalism goes further, precluding the composition of more than one entity out of the same entities by any chains of membership. For the extensionalist, two entities are identical if they break down into the same members; for the nominalist, two entities are identical if they break down in any way into the same entities. The extensionalist's restriction upon the generation of entities is a special case of the nominalist's more thoroughgoing restriction.

Nominalism describes the world as composed of individuals. To explain nominalism we need to explain not what individuals are but rather *what constitutes describing the world as composed of them.* So to describe the world is to describe it as made up of entities no two of which break down into exactly the same entities. What this means I have just explained, but a somewhat more technical formulation may be helpful.

Suppose we have two constructional systems, having one or more (but not necessarily the same or even the same number of) atoms. Entities other than atoms are generated in system **I** as classes, and in system **II** as sum-individuals. Let us now obliterate all purely notational differences between the two systems. We may suppose from the start that each system uses but one style of variable.[7] Then let us remove all remaining telltale signs from system **I** other than "ϵ*" (for the proper ancestral of "is a member of") by expansion in terms of "ϵ*", and similarly let us remove all peculiar signs of system **II** other than "$\langle\langle$" (for "is a proper part of") by expansion in terms of "$\langle\langle$". Finally, let us put "R" in for every occurrence of "ϵ*" in system **I**, and for every occurrence of "$\langle\langle$" in system **II**. No purely notational distinction between the two systems remains; and "R" in each is irreflexive, asymmetric, and transitive. (If system **I** is a one-sorted system in which "ϵ" is not definable in terms of "ϵ*", we need take into account only the theorems upon "ϵ*".) Will anything now reveal which system is which?

For each system, x is an atom if and only if nothing stands in the relation R to x;[8] and x is an atom of y (symbol: "Axy") if and only if x is an atom and is identical with or bears the relation R to y. Now in a nominalistic but not in a platonistic system, entities are the same if their atoms are the same. Thus the disguised systems will be distinguishable from each other by the fact that the nominalistic system satisfies, while the platonistic system violates, the principle:

$$(x)\,(Axy \equiv Axz) \supset y = z.{}^{9}$$

7. The aim is to take systems as nearly alike as possible, in order to isolate the critical difference.

8. Any null class of system **I** will thus appear simply as one of the atoms of the disguised version of **I**, and thus leave no revealing trace.

9. Both systems will satisfy the converse principle; under nominalism and platonism alike, if x and y are identical they have the same atoms.

Obviously the disguised **I** will violate this principle if the system acknowledges more than $2n - 1$ entities, where n is the number of its atoms; or again, if **I** acknowledges any unit-classes, since the unit-class and its member will have the same atoms. But even if **I** is a platonistic system so restricted as to be distinguished on neither of these two scores, it will still be detectable in its disguised version through violation of the stated principle. And if **I** admits no two such classes, then indeed it is not platonistic at all, regardless of its notation.

This, I think, disposes of the charge that the distinction between nominalism and platonism is a mere matter of notation,[10] and also clarifies the nominalist's dictum: "No distinction of entities without distinction of content." For a nominalistic system, no two distinct things have the same atoms; only from different atoms can different things be generated; all non-identities between things are reducible to non-identities between their atoms.

The further question must be raised whether the distinction between nominalism and platonism can be made *purely* formal. In the case we have just considered, the problem was how to determine whether a given system is nominalistic or platonistic when we know that a given one of its relations is either ϵ^* or $\langle\langle$. Suppose now that we are confronted with a system without knowing anything about the interpretation of its predicates; or better, suppose we are given only the arrow-diagrams of the relations of the system. Can we determine whether the system is nominalistic or platonistic? The answer is *no*. We need to know which relation is the 'generating' relation[11] of the system—and hence which ele-

10. E.g., by Wang on p. 416 of "What is an Individual?" in *Philosophical Review*, Vol. 62 (1953), pp. 413–420.

11. A necessary but not sufficient condition for the generating relation of a system is that if and only if x is a non-atomic element of the system will there be some element y that stands in that relation to x. Given the generating relation, the atoms are always determined. Given the atoms, the generating relation is not always determined, but in some cases such as the one here described may be so determined. (See further the appendix to this article.) The generating relation G of a system is the relation that obtains between two elements x and y of the system if and only if x and y are connected by a sequence of pairs such that the first element of each pair is either a proper part or a member of the second.

ments are atoms of the system. Take, for example, the following diagram for a system with a single relation:

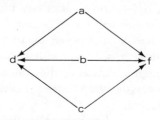

If we know that *a, b,* and *c* are the atoms of the system, or that the relation mapped is a generating one, then we know that the system is platonistic—since the distinct elements *d* and *f* then have exactly the same atoms. On the other hand, if we know that *a, b, c, d,* and *f* are all atoms of the system, then we know that the system is nominalistic. But if we do not know what the atoms are or whether the relation is a generating relation, we cannot tell whether the system is platonistic or nominalistic. Notice, though, that without such knowledge, *neither* can we tell whether a system is *extensional* or not. The system diagrammed is extensional if the relation is that of child to parent but surely not extensional if the relation is that of member to class.[12] Lest anyone gleefully welcome the apparent opportunity to dismiss both "nominalistic" and "extensional" as not purely formal characterizations of systems, I hasten to point out that no characterization of systems is purely formal in the sense implied. For if we are given just an arrow-diagram, without any interpretative information whatever, then we do not even know that the arrows represent relationships or that the letters represent elements. We can tell nothing at all about the system in question or even that there *is* a system in question; the diagram might be a hex sign or a complex character serving as the proper name of a single element. A classification of symbolic systems becomes significant only when at least some restrictions are imposed upon the interpretation of the symbols. The criterion

12. The system diagrammed, in fact, is extensional only if it is nominalistic, although obviously this is not true of all systems. Every system, of course, is nominalistic only if it is extensional.

for nominalism is formal to the same rather high degree as the usual criterion for extensionality.

What I have tried to do so far is to explain my version of nominalism. In outline, I have said that the nominalist insists on the world being described as composed of individuals, that to describe the world as composed of individuals is to describe it as made up of entities no two of which have the same content, and that this in turn is to describe it by means of a system for which no two distinct entities have exactly the same atoms.

Now, by way of justifying and defending the nominalism thus explained, I want to consider a number of objections to it.

3. Answers to Objections

(i) *Objection:* The nominalism described is not really nominalism in the traditional sense.

Answer: Doubtless a good many different theses are equally legitimate descendants of earlier nominalism. I claim no more than that the principle I have set forth is one reasonable formulation of the traditional injunction against undue multiplication of entities. And I willingly submit this claim to Father Bochenski for adjudication. If he rules against me, he deprives me of nothing but a label that incites opposition.

(ii) *Objection:* The principle of nominalism set forth is false as a statement, and groundless as a stipulation; for we know from everyday experience that different things often *are* made out of the same material, or the same particles, at different times.

Answer: The catch here in the phrase "at different times". Of course, different figures are often made out of the same lump of clay at different times; and of course, the same atoms often combine into different articles at different times. Likewise, different rooms are, so to speak, often made out of the same building at different places; and the same roads sometimes make up different crossings at different places. Admittedly, it is (spatially) different parts of the building or of the roads that are comprised in the two different rooms or the two different crossings; but so likewise, it is (temporally) different parts of the clay or the atoms that are comprised in the different figures or the different articles. We are at liberty to disregard the temporal or any other dimension we please; but if we were to rule out the spatial divisibility of buildings, or of roads, then we could not very consistently speak of the building, or a road, at different places. Similarly, if we rule out temporal divisibility, then we cannot very consistently speak of the clay, or of the atoms, *at different times.* The common experience of (different temporal parts of) the same clay making up different figures no more discredits the principle of nominalism than does the common experience of (different spatial parts of) the same building making up different rooms.

A variation on this objection points to ordered pairs like *Washington, Lincoln* and *Lincoln, Washington* as clearly illustrating the composition of different entities out of the same individuals.[13] To be pertinent, of course, this objection must not rest on any appeal to the logician's usual manner of defining these ordered pairs as distinct classes of classes; for the legitimacy of such multiple generation of classes out of the same individuals is just what is in question. Rather the argument must be that, regardless of how ordered pairs are defined in any formal system, we have here an everyday instance of distinct things being composed of the same things. But surely this claim is not true. Normally we no more conclude that we describe different composite entities when we name two people in different order than we conclude that a house from top to bottom and the house from bottom to top are different entities, or that the capital of Massachusetts and the largest city in New England are different things. We do not take the varied histories of the Battle of Bull Run as recounting different occurrences. In daily life a multiplicity of descriptions is no evidence for a corresponding multiplicity of things described.

Thus I find in common experience nothing discordant with the principle of nominalism.

(iii) *Objection:* Observance of the stated principle of nominal-

---

13. Cf. p. 110 of C. G. Hempel's article "Reflections on Nelson Goodman's *The Structure of Appearance*", in the *Philosophical Review,* Vol. 62 (1953), pp. 108–116.

ism is no sufficient guarantee of soundness or sense in a philosophical system; for trash of almost any kind can still be brought
in on the ground floor as admitted atoms of the system.
Answer: Granted. Nominalism no more guarantees philosophical soundness than the refusal to eat poison guarantees physical
well-being. Many additional rules must be observed if we are to
achieve either philosophical or physical health. Indeed, in some
cases a moderately platonistic system with a wholesome atomic
ontology may be a lesser evil than a nominalistic system that takes
monstrous vacuities as its atoms—just as a very tiny dose of poison
may be less harmful than a bullet in the head.

Nominalism is a necessary rather than a sufficient condition for
an acceptable philosophic system. To build well we must also exercise the most scrupulous care in choosing our raw materials. A
given philosopher's choice of atoms may very likely be guided by
attitudes or principles that are associated with nominalism by
temperament or tradition; but such associated principles are independent of nominalism as I have defined it. Nominalism does not
protect us from starting with ridiculous atoms. It does protect us
from manufacturing gimcracks out of sound atoms by the popular
devices of platonism. Nominalism, in other words, is a restrictive
rule of processing that won't select our raw materials or help us
make good things out of bad materials but will help keep us from
making bad things out of good materials.

(iv) *Objection:* To keep the rule of nominalism by generating
wholes, rather than classes, of individuals costs as much as it pays;
for it often means forcing the imagination to accept as individuals
some scattered or heterogeneous conglomerations that are never
in practice recognized as single units and are surely incomprehensible if classes are.[14]

Answer: This is perhaps the most chronic complaint against
nominalism: that a progressively and in the end hopelessly
strained analogy is involved in extending the application of such
terms as "part", "whole", and "individual" beyond the realm of

---

14. This objection is urged, for example, by Lowe in the article cited in
footnote 1 above; and is also put forth by Quine on p. 559 of his review of *SA*,
in the *Journal of Philosophy*, Vol. 48 (1951), pp. 556–563.

well-demarcated spatio-temporally continuous lumps. Yet as I have suggested earlier, I think this objection can be flatly and finally answered. The terminology of a system is irrelevant to the classification of the system as nominalistic or platonistic by the criterion I have explained. So long as a system admits no two distinct entities having exactly the same atoms, it is nominalistic no matter whether its generating relation is called "ϵ^*" or "$\langle\langle$" or just "R", and no matter whether the values of its variables are called "classes" or "individuals" or just "entities". The words and symbols used in a system do not make it platonistic; it becomes platonistic only when it admits different entities having just the same atoms.

Thus a nominalistic system cannot put any burden on the imagination that a platonistic system does not. For the nominalist's apparatus is simply part of the platonist's apparatus. A nominalistic system can be mapped into a platonistic one. A nominalistic system is a platonistic system curtailed in a specific way.

Whatever new charges may be brought against nominalism, this best-loved of all objections now deserves to be laid to rest.

(v) *Objection:* Nominalism is trivial for a finitist and pointless for a nonfinitist, since any system with a finite ontology can easily be made nominalistic while a system with an infinite ontology is repugnant to any nominalist.

Answer: Take the last point first. The nominalist is unlikely to be a nonfinitist only in much the same way a bricklayer is unlikely to be a ballet dancer. The two things are at most incongruous, not incompatible. Obviously, by the stated criterion for nominalism, some systems with infinite ontologies are nominalistic, and some systems with finite ontologies are platonistic.

But now, Hao Wang argues,[15] any finitistic platonistic system can be easily nominalized. He does not suppose that this can be done by any immediately obvious method, but refers to an ingenious device invented by Quine.[16] Now for the moment let us suppose that this device is entirely successful. Does this mean that the nominalistic program is thereby rendered pointless and triv-

15. See the article cited in footnote 10 above.

16. In Quine's article "On Universals" in the *Journal of Symbolic Logic,* Vol. 12 (1947), pp. 78–84.

ial? On the contrary it means that an important part of the nominalistic program has been accomplished. The nominalist, after all,
is looking for a nominalistic translation of everything that seems
to him worth saving. The more he succeeds in finding ways of
supplanting platonistic constructions by nominalistic ones, the
fewer will be the cases where platonistic apparatus need be
eschewed; for we can use without qualms whatever we know how
to eliminate. When Wang in effect says: "So you see these occurrences of platonism are harmless after all", he completely dis-
counts the fact that only the nominalist's efforts removed the sting.
One might as well say that the program for eradicating smallpox
in the United States is trivial because there is no smallpox around.
In one sense, of course, any completed program is trivial—in just
the sense that the goal of any program is to trivialize itself.

Unfortunately, however, the nominalistic program has not been
so fully accomplished for all finite systems. Quine, after presenting
his device, explicitly points out its fatal defects. The device can
never be used in a system with an ontology embracing the entire
universe; for more inscriptions will be needed to write out even
a single universally quantified statement than there are things in
the universe. Quine offers his device as an interesting but unsuccessful attempt, and drops it forthwith.

Thus Wang is wrong about the facts concerning Quine's device;
and even if the facts were as Wang supposes, they would not support the conclusion he tries to draw.

(vi) *Objection:* Nominalism is impossible.

Answer: This neatly complements the charge of triviality just
discussed. Call a program impossible until it is completed, and call
it trivial afterwards, and you have a well-rounded defense against
it. In the formal sciences we have proofs that certain problems cannot be solved—for example, the trisection of angles with straightedge and compass alone. But nothing even resembling proof is
available for the impossibility of nominalism. And parts of the program that were once confidently cited as impossible have recently
been accomplished; in particular the nominalistic and even finitistic treatment of most of classical mathematics, including general definitions for "proof" and "theorem".[17]

17. In the joint article cited in footnote 2 above.

Even if full realization of the nominalistic program ultimately does turn out to be impossible, the efforts expended on it may not be unfruitful. The impossibility of trisecting the angle with straight-edge and compass hardly detracts from the value of Euclidean geometry, or leads us to conclude that Euclid was too frugal in his choice of tools.

In the end, the nominalist may not be quite able to live within his means, but he is going to keep on trying as long as he can. Before he resorts to larceny he wants to make very sure that, and how much, he needs to steal.

(vii) *Objection:* Nominalism would hamper the development of mathematics and the other sciences by depriving them of methods they have used and are using to achieve some of their most important results.[18]

Answer: Not at all. The nominalist does not presume to restrict the scientist. The scientist may use platonistic class constructions, complex numbers, divination by inspection of entrails, or any claptrappery that he thinks may help him get the results he wants. But what he produces then becomes raw material for the philosopher, whose task is to make sense of all this: to clarify, simplify, explain, interpret in understandable terms. The practical scientist does the business but the philosopher keeps the books. Nominalism is a restraint that a philosopher imposes upon himself, just because he feels he cannot otherwise make real sense of what is put before him. He must digest what is fed him before he can assimilate it; but he does not expect it all to be pre-digested.

All the same, the advantages to the scientist of abundant and intricate apparatus are easily overestimated. Paucity of means often conduces to clarity and progress in science as well as in philosophy. Some scientists indeed—for example, certain workers in structural linguistics[19]—have even imposed the full restriction of nominalism upon themselves in order to avoid confusion and self-

18. E.g., see p. 40 of Carnap's "Empiricism, Semantics and Ontology" in the *Revue Internationale de Philosophie,* Vol. 4 (1950), pp. 20–40. (Reprinted in *Semantics and the Philosophy of Language,* ed. Linsky, University of Illinois Press, 1952, pp. 202–228.)

19. In particular, Zellig Harris and Noam Chomsky. See, for instance, the latter's "Systems of Syntactic Analysis" in the *Journal of Symbolic Logic,* Vol. 18 (1953), pp. 242–256.

deception. The policy of 'no holds barred' may be exhilarating, but it can sometimes result in a terrible tangle.

(viii) *Objection:* Nominalism is bigoted. In adopting or rejecting systematic apparatus or a system-form, we ought to be governed not by a supposed insight into its intrinsic merits and defects but solely by the results we are enabled to achieve. Languages and system-forms are instruments, and instruments are to be judged on how well they work. The philosopher must not handicap himself by prejudiced or dogmatic repudiations of anything that will serve his purpose.

Answer: This point is strongly urged by Carnap[20] and seems also to have been responsible for Quine's somewhat tentative defection from nominalism. But surely the nominalist does not want to exclude anything that will serve the purpose of philosophy. His critics seem to conceive of that purpose as consisting of correct prediction and the control of nature. These are certainly among the major concerns of daily life, technology, and science; but they do not constitute the primary goal of philosophy—nor, I think, of science in its more philosophical aspects. Obviously a system that predicted future events correctly but reported past events erroneously would be quickly dropped by any theoretical scientist or philosopher in his right mind. But even a true and detailed account of facts past, present, and future will leave the philosopher's work undone. As I suggested a moment ago, his task is to interrelate, systematize, interpret, explain. He is driven not by practical needs but by an impractical desire to understand. He, too, will judge a system by how well it works; but a system works for him only to the extent that it clarifies. The nominalist shuns platonistic devices precisely because he feels that their use would defeat rather than serve the purpose of philosophy. A clear story cannot be told in unintelligible language.

The nominalist cannot demonstrate the need for the restrictions he imposes upon himself. He adopts the principle of nominalism in much the same spirit that he and others adopt the principle of extensionality or that logical philosophers in general adopt the law of contradiction. None of these is amenable to proof; all are stipulated as prerequisites of soundness in a philosophic system. They

20. In the article cited in footnote 18 above.

are usually adopted because a philosopher's conscience gives him no choice in the matter. This does not mean that he need deny that he might some time change his mind. If the neopragmatist pushes me hard enough, I will even concede that I might some day give up the law of contradiction in the interests of getting better results— although if I should give up the law I am puzzled about what the difference would then be between getting results and not getting results. But I make this concession only if the pragmatist concede in return that we might some day even give up his Law of Getting Results. Or does he want to exempt this as constituting the essence of the human mind?

Carnap protests eloquently against what he considers narrow-mindedness in philosophy, concluding with the exhortation: *"Let us be cautious in making assertions and critical in examining them but tolerant in permitting linguistic forms";* and Quine agrees that "the obvious counsel is tolerance and an experimental spirit".[21] Reluctant as I am to cast a shadow on all this sweetness and light, there are limits to my tolerance of tolerance. I admire the statesman tolerant of divergent political opinions, and the person tolerant of racial and educational differences; but I do not admire the accountant who is tolerant about his addition, the logician who is tolerant about his proofs, or the musician who is tolerant about his tone. In every activity, satisfactory performance requires meticulous care in some matters; and in philosophy, one of these matters is the choice of systematic apparatus or 'linguistic form'. Thus in place of Carnap's exhortation, I propose another: *"Let us, as philosophers, be utterly fastidious in choosing linguistic forms."*

What choices fastidiousness will dictate varies with the individual philosopher. But if that were good reason for indifference, then variations in taste and belief would be good reason for indifference about quality in art and about truth in science.

4. Au Revoir

I have explained my version of nominalism, and dealt with objections to the effect that it is not nominalism at all, that it is false

21. *From a Logical Point of View* (see footnote 4 above), p. 19.

or groundless, that it is too weak, that it is too strong, that it is trivial, that it is impossible, that it cripples the sciences, and that it is bigoted. Yet I by no means suppose that I have answered all the criticisms that will be, or even all that have been, made. Nominalism generates few entities but it arouses endless objections. The nominalist is looked upon as an intellectual vandal; and all the good neighbors rush to protect the family heirlooms against him. But the nominalist can go about his business undismayed; for his position is virtually unassailable. Every device he uses, every step he takes, is acceptable to his opponents; he makes no move that is not entirely legitimate by platonistic standards. When the nominalist and the platonist say *au revoir*, only the nominalist can be counted on to comply with the familiar parting admonition they may exchange: "Don't do anything I wouldn't do."

Appendix[22]

A system is nominalistic, in the precise sense I have recently defined, if no two of its entities are generated from exactly the same atoms. In order to apply this test we need to know what relation of the system is its "generating" relation, and hence what are the atoms of the system; i.e., what entities of the system do not belong to the converse domain of the generating relation. The generating relation of the system is the ancestral of the logical sum of the proper-part relation and the membership relation, as these occur in the system.

The point of the criterion of nominalism I have presented is its independence of notation. One may use the sign "ϵ" and speak of classes and yet have a nominalistic system if severe restrictions upon the admitted classes are observed. And if these restrictions are violated, one cannot escape the charge of platonism by using some other sign, say "R", in place of "ϵ".

Since the class of generating relations is defined by reference to particular relations—proper-part and membership—the criterion of nominalism falls short of being purely formal. Before we can

22. This appendix was first published as a note entitled "On Relations that Generate", *Philosophical Studies*, 9 (1958), 65–66.

apply the criterion we must know which, if any, of the relations of the system is the generating relation. But we likewise have to know this before we can determine whether a system is extensional or not. The criterion of nominalism is thus no less formal than the criterion of extensionalism. And indeed, nominalism as I define it might appropriately be termed "hyper-extensionalism".[23]

All this is a restatement of what I hoped I had made clear in my earlier article. But Professor Hempel,[24] supposing that I use the term "generating relation" in some much broader sense than I do, has complained that I do not clearly define this broader sense and has proposed the relation of parent to child as a generating relation. This relation no more meets my requirements for a generating relation than does the relation of child to parent discussed in my earlier article. Accordingly, Hempel is mistaken in saying that the system he has described, with a parent-child relation as the only one involved, will be platonistic by my criterion. Such a system has no generating relation, has all its entities as its atoms, and is therefore nominalistic.

23. I am indebted to Professor Quine for this apt term.

24. *Journal of Symbolic Logic*, Vol. 22 (1957), pp. 206–207.

2

Steps Toward a Constructive Nominalism

with W. V. QUINE

1. Renunciation of Abstract Entities

We do not believe in abstract entities. No one supposes that abstract entities—classes, relations, properties, etc.—exist in spacetime; but we mean more than this. We renounce them altogether.

We shall not forego all use of predicates and other words that are often taken to name abstract objects. We may still write "x is a dog", or "x is between y and z"; for here "is a dog" and "is between ... and" can be construed as syncategorematic: significant in context but naming nothing. But we cannot use variables that call for abstract objects as values.[1] In "x is a dog", only concrete objects are appropriate values of the variable. In contrast, the variable in "x is a zoological species" calls for abstract objects as values (unless, of course, we can somehow identify the various zoological species with certain concrete objects). Any system that countenances abstract entities we deem unsatisfactory as a final philosophy.

Renunciation of abstract objects may leave us with a world composed of physical objects or events, or of units of sense experience, depending upon decisions that need not be made here. Moreover, even when a brand of empiricism is maintained which acknowledges repeatable sensory qualities as well as sensory events,[2] the philosophy of mathematics still faces essentially the

---

1. That it is in the values of the variables, and not in the supposed designata of constant terms, that the ontology of a theory is to be sought, has been urged by W. V. Quine in "Notes on Existence and Necessity", *The Journal of Philosophy,* Vol. 40 (1943), pp. 113–127; also in "Designation and Existence", ibid., Vol. 36 (1939), pp. 701–709.

2. As for example in *SQ.* Qualitative ('abstract') particles of experience and spatio-temporally bounded ('concrete') particles are there regarded as equally acceptable basic elements for a system. Devices described in the present paper will probably make it possible so to revise that study that no construction will depend upon the existence of classes. [This has since been carried out in *SA.*]

same problem that it does when all universals are repudiated. Mere sensory qualities afford no adequate basis for the unlimited universe of numbers, functions, and other classes claimed as values of the variables of classical mathematics.

Why do we refuse to admit the abstract objects that mathematics needs? Fundamentally this refusal is based on a philosophical intuition that cannot be justified by appeal to anything more ultimate. It is fortified, however, by certain *a posteriori* considerations. What seems to be the most natural principle for abstracting classes or properties leads to paradoxes. Escape from the paradoxes can apparently be effected only by recourse to alternative rules whose artificiality and arbitrariness arouse suspicion that we are lost in a world of make-believe.[3]

2. Renunciation of Infinity

We decline to assume that there are infinitely many objects. Not only is our own experience finite, but there is no general agreement among physicists that there are more than finitely many physical objects in all space-time.[4] If in fact the concrete world is finite, acceptance of any theory that presupposes infinity would require us to assume that in addition to the concrete objects, finite in number, there are also abstract entities.

Classical arithmetic presupposes an infinite realm of numbers. Hence if, in an effort to reconcile arithmetic with our renunciation of abstract entities, we were to undertake to identify numbers arbitrarily with certain things in the concrete world, we should

3. The simple principle of class abstraction, which leads to Russell's paradox and others, is this: Given any formula containing the variable "x", there is a class whose members are all and only the objects x for which that formula holds. See W. V. Quine, *Mathematical Logic,* pp. 128–130. For a brief survey of systems designed to exclude the paradoxes, see pp. 163–166, op. cit.; also "Element and Number", *Journal of Symbolic Logic,* Vol. 6 (1941), pp. 135–149.

4. According to quantum physics, each physical object consists of a finite number of spatio-temporally scattered quanta of action. For there to be infinitely many physical objects, then, the world would have to have infinite extent along at least one of its spatio-temporal dimensions. Whether it has is a question upon which the current speculation of physicists seems to be divided.

thereby drastically curtail classical arithmetic; for, we cannot assume there are infinitely many such things.

Classical syntax, like classical arithmetic, presupposes an infinite realm of objects; for it assumes that the expressions it treats of admit concatenation to form longer expressions without end. But if expressions must, like everything else, be found within the concrete world, then a limitless realm of expressions cannot be assumed. Indeed, expressions construed in the customary way as abstract typographical shapes do not exist at all in the concrete world; the language elements in the concrete world are rather inscriptions or marks, the shaped objects rather than the shapes.[5]

The stock of available inscriptions can be vastly increased if we include, not only those that have colors or sounds contrasting with the surroundings, but all appropriately shaped spatio-temporal regions even though they be indistinguishable from their surroundings in color, sound, texture, etc. But the number and length of inscriptions will still be limited insofar as the spatio-temporal world itself is limited. Consequently we cannot say that in general, given any two inscriptions, there is an inscription long enough to be the concatenation of the two.

Furthermore, there can be at most only as many inscriptions as concrete objects. Hence, if concrete objects are finite in number, there are bound to be some for which there are no names or descriptions whatever. Otherwise every concrete object would have to be the name or description of a unique and distinct concrete object; and we should thus be deprived of all predicates and connectives, to say nothing of synonyms, duplicate inscriptions, and non-inscriptions.

3. The Nominalist's Problems

By renouncing abstract entities, we of course exclude all predicates that are not predicates of concrete individuals or explained in terms of predicates of concrete individuals. Moreover, we reject any statement or definition—even one that explains some predi-

---

5. A nominalistic syntax language may, of course, still contain shape-predicates, enabling us to say that a given prescription is, for example, dot-shaped, dotted-line-shaped, Odyssey-shaped. See 5 and 10 below.

cates of concrete individuals in terms of others—if it commits us to abstract entities. For example, until we find some way of construing "is an ancestor of" in terms of "is a parent of" other than the way the ancestral of a relation is usually defined in systems of logic,[6] the relationship between these predicates remains for us unexplained.

We shall, then, face problems of reducing predicates of abstract entities to predicates of concrete individuals, and also problems of constructing certain predicates of concrete individuals in terms either of certain others or of any others that satisfy some more or less well-defined criteria. Apart from those predicates of concrete objects which are permitted by the terms of the given problem to appear in the definiens, nothing may be used but individual-variables, quantification with respect to such variables, and truth-functions. Devices like recursive definition and the notion of ancestral must be excluded until they themselves have been satisfactorily explained.

We are not *as nominalists* concerned with the motives behind the demand that a given predicate of concrete individuals be defined in terms of certain other such predicates. Naturally the demand may often arise from a feeling that the latter predicates are in some sense the clearer, and we may as persons often share this feeling; but purely as nominalists we know no differences of clarity among predicates of concrete individuals.[7] Our problem is solely to provide, where definitions are called for, definitions that are free of any terms or devices that are tainted by belief in the abstract. We shall naturally first try to find definitions where, for varied reasons, we feel they are most urgently needed; and we shall not waste time looking for definitions in terms of predicates that we suppose to be ambiguous or self-contradictory. But, as has

6. The usual definition, which was first set forth by Frege in 1879 (*Begriff-schrift*, p. 60), has become well known through Whitehead and Russell and other writers. It is presented once more in the next section.

7. It might be supposed that the nominalist must regard as unclear any predicate of individuals for which there is no explanation that does not involve commitment to abstract entities. But unless 'explanation' as here intended depends upon standards of clarity, which do not concern the nominalist as nominalist, a suitable explanation can always be supplied trivially by equating the predicate in question with any arbitrarily concocted single word.

perhaps been illustrated by the case of "ancestor" and "parent", it cannot be said that the explanation of one predicate in terms of another is of interest only if the latter is regarded as clearer. Indeed, if we have only a pseudo-explanation (involving abstract entities) relating predicates of individuals, the problem of replacing it by a genuine construction has as immediate interest as the problem of defining a given predicate in terms of others that come up to a certain standard of clarity, or the problem of explaining a predicate of abstract entities.

4. Some Nominalistic Reductions

Some statements that seem to be about abstract entities can be rephrased in well-known ways as statements about concrete objects. Thus, where "A" and "B" are thought of as fixed terms and not as bindable variables, the statement:

Class A is included in Class B

may be rephrased as:

Everything that is an A is a B.

The phrases "is an A" and "is a B" here are predicates of concrete objects, and are regarded as naming nothing in themselves; that is to say, the positions that they occupy are treated as inaccessible to bound variables.

Certain statements that even involve explicit quantification over classes are replaceable by equivalent statements that conform to the tenets of nominalism. To take a simple example, the statement:

Class A is included in some class other than A

is equivalent to:

Something is not an A.

Statements purporting to specify sizes of finite classes of concrete objects are also easily accommodated. Thus the statement:

Class A has three members

may be rendered:

There are distinct objects x, y, and z such that anything is an A if and only if it is x or y or z;

i.e.:

$$(\exists x)(\exists y)(\exists z)(x \neq y . y \neq z . x \neq z .$$
$$(w)(Aw \equiv: w = x \text{ .v. } w = y \text{ .v. } w = z)).$$

Obviously any statement affirming or denying that there are just, or at least, or at most, a certain number of concrete individuals satisfying a given predicate can be readily translated in similar fashion, provided the translation is short enough to fit into the universe.[8]

The definition of ancestorhood in terms of parenthood according to Frege's method seems to involve a class-variable even more essentially. The definiens of "b is ancestor of c" would run thus:

b is distinct from c; and, for every class x, if c is a member of x and all parents of members of x are members of x then b is a member of x;

i.e.:

$$b \neq c . (x)\{c \in x . (y)(z)(z \in x . \text{Parent } yz . \supset . y \in x) . \supset . b \in x\}.$$

But we can translate this sentence also with the help of the notation "Part st", meaning that the individual s is part (or all) of the individual t.[9] We need only replace "class" by "individual", and

8. The nominalist need not necessarily regard such a sentence as "There are 10^{1000} objects in the universe" as meaningless, even though there be no translation along these lines. For, this sentence can be translated as "The universe (as an individual) has 10^{1000} objects as parts" where "has 10^{1000} objects as parts" is taken as a primitive predicate of individuals. But while this translation satisfies purely nominalistic demands, there may be extra-nominalistic reasons of economy or clarity for wanting a translation that contains no such predicate. And wherever and for whatever reasons a translation of an expression is wanted in terms of certain predicates or a certain kind of predicates, the search for such a translation is a problem for the nominalist—though of course neither he nor anyone else claims that every predicate can be defined in terms of every possible set of others.

9. A systematic treatment of "part" and kindred terms will be found in "The Calculus of Individuals and its Uses" by Henry S. Leonard and Nelson Goodman in *Journal of Symbolic Logic*, Vol. 5 (1940), pp. 45–55. Earlier versions were published by Tarski and Leśniewski. Although all of these would have to undergo revision to meet the demands of nominalism, such revision is for the most part easily accomplished and does not affect any of the uses to which the terms in question are put here. [See *SA II*].

"member" by "part", provided we also stipulate that b be a parent and c have a parent. This added stipulation insures that b and c be single whole organisms, rather than fragments or sums of organisms. In symbols, "b is ancestor of c" becomes:

$$b \neq c \,.\, (\exists u) \text{ Parent } bu \,.\, (\exists w) \text{ Parent } wc \,.\, (x)\{\text{Part } cx \,.$$
$$(y)(z)(\text{Part } zx \,.\, \text{Parent } yz \,.\, \supset \text{ Part } yz) \,.\, \supset \text{ Part } bx\}.$$

Clearly the above method of translation presupposes that an individual may be spatio-temporally scattered, or discontinuous. It presupposes that continuity is not necessary for concreteness. A broken dish is no less concrete than a whole one, but merely has more complicated boundaries; and any totality of individuals, however disperse in space and time, counts as an individual in turn. Individuals, thus liberally construed, serve some of the purposes of classes, as is evident from the above treatment of "ancestor". But it is by no means true that we can in general simply identify any class of individuals with a scattered single individual, and reconstrue "member" as "part". The individual composed of all persons, e.g., has many parts that are not persons; some of these parts are parts of persons, and some consist of many persons or of parts of many persons. In the above analysis of "ancestor", we were able to overcome this difficulty by inserting the clause "$(\exists u)$ Parent bu . $(\exists w)$ Parent wc". Commonly, however, this kind of difficulty admits of no such simple solution.

The two-place predicate "is ancestor of" is, to borrow terminology from the platonistic logic of relations, the (proper) *ancestral* of the two-place predicate "is parent of". We have seen, above, how it can be defined. But the scheme used there does not work for the ancestral of every two-place predicate of individuals. It works so long as every individual in the field of the predicate has some part that has no part in common with any other individual in that field. At the present writing we know of no way of defining the ancestral of *every* two-place predicate of individuals nominalistically.

A rather different problem is raised by such statements as:

There are more cats than dogs.

As pointed out earlier, we are already able to deal with such statements as "There is at least one cat and not at least one dog" and

"There are at least two cats and not at least two dogs". An alternation of enough successive statements will be true if and only if there are more cats than dogs, and because it will contain at least one component statement that is true in view of the actual number of cats and of dogs. Use of this method requires, first, knowledge that in all space-time there are not more than so many (say fifty trillion) dogs, and second, a prodigious amount of writing or talking. Even though the requisite knowledge be available, the practical difficulties of actually writing or speaking the translation of the statement about cats and dogs would be prohibitive.

A better method of translation makes use of the predicate "is part of" and another simple auxiliary predicate: "is bigger than". The predicate "is a bit" is then so defined that it applies to every object that is just as big as the smallest animal among all cats and dogs. In other words, "x is a bit" is defined to mean that for every y, if y is a cat or a dog and is bigger than no other cat or dog, then neither is x bigger than y nor is y bigger than x. For brevity we shall call x a *bit of* z when x is a bit and is part of z. Now if and only if there are more cats than dogs will it be the case that every individual that contains at least one bit of each cat is bigger than some individual that contains at least one bit of each dog. (Such an individual will of course be spatio-temporally scattered.) Accordingly we may translate the sentence "There are more cats than dogs" as follows:

Every individual that contains a bit of each cat is bigger than some individual that contains a bit of each dog.

(Symbolic transcriptions are omitted here, as they will be given later for parallel cases: D9–10.)

This method of translation has the great advantage, over the first method suggested, that there is no practical difficulty about writing down an actual translation, regardless of the multiplicity of individuals concerned. But, like our method of defining the ancestral, it is not completely general. It will still work if, in place of "is a cat" and "is a dog", we choose any other two predicates each of which is such that the individuals fulfilling it are discrete from one another. Thus it holds good for such a case as:

There are more human cells than humans,

and indeed for most cases where such numerical comparisons are made in ordinary discourse. It has an important use in nominalistic syntax, as we shall see later. Moreover, by a relatively simple change it can be made general enough to work wherever each individual fulfilling either of the two predicates has a part that has no part in common with any other individual fulfilling that predicate. And in addition there are ways of modifying the method to take care of certain cases where even this latter condition is not satisfied. But we have not found any general formulation that will cover all cases regardless of how the individuals concerned overlap one another.

The method will, however, help us in finding a nominalistic reduction for even so platonistic-sounding[10] a statement as:

There are more age-classes than grade-classes in the White School.

We just replace this by:

There are more age-wholes than grade-wholes in the White School,

where an age-whole is the *individual* composed of all pupils in the school who were born during a single calendar year, and a grade-whole is an individual composed of all pupils who receive equally advanced instruction. The new sentence is then readily translated in the same way as the one about cats and dogs.

A combination of devices already described enables us to translate a statement like:

There are exactly one-third as many Canadians as Mexicans.

Letting "the Mexican whole" stand for the individual that is comprised of all Mexicans, the translation runs:

There are some mutually discrete wholes x, y, and z such that each is comprised of Mexicans and such that $x + y + z =$ the Mexican whole; and there are exactly as many Canadians (in all) as there are Mexicans in x and as in y and as in z.

---

10. We use "platonistic" as the antithesis of "nominalistic". Thus any language or theory that involves commitment to any abstract entity is platonistic.

The last clause may then be further translated by a slight variation of the method used in the example of cats and dogs.

The foregoing samples will illustrate some of the means that remain in our hands for interpreting statements that *prima facie* have to do with abstract entities. Certainly we have not as yet reached our goal of knowing how to deal with every statement we are not ready to dispense with altogether. But there is as yet no convincing reason for supposing the goal unattainable. Some of the devices used above are rather powerful, and by no means all the possible methods have been explored.

Since, however, we have not as yet discovered how to translate all statements that we are unwilling to discard as meaningless, we describe in following sections a course that enables us—strictly within the limitations of our language and without any retreat from our position—to talk *about* certain statements without being able to translate them.

5. Elements of Nominalistic Syntax

It may naturally be asked how, if we regard the sentences of mathematics merely as strings of marks without meaning, we can account for the fact that mathematicians can proceed with such remarkable agreement as to methods and results. Our answer is that such intelligibility as mathematics possesses derives from the syntactical or metamathematical rules governing those marks. Accordingly we shall try to develop a syntax language that will treat mathematical expressions as concrete objects—as actual strings of physical marks.[11] Since one mark is as concrete as another, we can deal with such marks and strings as "ϵ" and "$(v)(v \epsilon v \mid v \epsilon v)$" quite as well as with ones like "(" or "Eiffel Tower". But our syntax language must itself be purely nominalistic; it must make no use of terms or devices that involve commitment to abstract enti-

---

11. We might, equally consistently with nominalism, construe marks phenomenally, as events in the visual (or in the auditory or tactual) field. Moreover, although we shall regard an appropriate object during its entire existence as a single mark, we could equally well—and even advantageously if we want to increase the supply of marks—construe a mark as comprising the object in question during only a single moment of time.

ties. It might seem that this program could be carried out without any difficulty once we have specified that we are dealing with concrete marks; but actually classical syntax has depended so heavily upon platonistic devices in constructing its definitions that the nominalist is faced with the necessity of finding new means of definition at almost every step. Not only subsidiary terms, but such key terms as "formula", "substitution", and "theorem" have to be defined by quite new routes.[12]

The platonistic object language that our nominalistic syntax is to treat of must contain notations for truth-functions, quantification, and membership. All we need for these purposes are parentheses, variables, the stroke "|" of alternative denial, and the sign "ϵ" of membership. Parentheses will serve both for enclosing alternative denials to indicate groupings and for enclosing variables to form universal quantifiers. To simplify our syntactical treatment, let us require that each alternative denial be enclosed in parentheses—even when it stands apart from any broader context. As variables we may use "v", "v'", "v''", etc., so that the simple typographical shapes of the object language reduce to six: "v", "$'$", "$($", "$)$", "$|$", and "ϵ".

As already mentioned, the characters of our language are not these abstract shapes—which we, as nominalists, cannot countenance—but rather concrete marks or inscriptions. We can, however, apply shape-predicates to such individuals; thus "Vee x" will mean that the object x is a vee (i.e., a "v"-shaped inscription), and "Ac x" will mean that x is an accent (i.e., a "$'$"-shaped inscription), and "LPar x" will mean that x is a left parenthesis, and "RPar x" will mean that x is a right parenthesis, and "Str x" will mean that x is a stroke (a "$|$"-shaped inscription), and "Ep x" will mean that x is an epsilon.

But it happens actually that left parentheses and right parentheses are alike in shape, and distinguishable only by their orientation in broader contexts. It would appear therefore that instead

---

[12] The idea of dealing with the language of classical mathematics in terms of a nuclear syntax language that would meet nominalistic demands was suggested in 1940 by Tarski. In the course of that year the project was discussed among Tarski, Carnap, and the present writers, but solutions were not found at that time for the technical problems involved.

of writing "LPar x", to mean that x is intrinsically a left parenthesis, we should write "LPar xy", meaning that x is a left parenthesis from the point of view of its orientation within the longer inscription y; and correspondingly for "RPar". Since however this exceptional treatment is made necessary solely by a typographical idiosyncrasy, we may disregard it. The reader may, if he likes, restore an intrinsic distinction between left and right parentheses by thinking of each left parenthesis as comprising within itself the straight uninked line joining its tips.

Our nominalistic syntax must contain, besides the six shape-predicates, some means of expressing the *concatenation* of expressions. We shall write "Cxyz" to mean that x and y and z are composed of whole characters of the language, in normal orientation to one another, and contain neither split-off fragments of characters nor anything extraneous, and that the inscription x consists of y followed by z. The characters comprising y and z may be irregularly spaced; furthermore the inscription x will be considered to consist of y followed by z no matter what the spatial interval between y and z, provided that x contains no character that occurs in that interval.

The two remaining primitives of our syntax language are abbreviations of the familiar predicates "is part of" and "is bigger than". "Part xy" means that x, whether or not it is identical with y, is contained entirely within y. "Bgr xy" means that x is spatially bigger than y.

Our syntax language, then, contains the nine predicates "Vee", "Ac", "LPar", "RPar", "Str", "Ep", "C", "Part", and "Bgr", together with variables, quantifiers and the usual truth-functional notations "$\vee$", "$\cdot$", etc. The variables take as values any concrete objects.

6. Some Auxiliary Definitions

We now proceed to define certain useful auxiliary predicates. First, it is convenient to have four-, five-, and six-place predicates of concatenation. The definitions are obvious:

D1.   C$xyzw$ = $(\exists t)$(Cxyt . Ctzw),[13]

13. The sign "=", when it occurs as the main connective in definitions in

D2. $\text{C}xyzwu = (\exists t)(\text{C}xyt . \text{C}tzwu),$

D3. $\text{C}xyzwus = (\exists t)(\text{C}xyt . \text{C}tzwus).$

Also, later definitions will be shortened considerably if we can say briefly that a given individual is a *character* of our object language. Since a character is any concrete object that is either a vee or an accent or a left parenthesis, etc., the definition runs:

D4.   Char $x =.$ Vee x v Ac x v LPar x v RPar x v Str x v Ep x.

Convenience is similarly served by the definition of an *inscription* as an object composed of whole characters in normal orientation to one another. In view of the interpretation of "C" above, the definition is easy:

D5.   Insc $x =.$ Char x v $(\exists y)(\exists z)\text{C}xyz$.

An inscription x is said to be an *initial segment* of another, y, if x is identical with y or there is some inscription z such that y consists of x followed by z.

D6.   InitSeg $xy =.$ Insc x . $x = y$ .v $(\exists z)\text{C}yxz$.

The definition of *final segment* is strictly parallel:

D7.   FinSeg $xy =.$ Insc x . $x = y$ .v $(\exists z)\text{C}yzx$.

An inscription x is said to be a *segment* of y if x is an initial segment of some final segment of y.

D8.   Seg $xy = (\exists z)(\text{InitSeg } xz . \text{FinSeg } zy)$.

A segment x—whether initial, final, or interior—of an inscription y will be continuous relative to y, in the sense that if x con-

---

this paper, is not to be thought of as expressing identity. It is to be regarded rather as constituting, in combination with the "D" which precedes each definition-number, a mark of definitional abbreviation; and it may occur between name-matrices and statement-matrices indifferently. The definition D1 is to be understood as a convention to this effect: "$\text{C}xyzw$" is to be understood as an abbreviation of "$(\exists t)(\text{C}xyt . \text{C}tzw)$"; and a similar understanding is to obtain when any other variables are used in place of "x", "y", "z", and "w", provided that a variable distinct from them is used in place of "t". Other definitions are to be construed analogously.

tains two characters of y then x must contain all the characters
that occur in y between those two. The characters of a segment
x of y may still be irregularly spaced, but only because of irregular
spacing in y itself.

We shall later want to be able to say that two inscriptions are
equally long, not in the sense that their ends are equally far apart
but in the sense that each inscription has as many characters as
the other. Since the characters comprising any inscription are discrete from one another, this numerical comparison can be handled
in a way explained in 4 above. We begin by so defining "Bit" for
our present purposes that "Bit x" means that x is just as big as
every smallest character.

D9. Bit $x =.\ (y)\,(\text{Char } y \supset \sim\text{Bgr } xy)\ .\ (\exists z)\,(\text{Char } z\ .\ \sim\text{Bgr } zx).$

It must not be supposed that, because accents are in general the
smallest characters of our object language, every accent will be
a bit. For accents may vary in size, and only the smallest characters, along with everything that is just as big, will be bits.

An inscription x is *longer than* another, y, if x contains more
characters than y. Using the same method as for the example of
cats and dogs in 4 above—where a verbal explanation is given—
we define:

D10. Lngr $xy =.$ Insc x . Insc y . $(z)\{(w)\,[\text{Char } w\ .\ \text{Seg } wx\ .\supset$
$(\exists u)\,(\text{Bit } u\ .\ \text{Part } uw\ .\ \text{Part } uz)]\ \supset\ (\exists t)\,[(r)\,(\text{Char } r\ .\ \text{Seg } ry\ .\supset$
$(\exists s)\,(\text{Bit } s\ .\ \text{Part } sr\ .\ \text{Part } st))\ .\ \text{Bgr } zt]\}.$

Two inscriptions are *equally long* if neither is longer than the
other.

D11. EqLng $xy =.$ Insc x . Insc y . $\sim$Lngr xy . $\sim$Lngr yx.

We can now define what we shall mean by saying that two inscriptions are *like* one another. Two characters are alike if both
are vees, or both are accents, etc. Two inscriptions x and y are
alike if they are equally long and if, for every two equally long inscriptions z and w such that z is an initial segment of x and w is an
initial segment of y, the segments z and w end in like characters.

D12. Like $xy =.$ EqLng xy . $(z)\,(w)\{\text{EqLng } zw$. InitSeg zx .
InitSeg wy .$\supset$ $(\exists s)\,(\exists t)\,(\text{FinSeg } sz..\text{FinSeg } tw : \text{Vee } s\ .\ \text{Vee } t$ .v.

Ac s . Ac t .v. LPar s . LPar t .v. RPar s . RPar t .v. Str s . Str t .v. Ep s . Ep t) }.

Note that only inscriptions can be 'alike', in the sense here defined, since only inscriptions can be equally long; and further, that likeness depends solely upon the component characters and their order of occurrence, not upon identical spacing.

7. Variables and Quantification

A variable of our object language is a vee, or a vee together with a string of one or more accents following it. We first define a *string of accents* as any inscription of which every part that is a character is an accent.

D13. AcString $x =$. Insc x . (z) (Seg zx . Char z . $\supset$ Ac z).

The definition of a *variable* is then readily formulated.

D14. Vbl $x =$. Vee x v $(\exists y)$ $(\exists z)$ (Vee y . AcString z . $Cxyz$).

A variable is a vee or the result of concatenating a vee with a string of accents.

A quantifier will be simply a variable in parentheses. But it is more useful to define a *string of* (one or more) *quantifiers* directly. A method for doing this becomes evident when we reflect that any inscription will be a string of quantifiers if it begins and ends with facing parentheses and is such that every pair of facing parentheses within it frames an inscription that is either a variable or contains parentheses back to back.

D15. QfrString $x = (\exists y)(\exists z)\{$LPar y . RPar z . $(\exists w)Cxywz$. $(s)(t)(u)(k)[$LPar t . RPar k . Seg sx . $\supset$: $\sim$Cstk : Cstuk . $\supset$. Vbl u v $(\exists p)(\exists q)(\exists r)$ (RPar q . LPar r . Cpqr . Seg pu)]$\}$.

Then let us call x a *quantification of* y if x consists of a string of quantifiers followed by y.

D16. Qfn $xy = (\exists z)$ (QfrString z . $Cxzy$).

8. Formulas

An atomic formula of the object language consists of two variables with an epsilon between them.

D17. AtFmla $x = (\exists w)(\exists y)(\exists z)(\text{Vbl}\, w \cdot \text{Ep}\, y \cdot \text{Vbl}\, z \cdot \text{C}xwyz)$.

We are supposing that the class logic to be developed in the object language will use one or another of the alternatives to the theory of types, so that the epsilons may grammatically occur between any variables without restriction.

The non-atomic formulas of the object language are constructed from the atomic formulas by quantification and alternative denial. In order to define an *alternative denial* we first need to be able to say that a given inscription x *contains exactly as many left as right parentheses*. This will be the case if x lacks parentheses altogether; and it will be the case also if the inscription which consists of all the left parentheses in x and the inscription which consists of all the right parentheses in x are equally long in the sense of D11. In symbols:

D18. EqPar $x =. (u)(\text{LPar}\, u \lor \text{RPar}\, u \cdot \supset \sim\text{Seg}\, ux) \lor (\exists y)(\exists z)$ $\{\text{EqLng}\, yz \cdot (w)(\text{Char}\, w \supset : \text{LPar}\, w \cdot \text{Seg}\, wx \cdot \equiv \text{Seg}\, wy : \text{RPar}\, w$ $\cdot \text{Seg}\, wx \cdot \equiv \text{Seg}\, wz)\}$.

Now for an inscription x to be the *alternative denial* of y and z it is necessary that x consist of a left parenthesis followed by y, then a stroke, then z, and finally a right parenthesis. But this is not enough. We must make sure that the beginning and ending parentheses are 'mates'—that is, that they are paired with each other and not with other parentheses that occur between them. Also we must make sure that the stroke between y and z is the main connective in x. We can accomplish all this by requiring that y contain an equal number of left and right parentheses, and similarly for z, but that this be true of no initial segment of x (except x itself).

D19. AD$xyz =. $ EqPar $y \cdot$ EqPar $z \cdot (r)(s)(\text{C}xrs \supset . \sim\text{EqPar}\, r)$ $\cdot (\exists t)(\exists u)(\exists w)(\text{LPar}\, t \cdot \text{Str}\, u \cdot \text{RPar}\, w \cdot \text{C}xtyuzw)$.

The *formulas* of the object language comprise the atomic formulas and every inscription constructed from them by means of quantification and alternative denial. Some ways in which one might naturally seek to reduce this to a formal definition are not feasible in a nominalistic syntax.[14] Our method is to begin by

14. Using essentially the method of Frege's definition of the ancestral of a

defining a *quasi-formula* as anything that is an atomic formula, an alternative denial, or a quantification of an atomic formula or alternative denial.

D20.   QuasiFmla x = ($\exists y$) (x = y .v Qfn xy : AtFmla y v ($\exists w$) ($\exists z$)ADywz).

A quasi-formula will not necessarily be a formula, since the components of the alternative denial are not required to be formulas. But in terms of this notion of quasi-formula we can now easily define *formula*:

D21.   Fmla x =. *QuasiFmla* x . (w) (y) (z) (ADwyz . Seg wx .⊃. QuasiFmla y . QuasiFmla z).

In other words, a formula is a quasi-formula such that every alternative denial in it is an alternative denial of quasi-formulas.

By requiring even the shortest alternative denials in a formula x to be alternative denials of quasi-formulas, the definition requires them to be alternative denials of atomic formulas or of quantifications of atomic formulas, and this makes them genuine formulas in the intuitively intended sense of the word. Accordingly, by requiring also the next more complex alternative denials in x to be alternative denials of quasi-formulas, the definition guarantees that these also will be formulas in the intuitively intended sense; and so on, to x itself.

---

relation, we might say that x is a formula if it belongs to every class that contains all atomic formulas and all quantifications and alternative denials of its members. But this definition is unallowable because of its use of quantification over classes; cf. 4 above.—There is indeed a completely general method, in syntax, of deriving ancestrals and kindred constructions without appeal to classes of expressions. This is the method of 'framed ingredients' which appears in Quine, *Mathematical Logic,* §56. The method consists essentially of these two steps: (1) the Frege form of definition is so revised that the classes to which it appeals can be limited to finite classes without impairing the result; (2) finite classes of expressions are then identified with *individual* expressions wherein the 'member' -expressions occur merely as *parts* marked off in certain recognizable ways. However, when as nominalists we conceive of expressions strictly as concrete inscriptions, we find the method of framed ingredients unsatisfactory, because its success depends too much on what inscriptions happen to exist in the world. Actually, though, the nominalistic definition of proof in the present paper will be simpler than that in terms of framed ingredients; for it will not require the lines of a proof to be concatenated, nor to be marked off by intervening signs.

9. Axioms and Rules

Now that we have specified the characters and formulas of the object language within our nominalistic syntax language, the next problem is to describe the sorts of notational operations that pass for logical *proof* among the users of that object language. A full solution of this problem would consist in the formulation, in our syntax language, of a condition that is necessary and sufficient in order that an inscription x be a *theorem* of the object language.

The theorems are those formulas of the object language that follow from certain axioms by certain rules of inference. The axioms should be so chosen that we can obtain from them, by the rules of inference, every formula that is valid according to the logic of alternative denial and quantification and, in addition, a goodly array of formulas whose alleged validity is supposed to proceed from special properties of class-membership. We cannot aspire to completeness in this last regard, in view of Gödel's result.

There are many essentially equivalent sets of axioms suitable to the above purposes. The axioms that we shall adopt fall under three heads: *axioms of alternative denial, axioms of quantification,* and *axioms of membership.* In setting them forth let us understand "$\sim \ldots$" as short for "$(\ldots \mid \ldots)$".

Axioms of alternative denial: All formulas of the form:

$$((P \mid (Q \mid R)) \mid ((S \mid \sim S) \mid ((S \mid Q) \mid \sim (P \mid S)))),^{15}$$

like letters being replaced by like formulas.

Axioms of quantification: All formulas of the forms:

(1) $((v)(P \mid \sim Q) \mid \sim ((v)P \mid \sim (v)Q)),$

(2) $(R \mid \sim (v)R)$ (where "v" is not free in "R"),

---

15. This is Łukasiewicz's simplification of Nicod's axiom schema. See Jan Łukasiewicz, "Uwagi o Aksyomacie Nicod'a i o 'Dedukcyi Uogólniającej'", *Księga pamiątkowa Polskiego Towarzystwa Filozoficznego we Lwowie,* 1931, pp. 2–7; also Jean Nicod, "A Reduction in the Number of Primitive Propositions of Logic", *Proceedings of the Cambridge Philosophical Society,* Vol. 19 (1917–1920), pp. 32–41.

(3) $((v)P \mid \sim S)$ (where "S" is the result of substituting some variable for "v" in "P").

If the reader reflects that the sign-combination " $\mid \sim$ " amounts to "$\supset$", he will recognize in the forms (1) — (3) a familiar set of axiom-schemata for quantification theory.[16] Like capitals in (1) — (3) are of course to be understood as replaced by like formulas, and the vees by like variables. The two brief provisos appended to (2) and (3), above, may be stated more precisely as follows: (i) the formulas supplanting the "R"s contain no free variables like the variables supplanting the vees, and (ii) the formula supplanting the "S" is like the formula supplanting the "P" except perhaps for containing other free variables, like one another, in place of all free variables like the variable supplanting the vee.

Axioms of membership: Here it happens that a limited list of specific expressions is adequate; e.g., Hailperin's.[17] Let us suppose such a list put over into the primitive notation of our object language and set down here; then our axioms of membership are all inscriptions like those in the list.

In addition to the axioms, we need two *rules of inference:*

(1) From any formula, together with the result of putting a formula like it for "P" and any formulas for "Q" and "R" in "$(P \mid (Q \mid R))$", infer any formula like the one which was put for "Q".[18]

(2) From any formula infer any quantification thereof.

To reach a definition of "Axiom" we must first be able to define what it means to be an axiom of any given one of the five kinds above described. A simple auxiliary definition will be useful:

D22. $Dxy = (\exists z)(\text{Like } yz \cdot ADxyz);$

16. They answer to 4.4.4, 4.4.5, and 4.4.6 of F. B. Fitch, "The Consistency of the Ramified Principia", *Journal of Symbolic Logic,* Vol. 3 (1938), pp. 140–149; also to *102–*104 of W. V. Quine, *Mathematical Logic,* p. 88.

17. Theodore Hailperin, "A Set of Axioms for Logic," *Journal of Symbolic Logic,* Vol. 9 (1944), pp. 1–19.

18. This is Nicod's generalization of *modus ponens;* see footnote 15.

i.e., that x is a *denial* of y means that x is the alternative denial of y and some other inscription exactly like y.

Definition of "AADx", meaning that x is an *axiom of alternative denial*, is achieved by stating formally what we can observe from the general schema already given: that every axiom of alternative denial is an alternative denial of two formulas; one of these two main components is an alternative denial of formulas of which one is an alternative denial of formulas; the other of the two main components is an alternative denial of formulas of which one is an alternative denial of a formula with a formula like the denial of that formula, while the other is . . . etc., etc. In symbols:

D23. AADx = $(\exists f)(\exists g)(\exists h)(\exists i)(\exists j)(\exists k)(\exists l)(\exists m)(\exists n)(\exists p)$ $(\exists q)(\exists r)(\exists s)(\exists t)(\exists u)(\exists w)(\exists y)(\exists z)$ (Fmla f . Fmla g . Fmla h . Fmla i . Like ki . Like lg . Like mf . Like ni . ADpgh . ADqfp . Dri . ADsir . ADtkl . ADumn . Dwu . ADytw . ADzsy . ADxqz).

Formulation of "AQ1 x", meaning that x is an axiom of quantification of kind (1), proceeds in the same way; we shall omit the definition.

Formulation of "AQ2 x" offers the one additional difficulty that in order to express stipulation (i), appearing in the above description of the axioms of quantification, we must have a definition of *free variable*. A variable x is a free variable in an inscription y if x is a segment of y not followed by any additional accents in y, and if furthermore x is not a segment of any segment of y that consists of a formula preceded by a quantifier consisting of a variable like x framed in parentheses.

D24. Free xy =. Vbl x . Seg xy . $(z)(w)$(Ac w . Czxw .⊃ ～Seg zy) . $(q)(r)(s)(t)(u)$ (LPar q . Like rx . RPar s . Fmla t . C$uqrst$. Seg uy .⊃ ～Seg xu).

The definition of "AQ2 x" is then quite straightforward and may be omitted here.

Formulation of "AQ3 x" offers a further complication for nominalistic syntax. The problem lies in the notion of *substitution*, involved in stipulation (ii). Let z and w be the respective formulas supplanting the "P" and "S" of (3), let y be the variable supplanting the "v", and let x be like the free variables which are to appear in w in place of the free variables like y in z. We have to find a way within nominalistic syntax of defining "Subst $wxyz$", meaning that *the formula w is like the formula z except for having free variables like x wherever z contains free variables like y.* Our method of definition depends upon the fact that the condition in the foregoing italics is equivalent to the following one: *What remains when all free variables like y are omitted from the formula z is like what remains when some free variables like x are omitted from the formula w.* The formal definition is as follows:

D25. Subst $wxyz$ =. Fmla w . Fmla z . $(\exists t)(\exists u)\{$Like tu .
(s) [Char $s \supset : (r)$ (Like ry . Free rz .$\supset$ $\sim$Seg sr) . Seg sz .$\equiv$ Seg
$su : (r)$ (Like rx . Free rw .$\supset$ $\sim$Seg sr) .$\supset$. Seg $sw \equiv$ Seg st] .
$(s)(r)$ (Like rx . Free rw . Seg sr . Seg st .$\supset$ Seg rt)$\}$.

It was largely for the purpose of this definition that we so defined likeness of inscriptions as to allow their characters to be differently spaced.

Now that this definition is accomplished, the definition of "AQ3 x" offers no further difficulty (and is omitted here).

Definitions of axioms of the fifth and final kind—the axioms of membership, "AM"—present no problem; we can specify them in our syntax simply by spelling them out explicitly with the help of our primitive predicates.

We are then ready for a general definition of what it means for x to be an *axiom* of our object language. It means simply that x is an axiom of one of the five kinds specified.

D26.   Axiom x =. AADx ∨ AQ1 x ∨ AQ2 x ∨ AQ3 x ∨ AMx.

An inscription x is called an *immediate consequence* of inscriptions y and z just in case x follows from y and z by one application of rule of inference (1), or from y by rule of inference (2).

D27. ICxyz = $(\exists r)(\exists s)(\exists t)(\exists u)(\exists w)$ (Like rx .
           Like sy . Like tz : ADurw . ADstu ∨ ADtsu .∨ Qfn rs).

10. Proofs and Theorems

An inscription is a theorem if it has a proof; and a proof is constructed by a series of steps of immediate consequence, starting from axioms. Roughly, a proof is describable as composed of one or more lines such that each is either an axiom or an immediate consequence of preceding lines. Actually we need not require that the so called 'lines' of a proof be at different levels on a page, or be segregated from one another by any other device. They could even be written end to end without intervening punctuation, and we could still single them out uniquely as separate 'lines'. For, the grammar of the object language is such that the result of directly concatenating two formulas z and w will never be a segment of a larger formula, nor will it contain as segments any formulas other than those that are segments of z alone or w alone. Accordingly it will be convenient in general to speak of x as a *line* of y (where y may or may not be a proof) if x is a formula that is part of y but not part of any other formula in y.

D28.   Line $xy = (z)$ (Fmla z . Part xz . Part zy .$\equiv$. $z = x$).

If a theorem is to be defined as a formula for which a proof exists, it is important not to demand that all lines of the proof be assembled in proper order in any one place and time. Accordingly we shall so define a proof as to allow it to consist of lines wherever they may be—perhaps scattered at random throughout the universe, and perhaps not even all existing at any one moment or within any one century.

According to the rough characterization of proof proposed two paragraphs back, each line must be either an axiom or an immediate consequence of *preceding* lines. The reason for the word "preceding" here is to rule out cases where every line is deducible from other lines, in circular fashion, while not all lines are deducible ultimately from axioms. However, we must now resort to some other expedient for excluding such circularity; for we have chosen to dispense with the ordering of lines of a proof, and this deprives us of the notion of a 'preceding' line.

An expedient which will be shown to meet the requirements is this: We stipulate that if any individual y contains as parts some lines of a proof x but none that are axioms, then some line of x that lies in y must be an immediate consequence of lines of x that lie outside y. The following, then, is our definition:

D29.   Proof $x = (y)\{(\exists z)$ (Line zx . Part zy) . (w) (Axiom w .

194

Line wx . $\supset$ $\sim$Part wy) . $\supset$ ($\exists s$) ($\exists t$) ($\exists u$) (Line sx . Part sy .
Line tx . $\sim$Part ty . Line ux . $\sim$Part uy . ICstu) }.

In order to establish that this definition is adequate to our purposes, we shall now show (1) that if x is a 'proof' in the sense of D29, then we can specify an order of 'precedence' among the lines of x such that every line is either an axiom or an immediate consequence of 'earlier' lines; and we shall show conversely that (2) if x is such that an order of precedence of the above kind can be specified among its lines, then x is a 'proof' in the sense of D29.

(1) is established as follows. Suppose x is a 'proof' in the sense of D29. We can begin our specification of an order of precedence among the lines of x by picking out, in an arbitrary order L_1, L_2 $\cdots$, L_k, all those lines of x that are axioms. Next, from among the remaining lines of x, we pick one, call it L_{k+1}, which is an immediate consequence of lines from among L_1, L_2, $\cdots$, L_k. (There will be such a line; for, by D29, that individual y which consists of all lines x except L_1, L_2, $\cdots$, L_k must contain a line that is an immediate consequence of lines of x outside y.) Next, from among the remaining lines of x, we pick one—call it L_{k+2}—which is an immediate consequence of lines from among L_1, L_2, $\cdots$, L_{k+1}. (There will be such a one, for the same reason as before.) Continuing this, we eventually specify an order of precedence of the required kind.

(2) is established as follows. Suppose the lines of x can be counted off in some order such that each line is an axiom or an immediate consequence of earlier lines. Now consider anything y that contains some lines of x but none that are axioms. From among those lines of x that are parts of y, pick out the one that is earliest according to the assumed order. It must be either an axiom or an immediate consequence of earlier lines of x. But it is not an axiom, for y contains none of the lines of x that are axioms. Hence it is an immediate consequence of earlier lines of x; and those earlier lines are not in y. We see therefore that y contains a line of x that is an immediate consequence of lines of x outside y. Since y was taken as *any* individual containing some lines of x but none that are axioms, it follows that x is a proof in the sense of D29.

So it is now clear that D29, without stipulating any order among lines, gives us an adequate version of 'proof'.

Note incidentally that D29 abstains even from any requirement that a proof consist wholly of formulas; the 'lines' of a proof x are indeed formulas, but x may contain also any manner of additional debris without ill effect. Proofs are not in general 'inscriptions', in the sense of D5.

If a theorem is any inscription for which there is a proof, then an inscription is a theorem if and only if it is a line of some proof. But this formulation is a little too narrow. Given any inscription y for which a proof x exists, it will be true that for each inscription z that is like y, and that lies outside of x, a proof will also exist, consisting for example of z together with those lines of x that are not identical with y. Hence if y is a theorem all such inscriptions like it will also be theorems. But suppose that some inscription w that is like y lies embedded within some line t in the proof x, and suppose that no other line like t exists; in this case there may be no proof for w, so that some inscriptions like the theorem y may not be theorems. To prevent this anomaly, we construct our definition so that an inscription will be a *theorem* if and only if it is *like* some line of some proof. ("Like" has of course been so defined as to be reflexive.)

D30. Thm $x = (\exists y)(\exists z)$ (Proof y . Line zy . Like xz).

With the definition so constructed, it follows that all immediate consequences of theorems are theorems. But some formulas may still fail to qualify as theorems solely because no inscription exists anywhere at any time to stand as a needed intermediate line in an otherwise valid proof. Such limitations would prove awkward if we had to depend upon the accidental existence of inscriptions that are perceptibly marked out against a contrasting background. But we may rather, as suggested earlier (2), construe inscriptions as all appropriately shaped portions of matter. Then the only syntactical descriptions that will fail to have actual inscriptions answering to them will be those that describe inscriptions too long to fit into the whole spatio-temporally extended universe. This limitation is hardly likely to prove embarrassing. (If we ever should be handicapped by gaps in the proof of an inscription wanted as a theorem, however, we can strengthen our rules of inference to bridge such gaps; for, the number of steps required in a proof depends upon the rules, and the rules we have adopted can be altered or supplemented considerably without violation of nominalistic standards.)

It may be interesting to observe in passing that the theoretical limitations just considered obtain under platonistic syntax as well, if that syntax construes expressions as *shape-classes* of inscriptions; for, shapes having no inscriptions as instances reduce to the null class and are thus identical.[19] The platonist may indeed escape the limitations of concrete reality by hypostatizing an infinite realm of abstract entities—the series of numbers—and then arithmetizing his syntax; the nominalist, on the other hand, holds that any recourse to platonism is both intolerable and unnecessary.

11. Conclusion

In our earlier sections we studied the problem of translating into nominalistic language certain nonsyntactical sentences that had appeared to be explicable only in platonistic terms. In 5–10 we have been concerned with giving such a translation for syntax. This syntax enables us to describe and deal with many formulas (of the object language) for which we have no direct nominalistic translation. For example, the formula that is the full expansion in our object language of "$(n)(n + n = 2n)$" will contain variables calling for abstract entities as values; and if it cannot be translated into nominalistic language, it will in one sense be meaningless for us. But, taking that formula as a string of marks, we can determine whether it is indeed a proper formula of our object language, and what consequence-relationships it has to other formulas. We can thus handle much of classical logic and mathematics without in any further sense understanding, or granting the truth of, the formulas we are dealing with.

19. According to the classical principles of syntax, any two expressions x and y have concatenate $x^\frown y$; and moreover $x^\frown y$ is always distinct from $z^\frown w$, unless the characters occurring in x and in y are successively the same as those in z and in w. This combination of principles is as untenable from the point of view of a platonistic syntax of shape-classes as from the point of view of nominalism.

The gains that seem to have accrued to natural science from the use of mathematical formulas do not imply that those formulas are true statements. No one, not even the hardiest pragmatist, is likely to regard the beads of an abacus as true; and our position is that the formulas of platonistic mathematics are, like the beads of an abacus, convenient computational aids which need involve no question of truth. What is meaningful and true in the case of platonistic mathematics as in the case of the abacus is not the apparatus itself, but only the description of it: the rules by which it is constructed and run. These rules we do understand, in the strict sense that we can express them in purely nominalistic language. The idea that classical mathematics can be regarded as mere apparatus is not a novel one among nominalistically minded thinkers; but it can be maintained only if one can produce, as we have attemped to above, a syntax that is itself free from platonistic commitments.

At the same time, every advance we can make in finding direct translations for familiar strings of marks will increase the range of the meaningful language at our command.

3

A Revision in
The Structure of Appearance

Mr. Burdick's point* is well taken. It does not touch the general criterion for constructional definitions as set forth in the first chapter of *The Structure of Appearance,* but only the special criterion for definitions belonging to systems framed entirely in the language of individuals, as formulated in the last section of that chapter. That special criterion may be dropped in favor of a much simpler one; and this will be done in the next edition of the book.

In systems of the kind in question, all the extralogical terms will, of course, be one-place or many-place predicates of individuals. The definitions in such a system will be acceptable if and only if uniform replacement of the individuals that are arguments of the definiendum-predicates will yield the arguments of the definiens-predicates. Uniform replacement consists of replacing each individual in all its occurrences by the same individual and replacing different individuals by different individuals. Identities and differences among the arguments of all the definiendum-predicates of the system will then be duplicated by identities and differences among the arguments of the definiens-predicates. In this form, the special criterion is merely a case of the general criterion.

Yet although extensional isomorphism, defined in terms of uniform replacement, is not in general symmetric, it will be symmetric in this special case; and this raises an interesting question. The nearest analogue in such a system to a class of individuals is the whole that is the individual-sum of them. Where classes are admitted, note that while an individual a may be replaced by the class of two other individuals b and c, the converse replacement is prohibited. But a may replace as well as be replaced by the individual-sum of b and c; for that sum, like a, is an ultimate factor.

* In "On a Nominalistic Criterion of Definition", *Journal of Philosophy,* Vol. 66 (1969), pp. 382–383.

Should we, then, disqualify such a sum as an ultimate factor in favor of the parts b and c, require uniform replacement for these, and thus ban replacement of the sum by a? Since b and c are not necessarily the only parts of the sum of the two, how are ultimate factors to be identified here? If we are to divide an individual into its least parts, the criterion cannot be applied where any individual is presystematically deemed to be infinitely divisible. If we are not to divide every divisible individual, where are we to stop?

Moreover, although identities and differences among classes of individuals are duplicated when their members are uniformly replaced, identities and differences among individuals are not in general duplicated when parts of them are uniformly replaced. When a, b, c, and d are uniformly replaced by r, s, t, and u, the sum of a and b may be different from the sum of c and d while the sum of r and s is identical with the sum of t and u; or vice versa. For example, let the first four be the quarters of a square, the second four the vertical and horizontal halves of the same square; or vice versa. This important disanalogy overrides the analogy that raised the question here under discussion. Thus the isomorphism criterion as stated holds even in the special case: it calls for uniform replacement of ultimate factors; but the ultimate factors here are the individuals that are arguments of the definiendum-predicates.

The criterion is intended to apply to all predicates other than those belonging to what I call the general apparatus of a system, but not to apply, for example, to the predicate for overlapping of individuals, which plays in systems framed in the language of individuals a role comparable to that of "ϵ" in systems framed in the language of classes. The interpretation of 'overlaps' (or "o") is assumed to be given for a system, and definitions of other predicates in terms of this primitive are taken to be as stated in the general calculus of individuals.

Supplementary Readings for Chapter IV
secondary to references within text and footnotes

Leonard, H. S., *Singular Terms* (Doctoral Thesis, Harvard University, 1930).

Leśniewski, S., "O Podstawach Matematyki", *Przegląd Filozoficzny,* Vol. 30 (1927), pp. 164–206; Vol. 31 (1928), pp. 261–291; Vol. 32 (1929), pp. 60–101; Vol. 33 (1930), pp. 77–105; Vol. 34 (1931), pp. 142–170.

Quine, W. V., *Word and Object,* Cambridge, Mass.: M.I.T. Press, and New York: John Wiley and Sons, 1960, §55.

V

Meaning

FOREWORD

In all these papers, analysis of meaning leads us to look beyond a
term, either to its several instances, which may differ in extension
and meaning, or to its compounds, which may have extensions
integral to its meaning.

The treatment of 'indicator-words' in the two sections taken
from the last chaper of *The Structure of Appearance* may be compared with Russell's treatment of 'ego-centric particulars' and
Reichenbach's of 'token-reflexive' terms. Russell's work and mine
on this topic were carried on simultaneously and independently.
We met and exchanged papers only in 1940, when his book *An Inquiry into Meaning and Truth*[1] was already at press, and my thesis
A Study of Qualities was in final stages of preparation. Reichenbach seems to have been working on the matter at about the same
time, but did not publish his results until 1947 in *Elements of
Symbolic Logic*,[2] after he had read the Russell book.

The central points made in my chapter have some bearing on
many philosophical questions concerning time, including those
raised by Aristotle's discussion of tomorrow's sea-battle. Among
the many recent papers on these questions, some, such as Richard
Taylor's,[3] have taken my chapter as their point of departure. Some
others, however, have missed applying its results where needed,

---

1. New York: Norton, 1940, Chaps. XVI, XVII, XXIV.

2. New York: Macmillan, 1947, pp. 284–298.

3. *E.g.* "Spatial and Temporal Analogies and the Concept of Identity",
Journal of Philosophy, Vol. 52 (1955), pp. 599–612; "Moving about in Time",
Philosophical Quarterly, Vol. 9 (1959), pp. 289–301.

and some[4] have merely duplicated one or another of those results. Perhaps the reappearance here of part of that chapter will make it more accessible. The selection below, although it originally appeared near the end of a rather technical book, can be read quite independently.

That the several replicas of a tensed verb or other indicator-word may have diverse extensions does not distinguish it from other ambiguous words. Concerning the 'delicate distinction' to be made here, this much may be said: (1) The ratio of the number of different extensions to the number of replicas is usually much smaller for other ambiguous words than for genuine indicators; (2) For each indicator-word, we can usually formulate rather simply the relationship that the place or time or utterer or addressee, etc. of each replica bears to what is denoted. But no tight formula general enough to cover all indicators and exclude other ambiguous terms is at present available. Further illumination on ambiguity and related problems may be expected from current studies by Israel Scheffler. (See also *LA IV, 2* and *3*).

Since much of "Talk of Time" is concerned with certain problems of translation, the question of criteria of translation arises there, and reference is made to the papers on meaning. However, my analysis of likeness of meaning, far from providing any fixed criterion of translation, shows that, and how, the criteria vary with context and purpose. In "Talk of Time", translation in a particular sphere and for a particular purpose is explicated by prescriptions for translating indicators into freely repeatable terms. Although translation of other ambiguous words is not considered in any detail, one thing is clear: the principles of translation adopted will themselves define ambiguity, for ambiguity obtains where replicas have different translations.

The criterion of likeness of meaning applies after all indicators and other ambiguous words have been eliminated by translation, so that only freely repeatable terms remain. For such terms the result is that *only*, and as Beverly Robbins has shown,[5] *all*, replicas of each other have exactly the same meaning. Obviously, preser-

---

4. *E.g.* J. T. Saunders, "A Sea Fight Tomorrow", *Philosophical Review*, Vol. 66 (1957), pp. 1–28.

5. "On Synonymy of Word Events", *Analysis*, Vol. 12 (1952), pp. 98–100.

vation of sameness of meaning is thus too strict a demand to make upon translation for most purposes; for translation would then consist solely of repetition. On the other hand, since for a freely repeatable term, all replicas do have the same meaning, we can say that in a very strong sense they are translations of one another; sameness of meaning is a sufficient though not necessary condition for translation.

The conclusion that no two different terms have the same meaning has often been hastily dismissed as counterintuitive. Accordingly, when "On Likeness of Meaning" was reprinted in an anthology,[6] the next to the last paragraph of the present version was inserted to point out that since our intuitive demands concerning meaning are incompatible with one another, they cannot all be satisfied. In the meantime, the sting of the conclusion of "On Likeness of Meaning" had been somewhat softened by the final paragraph of "On Some Differences about Meaning".

The papers on meaning focus attention upon certain compounds of terms. A compound is a larger term obtained by adding other words. For example, "picture of a house", "description of a house", "part of a house", "small house", "corner house", and "house of seven gables" are compounds of the term "house"; and each is also, incidentally, a compound of some other term—of "picture", "description", "part", "small", "corner", and in the final example "gable", "seven", and "of seven gables". The compounds relevant to meaning-comparison are all among those such that their extensions are not included in the extensions of the term compounded; for if two terms such as "centaur" and "unicorn" are coextensive their difference in meaning is not revealed in such equally coextensive parallel compounds as "small centaur" and "small unicorn" but in such extensionally divergent parallel compounds as "picture of a centaur" and "picture of a unicorn". When parallel compounds of two terms thus differ in extension, the terms themselves are said to differ in secondary extension. What intensionalists point to as making a difference in meaning can often be more explicitly formulated as difference in secondary extension.[7]

6. *Semantics and the Philosophy of Language,* ed. L. Linsky (Urbana, Illinois: University of Illinois Press, 1952).

7. *E.g.* see Carnap, *Meaning and Necessity* (2nd ed., Chicago: University of Chicago Press, 1956), p. 238.

The 'language theory of pictures' suggested in "On Likeness of Meaning" has undergone some modification with time. Rejection of the view that the distinction between descriptions and pictures is a matter of presence or absence of conventionalization holds firm; but while in "On Some Differences about Meaning" the distinction is taken to be a difference in *degree* of conventionalization, seven years later in "The Way the World Is" (I,2 above) the distinction is held to be rather a matter of *different* conventions. In *Languages of Art,* the specific features distinguishing descriptions from pictures, as well as the features common to them as symbols, are studied in detail.

The basic idea used for dealing with pictures of centaurs and descriptions of unicorns in "On Likeness of Meaning" recurs in my later work, especially in the treatment of rhetorical aboutness in "About" (VI,1 below) and the treatment of fictive representation and of representation-as in *Languages of Art,* as well as in some unpublished correspondence about hunting non-existent lions. Much the same idea is used by Quine in construing belief-contexts,[8] and by Meyer and Lambert in the course of a paper on freeing logic from existential assumptions.[9] Scheffler, however, in his analysis of indirect discourse,[10] takes his cue rather from the treatment of inscriptions and replicas in "Talk of Time", and has convinced Quine,[11] that this may provide a better way of handling belief-contexts.

8. *Word and Object* (Cambridge, Mass.: M.I.T. Press, 1960), §44, especially p. 216.

9. "Universally Free Logic and Standard Quantification Theory", *Journal of Symbolic Logic,* Vol. 33 (1968), pp. 8–26.

10. "An Inscriptional Approach to Indirect Quotation", *Analysis,* Vol. 14 (1954), pp. 83–90; "Inscriptionalism and Indirect Quotation", *Analysis,* Vol. 19 (1958), pp. 12–18; and "On Synonymy and Indirect Quotation", *Philosophy of Science,* Vol. 22 (1955), pp. 39–44.

11. See *Words and Objections,* ed. D. Davidson and J. Hintikka (Dordrecht: D. Reidel, 1969), p. 334.

1

Talk of Time

Time and Language

In ordinary discourse we often indicate the time of events not by explicit description but by such a word as "now", "yesterday", "next week", "past", "later", or by the tense of a verb. As a result, we have quite unequivocal statements that nevertheless seem, paradoxically, to change in truth value. For example, when I say "The Red Sox now lead the American league", I am being quite definite; I am not saying that they lead at some unspecified time but am indicating the time unmistakably. What I utter is thus not an open statement like "x is yellow" but a closed statement that is either true or false. And yet although it be true when I first utter it, it may be false when I repeat it later.

The point is, of ocurse, that we must be more careful to distinguish between a statement and other statements that resemble it. In the last example, we have two statements, not one. Each of the utterances is a distinct, definite statement; and the two in fact have different truth values. These utterances may be exactly alike in sound pattern; but it is each utterance and not anything common to the two that constitutes a statement. Similarly, it is each of the utterances of "now"—not anything common to the two— that constitutes a word and refers to a certain time. In platonistic terms, the distinction between the general pattern or *type* of a word or sentence and its particular instances or *tokens* was drawn many years ago by Peirce. Too often, however, those who have noticed the distinction have looked upon it as a matter of isolated academic interest and assumed that thereafter one need be concerned only with the types. More recently,[1] we have been forced to recognize that often—as in the example above—it is the tokens that function as words or sentences; for we find different tokens of the same type naming and affirming different things.

---

1. See, for example, *SQ*, pp. 594–623; and Reichenbach's *Elements of Symbolic Logic* (New York: Macmillan, 1947), pp. 284–298.

Indeed, it is the types that we can do without. Actual discourse, after all, is made up of tokens that differ from and resemble each other in various important ways. Some are "now"s and others "very"s just as some articles of furniture are desks and others chairs; but the application of a common predicate to several tokens—or to several articles of furniture—does not imply that there is a universal designated by that predicate. And we shall find no case where a word or statement needs to be construed as a type rather than as a token. The exclusion of types not only does away with some excess baggage but also results, I think, in clarifying our immediate problem.

Obviously the term "token" is no longer appropriate. It is both misleading and superfluous; for utterances and inscriptions are no longer to be regarded as mere samples but as the actual words or statements themselves, and the linguistic universals from which they were to be distinguished are no longer to be countenanced at all. Nevertheless, to emphasize the fact that words and statements are utterances or inscriptions—i.e., *events* of shorter or longer duration—I shall sometimes use such terms as "word-events", "noun-events", " 'here'-events", " 'Paris'-events" and so on, even though the suffix is really redundant in all these cases. "Paris"-events, of course, are not events in Paris but certain utterances and inscriptions—namely, the "Paris"s. A word-event surrounded by quotes-events is a predicate applicable to utterances and inscriptions; and any

" 'Paris' consists of five letters"

is short for any

"Every 'Paris'-inscription consists of five letter-inscriptions".

Although each utterance and inscription is a separate word (or statement or letter, etc.), the difference between two words often has no practical importance. For most purposes, we need not distinguish among the several "Pisa"s, all of which name the same thing, even though they differ widely in size, shape, color, sound, place, date, etc. On the other hand, we must carefully distinguish a "Pisa" from a "Paris". It is true that a given "Pisa" may be more like a given "Paris" than like some other "Pisa", just as a given mushroom may look more like a given toadstool than like some other mushroom; but in both cases we must discern just that overt difference that is correlated with a difference in appropriate use. In the case of "Pisa"s and "Paris"s, and in many other cases, some certain difference of shape or sound-pattern is the clue to a difference in what the words name.

Yet by no means every difference of extension is accompanied by a difference in shape or sound-pattern. The nominata of two "Paris"s that are exactly alike in shape may be as different as those of a "Paris" and a "Pisa"; for some "Paris"s name a city in France while others name a town in Maine. To note from its shape that a given word is a "Paris" thus is not enough. In order to determine which of two places the particular "Paris" in question names, we must look to the *context*—i.e., to the surrounding words and to certain attendant circumstances. Similarly, the various "this continent"s name six or more different individuals; the various "John Smith"s a still greater number; and the various "I"s name vastly many different individuals.

For convenience, let us speak of words (or letters or statements, etc.) that are catalogued under a single label as *replicas* of one another,[2] so that any "Paris" (or any "I say") is a replica of itself and of any other "Paris" (or "I say"). Roughly speaking, a word is an *indicator* if (but, as will be made clear later in this section, not necessarily only if) it names something not named by some replica of the word. This is admittedly broad, including ambiguous terms as well as what might be regarded as indicators-proper, such as pronouns; but delimitation of the narrower class of indicators-proper is a ticklish business and is not needed for our present purposes.

What has been said above will suggest that almost every name has a replica somewhere that names something different, and that therefore almost every name will be an indicator according to this criterion. But the distinction between indicators and nonindicators becomes effective when applied to a limited discourse. Within such

2. This usage differs from that of C. S. Peirce, who speaks of inscriptions or utterances as *replicas* of a word type; see *Collected Papers of Charles Sanders Peirce,* Vol. II (Cambridge, Mass.: Harvard University Press, 1932), p. 143.

a discourse there will normally be many names that are not indicators—although proper nouns as well as pronouns will still often
be indicators, and pronouns will occasionally be nonindicators.

Among the commonest indicators are the personal indicators,
the spatial indicators, and the temporal indicators. Of the personal indicators, an "I" or "me" normally refers to its own utterer;
a "we" or "us" refers to the utterer and certain others determined
by the context; a "you" applies to those addressed by the utterer,
and so on. Characteristically, even though there is no variation
in what a given personal indicator names, there is a wide variation
in what several replicas of that indicator name. Much more remains to be said, of course. For one thing, the person in question
is sometimes, as in ghostwriting, the ostensible rather than the
actual utterer; and the indicators appearing in a copy or transcrip-
tion relate not to the actual maker of these inscriptions but to the
maker of the original inscription or utterance. Furthermore, some
indicators, like the "his"s, not only name but serve a prepositional
purpose as well. Again, some words of the same shape as indicators are actually not indicators at all but simply variables; a
case in point is the "he" in an "If anyone disapproves, he may
leave". Finally, an inscription sometimes divides temporarily into
several different indicators; for example, if a given placard reading "I hate Hitler" is carried by different persons on three successive days, then the three day-parts of the enduring "I"-inscrip-
tion name different persons. But all this is by way of subscript to
the main point.

The location of a spatial indicator has to be taken into account
in much the same way as the producer of a personal indicator.
Some spatial indicators like the "here"s name regions they lie in,
while others like the "yonders" are discrete from the regions
they name. In most cases, just what region a given indicator names
depends partly upon its context, including such supplementary
aids as pointing. Even among the "here"s, one may refer to part of
a room while others refer severally to a town, a county, a state, a
continent, etc. Analogues of all the subsidiary remarks about
personal indicators apply to spatial indicators. For example, a
"here"-inscription in a personal letter normally refers to the place
where it was written; a "here" in a delivered telegram refers

rather to the place where the original was written or spoken; and if a "No Parking Here" sign is moved about, certain different temporal parts of the "Here" name different places.

But we are primarily concerned with the temporal indicators. Part of what is to be said concerning them is already evident from our glance at the personal and spatial indicators. The "now"s, for example, behave much like the "here"s; each "now" names a period in which it lies, and the periods named by different "now"s range from a moment to an era. Other terms, like the "yesterday"s and the "soon"s, name periods earlier or later than themselves; but in every case the time of utterance of a temporal indicator is relevant to what it names. We need hardly review the other points of analogy between temporal indicators and those already discussed, but certain temporal indicators require special attention.

In the first place, the "past"s, "present"s, and "future"s lend themselves to frequent abuse in theoretical discourse. Most "present"s function exactly like most "now"s, naming some period they lie in; and the various "present"s name many different periods of varying lengths, some of them remote from others. A "past", however, most often names *all* the time preceding—and a "future" all the time following—a certain period in which it lies. Thus the period named by a given "past" overlaps, and indeed includes or is included in, the period named by any other "past"; and the same holds for "future"s. This fact, that what is once past is always thereafter past (and that what is once future was always theretofore future), creates an illusion of fixity and leads to treating the "past"s (or the "future"s, or even the "present"s) as if, like the "Eiffel Tower"s, all named the same thing. Metaphysicians have capitalized on this confusion for some very purple passages on The Past, The Present, and The Future. We must be careful to remember that nonsimultaneous "past"s (or "present"s, or "future"s) commonly name different even if not discrete periods.

Very often, however, temporal indication is accomplished in a sentence not by any word devoted solely or chiefly to that purpose but rather by the tense of the verb. A "Randy ran" tells us not only who did what but also when, i.e., prior to the period of production of the sentence itself. The "ran", besides specifying the action performed, serves also as a temporal indicator; non-simultaneous "ran"s ordinarily indicate different periods of time. Incidentally, verbs in some languages may also serve the third purpose of personal indication; for example, a *creo* in Spanish indicates its utterer so definitely that the pronoun *yo* is customarily omitted.

A verb in the present tense normally indicates a period within which the verb is produced, while a verb in the future tense normally indicates the period after its own production. The interpretation of compound tenses and of combinations of tensed verbs with other temporal indicators sometimes requires care but is seldom really difficult. A

"Randy had been running"

tells us that the running took place prior to a moment—presumably further specified in the context—that is in turn prior to the time of production of the sentence itself. An isolated

"World War II was present",

however, tells us simply, as does a

"World War II is past",

that World War II is prior to the sentence in question. The "present" in an "is present" or a "was present" or a "will be present" in no way affects the temporal indication accomplished by the verb alone. On the other hand, an "is past" or an "is future" functions in the same way as, respectively, a "was" or a "will be". No exhaustive survey of such combinations need be attempted here; but it should be noted that some may result in virtually vacuous statements. For instance, a

"World War II was future"

—if unaccompanied by any context determining what prior moment is being affirmed to precede World War II—says only what may be said about any event that did not begin at the first moment of time. Likewise, of any event that does not run to the end of time, we may truly say that it will be past. Of course, a combination such as a "was future" or a "will be past" is usually set within a restrictive context.

In many statements the tense is merely grammatical, the verbs not actually functioning as temporal indicators. This is true more often than not in formal discourse. For one thing, generalizations are usually without effective tense; an

"All men have spines"

refers not only to all men contemporary with the statement but also to all who preceded or will follow it. In many singular statements also the verb, although in the present grammatical tense, is adequately translated by a purely tenseless symbol. For example, where an "*a*" and a "*b*" are proper names, a given

"*a* overlaps *b*"

may speak simply of the overlapping of the two individuals, without indicating anything about the date of their common part; that is, the sentence may just say that *a* **o** *b*. On the other hand, another

"*a* overlaps *b*"

may have effective tense, being used to affirm not just that *a* and *b* have some common part but that they have some common part that is contemporary with the sentence itself. The context makes the difference.

Now one may say that two things overlap [tenseless] if and only if they did or do or will overlap; an "*a* **o** *b*" is implied by an effectively tensed "*a* overlaps *b*" or "*a* overlapped *b*" or "*a* will overlap *b*", while an "*a* **o** *b*" implies none of these but only such a disjunction as an "*a* overlaps *b*, or *a* overlapped *b*, or *a* will overlap *b*". But parallel principles do not hold for all other verbs, indeed, an "*a* ⅂ *b*" obviously is not implied by an effectively tensed "*a* is discrete from *b*" or "*a* was discrete from *b*" or "*a* will be discrete from *b*", but implies them all. Moreover, even though each verb that is effectively in, say, the past tense indicates a period preceding the verb, the relationship affirmed to obtain between such a period and other individuals referred to in a sentence varies considerably with different verbs. While an

"a overlapped b"

places a common part of a and b within such a period, an

"a was earlier than b"

places a within such a period; a

"color c was at place p"

places the (color-spot) sum of c and p within such a period, and a

"color c matched color d"

seems to place c and d (but not their sum, of course—see *SA VII,2*) at a moment within such a period. These examples will perhaps be sufficient warning against certain kinds of hasty generalization about tense.

Like some verbs, some replicas of other temporal indicators are not themselves indicators. For example, in a

"We can know at a given time only what is past at that time or present at that time, not what is future at that time",

the "past", "present", and "future" name no times. Rather, the "is past at", the "is present at", and the "is future at" are tenseless two-place predicates that may respectively be translated by the tenseless predicates "is earlier than", "is at", and "is later than".

Effective tense does not by itself prevent a string of words from constituting a genuine statement. A tensed statement has as constant a truth value as a tenseless one; and a tenseless statement, no less than a tensed one, is an event in time. The difference is that tensed statements and other statements with indicators are not, so to speak, 'freely repeatable'. Now of course no term or statement is ever repeated in the way a quale is repeated; for a term or statement is a particular event and not a universal. On the other hand, nearly all terms and statements are much repeated in that they have many replicas. But a term or statement is said to be freely repeatable in a given discourse if all its replicas therein are also translations of it. Indicators and statements containing them are not freely repeatable.

Ordinarily, when we want to make continued or renewed use of a given term or sentence that occurs earlier in our discourse, we just repeat it, i.e., introduce a replica to take its place. If the term or sentence is freely repeatable, then for most purposes we need not distinguish between it and its replicas; we proceed as if all were numerically identical. But in the case of an indicator or a sentence containing one, where not all the replicas are translations, this is obviously dangerous. Often, indeed, no available replica of a given term or sentence is a translation of it, so that an inaccessible original cannot, in effect, be brought back into play by repeating it. For this reason, although indicators are of enormous practical utility, they are likely to be awkward for formal discourse. Various remedies may be applied. One lies in supplying a freely repeatable name (or description) of the indicator, or of the sentence containing it, and thereafter, instead of repeating the term or sentence, referring to it by means of a replica of this name. For example, a given "now" might be identified by any

"The 937th word uttered by George Washington in 1776".

A later repetition of that "now" is not a translation of it; but any replica of this descriptive name is a translation of every other, and names just the particular "now" in question. And using such a name, we can readily arrive at a repeatable *translation* of the indicator; e.g., the "now" in question is translated by any

"The period referred to by the 937th word uttered by George Washington in 1776";

or alternatively, if the period is a day, by any

"The day on which George Washington uttered his 937th word in 1776".

Or we may seek a translation that contains no name of the indicator itself, but rather another name for what the indicator names. Thus a certain "here" is translated by any "Philadelphia"; and a certain "ran" is translated by any

"runs [tenseless] on January 7, 1948 at noon EST".

Against such translations, it is sometimes urged that they do not really convey the content of the originals. A spoken

"Randy is running now"

tells us that the action takes place at the very moment of speaking, while a

"Randy runs [tenseless] on October 17, 1948, at 10 P.M., EST."

does not tell us that the action takes place simultaneously with either utterance unless we know in addition that the time of the utterance is October 17, 1948 at 10 P.M., EST. Since—the argument runs—we recognize the tenseless sentence as a translation of the tensed one only in the light of outside knowledge, we have here no genuine translation at all. But this seems to me no more cogent than would the parallel argument that "L'Angleterre" is not a genuine translation of "England" because we recognize it as a translation only if we know that L'Angleterre is England.

A different question may arise from the auxiliary function of tensed verbs as indicators. If two tensed predicates are coextensive but indicate different times, are they translations of one another? Do we demand that the two agree in what they apply to, or do we demand that they agree also in what they indicate? It is to be noted that ordinarily predicates that indicate different times differ also in extension; for to say that a tensed predicate indicates a time is a convenient way of saying that the application of a tensed predicate is restricted to individuals at that time. Nevertheless in some cases predicates that—according to the looser locution—'indicate different times' may agree in extension. A clear if unimportant example is that of a

"stood still while walking"

and a simultaneous

"will stand still while walking".

Since neither applies to anything, they are coextensive. The question whether they are translations of each other is quite analogous to the question whether

"orders a centaur steak"

216

and

"orders a unicorn steak"

are translations of each other. Both questions illustrate a general problem concerning the criteria for the use of "translation". That general problem lies outside my province here. I can only remark in passing that I think (1) the appropriate criteria may vary considerably with the nature and purpose of the discourse and (2) criteria much more stringent than simple coextensiveness can be formulated within the framework of extensionalism.[3]

The Passage of Time

We have still to deal with statements that seem most patently to reflect the temporal flow of events. One speaks of time passing, of events moving from the future into the present and on into the past, of things growing steadily older. How is such language to be interpreted?

To say that time passes seems to amount to saying that a moment of time progresses constantly in a future-toward-past direction. Yet obviously a time does not shift its position with respect to other times; it is identified with its position in the temporal series, and if any time moves then all move together. Now we have seen how a

"Time t is future",

a later

"Time t is present",

and a still later

"Time t is past"

may all be true; and how the conjunction of the three might have as a translation any

"Washington's 27th 'future' is earlier than time t; his 13th 'present' is at time t; and his 49th 'past' is later than time t"

3. For a further discussion, see the other articles in this chapter.

(where each "is" is tenseless). The motion of time t ostensibly expressed here consists simply in the fact that t has different relationships of precedence to different verbal events. Again a

"Time t was future, is now present, and will be past"

says merely that this utterance is at time t, is later than some earlier time, and earlier than some later time. On the other hand, a statement like

"A time is at first future, then becomes present, then becomes past"

is quite a different matter. The final clause, for example, says neither that a time is earlier than this particular "past" nor that it is earlier than some "past" or other. The clause says rather that a time is past at some time or other; and this, as we have seen, just says that a time is earlier than some time or other. What the clause in question says thus does not depend on the time of its own or any other utterance. Indeed the whole sentence contains no actual indicators at all but is freely repeatable. Of course we may quite understandably want a translation of it free of words having many replicas that are actual indicators; and such a translation is readily provided:

"A time is later than some time x, identical with some time later than x, and earlier than some still later time".

In the case of a

"Time t is past and constantly recedes further into the past",

uttered at time s, the first "past" is an actual indicator while the second is not. The sentence says that time t is earlier than s; and that if q and r are times later than s, and q is later than r, then t precedes q by more than t precedes r. What has been said here of statements concerning times can easily be adapted to the interpretation of parallel statements concerning events.

So far I have not considered statements like

"While it endures, a thing constantly grows older".

This again is normally a tenseless, freely repeatable statement, saying in effect that if two times r and s are within the period of duration of a thing, and r is earlier than s, then a larger part of that period precedes s than precedes r.

Thus are sentences that express the passage of time or the flow of events translated by sentences that merely describe relationships of precedence in the temporal series. The suggestion of flow or of passing or of ageing disappears; and just for this reason, it may be felt that we are missing something important about time. Most efforts to formulate just what is missed end in vague poetry or in hopeless confusion over temporal indicators. Yet I think that underlying these efforts there is a certain peculiarity of time that deserves attention. Strangely enough it turns out not that time is more fluid than (say) space but rather that time is more static.

We saw that the analogy between space and time is indeed close. Duration is comparable to extent. A thing may vary in color in its different spatial or in its different temporal parts. A thing may occupy different places at one time, or the same place at different times, or may vary concomitantly in place and time. The relation between the period of time occupied by a thing during its entire existence and the rest of time is as fixed as the relation between the region the thing covers during its entire existence and the rest of space. And yet there is this difference: two things may approach and then recede from each other in space, may grow more and then less alike in color, shape, etc.; but two things never become nearer and then farther apart in time. The location or the color or the shape of a thing may change, but not its time.

This may seem to depend on a mere verbal accident. Why not simply generalize the use of "change" a little so that a thing changes in a given respect if different parts of the thing have different qualities of the kind in question? Because, it may be fairly answered, this ignores the distinction between a minute mobile thing that travels over a given region, and a spatially large thing that occupies a comparable region at a single instant. Each of the two things has parts that differ from one another in location; but according to ordinary usage, only the former undergoes change.

By applying the term "change" in the one case but not the other, ordinary usage marks an important distinction.

In other words, change is concomitant variation in time and some other respect. Since time is always one of the variant factors in change, we speak of *change in* whatever is the other variant factor in the given case. Thus although there is no change that does not involve time, there is no change in time.

2

On Likeness of Meaning

{Every so often someone steers me into a quiet corner and asks whether I am really in earnest about my paper "On Likeness of Meaning". There is perhaps some ground for the feeling that I am rather less in earnest about it than are some of my opponents. The problems it deals with do not seem to me to have quite the paramount importance that is commonly attached to them these days. And while I am increasingly convinced that any reasonably adequate explication of the misbegotten notion of synonymy is likely to yield the conclusion that no two terms in a natural language are exactly synonymous, I care very little whether that particular conclusion stands or falls.

Nevertheless my paper is a serious and I hope not wholly unsuccessful attempt to deal with what I consider an interesting question. If we resolve to confine ourselves to terms and the things they refer to, renouncing concepts, intensions, senses, meanings, criteria in mind, and the like, how are we to do justice to the ostensible difference in meaning between two words, such as "centaur" and "unicorn", that have the same extension?

Since my second paper was published, my attention has been called to two further points that may need clarifying.

First, if all we seek is some difference between "centaur" and "unicorn", why not point simply to their shape or their spelling? The answer is that degrees of difference in shape or spelling do not correspond even approximately with what we ordinarily regard as degrees of difference in meaning. Comparison of the extensions of the various parallel compounds into which the two terms enter is much more pertinent. And when simple extensional agreement of two terms is not a strong enough relation for a given purpose, what is usually wanted in addition is extensional agreement of certain parallel compounds. The set of compounds for

I am deeply indebted to Morton G. White and W. V. Quine, with whom I have frequently and profitably discussed the problem dealt with in this paper.

which this demand is made—and what in practice constitutes sufficient synonymy—varies from discourse to discourse.

The second objection is that precisely by entertaining expressions like "picture of a centaur", where replacement of "centaur" by an extensionally identical term like "unicorn" will change the extension of the whole, I have already transgressed the boundaries of extensional language and thus forfeited my goal. But I did not at all want to propose keeping within the confines of extensionality so construed. Rather, I have tried to suggest how the recognition of certain contexts that are indeed non-extensional by this criterion nevertheless enables us to explain the difference in meaning between such words as "centaur" and "unicorn" without involving us in any of the more distressing aspects of intensionalism. (1954) }

Under what circumstances do two names or predicates in an ordinary language have the same meaning? Many and widely varied answers have been given to this question, but they have one feature in common: they are all unsatisfactory.

One of the earliest answers is to the effect that two predicates have the same meaning if they stand for the same real Essence or Platonic Idea; but this does not seem to help very much unless we know, as I am afraid we do not, how to find out whether two terms stand for the same Platonic Idea.

A more practical proposal is that two terms have the same meaning if they stand for the same mental idea or image; or in other words, that two predicates differ in meaning only if we have a mental picture of something that satisfies one but not the other of the two. Thus even though in fact all and only pelicans have gallon-sized bills, we can easily imagine a sparrow or a kangaroo with a gallon-sized bill; and thus the predicates "is a pelican" and "has a gallon-sized bill", even though satisfied by exactly the same actual individuals, do not have the same meaning. There are two familiar difficulties with this theory. In the first place, it is not very clear just what we can and what we cannot imagine. Can we imagine a man ten miles high or not? Can we imagine a tone we have never heard? To decide these cases is only to be confronted by new and harder ones. But the second and more serious difficulty is that of predicates that pretty clearly have no corresponding image, such as "clever" or "supersonic". Of course there is imagery associated with these terms; but that is hardly to the point. There is imagery associated with nonsense syllables.

⎣The image theory thus sometimes gives way to the concept theory: the theory that two predicates differ in meaning if and only if we can conceive of something that satisfies one but not the other⎤ This enables us to transcend the narrow boundaries of imagination, but unfortunately it hardly seems to provide us with any criterion at all. Presumably we can conceive a five-dimensional body since we can define it although we cannot imagine it. But similarly we can define a square circle very easily (as a rectangle with four equal sides and such that every point of it is equidistant from a center) or a five-sided triangle. If it be objected that because such definitions are not self-consistent they do not represent genuine concepts, I must point out that the claim of inconsistency here can be supported only by appeal to just such meaning-relationships as we are trying to explain. We cannot use them in trying to define them. If the objection is put rather in the form that although we can define a square circle there is no possible thing that can satisfy the definition, then it is clear that we are not judging possibility by conceivability but rather judging conceivability by possibility. Our criterion of sameness of meaning has thus changed: we are saying that two predicates have the same meaning if and only if there is nothing possible that satisfies one but not the other.

The possibility theory is somewhat ambiguous. Does it say that two terms differ in meaning only if it is possible that there is something that satisfies one but not the other? If that is all, then any two terms we know to have the same extension have the same meaning. If I know that Mr. Jones is in New York, I no longer regard it as possible that he is not in New York; and similarly if I know that two predicates are satisfied by exactly the same individuals, the possibility is excluded that they are not satisfied by the same individuals. But this formulation seldom satisfies proponents of the possibility theory, who will cite cases of terms that, even though acknowledged to have the same extension, have different meanings. The thesis, they say, is rather that two predicates differ in meaning if there 'might have been' something that satisfied one but not the other; or in other words, if there is a possible but non-actual entity that does satisfy one but not the other predicate. The notion of possible entities that are not and cannot be actual is a hard one for many of us to understand or accept. And even if we do accept it, how are we to decide when there is and when there is not such a possible that satisfies one but not the other of two terms? We have already seen that we get nowhere by appealing to conceivability as a test of possibility. Can, we then, determine whether two predicates *"P"* and *"Q"* apply to the same possibles by asking whether the predicate "is a P or a Q but not both" is self-consistent? This is hardly helpful; for so long as *"P"* and *"Q"* are different predicates the compound predicate is logically self-consistent, and we have no ready means for determining whether it is otherwise self-consistent. Indeed the latter question amounts to the very question whether *"P"* and *"Q"* have the same meaning. And since we began by asking how to determine when two predicates have the same meaning, we are back where we started.

All these difficulties suggest that we might try the very different and radical theory that two predicates have the same meaning if and only if they apply to exactly the same things—or in other words, have the same extension. This thesis has been attacked more often than it has been advanced; but some of the familiar arguments against it seem to me worthless. An example is the absurd argument that the extension of a term is different at different times and that there by this thesis two terms may be synonymous at one time and not at another. The extension of a predicate consists, of course, of everything past, present, and future to which the term applies; neither the making or the eating of cakes changes the extension of the term "cake".

Certain other similar arguments apply not against the thesis that two terms have the same meaning if they have the same extension, but against the different thesis—that does not concern us here—that the extension of a term is its meaning. For example, against the latter thesis, one may argue as follows: before we can investigate whether a given predicate *"P"* applies to a given thing *a* we must know what *"P"* means, and if the meaning of *"P"* is its extension we must know the extension of *"P"*—and therefore must know whether it applies to *a*—before we can set about finding out whether *"P"* applies to *a*. But this argument does not apply against the weaker thesis that two predicates have the same meaning if they have the same extension; for obviously we may decide by induction, conjecture, or other means that two predicates have the same extension without knowing exactly all the things they apply to.

And yet, while many of the apparent objections seem to me unsound, I think we cannot maintain the unqualified thesis that two predicates have the same meaning if they have the same extension. There are certain clear cases where two words that have the same extension do not have the same meaning. "Centaur" and "unicorn", for example, since neither applies to anything, have the same (null) extension; yet surely they differ in meaning. I do not mean to suggest that identity of extension with difference of meaning occurs only where the extension is null, but such cases are enough and are the most striking.

Now the precise way in which the proposed thesis failed must be particularly noted. Obviously if two terms have the same meaning they have the same extension; the trouble is that two terms may have the same extension and yet not have the same meaning. Extensional identity is a necessary but not a sufficient condition for sameness of meaning. In other words, difference of extension does not draw distinctions as fine as those drawn by difference of meaning.

Does this mean, then, that we must return to the dismal search through Never-Never land for some ghostly entities called "meanings" that are distinct from and lie between words and their extensions? I don't think so. Despite the obvious inadequacy of the thesis we have been considering, I think that difference in meaning between any two terms can be fully accounted for without introducing anything beyond terms and their extensions. For while it is clear that difference in meaning of two terms *"P"* and *"Q"* is not always accompanied by difference in extension, I think it is always accompanied by difference in the extension of certain terms other than *"P"* and *"Q"*. Let me explain.

Since there are no centaurs or unicorns, all unicorns are centaurs and all centaurs are unicorns. Furthermore, all uncles

of centaurs are uncles of unicorns; and all feet of unicorns are
feet of centaurs. How far can we generalize on this? Leaving
aside absurd or ungrammatical variations, we must exclude the
analogues in terms of "thoughts" or "concepts" or even "meaning" itself; for there is no guarantee that thoughts of centaurs are
thoughts of unicorns. This is usually attributed to the mental reference or the vagueness of such terms. We have in logic the theo-
rem that if all α's are β's, then all the things that bear the relation
P to an α are things that bear the relation P to a β (see *Principia
Mathematica*, 37.2); and it might naturally be supposed that this
guarantees the truth of sentences like those we have been considering about centaurs and unicorns, provided the phrases involved apply only to physical objects if to anything. But actually
this is not the case; for *pictures*—i.e. paintings, drawings, prints,
statues—are physical objects, yet not all pictures of centaurs are
pictures of unicorns, nor are all pictures of unicorns pictures of
centaurs. At first sight this seems to violate the cited theorem of
logic. Actually, what it shows is that "picture of" is not always a
relation-term like "foot of" or "uncle of". If x is a foot of a centaur,
then x bears the relation "foot of" to some y that is a centaur. Thus
if there is any foot of a centaur or any uncle of a centaur then there
is a centaur. But in contrast, if there is—and indeed there is—
something that is a picture of a centaur, we cannot infer that there
is some centaur—as there certainly is not. A phrase like "picture
of a centaur" is a single predicate, and the fact that it applies to
one or many things plainly does not enable us to conclude that
there are objects that these things are pictures of. To avoid the
temptation to make such unjustified inferences, perhaps we had
better speak during the rest of our discussion not of 'pictures of'
centaurs or unicorns but rather of 'centaur-pictures' and 'unicorn-
pictures', etc.

A centaur-picture differs from a unicorn-picture not by virtue
of its resemblance to a centaur and lack of resemblance to a unicorn; for there are neither unicorns nor centaurs. "Centaur-
picture" and "unicorn-picture" merely apply to different objects
just as "chair" and "desk" apply to different objects, and we need
no more ask why in the one case than in the other. The simple fact
is that although "centaur" and "unicorn" apply to nothing and so

have the same extension, the term "centaur-picture" applies to many things and the term "unicorn-picture" applies to many others.

Now the important point here is this: although two words have the same extension, certain predicates composed by making identical additions to these two words may have different extensions. It is then perhaps the case that for every two words that differ in meaning either their extensions or the extensions of some corresponding compounds of them are different. If so, difference in meaning among extensionally identical predicates can be explained as difference in the extensions of certain other predicates. Or, if we call the extension of a predicate by itself its *primary* extension, and the extension of any of its compounds a *secondary* extension, the thesis is formulated as follows: Two terms have the same meaning if and only if they have the same primary and secondary extensions. Let us, in order to avoid entanglement with such terms as "thought of . . .", "concept of . . .", "attribute of . . .", and "meaning of . . .", exclude from consideration all predicates that apply to anything but physical things, classes of these, classes of classes of these, etc. If the thesis is tenable, we have answered our question by stating, without reference to anything other than terms and the things to which they apply, the circumstances under which two terms have the same meaning.

This explanation takes care of well-known cases discussed in the literature. For instance, Frege has used the terms "(is the) Morningstar" and "(is the) Eveningstar" as examples of two predicates that have the same extension—since they apply to the same one thing—but obviously differ in meaning. This difference in meaning is readily explained according to our present thesis, since the two terms differ in their secondary extensions. There are, for example, Morningstar-pictures that are not Eveningstar-pictures—and also, indeed, Eveningstar-pictures that are not Morningstar-pictures.

But is our thesis satisfactory in general? Perhaps the first question that arises is whether it takes care of cases where we have two terms "P" and "Q" such that there are no P-pictures or Q-pictures—say where "P" and "Q" are predicates applying to odors or electric charges. These present no difficulty; for the secondary extensions of a predicate "Q" consist not merely of the extension of "Q-picture" but also of the extensions of "Q-diagram", "Q-symbol", and any number of other such compound terms. Indeed *actual word-inscriptions* are as genuine physical objects as anything else; and so if there is such an actual physical inscription that is a P-description and is not a Q-description, or vice-versa, then "P" and "Q" differ in their secondary extensions and thus in meaning.

This makes it appear more and more as if every difference in meaning will be reflected by a difference in primary or secondary extension. Indeed, I think we can now show this to be true. For, given any two predicates whatsoever, say "P" and "Q", do we not have in an inscription of the phrase "a P that is not a Q" something that is a P-description and not a Q-description? Clearly the predicate "centaur-description" applies while the predicate "unicorn-description" does not apply to an inscription of "a centaur that is not a unicorn". Likewise, the predicate "pungent-odor-description" applies while the predicate "acrid-odor-description" does not apply to an inscription of "a pungent odor that is not an acrid odor"; and thus the two predicates "pungent-odor" and "acrid-odor"—whatever may be the relationship of their primary extensions—differ in secondary extension and thus in meaning. Again "triangle" and "trilateral" differ in meaning because "triangle that is not trilateral" is a triangle-description but not a trilateral-description. We do not, however, get the absurd result that "triangle" differs in meaning from "triangle"; for of course it is not the case that "triangle that is not a triangle" is and is not a triangle-description.*

But now see how far we have come. If difference of meaning is explained in the way I have proposed, then *no two different*

---

* One basic principle is: *any phrase such as "—— that is . . . " is a ——
-description and a . . . -description.* Thus "—— that is not a . . ." is both a
—— -description and a not-a- . . . -description. Being a not-a- . . .-description is not a sufficient condition for not being a . . . -description. By a second principle, however, a not-a- . . . -description is not a . . . -description unless the first principle (or some other) makes it also a . . . -description. Formulation of complete and exact principles deciding whether any phrase is or is not a . . . -description would be difficult and is neither possible nor necessary here.

words have the same meaning. We have assuredly answered the complaint that in terms of extensions alone we cannot draw fine enough distinctions. Here we get distinctions that are as fine as anyone could ask. But now we risk the opposite complaint: for can we accept the conclusion that a word has the same meaning as no word other than itself?

Before we decide that we cannot tolerate this conclusion, let me note that in the course of developing our criterion we have incidentally shown that there are no two predicates such that each can be replaced by the other in every sentence without changing the truth-value, *even if we exclude the so-called intensional contexts in which such words as* "necessary", "possible", "attribute of", or "thought of" occur. Thus if we maintain that two different words have the same meaning, their lack of interreplaceability in some context other than these can immediately be offered as evidence that the words do not have the same meaning. It seems apparent, therefore, that the demands we commonly make upon a criterion of sameness of meaning can be satisfied only if we recognize that no two different predicates ever have the same meaning.

Theoretically, then, we shall do better never to say that two predicates have the same meaning but rather that they have a greater or lesser degree, or one or another kind, of *likeness* of meaning. In ordinary speech when we say that two terms have the same meaning, we usually indicate only that their kind and degree of likeness of meaning is sufficient for the purposes of the immediate discourse. This is quite harmless. But we must remember that the requirements vary greatly from discourse to discourse; often it is enough if two terms have the same primary extension; in other cases, identity in certain secondary extensions or others is also required. If we overlook this variation and seek a fixed criterion of sameness of meaning that will at once conform to these differing usages and satisfy our theoretical demands, we are doomed to perpetual confusion.

To repeat, it is commonly supposed that a satisfactory definition of synonymy must meet two requirements: that some predicates be synonymous with others, and that either of a pair of synonyms be replaceable by the other in at least all non-intensional contexts without change of truth-value. But we have seen that *these two requirements are incompatible.* The sound course seems to be to construe degree of synonymy as, so to speak, degree of inter-replaceability—along lines above suggested—and to recognize that the relation of exact synonymy between diverse predicates is null.

Just a few further words to suggest a bearing this paper has on another question. It is sometimes said that a sentence like "All *A's* are *B's*" is *analytic* if the meaning of *B* is contained in that of *A*. Our investigation has shown not only that two different predicates like "*A*" and "*B*" never have quite the same meaning; but further that, so to speak, neither is meaning-included in the other; for there is an *A*-description that is not a *B*-description, *and* a *B*-description that is not an *A*-description. Thus, at least according to the suggested interpretation of "analytic", no non-repetitive statement will be analytic. The most we can say is that it is more, or less, nearly analytic. This will be enough to convince many of us that likewise a non-repetitive statement is never absolutely neces-sary, but only more or less nearly so.

3

On Some Differences about Meaning

In the light of many discussions of my paper "On Likeness of Meaning", I want to clarify and amplify some of its main points, then (in 2 below) answer briefly certain specific comments, and finally (in 3 below) suggest a minor but perhaps welcome amendment.[1]

1

The hopeless confusion of attempts to define synonymy in terms of images, concepts, possibilities, etc. leads us to seek a definition solely in terms of actual, even of physical, objects. Yet we must face the fact that some clearly non-synonymous names or predicates apply to exactly the same objects; the most striking but not the only examples are those where, as in the case of "centaur" and "unicorn", neither term applies to anything.

One main point of my earlier paper is that difference in meaning even between such terms can be explained without reference to anything but physical objects. Pictures, for example, are physical objects and yet some (indeed most) pictures of centaurs are not pictures of unicorns. In other words, while "centaur" and "unicorn" apply to exactly the same objects, "picture-of-a-centaur" and "picture-of-a-unicorn" do not by any means apply to exactly the same objects. This suggests that we should take into account not only what is denoted by a given term itself but also what is denoted by compounds containing that term (otherwise

---

1. Concerning two articles published since the first appearance of the present paper, one by Lester Meckler in *Analysis*, Vol. 14 (1954), pp. 68–78, and one by David Shwayder in *Philosophical Studies*, Vol. 5 (1954), pp. 1–5. I can say only that these writers have, in different ways, seriously misunderstood me.

than in quotation marks). My proposal is that two terms are synonymous if and only if

(a) they apply to exactly the same objects, and

(b) each compound term constructed by combining certain words with either of the terms in question applies to exactly the same objects as the compound term constructed by combining the same words in the same way or with the other of the terms in question.

This criterion recommends itself by accounting, without reference to anything but physical objects, for differences in meaning between coextensive terms. But if we can picture these differences that are not exemplified in actuality, just where does the power of pictorial differentiation end? The limits of realistic or representational depiction may seem rather narrow; but as a matter of fact there is no purely representational depiction. Conventionalization to some degree is always present, and increases rather gradually from the realistic painting through the sketch, the semi-abstract picture and the ideographic sign to the word in ordinary language. The string of inscriptions that we call a description is in effect merely a highly conventionalized picture. But description, or word-picturing, is so delicate and potent an instrument that there is virtually no limit on the distinctions it can make. The difference between a man twenty feet tall and a man twenty and one one-hundredth feet tall is hard to paint but easy to state. Indeed, we can even find triangle-descriptions that are not trilateral-descriptions. A couple of rather clear examples are:

(i) plane figure or three angles and four sides
(ii) triangle that is not a trilateral.

That these apply to nothing doesn't matter; centaur-descriptions likewise apply to nothing. And, even if we allow ourselves to speak of possibility for the moment, it doesn't matter that these descriptions apply to nothing possible. All that matters is that despite the nonexistence and even impossibility of triangles that are not trilaterals we have actually before us in (i) and (ii) *descriptions* of such triangles. "Triangle-description", then, applies to some strings of inscriptions that "trilateral-description" does not. Thus "triangle" and "trilateral" differ in at least one of their corresponding secondary extensions, and accordingly differ in meaning by our criterion. By similar argument, every two terms[2] will differ in meaning.

Now of course I cannot define descriptions precisely any more than I can define pictures precisely. Exact and inclusive definition of pictures of centaurs would be no less difficult than exact and inclusive definition of descriptions of triangles. But the most that is required here is that there be an appreciable number of clear cases, and that anomalous and paradoxical cases can be dealt with by reasonable rules. In the next section, I shall discuss some questions that have been raised concerning the applications of "triangle-description"; but there are other compound terms, having more easily specifiable ranges of application, that may equally well be used in carrying through the argument of the preceding paragraph. For example, "literal English triangle-word" may be taken as applying just to those inscriptions that are tokens of "triangle",[3] and "literal English trilateral-word" as applying just to tokens of "trilateral". Since these corresponding compounds have different extensions, the terms "triangle" and "trilateral"—and, by similar argument, every two terms—differ in meaning.

Now I am well aware that various plausible grounds for ruling out these examples need to be considered (see 2 below); but proving that every two terms differ in meaning is no part of my primary goal. The paramount problem is to deal with comparisons of meaning without reference to intensions, attitudes, or modalities. The proposed criterion in terms of primary and secondary extensions meets this requirement and yet successfully explains evident differences in meaning even between coextensive terms like "centaur" and "unicorn". In view of these virtues, I am willing to accept the apparent consequence that no two terms are synonymous. Anyone who shows that this conclusion does not follow at all, or that it can be precluded by suitable provisos,

2. That is, every two names or predicates in a natural language like English. Restricted artificial languages can easily be so constructed that some terms will have the same meaning as others by this criterion.

3. Whereas "literal English 'triangle'-term" applies to tokens of " 'triangle' ".

will simply render my criterion more generally acceptable. But I hold that the criterion is not, anyhow, disqualified by the result that no two terms are absolutely synonymous; for this result seems to me unfamiliar rather than intolerable. The extreme difficulty of finding in practice any two terms that surely have exactly the same meaning opens the way to acceptance of the view that there are no absolute synonyms but only terms that have a greater or lesser degree, or one or another kind, of likeness of meaning.

2

Richard Rudner is correct in saying[4] that I should want any final statement of my views to be formulated in terms of a strict nominalism that regards words as actual inscriptions or events, some of which are said to be *replicas*[5] of one another rather than 'tokens' of a common type. But I now think that Mr. Rudner is wrong and Beverly Robbins[6] right about the consequences of such a restatement. What follows is not that every two word-events differ in meaning but only that every two word-events that are not replicas of each other differ in meaning.

The "wild results" that C. D. Rollins cites[7] are therefore not forthcoming. His chief objection, however, is that a definition of synonymy that makes every two terms differ in meaning departs too far from ordinary usage. *Prima facie* this is reasonable enough; but the departure from ordinary usage is less drastic and better motivated than at first appears. Suppose we have a pile of logs, some of them being for all practical purposes of the same length as others. Will Mr. Rollins reject a process of measurement that gives the result that no two of these logs are of exactly the same length? A certain conformity to ordinary usage is indeed demanded of any definition; but even where the usage is much

4. "A Note on Likeness of Meaning", *Analysis*, Vol. 10 (1950), pp. 115–118.

5. See V,1 above.

6. "On Synonymy of Word-events", *Analysis*, Vol. 12 (1952), pp. 98–100.

7. "The Philosophical Denial of Sameness of Meaning", *Analysis*, Vol. 11 (1950), pp. 38–45.

clearer and more constant than in the case of meaning, what is commonly spoken of as sameness may turn out, according to a perfectly good definition, to be only approximate sameness.[8] And resistance to the conclusion that no two terms are exactly alike in meaning ought to be softened considerably by the recognition that some terms like "triangle" and "trilateral"are, through being interreplaceable in most compounds, very much alike in meaning.

Thus I think the second of Kingsley Price's[9] objections can be answered by saying that dictionary definitions are useful because they join expressions that are much alike in meaning—although the degree of likeness varies considerably. Mr. Price's first objection I cannot follow. He says that "glub" and "gloob" differ in meaning by my criterion because "glub that is not a gloob" will be a glub-description but not a gloob-description. But I am dealing with names or predicates in a language. When nonsense syllables are incorporated like words in a phrase, the phrase itself is nonsense. Or in other words, if "glub" is not in the language then neither is "glub-description".

Mr. Thomson says[10] that two words are synonymous because they have the senses they have. This is much like saying that a city is north of another because of the locations they have; and it seems to me misleading and irrelevant. It obscures the fact that cities in quite other places are such that one is north of the other; and it appears to deny that we can define the predicate "is north of" in an appropriate and useful way without reference to the location of any particular city. Mr. Thomson seems to be objecting to all definition of general terms rather than pointing to any special difficulty about synonymy. Nor can I accept Mr. Thomson's argument that if I am willing to use "centaur-picture" without being able to define it precisely, I should be equally willing to use "Platonic Idea of a centaur". One difference is that

---

8. Mr. Wienpahl, I take it, in "More about the Denial of Sameness of Meaning"—*Analysis*, Vol. 12 (1951), pp. 19–23—is making this same general point that clarification as well as conformity is required of a definition.

9. "A Note on Likeness of Meaning", *Analysis*, Vol. 11 (1950), pp. 18–19.

10. "Some Remarks on Synonymy", *Analysis*, Vol. 12 (1952), pp. 73–76.

I do know some things to which the term "centaur-picture" clearly applies and I don't know anything to which the term "Platonic Idea of a centaur" applies. I should be glad to have a full explication of "picture" in order to settle borderline cases; but I need an explication of "Platonic Idea" before I can apply it all.

Many questions have been raised about what constitutes a description.[11] No complete definition is needed. If the animal before us is clearly a polar bear, the question whether there are polar bears on our island is settled even though we neither know how to define "polar bear" nor are sure whether it applies to certain other animals. To show that two secondary extensions differ we need only a case in point. Now if we remember that we can perfectly well describe what is not actual or even possible, then "isosceles triangle", "triangle with angles totalling 110 degrees", and "triangle that is not a trilateral" are all triangle-descriptions according to ordinary usage. In other cases, like that of "triangle that is not a triangle", direct appeal to ordinary usage may yield no firm decision. Then we must formulate rules that fit ordinary usage where it is clear and that can be projected to decide these doubtful cases. There is no one correct way of doing this, but a reasonable rule covering the present question runs as follows: Any phrase of the form "— that is . . ." is both a — description and a . . . description; and a not-a-soandso-description is not a soandso-description unless required to be by the first clause of this rule. Thus "triangle that is not a triangle" is both a triangle-description and a not-a-triangle-description, while "trilateral that is not a triangle" is a trilateral-description and is not a triangle-description. As explained above, we may avoid all these complications about descriptions by choosing certain other compounds as our examples.

Mr. Clarke argues[12] that a compound such as "triangle-descrip-

11. For example, by Mr. Church in the *Journal of Symbolic Logic,* Vol. 15 (1950), pp. 150–151. The various suggestions that Mr. Smullyan despatches so easily in "ϕ-Symbols"—*Analysis,* Vol. 11 (1951), pp. 69–72—are too far afield to have called for consideration in the first place. As my example of centaur-pictures and unicorn-pictures was designed to show, we cannot define "P-picture" or "P-description" solely in terms of what "P" applies to.

12. "Reflections on Likeness of Meaning", *Philosophical Studies,* Vol. 3 (1952), pp. 9–13.

tion" ought to be ruled out on the ground that it implicitly mentions the word "triangle" in much the same way that "John is so-called . . ." implicitly mentions the word "John". A phrase implicitly mentions a term, in his view, if the expansion of the phrase explicitly mentions it. He would, of course, regard my example of "literal English triangle-word" as even more obviously open to this criticism. Turning Mr. Clarke's own argument against him, one might well contend that the expansion of "the expansion of" explicitly refers to synonymy and that his argument thus begs the whole question. But unlike Mr. Clarke, I am unwilling to rest my argument on the notion of *the expansion of* a phrase. Let us grant —overlooking the point about implicit reference to synonymy— that any given phrase can, so to speak, 'be rewritten' in various longer ways. Still, in the absence of any formal systematization, any of these longer phrases qualifies as well as any other as *an* expansion of the phrase in question. Now does Mr. Clarke exclude compounds having some expansion that mentions the term in question? Then he excludes all compounds; for even "white boat" can be rewritten "white thing to which 'boat' applies". Or does he exclude, rather, compounds of which every expansion applies to expressions containing the term in question? Then, since an expansion must obviously apply to just what the original compound applies to, he could have dispensed with all talk of expansions and simply ruled out compounds that apply to such expressions. Even so, the exclusion is ineffectual; for if it bars "triangle-description" and "literal English triangle-word", it does not bar "non-English triangle-description" or "literal German triangle-word", which serve the same purpose. Stronger prohibitions that readily suggest themselves likewise prove to be inadequate.

3

The reader may still feel that the compounds cited in deriving the conclusion that every two terms differ in meaning are somehow exceptional and trivial, and that a feasible way of ruling them out must eventually be found. This feeling I can understand; when a single form of compound has a different extension for every term, the fact that it has different extensions for two given terms is of no striking or special interest. Let us, then, simply exclude every compound for which the corresponding compounds of every two terms have differing extensions. We do not, indeed, thereby insure ourselves against the result that no two terms are synonymous, since for each two terms we may well be able to find corresponding compounds having different extensions. But we honor the feeling or principle that the interesting differences between two terms are just those that are not shared by every two terms. The net change effected is not great, amounting merely to this: instead of saying that every two terms differ in meaning but that some may not differ in interesting ways, we say that two terms differ in meaning only if they differ in certain interesting or peculiar ways. While it may be true that every two terms differ in meaning in some interesting way, this way of putting the matter may nevertheless alleviate some discomfort.

4

On a Pseudo-Test of Translation

When the question arises whether two given sentences are translations of one another, we often find a negative answer defended by the argument that we might know the truth of one without knowing the truth of the other.* If this argument is taken literally, then no sentence can translate another in a different language. Indeed, any two different sentences, even in the same language, are such that we might know the truth of one without knowing the truth of the other.

Perhaps, then, the principle is that two sentences *that we understand* differ in meaning if we might know the truth of one without knowing the truth of the other. But then it becomes utterly pointless. The earlier version suggests that if we are not sure whether two sentences differ in meaning, we can find out by asking whether we might know the truth of either without knowing the truth of the other. Now we discover that this test applies only to sentences we understand. And to understand merely to the extent of being able to use a sentence properly in some contexts is not enough; for plainly we might understand each of two synonymous sentences in this way and yet know the truth of one without knowing the truth of the other. But if we understand two sentences fully, if we 'know the meaning' of each, then we already know, without any further test, whether they have the same meaning.

Talk about meaning is usually obscure. The clarification ostensibly achieved by the supposed test in terms of possible knowledge of truth-values is wholly illusory.

* A recent example occurs in a book review by Professor Roderick Chisholm in the *Philosophical Review,* Vol. 61 (1952), p. 247. One revision in the present note was occasioned by a comment by W. V. Quine.

Supplementary Readings for Chapter V
secondary to references within text and footnotes

Montague, R., "Pragmatics" in *Contemporary Philosophy, a Survey* (R. Klibansky, ed.), Florence, Italy: La Nuova Italia Editrice, 1968, pp. 101–122.

Quine, W. V., "Identity, Ostension, and Hypostasis", *Journal of Philosophy*, Vol. 67 (1950), pp. 621–633; reprinted in *from a logical point of view*, Cambridge, Mass.: Harvard University Press, 1964, pp. 65–79.

———., *Word and Object*, Cambridge, Mass.: M.I.T. Press, and New York: John Wiley and Sons, 1960, Secs. 21, 36, 40, 42.

Smart, J. C. C., ed., *Space and Time*, New York: Macmillan, 1964.

VI

Relevance

FOREWORD

The encounter in philosophy between the demands of intuition and those of logic is nowhere better illustrated than in the task of answering the general question what a statement is about. Yet only quite recently has the question been seriously examined; and in the vast literature on meaning, hardly a dozen items deal specifically with this aspect of the problem. The question here is not what a statement says about something but rather what it says something about. And the question is not what a statement mentions; for a statement may say something about things it does not mention and may mention things it says nothing about.

Hilary Putnam's article[1] attacked the question by developing a measure of the amount of information a statement S gives about k. The whole approach is quite different from mine, and there are diametric differences on particular matters; for example, for me but not for him, "All ravens are black" is about black things as well as about ravens. However, he tells me that he believes he can show that if a statement S gives, by his measure, more than zero information about k, then S is absolutely about k by my criterion.

J. S. Ullian[2] tried to solve the surprisingly stubborn problem of proving that the negate of any sentence absolutely about k is also absolutely about k; but a full proof had to await the joint article by Putnam and Ullian.[3] In the course of that paper they

1. "Formalization of the Concept 'About'", *Philosophy of Science,* Vol. 25 (1958), pp. 125–130.

2. "Corollaries to Goodman's Explication of 'About'", *Mind,* Vol. 71 (1962), p. 545.

3. "More About 'About'", *Journal of Philosophy,* Vol. 62 (1965), pp. 305–310.

make an intensive and interesting study of details of my criterion of absolute aboutness.

Thomas Patton's criticisms[4] seem to me quite mistaken. On my view, "All ravens are black" is about non-ravens since from (1) "$(x)(Rx \supset Bx)$", the statement (2) "$(x)(\sim Bx \supset \sim Rx)$" follows differentially with respect to non-ravens. Patton argues in effect that this depends upon replacing "$\sim R$" by a universally quantified variable in making the test; and this treatment of an expression containing a logical constant he finds objectionable. What he quite overlooks is that a statement T follows from S differentially with respect to k if and only if T, but not the universal generalization of T with respect to *any part of* the expression designating k in T, follows logically from S. Thus, if we allow universal generalization with respect to non-logical constants only, the fact that (2) but not "$(Q)(x)(\sim Bx \supset \sim Qx)$" follows from (1) means that (2) follows from (1) differentially with respect to non-ravens, and hence that (1) is about non-ravens. On the other hand, (1) is not about the class of non-ravens or cows even though (3) "$(x)(\sim Bx \supset \sim Rx \vee Cx)$" follows logically from (1); for since "$(Q)(x)(\sim Bx \supset \sim Rx \vee Qx)$" also follows logically from (1), (3) does not follow from (1) differentially with respect to the class of non-ravens or cows.

Concerning my inclusion of the phrase "any part of" in the definition of differential consequence and hence of absolute aboutness, Patton contends (page 324) that I offer "... no argument whatever for this *ad hoc* addition" and that it "... has no rationale—in particular, it bears no detectable relation to the former core of Goodman's analysis, his 'requirement of selectivity' ". Actually, satisfaction of that requirement is the clear rationale for including the phrase in question, since I have shown that the definition of absolute aboutness without that phrase yields just the consequence the requirement of selectivity prohibits: that every statement about anything is about everything.

Others have suggested replacing the somewhat complicated definition of absolute aboutness by some such simpler formula as that S is absolutely about k if and only if some expression men-

4. "Some Comments on 'About' ", *Journal of Philosophy*, Vol. 62 (1965), pp. 311–325.

tioning k can be made up solely of extralogical expressions in S and logical expressions. This will not work. Consider, for example, the statement, "John is a parent of George." Both my definition and the proposed alternative have the quite proper result that this statement is absolutely about (among other things) John, George, the relation of parent of, the parents of George, and those of whom John is a parent. That the proposed alternative is not nearly restrictive enough, however, is illustrated by the fact that, unlike my definition, it has the quite improper result that the statement is also absolutely about the parents of John.

In defining absolute and relative aboutness, the concepts of differential consequence and unitary consequence had to be devised in order to filter out noise—that is, to neutralize the interference caused by terms occurring extraneously in statements and by irrelevant consequences drawn from merely lumping statements together. Interference of this sort is common enough in philosophical analysis to sustain my conjecture that these or similar devices may prove helpful in dealing with other problems.

On the other hand, all through "About" are questions calling for further study. For example, the complex and limited definition of relative aboutness needs to be simplified and made more general; and theorems are wanted concerning the relationship between cases where the conjunction of two statements not absolutely about k is about k and the cases where two statements not absolutely about k are about k relative to each other. A question of a different sort is what bearing the definitions proposed in "About" have upon the design of systems for information storage and retrieval. Since a promised paper on this subject was never written, the following remarks will have to serve in its place.

Whether or not a statement is about, say, Maine does not depend upon mere presence or absence of the word "Maine". We need, first, a dictionary that groups terms together according to what they designate. Such a dictionary can be complete only for a limited corpus of material. Yet whether or not a statement is about Maine does not depend even upon presence or absence of a term designating Maine, but upon whether the statement yields any statement differentially with respect to Maine—often a much harder matter to determine.

Furthermore, decisions must be made about the size of the passages or units to be stored. A book may be about Maine through containing a chapter discussing Maine; but filing (reference to) the book would not locate precisely enough the information we want. On the other hand, filing separately every sentence in the chapter would make for needless and unmanageable multiplicity. What is more serious, by dealing with units of the wrong size, we may lose relevant information or retain bogus information. If we work statement by statement we may for example reject two statements that are not about k and thereby eliminate their conjunction, which may be about k. Or we may accept a statement as about k even though the next statement contradicts it, or universally generalizes it with respect to k, so that no information about k is forthcoming. On the other hand, if we deal with longer passages, we may reject—because of a contradiction somewhere in it—an entire passage that also contains worthwhile information about it. Thus we need some such rules as the following:

Starting from a whole text T or largest feasible parts of it,

1) remove every minimal contradiction; i.e., every self-contradictory passage that contains no shorter self-contradictory passage.

2) remove every statement about the topic k in question such that the universal generalization of this statement with respect to k follows from T. Then, taking from T a passage P provisionally deemed of appropriate size for filing,

3) if it is about k, so file it; but

4) if it is not about k, find if possible in T an additional passage P' such that P' is not about k, and the conjunction of P with any proper part of P' is not about k, while the conjunction $P \cdot P'$ is about k; and so file $P \cdot P'$.

Admittedly, these rules for avoiding trouble are no handy recipes.

So far, I have been considering only statements that are absolutely about a topic k; but often we ask our files for information that is only relatively about k. For example, many statements about New England may be pertinent to a study of Maine. Yet we cannot file together all statements that are relatively about k; for almost any statement about anything is about k relative to some other statement. And to make a selection requires predicting what information relative to k we shall want on future occasions. In practice, with only statements absolutely about k filed as about k, we find our way through our files by proceeding, according to our interests, from statements that are absolutely about k and also about other topics to statements absolutely about these other topics. But the more complete our file of statements absolutely about k, the less we need thus go beyond them. For statements are about k relative to each other only by virtue of yielding a consequence of a certain kind that is absolutely about k; and the information they provide about k is comprised in such consequences.

The file for a term like "Pickwick" will consist of papers neither absolutely nor relatively but, rather, rhetorically about Pickwick. And for special purposes, statements that bear to a topic the second power or higher powers of the relation of absolute aboutness may need to be filed.

1

About

1. Introduction

The philosopher of science or of history, when he speaks of all statements about a given event or object, is sometimes uneasily aware that he would have a hard time specifying just what statements this covers, and an even harder time giving any general rule for deciding whether a given statement is or is not about a given thing. The plausible formulae that come most readily to mind yield anomalous consequences almost as readily.

Although the philosopher repeatedly encounters this problem while on other business, he has only sporadically focused attention on it. Such discussions as those of Ryle, Carnap, and Putnam[1] leave us still, I think, without any adequate formulation of the elementary logic of the ubiquitous word "about". The present paper is an effort toward such a formulation. The aim is not to describe in detail the everyday use of "about", but rather to define one or more technical counterparts that will be serviceable in precise discourse. Some sharp divergence from our ordinary notions concerning "about" is inevitable, since these notions are readily shown to be inconsistent. Nevertheless, the acceptability of any definitions proposed, and of the way they resolve conflicts and ambiguities, will depend not only on their consistency and simplicity, but also upon how successfully they elicit and embody the most important features of the ordinary use of "about". The law must derive its authority from the people even though it must treat some of them harshly.

1. G. Ryle, " 'About' ", *Analysis,* Vol. 1 (1933), pp. 10–11; and "Imaginary Objects", *Proceedings of the Aristotelian Society,* supplementary, Vol. 12 (1933), pp. 18–43. R. Carnap, *The Logical Syntax of Language* (London: Routledge and Kegan Paul Ltd., 1937), pp. 284–292. H. Putnam, "Formalization of the Concept 'About' ", *Philosophy of Science,* Vol. 25 (1958), pp. 125–130. Putnam here takes a different approach from mine, his basic concepts being those of a *state-description* and of *amount of information.* Where he touches on the same problems I consider here, his conclusions are in general also quite different from mine.

The task to be undertaken here is not that of determining what expressions are names, or what (if anything) an expression names, or what the ontological commitment of a statement is. How our problem is distinguished from and related to questions like these will become clearer as we proceed.

2. A Dilemma

The statement
> Maine has many lakes

is obviously about Maine. Since Aroostook County is in Maine, the statement
> Aroostook County grows potatoes

seems also to be about Maine. So also, since Maine is in New England, do the two statements
> New England is north of Pennsylvania
> New England States are small.

Apparently we speak about Maine whenever we speak about anything contained in (whether as part, member, member of member, etc.), Maine, and whenever we speak about anything that contains Maine. But to accept this principle is to overlook an obvious Hempel syndrome[2] and to be saddled with the conclusion that any statement about anything is a statement about Maine. Consider the statement
> Florida is Democratic.

According to the principle stated, this is about the United States and therefore about Maine. The statement
> Satellites are planets,

since it is about the universe and thus about whatever is in the universe, would also be about Maine.

Just where did we go wrong? Perhaps we generalized too fast; perhaps only some, not all, statements about what contains or is contained in Maine are about Maine. For example,
> New England borders on New York

does not say that Maine borders on New York; nor does
> Portland is without lakes

---

2. The paradox arising here is analogous to that pointed out by C. G. Hempel in a quite different connection. See his "Studies in the Logic of Confirmation", *Mind*, Vol. 54 (1945), pp. 102–104.

say that Maine is without lakes. Yet to say of the biggest city in Maine that it has no lakes, or to say of the section of the United States containing Maine that it borders on New York, is pretty clearly to say something about Maine.

Our dilemma is rather deep-seated. Given any statement, we can argue plausibly that it is about Maine. On the other hand, to admit that every statement is about Maine is to make utterly pointless any assertion that a given statement is or is not about anything in particular.

The way out, I think, is to distinguish between two cases: the one, of a statement that is independently or *absolutely* about a given thing; the other, of a statement that is, *relative to* certain other statements, about a given thing. Let us begin, then, by trying to formulate accurately enough what it is for a statement to be absolutely about an object.

3. Absolutely About

Certain words or combinations of words in a sentence designate. Just which expressions are taken as designating, and what they are taken as designating depends upon how the sentence is construed and upon what view is held concerning predicates. For example, in

Maine is smaller than Texas

the first and last words may be taken as designating States, the middle three as designating a dyadic relation, the first four as designating a class, and the last four as designating another class. All but two of these are excluded, however, if we insist upon treating the last four words as an indissoluble one-place predicate of which no component word designates. And others are excluded or supplanted if we regard predicates as not designating anything or as designating attributes rather than classes. But it is no part of our task here to decide such questions, either in a particular case or in general. Our sole problem (and it will prove troublesome enough) is to determine what a sentence is about, *given* what its terms designate. Purely for purposes of illustration in most of what follows, any normal analysis of a sentence into predicates and arguments will be considered admissible, and a predicate will be considered to designate its extension: the class of those elements it applies to or denotes.[3]

A sentence may be said to mention whatever any expression in it designates. Thus

> Maine prospers
> Utah is west of the Pine Tree State
> The Atlantic State farthest from Florida
> is agricultural

all mention Maine, by name or description. The first also mentions the class of things that prosper; the second mentions Utah, the class of things west of Maine, the class of things of which Utah is west, and the relation (class of pairs) designated by "is west of"; and the third sentence mentions another State and several other classes and relations.

That a statement mentions a class does not by any means imply that it mentions every, or even any particular, member of that class. For example, a sentence mentions what a predicate in it designates (the whole extension of the predicate) but not necessarily what that predicate denotes (the several things the predicate applies to). Mention of the New England States does not constitute mention of Maine. Nor, conversely, does mention of Maine constitute mention of the New England States. Furthermore, a sentence mentions only what an expression in it is used to designate in that sentence, not what that expression may elsewhere or normally designate; for instance,

> "Maine" has five letters

mentions a word but not a State.

As a first attempt to explain absolute aboutness in terms of mention, we might say that a statement S is absolutely about Maine if some statement T that mentions Maine follows logically from S. But this will need a good deal of amendment. The statement

---

3. But in 8 below, I shall discuss the modifications called for in the treatment of "about" if we countenance nothing but individuals. This nominalistic position, which I favor, is explained and defended in my paper "A World of Individuals" [IV,1 above]. In the usage of "designate" and "denote" above, I follow Quine's in "Designation and Existence", *Journal of Philosophy*, Vol. 36 (1939), pp. 701–709. Like him, I also here identify the unit-class of an individual with its member, so that a predicate having such a unit-class as its extension designates what it denotes.

(1) It either is or is not the case that Maine prospers

mentions Maine without saying anything about it. Moreover, since (1) follows logically from any statement whatever, even from

(2) Florida is Democratic,

every statement would qualify by this criterion as being absolutely about Maine.

The remedy that immediately suggests itself is to require that the T in question must not follow from logic alone, must not be logically true. But this will not suffice; for from (2) follows the conjunction of (1) and (2), which mentions Maine and is not logically true. Thus (2)—or any other sentence that is not logically true—will still qualify as absolutely about Maine.

To exclude as a permissible T every statement that contains a logically true clause, or a 'non-essential' occurrence of an expression designating Maine, will accomplish very little. For this requirement and all others so far imposed will be met by another consequence of (2), namely

(3) Maine or Florida is Democratic.

Clearly some such statement mentioning Maine follows from any S that is not logically true; and every statement that is not logically true will thus satisfy all the stated conditions for being absolutely about Maine.

Why, now, even though (3)—unlike (1), and unlike the conjunction of (1) and (2)—is surely about Maine, are we unwilling to accept the fact that (3) follows from (2) as showing that (2) is genuinely about Maine? Notice that we can put for "Maine" in (3) a name or description of anything (or even a universally quantified variable) and still have a statement that follows from (2). In other words, whatever (2) says about Maine it says about everything else as well. Now we must seriously raise the question whether a statement can properly be regarded as saying about any particular thing what it says about everything else. Or is a statement genuinely about Maine only if it says something about Maine that it does not say about something else?

Offhand, the answer might seem to be dictated by an elementary principle of logic. From "Every x is P" we can infer "m is P" by the rule of instantiation upon universal statements. What

holds for everything holds for each particular thing. Surely, it
follows that if a statement S is about every x, then S is about
Maine. But this does not quite settle the matter; for "about" behaves somewhat as "choose" does. If I ask Johnny to choose
some presents and he replies "I choose everything", he has not
chosen anything. Choosing something involves not choosing
something else. That Johnny chooses every x is always false.
Likewise, saying so and so about an object involves not saying
so and so about some other. Nothing said about every object
is said about Maine. Yet no violation of the rule of instantiation
occurs here. What holds for every x holds indeed for m; but never
does it hold for every x that Johnny chooses x, or that a statement says so and so about x.

However, although nothing can be said about every x, much
can be said about the class of all things. Such a statement as
           The universal class is infinite
says something about the universal class that it does not say
about all other classes; thus it is selectively and hence genuinely
about the universal class. But a statement about a class, whether
the universal class or some other, is not thereby about any member of that class. Many questions remain, of course, concerning
just what statements are about 'everything' in the sense of being
about the universal class, and these I shall come to presently. At
the moment we need only note that what a statement says about
everything (about the universal class, V) it does not say about
any particlular object m; that what a statement says about a particular object m, it does not say about everything (V); and that
nothing can be said about every object, or about every class of
objects, or about every class of classes of objects, etc.

In sum, the trouble with our definition of absolute aboutness
lies in the absence of any requirement of selectivity. That S
yield logically a statement mentioning Maine is not a sufficient
condition for S to be absolutely about Maine; S must, roughly
speaking, yield such a statement without yielding a parallel statement for everything else. To be able to put this more precisely,
we shall need to make use of the notion of the generalization of a
statement with respect to a given expression. Such a generalization of a sentence Q with respect to an expression E is arrived at

by putting an appropriate variable for E everywhere in Q and prefixing to the result a universal quantifier governing that variable. Now a statement S is absolutely about Maine only if S yields logically some statement T in which some expression designates Maine, without so yielding the generalization of T with respect to that expression.

In the cases considered above, although (3) follows from (2), the generalization of (3) with respect to "Maine"—*viz.* "(x) (x or Florida is Democratic)"—also follows from (2). Hence the fact that (3) follows from (2) cannot now be adduced to show that (2) is absolutely about Maine. Again, although (1) and the conjunction of (1) and (2) follow from (2), so also does the generalization of each of these with respect to "Maine"; thus we need no further provision to discount a T that is logically true or that contains only non-essential occurrences of an expression designating Maine.

Nevertheless, our formula still needs strengthening in one way. From the statement

(4) Aroostook County grows potatoes

follows the statement

(5) Everything that is a State and contains Aroostook County contains a county that grows potatoes.

Our present formula rightly precludes taking (5) as evidence that (4) is about the class of States, for the generalization of (5) with respect to "State"—namely,

(6) (α) (Everything that is an α and contains Aroostook County contains a county that grows potatoes)

—also follows from (4). However, (5) also has in it the expression "State and contains Aroostook County"; and the generalization of (5) with respect to this—namely,

(7) (α) Everything that is an α contains a county that grows potatoes)

—certainly does not follow from (4). Hence (5) may still be cited as showing that (4) is absolutely about whatever is a State and contains Aroostook County—that is, about Maine. Furthermore, by use of this same device, we could show that (4) is about anything that contains or is contained in Aroostook County. We must rule out statements like (5) as evidence that statements like (4) are about Maine (or about other things containing or contained in Aroostook County) on the ground that the generalization of (5) with respect to a part of the expression designating Maine in (5) also follows from (4).

Let us say that a statement T follows from S differentially with respect to k if T contains an expression designating k and follows logically from S, while no generalization of T with respect to any part of that expression also follows logically from S. Then our final definition of absolute aboutness runs: S *is absolutely about* k if and only if some statement T follows from S differentially with respect to k.

Furthermore, the consequences that a statement yields differentially with respect to k embody what that statement *says about* k. What S says about k and what Q says about j are the same if and only if the consequences that S yields differentially with respect to k and the consequences that Q yields differentially with respect to j are the same except for the expressions in them designating k and j. What S and Q say about k is the same if the consequences they yield differentially with respect to k are the same except (at most) for the expressions in them designating k.

By our definition of absolute aboutness, the statement

        (8) Crows are black

is about black things as well as about crows;[4] and this seems to me quite as it should be. Ryle and Putnam treat (8) as about crows but not about black things; and no doubt it is often thought of as 'telling us something about' the one but not the other. But whether we consider it on a given occasion as telling us about crows or black things may depend upon whether the statement occurs as an answer to a question like "What is the color of crows?" or to a question like "What are some black things?" By our definition above, absolute aboutness is purposely made independent of such shifting psychological emphasis and of the grammatical position of the designating expressions in a sentence.

Since absolute aboutness has been defined in terms of certain logical consequences, what a statement is absolutely about will

---

4. That is, about the class of black things and the class of crows. I shall usually omit "class of", as understood, between "about" and a plural noun.

depend in part upon what logic is presupposed; and this is to some extent aribtrary. No satisfactory criterion for distinguishing just what is logic from what is not has been discovered. Rather, logic is specified by listing the signs and principles that are to be called logical; and the lists given by different logicians are not all the same. A major point of difference concerns the theory of membership. I here regard logic as including the usual theory of statements and all of quantification theory (with identity), but as stopping short of the full theory of classes. Thus although logical constants are here treated as non-designatory, the signs "V" and "Λ", for example, are treated as non-logical terms designating the universal and the null class. However a different specification of logic may perfectly well be used in conjunction with the above definition of absolute aboutness.

Even with the boundaries of logic explicitly drawn, what a statement in ordinary language is absolutely about can be determined only after its interpretation has been settled with regard both to its logical form and to the particular designation of its terms. The remarks on this point earlier in this section will bear some further illustration. The statement

> Men are earthbound,

if construed as of the form "$(x) (Mx \supset Ex)$", is about men and earthbound things; but if construed as of the form "$(x) (Mx \supset Bxe)$", is about the earth, men, and the relation of being bound. We are safe in saying that

> (9) Paris is growing

is absolutely about Paris; but we cannot tell whether it is about the capital of France or about a certain town in Maine unless we know which place is named by the particular "Paris"-inscription[5] occurring in (9). That is, baldly: what ambiguous statements are about is ambiguous. But while (9) would rarely be used unless the context resolved the ambiguity, many statements in ordinary discourse remain ambiguous in a way that gives little practical difficulty. In

> Maine prospers

---

5. Concerning the difference in reference and truth-value that may obtain among the several utterances of a statement, see VI,1 above.

the word "Maine" may normally be taken equally well as naming
an individual, or any one of a number of classes (*e.g.* a certain
class of counties), or any one of a number of classes of classes, etc.
Seldom does the context remove the ambiguity completely, and
we may usually decide at our convenience which of several alternatives the sentence mentions and is about. A similar case is that
of statements like

Everything is material,

where we are normally free to regard "everything" equally well
as naming the universal class or as playing the role of a universally
quantified variable. But none of this raises any difficulty for our
definition of absolute aboutness.

All this discussion of what a sentence mentions should not obscure the fact that mention of k by S is neither a necessary nor a
sufficient condition for S to be absolutely about k.[6] That mention
is not a necessary condition is most easily illustrated by pointing
out that a statement like

Cows are animals

is absolutely about non-cows,[7] since this statement yields differentially with respect to non-cows the consequence

Non-animals are non-cows.

That mention is not a sufficient condition is evident from such
logical truths as (1), and from such contradictions as the denial
of (1), which mention but are not absolutely about Maine; and
also from such a statement as

Maine and everything else prospers,

which mentions Maine and is neither logically true nor contradictory and yet, since it yields no consequence differentially with
respect to Maine, is not absolutely about Maine.

Merely by putting for one expression a suitably chosen expression with the same designation, we can transform any statement

---

6. *Contra* Carnap, who (in the passage cited in footnote 1) regards mention of Babylon by S as both a necessary and a sufficient condition for S
to be about Babylon. Carnap's definition does not meet the requirement
that logically equivalent statements are about the same things. My definition
is designed to meet this requirement without yielding the anomalous result
that every statement about anything is about everything.

7. See 4 below for further discussion of this result and its acceptability.

that is absolutely about Maine into another that says the same thing about Maine and yet is also about, say, Florida. For example, although both the statement

(10) Maine prospers

and the statement

(11) The Atlantic State farthest from Florida prospers

are absolutely about Maine, and although what they say about Maine is the same, (11) is also absolutely about Florida. However, (11) does not follow logically from (10); the additional premiss

Maine is the Atlantic State farthest from Florida

would be needed. Accordingly, (11) cannot be cited to show that (10) is absolutely about Florida; and no paradox arises. Furthermore, absolute aboutness as defined above is *purely extensional:* if S is absolutely about k, and k is identical with j, then S is absolutely about j. The question of intensional contexts of "about" will have to be dealt with later, in 7, but much else needs to be done first.

4. Some Consequences

A self-contradictory or a logically true statement is not absolutely about anything. No statement follows from it differentially with respect to k; for a self-contradictory statement yields all statements as consequences, while for every consequence a logically true statement yields, it also yields a generalization of that consequence with respect to an expression designating k. Furthermore, the conjunction of any statement with a self-contradictory one is not absolutely about anything. But the conjunction of a statement S with a logically true statement is absolutely about just what S alone is absolutely about. Since a compound of two statements, neither of them self-contradictory or logically true, may be self-contradictory or logically true, the compound may not be absolutely about k even though one or each of the component statements is.

Even if a conjunction of statements is not self-contradictory or logicaly true, and one or each is absolutely about k, still the conjunction may not be absolutely about k. Consider the statements:

(12) Maine is material

(13) Everything is material

(14) Everything but Maine is material.

Although (12) and (14) are absolutely about Maine, their conjunction is not; nor is the conjunction of either with (13)—nor,
for that matter, is the conjunction of all three. Thus from the fact
that a conjunction is not absolutely about k, we cannot conclude
that its conjuncts are not.

Conversely, from the fact that a conjunction *is* absolutely about
k we cannot conclude that any conjunct of it is. For example, the
conjunction of the two statements

(15) Northern states are cool

(16) Atlantic states are cool,

yields the statement

States that are either northern or Atantic are cool

differentially with respect to the class of states that are either
northern or Atlantic. The conjunction of (15) and (16) is therefore absolutely about this larger class. Thus a conjunction of
statements that are not absolutely about k may itself be absolutely
about k.

An atomic as well as a molecular statement absolutely about k
may of course follow from, and yield, statements that are not
absolutely about k. For example, neither of the statements

Something is material

Everything is material

is absolutely about Maine, though they respectively follow from
and yield (12). But if a statement T follows from S differentially
with respect to k, then T (as well as S) is absolutely about k; and,
moreover, T then follows from itself differentially with respect to
k. Every statement that follows from a statement differentially
with respect to k, mentions k, but the converse does not hold.
Accordingly, every statement absolutely about k has a consequence T such that T follows from T differentially with respect
to (and hence mentions) k.

We have seen that no statement is absolutely about every x but
that a statement like

(17) Everything ages

257

may be construed as saying that the universal class is identical with the class of things that age, and therefore as being absolutely about the universal class. Again, from the statement

All minnows are fish

the statement

Everything is either a fish or not a minnow,

which may be construed as saying that the universal class is identical with the class of things that are either fish or non-minnows, follows differentially with respect to the universal class. Obviously, singular and existential statements can be shown in similar fashion to be about the universal class. Indeed, every statement that is absolutely about any object or class of objects is absolutely about the universal class; and furthermore, every such statement is also about the null class.

Logically equivalent statements are absolutely about exactly the same things. Hence since (10) ("Maine prospers") is equivalent to

Everything that does not prosper is not Maine,

(10) is absolutely about the class of things that are not Maine, as well as about Maine. And

(18) All crows are black,

in view of the equivalent

Everything is either a black crow or a black non-crow
or a non-black non-crow,

is absolutely about the class of non-crows, the class of non-black things, the class of black non-crows, the class of things that are either black crows or non-black non-crows, and so on. In general, a statement absolutely about any class or classes is absolutely about each Boolean function of them.[8]

That logically equivalent statements should thus be about just the same things would seem a minimal condition of adequacy that any acceptable definition of aboutness must satisfy. And

8. A further question I left open when this paper was submitted for publication has since been settled by Hilary Putnam and Joseph Ullian, who have proved that the negate of a statement absolutely about k is always also absolutely about k. See their "More About 'About'", *Journal of Philosophy*, Vol. 62 (1965), pp. 305–310.

although a statement about k will therefore also be about the class of all other things, we have already seen why this does not imply, under our definition, that the statement is about every particular thing. Yet the result that a statement absolutely about a class is absolutely about the complementary class may not seem altogether welcome. Is there no reasonable sense in which a statement may be about a given class and yet not about the complementary class? Such a sense may indeed be readily defined. A statement S may be called *immediately about* k if S follows from itself differentially with respect to k—and therefore both mentions and is absolutely about k. By this definition, statement (18) will be immediately about the class of crows but not immediately about the class of non-crows. Statement (18) does not follow from itself differentially with respect to the class of non-crows; it does not mention though it is absolutely about that class. This increased narrowness had to be achieved, however, by sacrificing the equivalence principle; logically equivalent statements are not always immediately about the same things. As a result, the usefulness of the notion of immediate aboutness is severely limited. For example, while a statement may in this sense be about a class without being about the complementary class, no statement can have consequences that are immediately about a class without having equivalent consequences that are immediately about the complementary class. On the whole, then, immediate aboutness has only occasional utility and moderate theoretical interest, and need not detain us longer here.

Obviously a statement may be absolutely about another statement as in the case of the four statements:

> John said, "Maine prospers"
> "Maine prospers" is true
> Statement S is short
> Statement S is absolutely about k.

Other examples are:

> (19) Statement S is not absolutely about k
> (20) Statement S is false.

But if S itself happens to be (19), it is false; while if S happens to be (20), it is self-contradictory and so not absolutely about anything.[9]

A statement that is absolutely about a statement that is absolutely about Maine bears to Maine the second power, or square, of the relation of absolute aboutness. The statement

"Maine prospers" is about Maine

bears to Maine both the first and second powers of the relation. Obviously, any higher power of the relations may occur. However, a statement like

"Maine and everything else is material" is doctrinaire

bears to Maine no power of absolute aboutness, but is simply a statement absolutely about a statement that is *not* absolutely about Maine.

5. Relatively About

Many statements that are not absolutely about Maine are nevertheless in some important sense about Maine. Such a statement as

(21) Aroostook County grows potatoes,

while not absolutely about Maine, is about Maine *relative to* the statement

(22) Aroostook County is in Maine.

That is, (21) yields no statement differentially with respect to Maine; but (21) and (22) together yield differentially with respect to Maine a statement that neither yields by itself:

(23) Some county in Maine grows potatoes.

Similarly (21) is about New Hampshire relative to

Aroostook County borders on New Hampshire;

and other examples of relative aboutness come readily to mind.

Tentatively, then, S is about k relative to Q if and only if there is some statement T that follows differentially with respect to k from S and Q together but not from either alone. But by this criterion, as it stands, almost any statement about anything would

---

9. Whether a statement like "John asserted that Maine prospers" is absolutely about "Maine prospers" or not will depend upon how one chooses among the various ways proposed (e.g. by Carnap, Church, Scheffler) for interpreting indirect discourse.

be about Maine relative to almost any other statement that is absolutely about Maine. For example,

(24) Ghana is tropical

would have to be counted as about Maine relative to

(25) Maine prospers,

since the conjunction of (24) and (25) follows differentially with respect to Maine from the two together but not from either alone, and so qualifies as T.

The remedy for this trouble is not simple. Merely to rule out $S \cdot Q$ as an admissible T will not suffice; for $S \equiv Q$—or, in our example,

Ghana is tropical if and only if Maine prospers

—likewise follows from S and Q together but not from either alone. The more stringent requirement called for is, I think, that T be a *unitary* consequence of $S \cdot Q$ in a sense that must now be explained. For convenience, I shall consider only statements in which no scope is governed by more than one quantifier, although completeness would demand treatment of cases of multiple quantification as well.

In the first place, a statement U is an explicitly unitary consequence of W only if U is expanded to eliminate all descriptions and class-abstracts, all statement-connectives other than conjunction and disjunction, and all negations applied to expressions containing another negation, a quantifier, a conjunction or a disjunction. Every statement has a logical equivalent satisfying this requirement. In the second place, every disjunction-sign in U must be outside the scope of every existential quantifier. Here again, every statement may readily be transformed to meet this condition, which is imposed for the sole purpose of simplifying the formulation of the third and crucial requirement. This third requirement is that every conjunction-sign in U be, with reference to W, irrevocably within the scope of an existential quantifier. Conjunction-signs are thus *captive* only if they can be neither freed from the scope of existential quantifiers nor eliminated.

Now in the present context there are four circumstances under which conjunction-signs can be so removed from the scope of existential quantifiers: (i) if any of the conjoined clauses duplicates another; for example, "$(\exists x)(Ax \cdot Bx \cdot Ax)$" can be supplanted by "$(\exists x)(Ax \cdot Bx)$"; (ii) if any of the conjoined clauses lacks the variable governed by the quantifier; for example, "$(\exists x)(Ax \cdot Bc)$" can be supplanted by "$(\exists x)(Ax) \cdot Bc$"; (iii) if any of the conjoined clauses identifies the governed variable with a constant; for example, "$(\exists x)(Ax \cdot x = c)$" can be supplanted by "$Ac$"; (iv) if merely exchanging the existential quantifier for a universal one results in a statement that still follows logically from W; for example, "$(\exists x)(Ax \cdot Bx)$" can be supplanted in the present context by "$(x)(Ax \cdot Bx)$"—although the two are of course not equivalent—provided the latter is likewise a consequence of W. If none of these four circumstances obtains, then all conjunction-signs within the scope of the existential quantifier are captive.[10]

In short, an explicitly unitary consequence of a statement is a consequence expanded in the way described and such that all its disjunction-signs are free of the scopes of its existential quantifiers and all its conjunction-signs are captive. Since any consequence can be transformed to meet the first two conditions, the third is the really effective requirement. Its motivation is clear. We want to exclude any consequence that is merely a loose composite of statements that derive separately from two others. The requirement that all conjunction-signs be captive guarantees that, so to speak, the consequence cannot be broken in two, that it does not consist of two statements lightly stuck together. A unitary consequence may now be defined as one that is logically equivalent to some explicitly unitary consequence. Thus T is a unitary consequence of $S \cdot Q$ if and only if T is logically equivalent to some explicitly unitary consequence of $S \cdot Q$.

This definition will not determine whether T is a unitary consequence of $S \cdot Q$ until the logical structure of the statements concerned is settled. As observed earlier, there is usually some

10. One might expect that a conjunction-sign could also be freed in the relevant sense if a statement that likewise follows from W is obtained by dropping the existential quantifier and replacing the variable by a constant throughout the scope. But this gives unwanted results. The pertinent difference between this and the fourth case above seems to be that introduction of a non-logical constant would be involved here but is not involved in the mere exchange of an existential for a universal quantifier.

leeway in deciding the logical structure of a statement in ordinary language. The statement

(26) Maine prospers and Ghana is tropical

might be construed not as a conjunction but as an atomic statement with a single one-piece or two-place predicate. But this will not at all affect the operation of our criterion of relative aboutness; for (26), if thus taken as atomic, will not follow logically from (24) and (25) and so will fail to meet the conditions for T here anyway. Thus (26), no matter which logical structure it is deemed to have, cannot be adduced under our present definition to support the unwelcome conclusion that (24) is about Maine relative to (25).

We have now arrived at a definiens for relative aboutness that is entirely symmetrical with respect to S and Q, and that may be put: S and Q are about k relative to each other if and only if some unitary consequence T of $S \cdot Q$ follows differentially with respect to k from $S \cdot Q$ but not from either S or Q alone.

Incidentally, while we have concentrated so far upon cases where a statement not absolutely about k is about k relative to another statement, the definition given operates equally well to determine whether a statement that *is* absolutely about k is also about k relative to another statement. For example, (25) is about Maine relative to either of the statements

What prospers grows

If Maine prospers, Maine votes Republican,

but not relative to (24) or to either of the following:

Maine has many lakes

Maine prospers and grows.

At the beginning of our study, we found ourselves in a dilemma. On the one hand, the question whether a given statement S is about a given object k seemed to be a perfectly genuine one. On the other hand, we seemed forced to the conclusion that any statement is about anything. The resolution of this dilemma is now clear. Only statements of a certain well-defined class are absolutely about k. But any statement about anything is about k relative to some statement or other. The question whether a given statement S is absolutely about a given object k is complete and unambiguous. The question whether S is relatively about k

is incomplete; rather we must ask whether S is about k relative to some other given statement Q.

6. Some Further Consequences

Suppose S and Q are about k relative to each other. Then if h is identical with k, S and Q are about h relative to each other. And if W is logically equivalent to Q, then S and W are about k relative to each other.

As already noted, relative aboutness is symmetrical with respect to S and Q. It is irreflexive, since $S \cdot S$ yields nothing that S does not. The relation is non-transitive, as will be evident from the following example: of the three statements,

> Houlton is in Aroostook County
>
> Aroostook County is in Maine
>
> Caribou is in Aroostook County,

the first and second are about Maine relative to each other, and so are the second and third; but the first and third are not.

If one or each of S and Q follows from the other, then they are not about anything relative to each other; for their conjunction will then yield no statement not yielded by at least one of them alone. Since every statement follows from a contradiction, and since a logically true statement follows from every statement, no statement is about anything relative to any contradiction or logical truth. And of course, two statements that contradict each other are not about anything relative to each other; for their conjunction is not absolutely about anything.

All relative aboutness traces back to absolute and even to immediate aboutness; for two statements are about k relative to each other only if their conjunction is absolutely about k, and in that case the conjunction yields a statement that is immediately about k. Obviously, however, from the fact that a conjunction of the two statements is absolutely about k, we cannot infer that they are about k relative to each other.

Furthermore, that two statements are about k relative to each other does not imply that either is absolutely about k. For example, neither of the following two statements:

> Northern States are cool

       Atlantic States are damp, and States that are both cool
       and damp are foggy

is absolutely about the class of States that are both Northern and
Atlantic. Yet these statements are about this class relative to each
other, since their conjunction yields differentially with respect to
this class the unitary consequence

       States that are both Northern and Alantic are foggy.

Thus from the fact that neither of two statements is absolutely
about k, we cannot infer that they are not about k relative to each
other.

Obviously two statements may, relative to each other, be about
a statement. Also there are second and higher powers of relative
as well as of absolute aboutness. And laminations of absolute and
relative aboutness intermixed occur, as in a statement that is
absolutely about a second that is, relative to a third, about a
fourth that is absolutely about k. The reader who does not want
to leave it at that may construct his own illustrations.

7. Rhetorically About

So far, we have been dealing solely with the relation between a
statement and something that it is about. All our definitions have
construed "about" as a semantic two-place predicate. No provision has been made for statements about fictions like Pegasus, Mr.
Pickwick, or centaurs. How can we say that the statement

       (27) Pickwick fell

is about Pickwick, when there is no Pickwick for it to be about?

Ryle concludes that such a statement only seems to be about
Pickwick; but the matter can hardly be left there. In the first
place, if there is no such thing as Pickwick for the statement to
be about, neither is there any such thing for the statement to
seem to be about. In the second place, to say merely that the
statement seems to be about Pickwick glosses over the distinction
between cases like this and very different ones like

       Maine and everything else is material,

which may seem to be about Maine, or like a certain utterance of

       Paris is growing

that is about a town in Maine but may seem to be about a city in

France. Some more satisfactory account must be given of the
sense in which (27) is about Pickwick and not about Pegasus,
centaurs, or Maine.

A glance at a closely analogous situation may help.[11] A picture
of Abraham Lincoln is an object that bears a certain relation to a
person. But what about a picture of Pickwick? We can compla-
cently deny that it is a picture of anything, since there is no Pickwick; but this leaves us without any account of the sense in which
the object in question is a picture of Mr. Pickwick and not a picture
of Micawber or Abraham Lincoln. What we must recognize is that
while

(28) The frontispiece is a picture of Lincoln

may be construed as applying the two-place predicate "—is a
picture of . . ." to a pair of objects (the frontispiece and Lincoln),
the statement

(29) The frontispiece is a picture of Pickwick

is rather to be construed as applying the one-place predicate
"—is a picture of Pickwick" to a single object (the frontispiece).
From (28) but not from (29) we can legitimately infer that there is
something of which the frontispiece is a picture. For (29) says
in effect that the frontispiece is a Pickwick-picture; the "Pickwick" occurs here as an inseparable part of a longer predicate and
can no more be treated as an independently designating term than
can one of its syllables or letters.

Just as the frontispiece is not a picture of anything and yet is
a picture of Pickwick—or better, is a Pickwick-picture—so (27)
is not about anything and yet is about Pickwick—or better, is
Pickwick-about. In saying

"Maine prospers" is about Maine

we are applying a semantic two-place predicate to relate a statement to an object; but in saying

"Pickwick fell" is about Pickwick

we are applying a syntactic one-place predicate to a statement.
And since we cannot validly infer that there is something that
(27) is about, we may well keep this in mind hereafter by saying
rather that (27) is Pickwick-about.

11. *Cf.* my paper "On Likeness of Meaning" [V,2 above].

If this suggests an approach, the characteristic of being Pickwick-about still has to be defined. As a first try, we might say that S is absolutely[12] Pickwick-about if and only if some statement T that contains the expression "Pickwick" follows from S while the generalization of T with respect to "Pickwick" does not. This is too loose, however; for "Pickwick" must not merely be somehow contained in T but must occur as a genuine term of T rather than in some such oblique way as in quotation marks or in "Pickwick-picture"—or, for that matter, in "Pickwick-about". Obviously we cannot stipulate that "Pickwick" designate in S; the needed restriction must be effected in some other way. Let us say that an expression E occurs as a term of S if and only if E either is a predicate in S or occupies one of the argument places of a predicate in S. Occurrence of an expression in quotation marks, or as part of a word, etc. does not constitute occurrence as a term. A statement T follows *term-differentially* from S with respect to a term E of T if and only if T, but no generalization of T with respect to any term of T that is part of E, follows logically from S.[13] Our definition of "Pickwick-about" may now run: S is Pickwick-about if and only if it yields some statement T term-differentially with respect to "Pickwick".

"Pickwick-about" is one of a large family of predicates that end in "-about"; and the definition given is a sample application of a general schema for defining any such predicate. S is ———-about if and only if some statement T follows from S term-differentially with respect to "———", where both blanks are filled in any one case by the same expression. The expression in question must occur as a term of T, but may or may not designate. Hence the schema may be used to define "Maine-about" as well as "Pickwick-

12. The distinction between absolute and relative Pickwick-aboutness parallels that between absolute and relative aboutness. But I shall often omit, as understood, the modifiers "absolute" and "absolutely".

13. Note that for T to follow from S term-differentially with respect to E, E must occur as a term of S; but for T to follow *differentially* from S with respect to k, even if k is an expression, T must rather contain a term designating k. *Occurrence as a term* and *designation* are related in the following way: if E occurs as a term of S, and if the result of putting an appropriate variable for E in S and prefixing an existential quantifier governing that variable is a statement that follows from S, then E designates in S.

about"; and even though "Maine" designates, saying that S is about Maine is not equivalent to saying that S is Maine-about. For example

> The Pine Tree State prospers

is about Maine but not Maine-about. (Incidentally,

> The usual name of the most northeasterly State has five letters

is about "Maine" but not "Maine"-about; while

> "Maine" has five letters

is about "Maine" and is "Maine"-about.)

We saw that absolute aboutness as defined earlier is extensional; *i.e.* if S is absolutely about k, and k is identical with h, and S is identical with Q, then Q is absolutely about h. Now clearly, a statement that is Maine-about may not be Pine-Tree-State-about even though Maine is identical with the Pine Tree State. But this no more shows that "Maine-about" is non-extensional than the fact that an object that is a cane may not be a tine, even though tin and can are identical, shows that "cane" is non-extensional. "Maine" is an inseparable part of the one-place predicate "Maine-about" as "can" is of the one-place predicate "cane". And just as "cane" is extensional in that if a is identical with b then a is a cane if b is, so "Maine-about" is extensional in that if S is identical with Q then S is Maine-about if Q is. The extensionality of the rhetorical "-about" predicates is gained, of course, at the price of having a multiplicity of them.

A statement that is Homer-about is absolutely about Homer only if "Homer" designates Homer; and even if "Homer" designates Homer, a statement absolutely about Homer is not necessarily Homer-about. Thus, whether or not "Homer" designates Homer, being Homer-about is not equivalent to being absolutely about Homer. The positive relationship between absolute aboutness and the "-about" predicates can be summarized in two schematic principles. If S is ——-about and "——" designates k, then S is absolutely about k. If S is absolutely about k, then for some expression "——" that designates k, S is ——-about.

The question whether or not a statement is ——-about and the question whether or not that statement is about what "——" designates assume different relative importance with different terms. Since "Pickwick" does not designate, the answer to the

question whether a statement is about Pickwick is always
negative, and thus only the first question counts. On the other
hand, once the question whether a statement is about Maine is
answered, the question whether it is Maine-about—which in
effect merely asks further concerning what words happen to be
employed—is of minor interest. However, the same cannot be
said for all terms that designate. "Unicorn" designates the (null)
class of unicorns; and the statement

Every unicorn has a horn

is about the class of unicorns, hence about the null class, hence
about the class of centaurs. But this is not very informative,
since every statement about any object or class of objects is
about the null class and hence about the class of unicorns and the
class of centaurs. What matters here is that the statement is
unicorn-about rather than null-class-about or centaur-about.
Again, if "material" designates the universal class, the statement

Everything material is tangible

is about the universal class; but so are all statements that are
about any object or class of objects, and the important point here
is that this statement is material-about. In general, the question
of absolute aboutness takes precedence in our interest over the
question of the application of the predicate "—— -about" except
where "——" designates the null class or the universal class or
does not designate at all.

Each "-about" predicate satisfies the equivalence condition: if
S and Q are logically equivalent then either is "—— -about" if
the other is. Predicates bearing to these "-about" predicates the
same relation that immediate aboutness bears to absolute aboutness may, of course, be defined; for example, S is immediately
Maine-about if and only if S follows from itself term-differentially
with respect to "Maine". However, many such predicates fail to
satisfy the equivalence condition, and their value is largely academic. But it is worthwhile to compare the following four
statements:

(30) S is absolutely about non-crows
(31) S is immediately about non-crows
(32) S is non-crows-about
(33) S is immediately non-crows-about

Statement (30) implies that S yields a statement containing (a) word(s) designating the class of non-crows; (31) implies that S itself contains (a) word(s) designating the class of non-crows; (32) implies that S yields a statement containing the word "non-crow(s)"; and (33) implies that S itself contains the word "non-crow(s)". (31) implies (30), and (33) implies (32). But only with the help of the additional premiss that "non-crows" designates the class of non-crows does (32) imply (30), and (33) imply (31) and hence (30).

I shall not take space to consider further theorems or such matters as relative rhetorical aboutness. It may be noted in passing that the practical man seldom needs to consider rhetorical aboutness. Where documents are to be filed, for example, he may simply assume that all terms of statements in these documents designate, and—wherever he can consistently—that what they designate is neither the null class nor the universal class.[14] It is the unworldly philosopher who has to deal with the grim fact of life that some terms that may seem to designate don't.

8. Nominalization

The language of platonism,[15] speaking of predicates and some other terms as names of classes, has been used freely up to this point. How would our treatment of aboutness have to be modified to meet the demands of nominalism? The nominalist can purify the definitions of "absolutely about" and "relatively about" simply by casting them in terms of utterances or inscriptions rather than expressions. But since for him there are only individuals for statements to be about, these two-place predicates will apply less often; and the rhetorical one-place "-about" predicates will play a correspondingly bigger role. However, the way of defining these "-about" predicates will have to be somewhat revised.

14. A memorandum concerning the bearing of the present paper upon problems of information retrieval is planned for The Transformations Project on Information Retrieval, at the University of Pennsylvania, sponsored by the National Science Foundation. [See FOREWORD to this chapter.]

15. Concerning the platonism and nominalism under discussion here see "A World of Individuals" (cited in note 3).

For the nominalist, there is no appropriate variable that may be put for a predicate or other ostensible class-name in a statement, and therefore no generalization of any statement with respect to any such term. Thus for no statement T that follows from S will any generalization of T with respect to any such term also follow from S. Hence if S yields a statement T in which "——" occurs as a predicate (or as filling a place of a predicate of classes), and no term of T that is part of "——" designates an individual, then S will yield T term-differentially with respect to "——". As a result, every statement whatsoever will be prosper-about, for example, since

Maine either does or does not prosper

will follow from every statement term-differentially with respect to "prosper".

The central feature of the remedy to be administered here is that rather than a generalization of T with respect to "——", we speak of statements obtained from T by putting for "——" any other expressions of the same syntactical category. Roughly, two terms are of the same syntactical category if either may replace the other without disrupting the syntactical structure of any statement. A fuller and more precise definition of the appropriate notion of being of the same syntactical category is wanted, of course, and it will have to be in terms of inscriptions or expression-occurrences rather than of expressions. This cannot be attempted here; but suggestions toward such a definition are to be found in the work of several recent writers on logic and structural linguistics.[16]

The next and final step is to revise the schema for defining the

---

16. See Tarski, *Logic, Semantics, Metamathematics* (Oxford: Clarendon Press, 1956), pp. 215 ff. and the discussions referred to in his footnote on p. 215. See also Zellig Harris, *Methods in Structural Linguistics* (Chicago: University of Chicago Press, 1951), Chaps. 15 and 16; and Noam Chomsky, "Systems of Syntactic Analysis", *Journal of Symbolic Logic*, Vol. 18 (1953), pp. 242–256. The structural linguists have undertaken the difficult task of providing a method for determining, given only samples of discourse in any language, whether two expressions in that language are of the same grammatical category. Our problem above is much simpler since we understand the language we are dealing with, know its general grammatical structure, and suppose it to consist of statements determinate in logical form.

rhetorical "-about" predicates to read: S is —— about if and only if S yields logically some statement T of which "——" is a term, while for no term E of T that is part of "——" does S yield logically every statement obtained from T by putting for E an expression of the same syntactic category. In this way, each "-about" predicate is defined nominalistically and yet so that it will apply to the same or virtually[17] the same statements as when defined according to the unrevised platonistic scheme.

9. Conclusion

In the foregoing pages, I have tried to suggest some of the difficulties and paradoxes that arise in setting forth seemingly obvious principles underlying our ordinary usage of "about", to define some consistent and serviceable and intuitively well-founded ways of using the term, and to outline some theoretical and practical consequences of these definitions. I have not discussed exclamations about, questions about, phrases about, etc.; but these should not present any grave new difficulties. The problem of thoughts about, beliefs about, feelings about, etc. is another matter.

I claim finality no more than completeness for what is offered above; the problem is too delicate, and its investigation in too early a stage. On the other hand, some of the devices employed, such as the ideas of a differential and of a unitary consequence, may prove useful in dealing with other problems.[18]

17. Depending upon the particular definition given for "same syntactic category".

18. The above text incorporates several suggestions made by Noam Chomsky, Burton Dreben, C. G. Hempel, and Israel Scheffler, who were kind enough to read the manuscript just before it went to press. I am particularly indebted to Dreben and Chomsky for comments leading to an important modification in the definition of a unitary consequence (5 above).

2

"About" Mistaken

Nicholas Rescher contends[1] that my definition[2] of "absolutely about" yields the anomalous result that the sentence "Pa" is absolutely about all individuals. His argument is entirely specious.

He begins by proposing that we adopt the postulate that there are at least two individuals in the world. Then, he says, "Pa" is by my definition absolutely about any other individual in the world, since for any such individual, say b, the statement "$(\exists x)(x \neq b \cdot Px)$" follows logically from "Pa".

Now the assumption that there are at least two individuals is not very risky or restrictive. But "follows logically from" is so used in my definition of "about" that one sentence follows logically from another only if the inference holds in every non-null universe of discourse. The fact or the assumption that the world contains two or millions of individuals does not affect this usage; and inferences depending on any assumption of more than two individuals cannot be counted as logical in determining what a sentence is absolutely about under my definition.

In the second place, Professor Rescher has concealed a premiss in the words "for any other individual". Either he must adopt some such general assumption as that no two individuals have the same name—a drastic assumption that is false for English—or he must admit "$a \neq b$" as an explicit premiss. From "Pa $\cdot$ a $\neq$ b" the statement "$(\exists x)(x \neq b \cdot Px)$" does follow logically; but this, far from showing that "Pa" will be absolutely about every individual, yields only the unobjectionable result that "Pa" is about b relative to the statement "$a \neq b$", or that "Pa $\cdot$ a $\neq$ b" is absolutely about b.

---

1. In "A Note on 'About'", *Mind*, Vol. 72 (1963), pp. 268–270.
2. In "About", *Mind*, Vol. 70 (1961), pp. 1–24.

Supplementary Reading for Chapter VI
secondary to references within text and footnotes

Patton, T., "A Reply to Rescher on Goodman's 'About' ", *Mind*, Vol. 74 (1965), pp. 592–593.

VII

Simplicity

FOREWORD

Simplicity, like "about", is a rather new topic for philosophy. With virtually no relevant literature available, no inherited respect for or even recognition of the problem, and no established guidelines, the problem itself had to be defined, its importance explained, and workable concepts and strategies developed, almost from scratch. In the course of the struggle, a number of interesting aspects of philosophical method were illustrated; for example, the search for a root principle in the criteria implicitly used in rejecting the first attempts at definition, the need for making some arbitrary, along with many grounded, decisions on the way from an intuitive notion to a technical concept, and the progressive building of a calculus by looking to the consequences of the initial axioms for cues to appropriate additional axioms. Since, however, each paper on the structural simplicity of sets of extralogical primitive predicates tends to be amended or superseded by the next, and since all my papers on the subject are superseded by the treatment in the second edition of *SA*, I have included only four of them here: two that are in effect surveys, one note that clears up a fairly common misunderstanding, and a review.

To amplify the review a little, William Craig's device for eliminating extralogical primitive predicates consists not in defining them but in providing a separate postulate for proving each theorem that amounts in effect to the expansion, under such definition, of a theorem containing them. While the number of primitive terms is thus decreased, the number of primitive propositions is increased. This might be remedied if these postulates could in turn be disposed of by the device of "Elimination of Extralogical

275

Postulates" but that device works only for finite sets of postulates, while the postulate sets to be dealt with here will normally be infinite. Thus Craig's procedure achieves simplicity and systematization of terms by sacrificing simplicity and systematization of statements.

Ramsey's device,[1] recently discussed by Bohnert[2] and by Scheffler,[3] makes possible the elimination of extralogical bases by dropping constant primitive predicates in favor of quantified predicate variables. Such reduction to zero of the complexity of extralogical bases depends upon use of a rich logic. For example, removal of a set of predicates of individuals will require quantification over variables for such predicates, and—depending on how these are related—may require quantification over variables of much higher type. Extralogical economy is thus paid for by complexity in the logical apparatus. Complexity of the latter sort is not measurable by our calculus of extralogical simplicity; but neither, contrary to what Bohnert seems to suggest, does the judgment of complexity here rest on nominalistic prejudice. By quite neutral standards, logic is the more complex, all else being equal, the higher its order.

Ramsey's proposal does have important bearing on the whole question of simplicity: (1) it reminds us that our calculus of extralogical simplicity should be applied only for comparing systems having the same logic—or only relative to a minimal logic adequate to both; (2) it raises the question how simplicity of extralogical basis and of logical apparatus are to be measured against one another. Here, I think, the fact that any finite set of primitives of a given type can be replaced by a single one of higher type suggests that raising the logical type increases complexity much more drastically than does adding extralogical primitives at lowel levels.

1. F. P. Ramsey, "Theories" in *The Foundations of Mathematics*, ed. R. B. Braithwaite (London: Routledge and Kegal Paul, 1931), pp. 212–236.

2. H. G. Bohnert, "In Defense of Ramsey's Elimination Method", *Journal of Philosophy*, Vol. 65 (1968), pp. 275–281; and "Communication by Ramsey-Sentence Clause", *Philosophy of Science*, Vol. 34 (1967), pp. 341–347.

3. *The Anatomy of Inquiry* (New York: Knopf, 1967), pp. 203–222; and "Reflections on the Ramsey Method", *Journal of Philosophy*, Vol. 65 (1968), pp. 269–274.

(3) It underlines the extravagance of unlimited logical apparatus by showing that with such apparatus available, extralogical simplicity hardly matters. With unlimited funds, who need worry about the cost of living?

While work on the simplicity of sets of primitive terms has resulted in some progress, "The Elimination of Extralogical Postulates" has up to now eliminated hope of progress toward measuring the simplicity of sets of primitive statements. Occasional attempts to dismiss the result of that paper have not, I think, touched the central point; and we are still very much where we were thirty years ago. Quine has recently[4] reaffirmed and expanded upon our conclusion and our despair.

My insistence that simplicity is of the essence of science has sometimes been misinterpreted as the claim that simplicity is the only or the always-overriding factor in the choice of basis. Obviously, considerations such as brevity, clarity, convenience, familiarity, and utility for a special purpose usually enter also, and may sometimes exact a considerable sacrifice of simplicity; but these other factors, unlike simplicity and truth, are minor aids rather than major aims. A scientific system may be cumbersome, difficult, strange; but with no simplicity we have no system and no science at all.

The remaining papers in this chapter are concerned with simplicity as an integral factor in the inductive rather than in the deductive aspects of science. Whenever we make any inference beyond the evidence, we must choose among countless alternative hypotheses; and the choice must favor simplicity. For just as every admission of an undefined term or unproved statement detracts from definitional or deductive systematization, so every admission of an exception in a hypothesis or of an irregularity in a curve tends to detract from the inductive subsumption of the particular under the general. Science proceeds by definition, demonstration, and generalization; and abhors the undefined, the unproved, and the *ad hoc*.

But just as a measure of structural simplicity must disallow the

4. "Implicit Definition Sustained", *Journal of Philosophy*, Vol. 61 (1964), pp. 71–74; reprinted in *The Ways of Paradox* (New York: Random House, 1966), pp. 195–198.

spurious gain that results from compressing a number of primitives into a single one-place predicate of higher type, so a measure of inductive simplicity must disallow the spurious gain that results from smoothing out a rough curve or hypothesis (such as "All emeralds are examined before t and green, or not so examined and blue") by use of specially contrived coordinates or terms (such as "grue"). What we must do is take into account the familiarity of the predicates along with the grammatical composition of the hypotheses. Of course, sheer familiarity cannot be taken as the measure. What we must do, as discussed further in VIII below and in *FFF*, is to develop—on the basis of familiarity in relevant contexts and other considerations—a criterion that does not exclude new terms wholesale and that allows for trading some elementary simplicity for higher-level simplicity and consequent overall simplicity of theory. Curiously enough, familiarity of another sort entered into the measurement of the structural simplicity of bases in a different way, by distinguishing between the routine replacement that does not and the non-routine replacement that may result in genuine economy.

Criteria for the simplicity of hypotheses will obviously have a direct bearing upon the distinction between significant and superficial similarity (see IX,2 below), between natural and artificial kinds, and between regular and random sequences. All these questions are part of the general scientific problem of classifying and ordering nature and making it lawful.

Long neglected, as a matter for effete and gratuitous speculation, simplicity has recently been taking on pressing importance. The response to the earlier papers was a deafening silence, and simplicity is still far from a popular topic among philosophers; but scientists and technologists are becoming acutely aware of the need to measure simplicity in the course of their own work. Publication of "The Test for Simplicity" brought inquiries from all fields of science from all over the world. "Uniformity and Simplicity" resulted from a request from geologists. Engineers and educators have asked for help. Unfortunately, while we know somewhat more about simplicity now than we did thirty years ago, we still know far too little to meet all such needs.

1

The Test of Simplicity

Simplicity is a test of the effectiveness of scientific theories; but what is the test of simplicity?

All scientific activity amounts to the invention of and the choice among systems of hypotheses. One of the primary considerations guiding this process is that of simplicity. Nothing could be much more mistaken than the traditional idea that we first seek a true system and then, for the sake of elegance alone, seek a simple one. We are inevitably concerned with simplicity as soon as we are concerned with system at all; for system is achieved just to the extent that the basic vocabulary and set of first principles used in dealing with the given subject matter are simplified. When simplicity of basis vanishes to zero—that is, when no term or principle is derived from any of the others—system also vanishes to zero. Systematization is the same thing as simplification of basis.

Furthermore, in the choice among alternative systems, truth and simplicity are not always clearly distinguishable factors. More often, simplicity is one test of truth. The martyr-bestrewn debate over what bodies in the universe are fixed has turned into the question: What choice of points of reference will give us the simplest description of their relative motions? And by now, after Duhem and Poincaré,[1] it is almost a commonplace that the refutation of a mode of scientific explanation such as the Ptolemaic or the Newtonian consists not in showing that it is inapplicable but in showing that its application would be intolerably complex.

The case can be put even more strongly. We want to select a system or hypothesis that not only agrees with the established evidence but also predicts correctly the outcome of further observations and experiments. Thus selection of a theory must always be made in advance of the determination of some of the facts it covers; and, accordingly, some criterion other than conformity with such

---

1. P. Duhem, *Système du Monde* (Paris, 1913); H. Poincaré, *Science et Methode* (Paris, 1908).

facts must be applied in making the selection. After as many points as we like have been plotted by experiment concerning the correlation of two factors (for example, of time and deterioration of radioactivity), we predict the remaining points by choosing one among all the infinitely many curves that cover the plotted points. Obviously, simplicity of some sort is a cardinal factor in making this choice (we pick the "smoothest" curve). The very validity of the choice depends upon whether the choice is properly made according to such criteria. Thus simplicity here is not a consideration applicable after truth is determined but is one of the standards of validity that are applied in the effort to discover truth.

Nature of the Problem

But if simplicity is a test of truth and systematization, what is the test of simplicity? Explication of the standards of simplicity constitutes one of the most pressing current problems in the philosophy of science. The scientist, however, may be inclined to ask why there is any *problem* here. Given two alternative systems covering the same subject matter, isn't it always pretty clear which, if either, is the simpler? How does any puzzle arise? There are two good answers.

In the first place, the difficulty and significance of formulating precise general criteria of simplicity no more depend upon trouble encountered in making particular judgments of simplicity than the difficulty and significance of codifying deductive logic depend upon trouble encountered in ordinary reasoning. The systematic logic developed by Aristotle, Boole, Whitehead and Russell,[2] and others is only incidentally a tool for drawing or correcting inferences needed in ordinary life or in the laboratory. Even the energetic investigation of inductive logic since Mill[3] aims much less at providing instructions for making predictions than at eliciting the laws of induction for their own sake. The utility that the results may have for the practicing natural scientist is as much a

2. G. Boole, *An Investigation into the Laws of Thought* (London, 1854); A. N. Whitehead and B. Russell, *Principia Mathematica* (Cambridge, England, 1910–1913).

3. J. S. Mill, *A System of Logic* (London, 1843).

by-product as the utility that the scientist's results may have for the technologist. Investigation of the canons of deduction or induction or simplicity no more derives its main interest from the help it may give to physicists or biologists than investigation of the laws relating mass and energy derives its main interest from the help it may give to munitions-makers or surgeons.

But in the second place, comparative simplicity is often not very readily and surely judged. Of course if we succeed in deriving one of a set of hypotheses or concepts from the others, the saving is obvious. But comparison of theories incorporating different hypotheses or concepts can offer great difficulty. For example, just when does introduction of the concept of a new fundamental particle simplify and when does it complicate physics? Sometimes different aspects of over-all simplicity may set up competing claims. Is a genuine simplification achieved by deriving mathematics from a few logical concepts at the cost of three big volumes of complicated formulae? We may smugly reply "yes", on the ground that what counts is the simplicity of the basic notions and postulates, and that the derivation is bound to be complicated just to the extent that the basis is simplified. But we seem to take the opposite view when we rate description of the motions of astronomical bodies in terms of ellipses as simpler than that in terms of circles; for the advocates of epicycles might argue that the more elaborate constructions and computations required by his system are the symptomatic result of the greater simplicity of his elementary concepts. If we are tempted to dismiss the idea that circles are simpler than ellipses as a mere superstition, we shall be embarrassed by the fact that, as remarked above, we employ some such notion of the relative simplicity of different curves when we choose one to fit to plotted points in order to extrapolate from determined data to untested cases. Plainly, simplicity is not a single easily estimated characteristic of systems but several different interrelated characteristics, few of them easy to estimate. Thus simplicity is a problem for the scientist as well as for the philosopher. Canons of simplicity need to be formulated not only for their intrinsic interest but also as means for making needed judgments in actual scientific investigation.

A more plausible excuse for neglecting the study of simplicity has been that the problem, far from being too easy, is hopeless.

Simplicity, the argument runs, is vague, ambiguous, variable, and subjective, and therefore too elusive for measurement. But exactly the same argument might have been urged in primitive times against the possibility of measuring temperature or size. Ordinary judgments of size vary with distance, perspective, atmosphere, color, eyesight, and even with interest. Size may mean total bulk, or it may mean maximum diameter, or it may mean height and length and breadth or any of many other quantities. And size changes with temperature, pressure, growth, and wear. The arguments against the measurability of simplicity would, indeed, have been equally strong against the measurability of almost anything. Precision, fixity of meaning, verifiability, and objectivity are the results of measurement, not preconditions of it.

What the problem of simplicity needs is a lot of hard work. So far, just a little has been accomplished; the entire bibliography of contributions to the subject hardly lists more than a dozen items,[4] most of them published during the past fifteen years. Thus the problem is not only one of the most important in the philosophy of science but also one of the newest to be tackled seriously. We are still seeking proper formulation of some aspects of the problem, still exploring avenues of approach to others. Yet this gives the whole matter added interest; for here we can observe philosophy, and therefore science, in the early, formative stages of a typical development from a nebulous cluster of difficulties into articulated questions and on towards an organized discipline.

Simplicity of Basic Terms

We must begin by staking out a very small part of the problem for concentrated attention.[5] A theory is a system of statements. I shall be concerned here solely with the simplicity of the set of

4. The articles mentioned in reference 5 together contain a fairly complete listing of relevant publications, from an article by Lindenbaum in 1935 to the present: Karl Popper's discussion in *Logik der Forschung* (Vienna, 1935) should be added to the list.

5. The treatment of simplicity to be outlined here has been developed in the course of several of my publications, from "On the Simplicity of Ideas", *Journal of Symbolic Logic*, Vol. 8 (1947), pp. 107–121, through "Recent Developments in the Theory of Simplicity" [VII,2 below]. [Further revisions were made in the second edition of *SA*, which appeared eight years after the present paper.]

concepts, or the vocabulary of terms, employed in these statements. Furthermore, since some words and symbols—like "and",
"or", "not", "if .... then", "all", "some", "$=$", or translations of
these—are logical apparatus common to all the systems in question, we need consider only the remaining, extralogical terms.
Such of these as are not defined in the system are called "primitive" and constitute the extralogical basis of the vocabulary of
the system. It is the simplicity of such extralogical bases that I
want to examine here.

Among the extralogical terms of a system may be property-
terms like ".... is acid", and relation-terms of various degrees,
like ".... is larger than ———" and ".... lies halfway between
——— and ....". The examples given are respectively a one-
place, a two-place, and a three-place predicate and may be abbreviated, in standard symbolic notation, as "$A(x)$", "$L(x,y)$", and
"$B(x,y,z)$". In general, an n-place predicate has n blanks or variables and stands for an n-adic relation.

Many of the most familiar terms occurring in scientific theories
are not predicates but rather nonassertive function-terms, like
"the father of ....", "the temperature of ....", "the distance between .... and ———". However, for every function of n arguments there is a corresponding $n+1$-adic relation; and for uniformity, let us suppose that in the extralogical bases under
consideration all function-terms have been eliminated in favor of
corresponding predicates. Thus the function-term "the father of
....", or "f_x" gives way to the predicate "——— is the father of
....", or "$F(x,y)$"; and the function-term "the distance between
.... and ———", or "$d_{x,y}$" gives way to the predicate "........... is
the distance between .... and ———", or "$D(x,y,z)$".

Some predicates, like ".... is wooden" and ".... is a more ancient fossil than ———", are predicates of things or individuals.
Others, like ".... are rare" and ".... is a subset of ———", are
predicates of classes of things. Still others are predicates of classes
of classes, numbers, and so on. Some predicates, like ".... is the
temperature of ———" and ".... is a member of ———", are
heterogeneous, relating numbers to things, or things to classes,
and so forth. To avoid having to deal at the start with differences
in simplicity arising from such differences in type, let us require
that in every case under consideration all the predicates be of

a single homogeneous type—that is, that all apply solely to things, or all apply solely to classes of things, and so on. Our results can afterwards be extended to cover cases where predicates of differing types are involved.

One more temporary assumption is that all predicates in a basis are applicable—that is, that none are like ".... is a centaur" or ".... is a square circle" in applying to nothing. Although this may seem a common-sense restriction, we may sometimes want to determine the simplicity of a predicate when we are not sure whether it applies to anything. However, the restriction can later be easily removed.

Still further specification of our immediate problem is needed. We are not concerned with the purely grammatical construction of predicates or with their length. Nor are we concerned with their relative familiarity or the ease of comprehending them. These aspects of simplicity and many others may be philosophically and scientifically significant, but our present concern is rather with that logical or structural simplicity of bases which pertains directly to the degree of systematization of theories founded upon them. Just what constitutes such structural simplicity is indeed part of our problem and will have to be made clearer as we proceed. But we may note here that predicates in different languages, or in entirely different words of the same language, or quite unlike in grammatical composition, may be equally simple in this sense, and that for two predicates to apply in exactly the same instances—that is, to have the same denotation or extension—is a sufficient though not necessary condition for their having the same degree of structural simplicity.

In summary, then, we want to find a way of measuring the structural simplicity of the set of undefined extralogical terms of a theory or system. That is, we want to be able to assign to any such set of terms a number that will indicate the complexity of that set and, accordingly, one significant aspect of the complexity of the theory. We begin by assuming that all the terms under consideration are applicable predicates belonging to some one homogeneous type. But they may have any number of places, and of course the several predicates in a given basis need not have the same number of places.

A Clue to an Answer

The first step toward measuring the size of objects must have been to fix upon a single elementary clue: the application of a yardstick of some sort directly to the object in a certain way. This at once abstracted from apparent differences resulting from variations in distance and perspective, picked out as standard certain among the innumerable dimensions of familiar objects, and provided a unit for the numerical expression of size. We seek some comparable clue to the problem of measuring the simpliicty of extralogical bases.

From the primitive predicates constituting the extralogical basis of a system, with the help of the specified logical apparatus, all other extralogical terms of the system are generated by definition. One might first think of measuring complexity by definitional yield, or defining-power, on the principle that if one set of predicates is definable from a second but the second is not definable from the first, then the second is more complex, and that interdefinable sets of predicates are equally complex. For example, we can define ".... differs by one from ———", among the natural numbers, from ".... is the immediate successor of ———" (as follows: "x differs by one from y if and only if x is the immediate successor of y, or y is the immediate successor of x") but not vice versa; hence a basis consisting solely of the former predicate would be rated simpler, according to this proposal, than a basis consisting solely of the latter predicate. Yet, plausible as this idea may be in a few such cases, it is quite mistaken as a general principle, for it would have the consequence that no simpler basis could be found for a system than that arrived at by merely taking all the extralogical terms of the system as primitive! For, since any adequate basis for a system must yield, through definition, all the terms of the system, the set of all these terms would, by the proposed criterion, be as simple as any adequate basis of fewer of these predicates. What is actually maximal complexity would be accounted maximal simplicity.

Counting the predicates in a basis seems, offhand, a better test of simplicity, but this likewise fails. For if the number of predicates in a basis were the sole measure of complexity, ultimate simplicity would always be achieved in a purely trivial way. Any number of predicates can be readily combined, so to speak, into a single predicate. A basis consisting of a one-place predicate (say, ".... is copper") and a two-place predicate (say, "——— is more durable than ....") can always be replaced by a single three-place predicate (say, ".... is copper, and ——— is more durable than ...."). And, taking all the predicates in a system, we can immediately construct a single many-place predicate from which all are definable by a routine procedure. If the total number of places in those original predicates is m, the single primitive thus arrived at will have m places. Obviously, no genuine increase in simplicity is effected in this way; many simpler predicates are replaced by a single correspondingly more complex one. The proposal to measure the complexity of bases by a mere counting of the predicates they contain fatally ignores all differences of complexity among predicates.

The idea that inevitably suggests itself next is to measure complexity by the total number of places in all the predicates in a basis. The spurious simplicity effected by artificially combining several predicates into one will thus be properly discounted. But the new proposal is again too hasty. While we have clear grounds for not regarding an m-place predicate as simpler than a set of several predicates with a total of m places, we have no such grounds for not regarding the set of predicates as simpler than the single predicate. Replacement of set by single predicate is always possible, but not replacement of single predicate by set. For example, the two one-place predicates ".... is a parent" and ".... has a parent" will not serve instead of the two-place predicate ".... is a parent of ———"; to say that x is a parent and y has a parent is not to say that x is a parent of y. The complexity of bases seems to vary not only with the number of places but also in some manner with the way this number is distributed among predicates in the basis. Several plausible formulas for this variation can easily be devised, but there is no immediately obvious method for choosing among them.

Not only have our efforts been unsuccessful so far, but trying out one rule of thumb after another begins to look like an unpromising method of attacking our problem. Yet, all the time, the clue we want has lain ready in our hands. In rejecting the mere counting of primitives as a measure of complexity, we argued that any set of predicates can always be replaced by a single predicate. We tacitly appealed to the principle that replacement of a basis by another effects no genuine simplification where such a replacement can always be made by a purely routine procedure. Other applications of the same principle come quickly to mind. Predicates can always be added to a basis without destroying its adequacy, and a predicate can always be replaced by another having more places; obviously, in neither case is simplicity increased. In other words, an elementary principle applied in judging proposed measures of complexity is this: If every basis like a given one can always be replaced by some basis like a second, then the first is not more complex than the second. This may seem too meagre and negative a principle to carry us very far, but it is the key to our problem. More carefully formulated, clarified, and supplemented, it will constitute the fundamental axiom of a calculus of simplicity.

First Axioms of Simplicity

Let us, then, adopt our first postulate:

P1. *If every basis of a relevant kind K is always replaceable by some basis of a relevant kind L, then K is not more complex than L* (that is, K does not have a higher complexity value than L—or, briefly, when "v" stands for "the complexity-value of", $vK \leqq vL$).

Now a good many points here call for explanation. In the first place, to say that every basis of kind K is *always replaceable* by some basis of kind L is to say not only that there always is some equivalent basis of kind L but also that we can always find one; that is, that given any basis B of kind K, with no further information than that B is of kind K, we can define in terms of B and the stated logical apparatus alone some basis B' of kind L such that we can redefine B from B' and the logic alone.

In the second place, our postulate speaks of the complexity of kinds rather than of bases. A kind has the highest complexity-value possessed by any basis of that kind, and a basis has the

287

complexity-value of the narrowest relevant kind to which the basis belongs.

In the third place, what are the *relevant kinds*? Structural kinds, certainly, since we are concerned with structural complexity. But not every structural difference constitutes a difference in relevant kind; for if that were the case, then, since definition from a basis always depends upon structural features, our postulate would in effect reduce to the test in terms of defining power that we have already rejected. What will constitute a relevant kind depends upon the fact that our postulate is intended to express the principle that *purely routine* replacement effects no genuine simplification.

Now, replacement of a basis B by another, B', is purely routine if every basis like B, or of the same broad sort or general kind as B, is always replaceable by some basis of the same general kind as B'. The ordinary notion of a "broad sort" or "general kind" is vague and has to be supplanted by something much more clearcut. As a first approximation, we may define such a relevant kind as any class of bases delimited by specifying the number of predicates in a basis and the number of places in each predicate, together with any or no information concerning the three most commonplace properties of predicates: reflexivity, transitivity, and symmetry. (At the moment, the reader need not understand what these properties are; they will be explained presently, and our tentative definition of relevant kinds will be somewhat revised.) Thus, for example, the class of all bases consisting of a two-place and a one-place predicate is a relevant kind; so also is the narrower class of bases consisting of a symmetric two-place predicate and a one-place predicate. Our tentative definition of relevant kinds will presently be further explained and somewhat revised.

One may ask what justifies this particular interpretation of "broad sort" or "general kind", this particular decision in spelling out the imprecise notion of purely routine replacement. Quite plainly, no precise interpretation can claim to be uniquely indicated. Developing any method of measurement is a process of forging a sharp and effective tool from rough practice. We must look to the practice where it offers us guidance and, at the same time, remove obscurities, resolve conflicts, and fill in gaps, by rulings designed to yield the most significant results. A method of measuring anything must meet taxing but somewhat elusive demands of faithfulness and serviceability, but no method is exclusively correct. Thus our chosen definition of relevant kinds must find its justification in the combination of its plausibility as a translation of the rough notion of "general kinds" with the overall acceptability of the calculus of measurement to which this interpretation is a contributing factor.

From postulate 1, we can show that two kinds are equally complex if every basis of each kind is always replaceable by some basis of the other kind, and we can derive complexity-value equations for many kinds of bases. But in order to derive inequalities—to show that certain kinds are more complex than certain others—we need something more. This is provided by a prosaic postulate to the effect that a basis consisting of some predicates is more complex than a basis consisting of none, and that the value of a basis can be computed by adding the complexity-values of the predicates in it.

P2. *Every predicate in an extralogical basis has a positive complexity-value, and the value of the basis is the sum of the values of the predicates in it.*

The second clause operates to exclude from consideration, in determining complexity-values, any interconnections among the predicates in a basis. But such interconnections will be taken into account later, after a primary scale of complexity-values has been established.

Development of a Calculus

Easily proved from these postulates are certain elementary theorems, such as that *where m is less than n, the complexity-value of the class of m-place predicates* (that is, the kind of basis that consists of a single m-place predicate)[6] *is less than the complexity-*

---

6. I shall often abbreviate such a locution as "the complexity-value of the kind of basis that consists of one two-place predicate" to "the complexity-value of two-place predicates" or to "the complexity-value of a two-place predicate".

value of the class of n-place predicates. But the further development of the calculus requires treatment of more specific properties of predicates and becomes highly complicated. I shall describe it here very sketchily, merely to suggest its general character and the results obtained.

1) Two-place predicates are *irreflexive* if they never relate anything to itself. Thus, ".... is a parent of ————" is irreflexive. On the other hand, the predicate ".... has the same blood type as ————" is reflexive, since everyone has the same blood type as himself. Some predicates, like ".... has a brother in common with ————", are neither reflexive nor irreflexive; every person with a brother, but no person without, has a brother in common with himself. One-place predicates are, degenerately, both reflexive and irreflexive.

Reflexive predicates are interreplaceable with irreflexive predicates and hence they are equal in complexity. A two-place predicate "P" that is neither reflexive nor irreflexive has the same complexity-value as a set of two irreflexive predicates: a two-place predicate that relates every two distinct elements, x and y, related by "P", and a one-place predicate applying to every x that "P" relates to x itself.

With predicates of more than two places, the varieties of reflexivity-properties multiply rapidly, for a many-place predicate may be reflexive or irreflexive or nonreflexive with respect to all or to any given selection of its places. But fortunately, *the complexity of any basis can be proved to be equal to that of a certain basis consisting solely of thoroughly irreflexive predicates* (that is, irreflexive with respect to all their places). Every other predicate of n places in the basis gives way to a set of one or more thoroughly irreflexive predicates, each having not more than n places. Thus we can confine our attention to thoroughly irreflexive predicates.

2) A two-place predicate, like ".... is greater than ————", is said to be *transitive,* since if x is greater than y and y is greater than z, then x is greater than z. However, transitivity proves to be less pertinent to complexity measurement than (and is now to be supplanted as a defining property of relevant kinds by) a stronger property of predicates that may be called *self-completeness.* If two

one-place predicates—say, ".... is red" and "———— is white"—
are compounded into one two-place predicate—say, ".... is red,
and ———— is white"—the latter is self-complete. In general, a self-
complete two-place predicate is such that if it joins x to y and also
z to w (and if all these except possibly y and z are different), then
it joins x to w. Predicates of more places may likewise be self-
complete with respect to all their places: for example, the predicate
".... is red, and ———— is white, and .... is square". Such
predicates (whatever their number of places) are, figuratively,
rather unstable; they break down easily into one-piece predicates.
For that reason, thoroughly self-complete predicates do not often
occur in actual systems; but for the same reason, their consideration is important for our present purposes. Their resolubility enables us to show that *the complexity-value of an n-place thoroughly self-complete predicate is equal to the complexity-value of
n one-place predicates*. This is a crucial step towards determination of the general relationship between the complexity-values of
predicates differing in number of places.

3) A two-place predicate is *symmetric* if it pairs elements in
both directions whenever it pairs them in either; for example,
".... is a sibling of ————" is symmetric, since everyone is a
sibling of anyone he or she has as a sibling. The three-place predicate ".... and ———— and .... are triplets" is also symmetric
with respect to all its places, and a predicate of more places that
is similarly entirely order-indifferent is likewise thoroughly
symmetric.

We saw that a self-complete two-place predicate has the same
complexity-value as two one-place predicates; but a *symmetric*
self-complete two-place predicate has the same value as a *single*
one-place predicate. Such a predicate merely pairs in both directions every two elements of a set. Likewise, *an n-place thoroughly
symmetric and thoroughly self-complete predicate merely combines in all directions (or applies to all permutations of) every n
elements of a set, and such an n-place predicate has the same
complexity-value as a single one-place predicate.*

4) Complications pile up fast when we consider predicates that
are only partially, rather than thoroughly, self-complete or symmetric. For instance, many-place predicates may be symmetric

with respect to some rather than all of their places. If x lies on a straight line between y and z, it follows that x lies on a straight line between z and y, but not that y lies on a straight line between x and z. Thus the three-place predicate ".... lies on a straight line between ———— and ...." is symmetric with respect to the last two, but not with respect to all, of its places.

Again, a predicate may be symmetric with respect to sequences of its places rather than with respect to its places severally. For example, if x is exactly as much greater than y as w is greater than z, then w is also exactly as much greater than z as x is greater than y. The four-place predicate in question here is not symmetric with respect to any two or more of its places severally but is symmetric with respect to pairs of its places: the pair of its first two and the pair of its last two places.

Similarly, self-completeness may occur with respect to sequences of places rather than with respect to places severally. And a single predicate may exhibit many varieties of symmetry and self-completeness at once.

All this makes the full treatment of our problem very intricate. Briefly, what we do is define the *symmetry index* of a predicate as a certain function of all the symmetries the predicate has, and also define the *self-completeness index* of a predicate in a comparable way. We then examine how complexity varies in relation to these indices.

5) This examination, carried out with the help of two supplementary postulates, yields the means for determining the complexity-value of any relevant kind of basis as a function of two constants (either but not both of which may occur vacuously): the complexity-value of one-place predicates and the complexity-value of two-place irreflexive predicates. In order to achieve a fully quantitative measure, a final postulate is needed to fix the numerical value of these constants. This postulate stipulates that all, and only, those kinds of bases that can be shown by preceding postulates to have the same value as one-place predicates shall have the value 1, and that all other kinds shall have the lowest integral value consistent with this requirement and with preceding postulates. Assignment of the value 1 is a mere convenience;

we might have used some arbitrary constant c. The choice of integral values is always indicated in any scheme of measurement where, as here, use of nonintegral values can be avoided.

Resultant Simplicity Formulae

Some of the resulting complexity-values are given by the following formulae:

1) The class of n-place thoroughly irreflexive predicates has value $2n - 1$.

2) The class of n-place thoroughly irreflexive and thoroughly self-complete predicates has the value n.

3) The class of n-place thoroughly irreflexive and thoroughly symmetric predicates has the value n.

4) The class of n-place predicates that are thoroughly irreflexive, self-complete, and symmetric has the value 1.

More generally, *the value of any kind of n-place irreflexive predicate is 2n − 1 minus an amount dependent upon its symmetry and self-completeness and their interrelation.*

When the limitation to irreflexive predicates is dropped, the values of relevant kinds are obtained, as suggested earlier, by computing the value of corresponding kinds of bases consisting of irreflexive predicates. These values rise very rapidly with the number of places; the class of all two-place predicates has the complexity-value 4, and that of all three-place predicates, the value 15.

Some temporary exclusions made earlier can now be removed. In the first place, the restriction to applicable predicates is easily eliminated without affecting any of our results; for since inapplicable predicates have zero complexity, adding them to a relevant kind cannot increase its complexity-value. In the second place, where the predicates in question are not all of one homogeneous type (but meet certain conditions of finitude), available methods of correlating each predicate with a set of predicates of the lowest type may be applied, and the complexity-values may then be readily calculated. Finally, our temporary exclusion from consideration of interconnections between predicates is compensated for by adoption of a secondary rule for choosing in certain cases between bases of different structure but of equal computed complexity-value.

Present Status of Simplicity Study

The calculus I have outlined is virtually complete; proofs for all theorems are currently being checked. However, some possibilities for improvement still need consideration, and other writers have entered some objections and have proposed modifications and alternatives.[7] Investigation of the measurement of the structural simplicity of the extralogical bases of theories is unlikely to reach its stage of ultimate stagnation for some time. But that can also be said of many an older scientific inquiry. I hope enough has been said to show that our problem has at least been carried some steps away from its stage of initial confusion.

We have been dealing, it must be remembered, with a very small corner of the big problem of simplicity. We have considered the simplicity of terms but not of postulates framed in these terms. We still have no measure of the overall simplicity of theories. Nor does our calculus answer the crucial questions involved in the fitting of curves and in induction generally.[8] But perhaps the progress made on one aspect of the problem will somewhat alleviate despair concerning the rest. If some of the remaining questions seem too vague to be amenable to precise formulation and treatment, we may well reflect that most scientific problems seemed that way once. The obscurities of problems are due less to the subject matter than to shortcomings in its investigation.

7. [For a discussion of these see the following paper in this volume.]

8. On this topic, see I. Scheffler, "Inductive Inference: A New Approach", *Science,* Vol. 127 (1958), pp. 177–181.

2

Recent Developments in the
Theory of Simplicity

We increase the degree of systematization achieved in our account of a given subject matter whenever we make any reduction in the set of terms left undefined. But since terms differ in complexity, the extent of the economy effected cannot be determined merely by counting the undefined terms. In a number of earlier publications,[1] I have investigated the problem of measuring the structural complexity of primitive extralogical vocabularies, or bases, of constructional systems. Recently several other papers on the subject have appeared and some new results obtained. I want here to comment on papers by Patrick Suppes, John Kemeny, and Lars Svenonius—in this order, which is the reverse of their order of publication. I shall answer the criticisms advanced by Suppes, point out some serious defects in the alternative measures of complexity proposed by Kemeny, and explain why the treatment of definability and replaceability offered by Svenonius seems to me an important contribution. In the course of discussing these papers, I hope also to make clearer some aspects of my own work. Finally, I want to outline an improvement in the system proposed

---

1. These, in order of publication, are: "On the Simplicity of Ideas", *Journal of Symbolic Logic*, Vol. 8 (1943), pp. 107–121; "The Logical Simplicity of Predicates", *ibid.*, Vol. 14 (1949), pp. 32–41; "An Improvement in the Theory of Simplicity", *ibid.*, Vol. 14 (1949), pp. 228–229; the third chapter of the first edition of *SA;* "New Notes on Simplicity", *Journal of Symbolic Logic,* Vol. 17 (1952), pp. 189–191; and "Axiomatic Measurement of Simplicity", *Journal of Philosophy,* Vol. 52 (1955), pp. 709–722.

The following errata in this last mentioned article should be noted: (a) p. 716, line 1, for "(1,3) (2,4)" read "(1,2) (3,4)". (b) p. 717, line 14, for "simplicity" read "symmetry". (c) p. 718, line 2 of T15, after "$(vK-vL)/c$" insert "and $(syL-syK)/c$"; and for "is" read "are". (d) p. 718, line 2 of P3, after "$(vK-vL)/c$" insert "or $(syL-syK)/c$". (e) p. 719, lines 2–4 of T16, for "$\leqq$" read "$<$"; and for "k" read "K". [Postulates, theorems, and definitions from this article that the reader will need to refer to can be found in the appendix to the present paper.]

in my "Axiomatic Measurement of Simplicity" (hereinafter referred to as *AMS*).

1. On Patrick Suppes's "Nelson Goodman on the Concept of Logical Simplicity"[2]

The economy of an extralogical basis is the ratio of its defining power to its simplicity. When two bases are of equal defining power, their economy is directly proportionate to their simplicity. Clearly, then, the simplicity in question here is not the mere inverse of defining power but a distinct factor that must be measured in some other way. This is the problem of measurement that has always concerned me. Nevertheless, Suppes writes:

> In my discussion I am assuming that the basic intuitive idea to be captured formally is that of structural *simplicity*. An entirely different notion of simplicity could concern itself with the relative complexity of predicate bases for the same structure, for instance, an evaluation of different sets of primitive notions for groups or Boolean algebras. Kemeny's two measures assign the same complexity value to different predicate bases yielding the same structure. My own feeling is that Goodman's paper suffers from a failure to distinguish clearly these two problems.

What Suppes here calls "an entirely different notion" is just the one I have always been considering. This is made very explicit in my first article on simplicity and again in my book;[3] but Suppes apparently knows only *AMS*, in which I had to presuppose some of the basic expositions contained in my earlier publications.

The two notions indeed differ drastically. Consider a set *S* of predicates of varying number of places. According to the Suppes notion of simplicity we can arrive at no simpler basis for *S* than we get by taking all the predicates of *S* as primitive. According to my notion, we may arrive at a much simpler basis—and structurally simpler, too, in my usage—if we discover how to define some predicates in terms of others.

Not surprisingly, Suppes's false start renders many of his criti-

2. *Philosophy of Science*, Vol. 23 (1956), pp. 153–159.

3. See p. 110 of the first article cited in footnote 1; and pp. 68–69 of *SA*.

cisms of my work utterly irrelevant. For example, the cases he cites in his Sections 1 and 2 to illustrate the counterintuitive results of my measurement of simplicity are quite beside the point, proving only that complexity in my sense does not vary uniformly with defining power. Likewise, the particular argument he brings against my Postulate 2 (which fixes the complexity-value of a basis as the sum of the complexity-values of the predicates in it) depends entirely on his misconception of what I am talking about.[4] Incidentally, some things he says convey the false impression that my method of measurement does not apply to bases consisting of several interconnected predicates. Actually the method applies to bases consisting of any number of predicates connected in any way.

Suppes's initial misunderstanding also infects his discussion of the notion of relevant kinds. He thinks the notion can well be dropped. But if the notion is dropped from my treatment, so that **P1** for example reads "If a basis B_1 is replaceable by a basis B_2, then B_1 is not more complex than B_2", then obviously no basis can ever be replaced by a simpler one, and we have a measure not of complexity in my sense but of defining power. The clue to my approach is that replacement of a basis B_1 by a basis B_2 is a replacement of a more complex by a less complex basis only if bases like B_1 cannot always automatically be replaced by bases like B_2. Where the replacement is purely routine, as is the replacement of six one-place predicates by one six-place predicate, no genuine simplification is effected. The notion of relevant kinds is a means of spelling out more explicitly such phrases as "a basis like B"; and thus it is only with the help of the notion of relevant kinds that a complexity-measure of the sort we want is defined.

The question remains, of course, whether the needed notion of relevant kinds is adequately defined. Suppes complains that it is not; and indeed no full and formal definition is given. What is given, rather, is a rough description, later filled in and modified by a study of certain properties of many-place predicates. In sum, the explanation given is as follows: A relevant kind of basis is de-

---

4. For further discussion of this postulate and the matter of connections among primitives, see 2 below.

limited by stating the number of predicates in such a basis and the number of places in each predicate, along with any or no information concerning the reflexivity, symmetry, and self-completeness[5] of these predicates; and any sum, non-null product, or non-null difference of two relevant kinds is also a relevant kind. This seems to me to specify the relevant kinds quite clearly. No new primitive is required, but writing out the full definition in ordinary notation would be excessively laborious.

One might ask why the line between relevant kinds and other classes of basis should be drawn just where I draw it. A proper answer would require a long discussion of the whole philosophy of measurement. All I can say here is that developing a precise method of measurement on the basis of rough practice is a process of forging a sharp and effective tool from ordinary intuitive judg-ments while striving to do them the least violence. This means being arbitrary and judicious at once; and it always is a very deli-cate question whether one has succeeded in being judiciously arbitrary. The particular way I have selected relevant kinds rep-resents an effort to give a precise and yet not unfaithful formula-tion of the rough distinction we commonly make between a merely mechanical replacement of a basis and a replacement that effects a genuine saving.

Suppes offers further criticism on other points. His passing re-mark that the notion of *numerically determined* is vaguely de-fined seems to me adequately refuted by the definition he quotes from my text: briefly, a quantity is numerically determined by given postulates when they fix a unique number for it. But he goes on to complain that it is 'not customary' for one postulate to refer to others, and that it is undesirable 'for a variety of reasons' to introduce a metamathematical notion such as *numerically deter-mined* into my postulates.

The reference to **P1** and **P2** in **T15** does indeed complicate the

5. Self-completeness is akin to, but stronger than, transitivity. A 2-place predicate "P" is self-complete if $(x)\,(y)\,(z)\,(w)\,(Pxy\,.\,Pzw\,.\,x \neq y\,.\,x \neq w\,.\,z \neq w\,.\, \supset\, Pxw)$. This differs from my earlier definition by the addition of the final two non-identity clauses to the antecedent. This change is made to preclude an anomaly that Lars Svenonius has shown to result from use of the earlier definition.

theorem and make the route of proof long and arduous. Later in this paper I shall explain how, without essentially changing the structure of the system, both **T15** and **P3** can be simplified to eliminate the reference to earlier postulates. However, when Suppes proposes the odd device of strengthening **P3** to incorporate what has already been established,[6] he shows that he has quite overlooked the positive purpose served by the atypical features of my set of postulates. If my aim had been to axiomatize an already accepted set of complexity-values, this could have been accomplished most effectively by taking as axioms some of the principles that come out as theorems (*e.g.*, **T21**) in my system. I was concerned rather to axiomatize the foundations from which a set of complexity-values could be derived. The problem was to develop a systematic method of measurement out of unsystematic comparative judgments; and a primary function of the axiomatization is full disclosure both of the elementary clues elicited from such judgments and also of the evolution of a system of measurement out of such clues. The fundamental clue I have adopted is the replaceability principle formulated in **P1**.[7] **P2** has the status of an auxiliary instrument. Just how far can we go without further assumptions? **T15** shows that we can go a good way: that for all the many varieties of predicate that can, so to speak, be taken apart and examined, complexity diminishes directly as symmetry increases. Our next step is to add **P3**, which is suggested by **T15** and projects the same principle over all other predicates as well.

6. He points to the lack of proof for T15 as partial justification of his proposal. I stated in *AMS* that I had no proof; but soon afterward I found a proof for an even stronger theorem, so that P3 could be weakened. This I explained during the discussion at the meeting of the American Philosophical Association on December 28, 1955, when *AMS* and the papers by Suppes and Kemeny formed the basis of a symposium. However, see the further proposal outlined in 4 below.

7. Note especially that the replaceability principle provides a sufficient but *not* a necessary condition for comparing complexity-values. Indeed, much of the subsequent development of the system is devoted to determining comparative values where no replaceability relationship obtains. This point is missed by people who suppose, for example, that to give bases consisting of a single 2-place predicate the same value as bases consisting of four 1-place predicates must be wrong because bases of neither kind are in general replaceable by bases of the other kind.

Thus **P3** is in effect a 'smooth extension' of **T15** and, more remotely, of **P1**. Such a dynamic development, with successive additions to the foundations being guided by the results of prior assumptions, may not be characteristic of axiomatizations of mathematical theories, but it seems peculiarly well-suited to the purpose in hand.

Finally, Suppes balks at adopting anything like my fifth postulate. What I should do, he thinks, is to state within what boundaries the first four postulates determine complexity values, and leave it at that. He holds that to add a postulate that turns the comparative theory into a quantitative one is to confuse "the axiomatic problem of formulating the intuitively essential conditions an adequate complexity measure should satisfy and the different problem of choosing one among the possible large number of measures satisfying the essential conditions". I cannot see that there is any such sharp distinction. Each successive postulate narrows further the range of admissible measures by bringing to bear an additional intuitive principle. Choice of some among the many measures that satisfy **P1–P3** is so accomplished by **P4**; and choice of some—in this case one—among the many measures that satisfy **P1–P4** is so accomplished by **P5**. Thus the role of **P5** is entirely parallel to that of the other postulates. The only question, then, is whether **P5** itself is intuitively well-founded; and this perhaps deserves to be explored here a little more fully than in my article.

The first four postulates provide for the complexity-value of each relevant kind an expression of the form "$xc + ys$", where "x" and "y" stand for positive integers (except that either but not both may be 0), and where "c" stands for the complexity-value of 1-place predicates (*i.e.*, for $v\{1$ pl.$\}$) and "s" for the complexity-value of 2-place irreflexive symmetrical predicates (*i.e.*, for $v\{2$ pl. irref. sym.$\}$). No non-numerical sign other than "c" and "s" occurs, regardless of how many places there are in predicates of the kind in question. Thus the first four postulates fix all complexity-values *relative to c and s*. Is there, now, any sound basis for selection among all the possible values for c and s?

First, consider c. No simpler extralogical basis can be found than a single one-place predicate; and the complexity-value of one-place predicates is the natural unit of complexity-measurement. We might assign c any numerical value, but there seems to be no good reason for choosing a value other than 1. However, there is no call to labor the point; for we can almost equally well leave c without any numerical assignment. The decision whether to give c the value 1 or leave it unvalued and express other values in terms of c makes no more difference than the decision whether, when measuring in miles, to assign a mile the value 1 and write our measurements $e.g.$, "13", "27", "584" or leave m without numerical value and write "$13m$", "$27m$", "$584m$".

Then the single crucial question left unresolved by the first four postulates is the fixing of s relative to c. Of course, since earlier postulates yield the equation:

$$s + c = v\{2\,\mathrm{pl.\,irref.}\},$$

a determination of the value of 2-place irreflexive predicates relative to c would serve equally well. As a matter of fact, determination of the value relative to c of any one relevant kind not restricted to self-complete predicates would do. But it is easiest to focus our discussion upon s. So far, we know from **P2** that s is positive. Let us see whether there are considerations that may help us to fix s relative to c.

In the first place, the very character of our subject matter invites integral measurement. The number of predicates in a basis and the number of places in a predicate are integral. Furthermore every predicate has the same value as an integral number of thoroughly irreflexive predicates; the self-completeness measure of a predicate is integral; and the symmetry measure of a predicate is a sum of multiples of the values of partitions of the predicate. [This no longer holds in the revised treatment of SA, 2nd ed. See the discussion of the combination factor on pp. 94–103 of that book.] Finally, we have already shown that the complexity-value of each relevant kind is expressible as the sum of a multiple of c and a multiple of s. In the face of all this and of the fact that integers are indicated anyway wherever other numbers are not clearly required, very strong reasons would be needed to introduce non-integers into this scheme. Accordingly, in fixing s we restrict ourselves to the positive multiples of c, or to integers if c be taken as 1.

Shall we now, set s at 1? Thus to give 2-place irreflexive symmetrical predicates the same value as 1-place predicates seems pretty plainly counterintuitive; but I should not like to rest the case very heavily on one particular judgment of this sort. I should add another and more general consideration: To set s at 1 would give 2-place irreflexive symmetrical predicates the same value as 2-place irreflexive symmetrical *self-complete* predicates. In other words, self-completeness would not reduce the complexity of 2-place irreflexive predicates. But from this together with **P1**–**P4**, it would follow that n-place irreflexive predicates in general have the same value as n-place irreflexive self-complete predicates and hence the same value as n 1-place predicates—in other words, that no degree of self-completeness whatever has any simplifying effect at all. Thus the distinctive feature of many-place predicates—that they select some among all the possible sequences of occupants of their places[8]—would be completely discounted. And this result is enough to condemn the proposal to set s at 1.

No such objection, however, lies against setting s at 2. This assignment has the virtue of being the lowest that avoids difficulties of this sort, and there seems to be no good reason for any higher assignment. But still more can be said. From our earlier postulates, it follows that the simplifying effect of symmetry is exactly the symmetry measure.* If we set s at 2, the simplifying effect of self-completeness will likewise be exactly the self-completeness measure.* That such a balanced system of valuation, reflected in **T21**, results from setting s at 2 is no inconsiderable point in favor of an assignment that recommends itself anyway at the lowest feasible one.

Here, then, is a sketch of the grounds for setting s at 2—or at $2c$. **P5** is one way—certainly not the only and perhaps not the best way[9]—of formulating these grounds and fixing this value. I have

---

8. For further explanation of this point see pp. 99–100 of *SA*.

9. Another way is to adopt a postulate that restricts our choice of values to integers and stipulates further only that $v\{2$ pl. irref. self-com.$\} < v\{2$ pl. irref.$\}$. Or, if a specific valuation happens to appeal as more directly intuitive than the general principles, one might simply adopt some such postulate as "$s = 2$" or "$v\{2$ pl. irref.$\} = v\{2$ pl. irref. self-com.$\} + 1$".

* [See the Appendix to this article, below.]

gone into some detail in order to illustrate how we have to feel our way along in developing a calculus of simplicity. The decisions to be made are often delicate ones, as I suspect has been the case in the development of any calculus of measure; and the reasons that can be brought to bear are often conducive rather than conclusive. We can hardly expect full proof for our postulates. Yet the decisions made here are by no means unmotivated, and they combine to reinforce one another. Moreover, I think they derive reflected support from the orderly, convenient, and acceptable system of values that results.

2. On John G. Kemeny's "Two Measures of Complexity"[10]

Since Kemeny's article was published simultaneously with *AMS*, his comments on my work refer only to earlier publications and are in some cases no longer relevant. For example, the version of the replaceability principle he quotes is much stronger than that incorporated as **P1** in my axiom system; and I no longer use the method of joints and segments. But he is also sometimes inaccurate in reporting on the earlier publications: he says, for instance, that I assign the value 2 to symmetric 2-place predicates and the value 3 to non-symmetric ('ordinary' in his terminology) 2-place predicates, even though in my 1952 article[11] I state explicitly that these values are for *irreflexive* predicates of these kinds. And he is simply in error in supposing that a symmetric 2-place predicate can always be replaced by a non-symmetric one.

However, his comments on my work are incidental to his main purpose of presenting "two new definitions of the complexity of a set of extralogical predicates". The first of these, he says, is a direct outgrowth of my work but more intuitive. The proposal is "to take the number of basic relations expressible by a predicate as its complexity-measure". He illustrates by the case of an ordinary 3-place predicate "S". The predicate can express the relations: $\hat{x}\hat{y}\hat{z}(Sxyz)$, $\hat{x}\hat{y}\hat{z}(Sxzy)$, and so on for all permutations of the arguments; also $\hat{x}\hat{y}(Sxxy)$, $\hat{x}\hat{y}(Sxyx)$, $\hat{x}\hat{y}(Syyx)$, and so on;

10. *Journal of Philosophy*, Vol. 52 (1955), pp. 722–733.

11. "New Notes on Simplicity" cited in footnote 1 above.

and finally $\hat{x}(Sxxx)$. The total count is 15. For a 3-place predicate that is not ordinary, some of these relations may be empty or be identical with or conflict[12] with others. Empty relations are not to be counted at all; and of two identical or conflicting relations, only one is to be counted. Thus a thoroughly symmetric 3-place predicate has the value 4. Kemeny provides a table showing other sample values that result.

Is this proposal intuitively sound in principle? The distinction between the relations that are and those that are not expressible by a predicate is not an obvious or familiar one; and Kemeny's decision where to draw it seems especially capricious. Why, for instance, are the relations expressible by "S" considered to be just those specified above and not also the relation $\hat{x}\hat{y}(\exists z)(Sxyz)$, the relation $\hat{x}((\exists y)(\exists z)(Sxyz))$, and many others? Kemeny offers no explanation. Of course, one must often draw arbitrary lines in setting up a system of measurement, and to this in itself I have no objection. What I am disputing here is Kemeny's claim of intuitive superiority for his proposal.

Next, let us look at the resulting values. From Kemeny's sample table, we see that he assigns 2-place asymmetric predicates the same value (1) as 1-place predicates. There are still more startling consequences. Consider some cases not in Kemeny's table. Three-place thoroughly asymmetric predicates will be assigned the value 1. Furthermore, 3-place thoroughly irreflexive, thoroughly symmetric predicates will also have the value 1. Indeed, *no matter how many places a predicate has, if it is thoroughly irreflexive and either thoroughly symmetric or thoroughly asymmetric, it will be assigned the value 1.* Even had Kemeny shown that there were *prima facie* intuitive advantages in his method of measurement, this result would condemn it.

Moreover, we can now easily show that his method is inconsistent. To illustrate his way of handling many-predicate bases, Kemeny considers 'families' consisting of f disjoint 1-place predicates that together exhaust the universe of discourse. We are first to take the conjunction "$P_1a.P_2a.P_3a.P_4a \ldots Pfa$" and all other

---

12. If for no x and y can "Rxy" and "Qxy" both be true, then Kemeny calls R and Q "contradictory" relations, though "contrary" would be more appropriate. Since I dislike applying either term to relations, which are not statements, I use the looser term "conflicting".

conjunctions constructed by negating one or more of these clauses; then eliminate all the conjunctions that cannot be true; and finally count the rest and take log_2 of this number as the complexity-value of the family. Obviously, the only conjunctions not eliminated will be those in which all the clauses but one are negated; and obviously there will be just f of these. Accordingly, the complexity of a family will be $log_2 f$; a family of four 1-place predicates, for instance, will have the value 2. But now, any family of f 1-place predicates can always be replaced by a single thoroughly assymmetrical f-place predicate; and as we have just seen, such a predicate has under Kemeny's method the value 1. Thus by the replaceability principle,[13] a family of 1-place predicates cannot have a value greater than 1. Hence for any family of more than two 1-place predicates, Kemeny's method requires both that the value be 1 and also that the value be not 1 but greater than 1.

Kemeny's first proposal must therefore be rejected. But one or two general points he urges along the way call for some comment.

In the first place, he objects to my view that in measuring the value of a basis we should take into account all relevant information about it. He maintains that we should consider only the analytic properties of the basis, the properties that follow from the meanings of the primitive predicates. Suppes holds rather that we should take into account just the information given in the postulates of the system. Even if we grant the distinction between analytic and synthetic, I think the case is quite clear for taking into account all information, whether analytic or synthetic, postulated or unpostulated, in evaluating any given basis. We can fix the value of a basis, under my procedure, just to the extent that we know to what relevant kinds the basis belongs. If we know—no matter how—that a particular basis B belongs to kind K, then we know that the value of B does not exceed that of K. And the lowest upper bound we can set for the complexity of B is the value of the least complex kind to which we know—no matter how—that B belongs. Suppose B consists of the single two-place predicate "likes" among members of a certain community; and suppose we know that everyone in this community likes everyone else.

13. Although Kemeny expressly adopts the stronger replaceability principle used in my book, I here need only the weaker principle embodied in P1 of *AMS*.

Kemeny will give B the same value as a 2-place predicate that is neither symmetrical nor self-complete. Suppes will agree, unless all or part of my information is embodied in postulates. But I say that since we know that B is symmetrical and self-complete, we know that its complexity value does not exceed $v\{2$ pl. sym. self-com.$\}$, which is 1. *How* we know that B is symmetrical and self-complete is quite irrelevant.

In the second place, Kemeny argues that connections among the predicates in a basis, as well as the properties of the separate predicates, are relevant in determining complexity. Take for example a basis consisting of two equivalent one-place predicates. Kemeny holds that such a basis, which can always be replaced by a single one-place predicate, should have the value 1. My method, as a result of **P2**, assigns this basis the value 2. I might defend my result here by saying that it is entirely consonant with the obviously sound recommendation not to use two primitives where one of them will do. But this may be countered by the argument that similar reasoning would call for giving a symmetrical self-complete 2-place predicate a higher value than a 1-place predicate, whereas my method assigns each of these the value 1. In short, Kemeny's contention put in its strongest form seems to be that any argument for or against considering connections between predicates in making complexity comparisons is equally an argument for or against considering connections within a predicate; and that we ought to take both or neither into account.

Not only am I inclined to agree with the principle thus formulated, but I had it explicitly in mind in developing my treatment of complexity. It is true that my five postulates result in assigning to a basis the sum of the values of the separate predicates in it, without regard to connections between them. But once the numerical values have been assigned, a supplementary rule[14]—which might, indeed, be formally adopted as an additional postulate—goes into operation to effect secondary comparisons of complexity among bases having the same numerical value. One consequence of this rule is that among predicates having the value 1, a 2-place symmetrical self-complete predicate is more complex than a

14. See the second paragraph of Section 9 of *AMS*, p. 721–722. The principle there stated supplants the several rules set forth under remark (3) on page 190 of "New Notes on Simplicity".

1-place predicate. Thus in the end, I treat both a basis consisting of two equivalent 1-place predicates and a basis consisting of one 2-place symmetrical self-complete predicate as structurally more complex than a basis consisting of a single 1-piece predicate. Kemeny's preference for the opposite course of treating all these bases as equally complex reflects the fact that he is concerned with measuring power rather than structural complexity.

My two-stage treatment, by which numerical values are first assigned and further comparisons then made among bases having the same numerical value, is perhaps not ideal. One might hold that we should seek a set of postulates that will at once represent all differences of complexity on a single numerical scale. While this may be a counsel of elegance rather than of strict adequacy to our purpose, I should certainly welcome a suitable modification of my system in this direction. But the task is not easy; and indeed the two-stage character of my treatment resulted from my need to divide the problem in order to conquer it.

Kemeny's second proposal for measuring complexity is based, he says, on a quite different idea from the first. "We are given a set of [extralogical] predicates, and we want to measure its complexity, *i.e.* the richness of description allowed by the set." This richness is the greater "the more detailed is the account we can give of our experience". The models for a language being the possible worlds it enables us to distinguish, "the number of models is a good measure of the richness of the extralogical vocabulary. We will count the number of models for the given language and let the complexity-value be some function of this number." For technical reasons, he decides that the function in question is to be that power of 2 that is the number of models—or in other words, $\log_2 m$.

Note first that since equivalent systems have the same models, the "richness" Kemeny speaks of here is not structural complexity in my sense but something more like power.[15] By his measurement, we have as simple a basis when we take as primitive all the extralogical predicates in a system as when we take only one as primitive and define the rest.

But is it indeed true that the number of models is a good mea-

15. Prof. Paul Henle first called my attention to this just before the symposium mentioned in footnote 6.

sure of the "richness" in question? Let "H" be short for the one-place predicate "is poorer than at least half the population", and let "T" be short for the one-place predicate "is poorer than at least nine-tenths of the population", where our universe consists of ten or more people. "H" has many more models than "T". But can we give a more detailed account of this universe in terms of "H" than of "T"? As a matter of fact, we make a much more specific statement when we apply "T" to an individual than when we apply "H"; the more specific predicate has not the more but the fewer models. I do not contend, however, that "T" enables us to give a more specific or detailed description of the universe than does "H"; for while the application of "T" to an individual is more specific than the application of "H", the denial of "T" to an individual is less specific than the denial of "H". It seems clear that "H" and "T" are equally rich in the sense Kemeny has explained. Furthermore, it would be easy to find examples of many-place predicates that likewise differ in their number of models without differing in the specificity of the descriptions they make possible. Plainly, the number of models is not a good measure of richness; and Kemeny's rationale for his second proposal thus collapses.

When we turn to Kemeny's table of sample values resulting from his second proposal, we must begin by correcting a rather serious mathematical error. The value he gives for 2-place asymmetric predicates in a universe of N individuals is $N(N - 1)/2$, which means that the number of models is 2 to this power. Where N is 3, the value would then be $(3 \cdot 2)/2$ and the number of models 8. But obviously the number of models of a 2-place asymmetric predicate in a universe of three elements is 27; since any selection of 0 or more of the six couples

$$
\begin{array}{ll}
a,b & b,a \\
b,c & c,b \\
a,c & c,a
\end{array}
$$

that contains no two couples from the same row constitutes a model. Accordingly the complexity-value ($\log_2$ of the number of models) is not 3 but somewhere between 4 and 5.

This correction makes a great difference; for it reverses the relative value of symmetric and asymmetric predicates for universes of more than a very few elements. According to Kemeny's table, symmetric 2-place predicates have higher value than asymmetric ones. According to the corrected table, for any universe of 5 elements or more the asymmetric 2-place predicates have a higher value than the symmetric ones.[16] Now by way of partial justification of his proposal, Kemeny has pointed to the fact that by his (uncorrected) table the value of an n-place asymmetric predicate is one-half the difference between the value of an ordinary predicate of n places and the value of an ordinary predicate of $n - 1$ places. But this does not hold for the corrected table. Kemeny's apparent satisfaction with the values given by the uncorrected table suggests that he might find some difficulty in reconciling himself to the corrected values.

Kemeny recognizes two disadvantages of the method of measurement described: it depends upon the usually unknown number N of elements in the universe of discourse, and it gives enormous numbers of complexity-values where N is even moderately large (for example, 160,000 as the value of an ordinary 4-place predicate where $N = 20$). He therefore suggests an alternative version of his second proposal. He writes that he has elsewhere

> presented a method which is applicable to such measure-function for an N whose exact size is unknown but which is known to be very large. The complexity-value must, according to this method, be thought of not as a number but as a function of N. Two such functions are then compared by their asymptotic behavior: If, for all sufficiently large N, $f_1(N) > f_2(N)$, then we say that $f_1 > f_2$.

This leaves open the question what we do when N is indeterminate but not guaranteed to be very large; and such cases are common, since many systems are so designed as to make minimal existential commitments.[17] Moreover, the suggested device be-

16. My own method of measurement gives n-place asymmetric predicates a higher value than n-place symmetric *irreflexive* predicates, but gives 2-place asymmetric predicates the same value as 2-place symmetric predicates in general.

17. Rather elaborate systems often yield no theorem to the effect that there is more than one element in the universe. And according to Kemeny's own principles, what counts is not what we may happen to know about the universe but what follows from the meaning of the primitive predicates of the system in question.

haves badly where N is known to be large. One result, as Kemeny points out, is that a single predicate having m places will be rated as more complex than any finite set of predicates each having fewer than m places. He argues:

> Since a predicate of more places can take the place of any 'reasonable' number of predicates of less places, there is some intuitive justification for these results.

But I am afraid this is no justification at all. We cannot always replace more than one 2-place predicate by a 3-place predicate; and we cannot always replace more than three irreflexive 2-place predicates by a 3-place predicate. Surely there is no justification here for the conclusion that every finite set of 2-place predicates is less complex than one 3-place predicate. Perhaps by the locution "can take the place of" he does not mean that a set of 2-place predicates can in my sense always be replaced by a single 3-place predicate, but only that there is some 3-place predicate (whether we can find it or not) from which all the 2-place predicates could be defined.[18] But insofar as this statement is true, the statement is equally true that for any set of predicates of *any* finite total number of places, there is a single 2-place predicate (whether we can find it or not) from which all the original predicates could be defined. Obviously, this lends no support to the conclusion that every set of 2-place predicates is less complex than a 3-place predicate. The price of adopting Kemeny's alternative version of his second proposal is thus not only that we must take functions as values but also that we must swallow some highly anomalous consequences.

So I think Kemeny's second proposal, like his first, must be rejected. The difficulties peculiar to each version of the second proposal are in addition to those already explained: (1) that for either version the actual mathematical results are different in important respects from the erroneous ones that Kemeny presents and considers intuitively satisfactory, and (2) that the proposal is founded upon the unsound claim that the number of models is a good measure of richness.

---

18. Further explanation of the distinction in question here, and of the argument in the following sentence, will be found in the next section.

3. On Lars Svenonius' "Definability and Simplicity"[19]

The penetrating study of definability and replaceability contained in this paper is a real contribution to the theory of simplicity.

Svenonius begins by observing that the extension of a predicate may be invariant with respect to certain permutations of elements in the universe; for example, if the universe consists of the elements a, b, c, and d, and the extension of a given predicate consists of the pairs a, b and a, c, then putting a for a, c for b, b for c, and d for d will give the same extension.

He then defines as *equally strong* any two extensions that are invariant with respect to exactly the same permutations. For example, in the same universe of four elements, the extension consisting of the pairs a,b and b,a is exactly as strong as the extension consisting of the elements c and d; for if any permutation of the elements in the universe leaves either of these extensions unchanged it will also leave the other unchanged.

He is now able to set forth a necessary condition for replaceability. Only if there is a regular two-way mapping between the possible extensions of bases of kind K and some subclass of the possible extensions of bases of kind L, and each two extensions correlated by this mapping are equally strong, will it be the case that every basis of kind K is always replaceable by some basis of kind L. Accordingly, if we can show that there is no such mapping, we can show that not every basis of kind K is always replaceable by some basis of kind L. Some method of proving negative replaceability theorems was clearly much needed; for while the fact that a replaceability relationship obtains can be established by producing the formulae effecting the replacement, mere failure to find any formulae hardly proves that no replaceability relationship obtains. This has been a handicap, since when the stronger replaceability principle is used, each application requires establishing absence of a replaceability relationship. And although application of the weaker replaceability principle adopted (as **P1**) in *AMS* requires only that positive replaceability relationships be

19. *Journal of Symbolic Logic*, Vol. 20 (1955), pp. 235–250.

established, the ability to prove negative replaceability theorems remains important, particularly for answering an objection that is often raised and that may well be considered now.

Various writers have devised ways of showing that every basis can in some sense 'be reduced to' some basis consisting of a single 2-place predicate.[20] One or another of the proposed devices is sometimes thought to constitute proof that the replaceability principle (in either version) must yield the result that no basis has a complexity-value greater than that of a single 2-place predicate. Actually none of these devices establishes the replaceability required by my way of measuring complexity; that is, none of them enables us always to find the requisite 2-place predicate without the help of existential or other assumptions that are not permitted in establishing always-replaceability in my sense. But the threat remained that some new inventions might do the trick or something like it. Svenonius has now shown that nothing of the sort is possible. Using the method outlined above, he has proved that it is not the case that every basis can always be replaced by some basis consisting of a single 2-place predicate, or even by some basis consisting of any finite number of 2-place and 1-place predicates. Indeed he has demonstrated the much more sweeping theorem that it is not the case that every basis containing at least one n-place predicate is always replaceable by some basis consisting of any finite number of predicates of fewer than n places.[21]

Svenonius quite incidentally proposes a definition of complexity that amounts to adoption of the stronger replaceability principle, with all logically specifiable classes of bases admitted as relevant kinds. So to admit all structure-classes as relevant kinds is to obtain a measure of power rather than of what I have called complexity. Furthermore, since Svenonius adopts no projective postulates or similar devices, his measure is a very incomplete one, with

20. *E.g.*, see W. V. Quine, "Reduction to a Dyadic Predicate", *Journal of Symbolic Logic*, Vol. 19 (1954), pp. 180–182, and the articles referred to in the first footnote of that article; also A. Tarski, "A General Theorem Concerning the Reduction of Primitive Notions" and "On the Reduction of the Number of Generators in Relation-rings", (Abstracts), *Journal of Symbolic Logic*, Vol. 19 (1954), pp. 158–159. [See further VII,3 below.]

21. Actually, he proves a slightly weaker theorem (his Theorem 22), from which the above is readily derived.

many kinds remaining incomparable in strength. And finally, use of the stronger replaceability principle no longer seems to me advisable; for it is inconsistent with some other rather natural and useful principles.[22] Nevertheless, Svenonius has made a beginning toward developing a measure of power; and a complete measure of power, combined with a complete measure of complexity (such as is proposed in *AMS*), would give a complete measure of economy of bases. But the main interest of his paper, for both author and reader, lies in the treatment of replaceability that I have outlined above.

Svenonius has recently obtained, but not yet published, two further interesting results; and he has given me permission to mention them here. First, he has proved an assertion I had made without proof: that if we make no assumption about applicability of the predicates concerned or about existence of more than one element in the universe, then we cannot always replace a set of predicates having a total of n places by a single n-place predicate. Second, he has advanced and proved the striking theorem that if we assume there are at least two elements in the universe, then we

---

22. Let K be the class of 2-place predicates and L the class of 2-place symmetrical predicates. Obviously every predicate of class L is always replaceable by some predicate of class K, while not every predicate of class K is always replaceable by some predicate of class L. Likewise, every predicate of class $K - L$ is always replaceable by some predicate of class K, while not every predicate of class K is always replaceable by some predicate of class $K - L$. Consequently, if K, L, and $K - L$ are relevant kinds, the stronger replaceability principle gives the results: $vK > vL$ and $vK > v(K - L)$. But this cannot be the case if the value of a kind is the value of its most complex members.

Such inconsistencies may be avoided in any of three ways: (a) by adopting a sufficiently exclusive policy of selection of relevant kinds that, for example, rules out K–L and does not in general accept every sum or product or difference of relevant kinds as a relevant kind; or (b) by denying that the value of a relevant kind is the value of its most complex members; or (c) by discarding the stronger in favor of the weaker replaceability principle.

Course (a) was adopted, though not very explicitly, in the first edition of *SA;* but it now seems to me too *ad hoc* and awkward. This course was not open to Svenonius, for whom all structure-classes of bases are relevant kinds; and he adopts course (b). But this obscures the relationship between the value of a kind and the values of its members; no longer can we regard such a statement as "$vM = 3$" as short for the statement "some members of M have the value 3 and no member has a higher value". It is partly for these reasons that in *AMS* I have rejected courses (a) and (b) and have adopted course (c).

can always replace any set of predicates having a finite total of n places by a single n-place predicate.

4. An Improvement in "Axiomatic Measurement of Simplicity"[23]

The system outlined in *AMS* can be appreciably improved without changing its general structure. Roughly speaking, Theorem **15** states that wherever the effect of symmetry or complexity can be numerically determined by Postulates **1** and **2**, the complexity-value is reduced by the symmetry-measure. The reference to **P1** and **P2** complicates the theorem and makes the proof laborious. We can shorten both theorem and proof, and clarify the development of the system, by eliminating reference to previous postulates in favor of a more explicit characterization of the cases covered. The cases where the relation between difference in symmetry-measure and difference in complexity-value can be precisely compared by means of **P1** and **P2** are those where the difference between kinds is a difference in symmetries whose subsequences

---

23. The definition of symmetry on page 716 of that article should be revised to read: A predicate is symmetrical with respect to a set S of its places if, wherever "P" applies to any sequence q of elements, "P" also applies to every sequence obtained from q by permuting in any way the elements of q occurring in the places of S while holding fixed the elements of q in the remaining places of "P".

Furthermore, the method of defining symmetry stretches on page 717 likewise needs revision. A *first-level stretch* of a predicate "P" is any set S of its places such that "P" is symmetrical with respect to all these but not with respect to all the places in any other set S' that includes S. An *m-level stretch* of "P" is any set S of m-length place-subsequences such that no two of them intersect any lower-level stretch, and such that "P" is symmetrical with respect to all these, but not with respect to all in any other set S' that includes S.

The procedure (p. 713) for finding the set of thoroughly irreflexive predicates to be used in computing the complexity-value of a given predicate also needs revision. Such a set need contain only one k-place predicate for each set of k-variegated primary patterns that are symmetrical with respect to each other. (Two k-variegated patterns of a predicate are symmetrical with respect to each other, if some permutation of all the sequences of each yields all the sequences of the other.) Thus the set for the predicate "x is the same distance as y from z" will consist of: one 3-place irreflexive predicate, symmetrical with respect to its first two places; and one 2-place irreflexive predicate. The 2-place predicate serves for both the patterns x,y,x and y,x,x. The patterns x,x,x and x,x,y are not primary, since the original predicate is totally reflexive with respect to these.

are partitions—that is, in what might be called 'molecular' symmetries. The older version of **T15** may thus be supplanted by:

T15a. *If K and L are relevant kinds of irreflexive n-place predicate and differ at most in molecular symmetry, then vK–vL = syL– syK.*

This is actually a stronger theorem than **T15**; for there are many cases where K and L differ at most in molecular symmetry but where $(vK-vL)/c$ is not numerically determinable from **P1** and **P2**.[24] Yet proof of the new theorem, though still rather lengthy, is simpler in principle. In brief outline, the proof is as follows: (1) If all molecular symmetries are disregarded, the value—call it x— of any relevant kind may be expressed as the sum of the values of the members of any set of mutually exclusive and jointly exhaustive partitions of a predicate of that kind. (2) Every molecular symmetry of k partitions, each having the value y, reduces the value x by $(k-1)y$. (3) The symmetry-measure of such a molecular symmetry is also $(k-1)y$. (4) The total difference between x and the value of the kind is equal to the total symmetry-measure of the molecular symmetries of the kind. (5) *Q.E.D.* Thus while the full proof involves some tiresome detail, the general route by which **T15a** derives from previous theorems (especially **T14**) is quite apparent.

T15a states in effect that any symmetry whose subsequences are partitions reduces complexity-value by exactly the symmetry-measure of this symmetry. The principle that complexity-value is reduced by the symmetry-measure now needs to be projected to the case of symmetries whose subsequences are within minimal partitions—*i.e.*, to 'atomic' symmetries.[25] However, we need postu-

---

24. *E.g.*: Let K be the kind of 5-place irreflexive predicate that is (1,2) (3,4) (5) self-complete and is without any symmetries. Let L be the kind of 5-place irreflexive predicate that is likewise (1,2) (3,4) (5) self-complete but is (1,2) (3,4)—and not otherwise—symmetrical. Now represent v {2 pl. irref.} by "x". Then $vK = 2x + c$, and $vL = x + c$; hence $vK-vL = x$. Also $syL = x$, and $syK = 0$; hence $syL-syK = x$. Thus even though P1 and P2 do not here numerically determine $(vK-vL)/c$, they do yield the equality of $vK-vL$ with $syL-syK$.

25. Note that an atomic symmetry need not be a first-level symmetry. For example, if a 4-place predicate is its own sole partition but is (1,2) (3,4) symmetrical, then its symmetry is second-level but atomic.

late this only for predicates that have but a single partition. The following replaces **P3**:

P3a. *If K and L are relevant kinds of irreflexive n-place predicate without self-completeness at any level and they differ at most in symmetry* (hence at most in atomic symmetry), *then vK–vL = syL–syK.*

We can then prove:

T15a.1. *If K and L are relevant kinds of irreflxive n-place predicate that differ at most in atomic symmetry, then vK–vL = syL–syK.*

And this together with **T15a** will yield the wanted general theorem:

T15a.2. *If K and L are relevant kinds of irreflexive n-place predicate and differ at most in symmetry, then vK–vL = syL–syK.*

These revisions, while simplifying the development of the system, preserve its step-by-step character. A consequence of the first two postulates is projected to further cases by adoption of a third postulate. One naturally asks whether comparable revisions might be made in **T16** and **P4**. The answer must await further study. So far I have not investigated at all thoroughly either the problem of proving **T16** as it stands or the question what form such revisions might take.[26]

Appendix: Some Postulates, Theorems, and Definitions from "Axiomatic Measurement of Simplicity"

P1. *If every basis of a relevant kind K is always replaceable by some basis of a relevant kind L, then K is not more complex than L* (*i.e., K does not have a higher complexity-value than L*—or, using obvious abbreviations, $vK \leq vL$).

26. [The definition and treatment of symmetry is further revised in *SA*, 2nd ed., pp. 88–94. Under this new treatment P3a above becomes a theorem, whereas T15a, T15a.1, and T15a.2 are dropped in favor of other theorems. Proofs of all retained theorems are now available.]

P2. *Every predicate in an extralogical basis has a positive complexity-value, and the value of the basis is the sum of the values of the predicates in it.*

T15. If K and L are relevant kinds of n-place irreflexive predicate, and $scK = scL$ and $syK \leq syL$, and $(vK - vL)/c$ and $(syL - syK)/c$ are numerically determined by P1 and P2, then $vK - vL = syL - syK$.

P3. *If two relevant kinds K and L are like those specified in T15 except that $(vK - vL)/c$ or $(syL - syK)/c$ is not numerically determined by P1 and P2, then $vK - vL = syL - syK$.*

T16. If K, L, M, N are relevant kinds of n-place irreflexive predicate, and $syK = syL$, and $syM = syN$, and $scK < scL$, and $scM < scN$, and $(vK - vL)/(vM - vN)$ is numerically determined by P1, P2, and P3, then $(vK - vL)/(vM - vN) = (scL - scK)/(scN - scM)$.

P4. *If relevant kinds K, L, M, N are like those specified in T16 except that $(vK - vL)/(vM - vN)$ is not numerically determined by P1 through P3, then $(vK - vL)/(vM - vN) = scL - scK)/(scN - scM)$.*

P5. *Just those kinds that are determined by preceding postulates to have the same value as {1-pl.} have the value 1; and every other kind has the lowest integral value consistent with this requirement and preceding postulates.*

T21. If K is a relevant kind of irreflexive n-place predicate, then $vK = (2n - 1) - (syK + scK)$.

Definition of self-completeness measure. A predicate that is not self-complete in the sense of footnote 5 above may still be self-complete with respect to a set of separate and jointly exhaustive subsequences of its places; for instance, the three-place predicate "Q" is self-complete with respect to the place-subsequences $(1, 3)$ and (2) if Qx,y,z whenever x, y, and z are different and Qx,v,z and Qs,y,t. Any place-subsequence that belongs to a set (of one or more) with respect to which a predicate is self-complete may be called a *partition* of the predicate. Thus the sequence of all the

317

places of a predicate is a partition of it; and any sequence of places that is exhaustively divisible into separate partitions of a predicate is also a partition of it. A *minimal* partition of a predicate is any one of its partitions that contains none of the others. The self-completeness measure of predicate "P" (sc$P$) is simply what might also be called the degree of self-completeness of a predicate; that is, the number of rifts between its minimal partitions. In other words, if k is the number of minimal partitions of "P", then sc$P = k - 1$.

Definition of symmetry-measure. If an m-level stretch (as defined in footnote 23 above) contains h m-length place-subsequences, each having the complexity-value k, then $(h - 1)k$ is the symmetry-measure of the stretch. And the symmetry-measure of a predicate "P" (sy$P$) is the sum of the symmetry-measures of all its stretches. We must now explain what is meant by the complexity-value of a place-subsequence of a predicate. Let $p, p', \ldots$ be k not necessarily consecutive places taken in order from a given n-place predicate "P". Now from each n-ad of "P" abstract a k-ad by taking in order just the components that occur in places $p, p', \ldots$ By the complexity-value of the place-subsequence $(p, p', \ldots)$, is meant the value of a k-place predicate having as its sequences just the k-ads so abstracted.

3

Condensation versus Simplification

Professor Quine writes in his new book[1] (page 232):

> Yet it is possible in general to subject general terms to a striking formal condensation. If the assumed universe of objects includes at least a modest fund of classes—actually none of more than two members are required for the purpose—then it can be shown that any vocabulary (finite or infinite) of general terms (absolute or relative) is reducible by paraphrase to a single dyadic term.;

and he refers us in a footnote to his "Reduction to a Dyadic Predicate".[2]

This remark seems to me likely to mislead the reader and perpetuate a widespread misunderstanding. Many people have supposed that my method of measuring the simplicity of a set of extralogical predicates[3] is undermined by such results as the reduction Quine cites here. If any set of predicates can be replaced by a single two-place predicate, does this not show that no set of predicates is more complex than a single two-place predicate? The objection has been answered with finality by Svenonius, who has proved[4] that it is not in general possible even to replace an n-place predicate of individuals by any set of predicates (of individuals) having fewer than n places each. From Quine's remark above, however, the reader may conclude that my calculus of simplicity has been saved by a mere technicality; that it breaks down if we accept a very parsimonius existential postulate. I should like to show, in one more effort to correct a persistent mistake, that such a conclusion is totally unfounded.

In the first place, the classes required for Quine's reduction are

1. *Word and Object* (Cambridge, Mass.: M.I.T. Press, 1960).

2. *Journal of Symbolic Logic,* Vol. 19 (1954), pp. 180–182.

3. See "Recent Developments in the Theory of Simplicity" [VII,2 above].

4. "Definability and Simplicity", *Journal of Symbolic Logic,* Vol. 20 (1955). See my summary of the point in the article cited in footnote 3 above.

modest neither in number nor in composition. We must assume
that every class of not more than two elements is itself an element
in the universe of our system. Thus if our individuals are physical
objects, our universe must contain not only all classes of not more
than two such objects, but also all classes of not more than two
such classes of objects, and so on *ad infinitum*. And since no type-
restrictions are imposed, all mixed-level classes of not more than
two members will be admitted as well. Even if the number of
individuals is finite, the number of classes will be infinite. Indeed,
the number of classes required is equal to the number of all con-
ceivable classes (just as the number of even integers is equal to
the number of all integers). "Modest" is hardly the word for it.
Furthermore, although no class will have more than two members,
some will embrace (as members of . . . members) all individuals
and many classes. Among the infinitely numerous classes required,
many are of awesome complexity.

In the second place, suppose the requisite assumption to be
granted, so that Quine's method of reduction can be used. Does
my calculus of simplicity then fail to work? Not at all. For if the
predicates of the set replaced are predicates of individuals, the
replacing two-place predicate will take classes as arguments; and
whatever may be the level of the arguments of the replaced predicates, the arguments of the replacing predicate will belong to a
higher level in the platonic hierarchy of classes. This in no way
conflicts with my result that a two-place predicate of individuals
is in general simpler than a three-place predicate or any set of
two or more many-place predicates of individuals. Moreover,
according to my calculus, any predicate of classes has a higher
complexity-value than any set of predicates of individuals; and a
predicate with arguments of any level has a higher value than any
set of predicates with lower-level arguments.[5] Thus, Quine's 'reduction' consists in replacing what is less complex by what is more
complex.

In sum, it seems to me that the second sentence of the passage
quoted above should be revised to read:

> If the assumed universe of objects includes a vast fund of classes—
> indeed, every class of not more than two objects must itself be con-

5. See *SA*, pp. 107–117, especially pp. 114–117.

sidered an object—then it can be shown that any vocabulary of general terms is exchangeable for a single dyadic relative term, which will, however, be more complex than the vocabulary replaced.

But then the 'striking formal condensation' effects no genuine gain in simplicity.

4

Review of Craig's
"Replacement of Auxiliary Expressions"

William Craig, "Replacement of Auxiliary Expressions", *The Philosophical Review,* Vol. 65 (1956), pp. 38–55.

If certain terms in an important discourse are suspect for one reason or another (e.g. as the 'theoretical' terms of a science are suspect to a phenomenalist), an effort may be made to show that they function as mere auxiliary devices enabling us to derive some sentences in non-suspect language from others. We may try to show how the use of these terms can be completely prescribed without commitment to the meaningfulness of any suspect term [as in IV,2 above], or try to show how all use of the suspect terms can be made unnecessary by defining them from non-suspect terms.

Craig outlines a different and general method for eliminating suspect terms from any formal system that has an effectively defined class of theorems and a basic logic that meets certain meagre requirements. Since his present paper is a less technical exposition and discussion of his earlier paper in the *Journal of Symbolic Logic,* Vol. 18 (1953), pp. 30–32, there is no need to give the details of his method here. What is important is that a formal system S, containing suspect language, is in each case replaced by a system S^* having as theorems all the statements in non-suspect language that are theorems of S. This is accomplished by a device that provides, for each such statement in S, a postulate in S^* that is a conjunction of a certain number of repetitions of the statement.

Craig explicitly disclaims any philosophical importance for this method of replacement. He acknowledges that his device is highly artificial and that it effects no clarification of the suspect terms eliminated. But this gives us small excuse for complacency. Artificiality is as yet a vague notion, and one may ask whether there is any need to clarify terms shown to be eliminable. While replacement by Craig's method does not satisfy the usual objectives of a replaceability program, we are hard put to it to say exactly why.

Evidently preservation of all theorems in non-suspect language is far from enough. What more, then, is required? For one thing, that the replacing system have an appreciable degree of deductive coherence or economy. The chief purpose of proof in a philosophical system is less to convince of truth than to integrate. If every theorem has its own postulate, no integration is achieved. But that is not the whole story. The fact that everything that can be said or established in non-suspect language in the replaced system can also be said or established in the replacing system leaves open the crucial question whether what can thus be done in non-suspect language is all that needs to be done. But the task of defining in general the nature of "what needs to be done" is a formidable one.

Thus the importance of Craig's paper lies in the challenge to explain why the device he offers is unimportant; for this raises the whole question of the objectives of philosophical replacement programs.

Although acknowledging that his method of system-for-system replacement is philosophically unsatisfactory, Craig thinks that definitional, or term-for-term, replacement programs are in general doomed to failure. He argues that certain plausible requirements for a term *"M"* to be a suitable replacement for *"N"* will be satisfied only if *"M = N"* is already a theorem of the original system. But this seems to the reviewer to show only that the roughly plausible requirements Craig lays down need reformulation; and this is not surprising, since the pitfalls of adopting oversimplified criteria of definition have been discussed before (Craig cites an article by Tarski; see also Chapter I of *SA*).

Craig goes on to make the currently popular remark that "empirical significance attaches to an entire framework of assertions of beliefs, and to individual expressions or concepts only indirectly, by means of that framework". This is salutary insofar as it reminds us that terms, phrases, or sentences must be interpreted in the light of their relationship to an entire framework, or warns us that a criterion of definition must refer to the relation between the entire set of definientia of a system and the entire set of definienda. But the holism that despairs of any expression-by-expression translation overreaches itself; for we can understand and use a language only when we can operate with relatively small particles of it. No one has gone far towards mastering Choctaw when he knows only that a given long discourse in Choctaw says just what a given long discourse in English says, if he is unable to make correlations between fairly small pieces of the one discourse and fairly small pieces of the other.

5

Elimination of Extralogical Postulates

with W. V. QUINE

1. Simple Cases of Eliminability

Under certain circumstances a postulate can be eliminated in favor of a mere definition, or convention of notational abbreviation. Suppose e.g. that a given system presupposes the machinery of ordinary logic and contains in addition a single extralogical primitive: the relation Pt, "is a spatial part of". Suppose this relation is governed by a single extralogical postulate, to the effect that Pt is transitive:

$$(1) \qquad (x)\,(y)\,(z)\,(x\,Pt\,y\,.\,y\,Pt\,z\,.\,\supset\,.\,x\,Pt\,z).$$

Now instead of Pt, the relation O of spatial overlapping might be taken as primitive; Pt could then be defined in terms of O as follows:

$$(2) \qquad Pt =_{\mathrm{df}} \hat{x}\hat{y}(z)\,(x\,O\,z\,.\,\supset\,.\,y\,O\,z).$$

The transitivity of Pt then follows by purely logical principles from the definition. The statement (1) with its "Pt" clauses expanded according to (2) is a purely logical theorem, demonstrable independently of any stipulations or assumptions concerning the properties of O. Thus, through a change involving neither increase nor decrease of primitive ideas, the need of adopting (1) as a postulate is removed.

Or again, consider a system comprising ordinary logic and the sole extralogical primitive S, the relation of simultaneity, governed by a sole postulate to the effect that S is symmetrical:

$$(3) \qquad (x)\,(y)\,(x\,S\,y\,.\,\supset\,.\,y\,S\,x).$$

Here instead of S the relation N, "is no later than", might be taken as primitive; S could then be defined in terms of N as follows:

$$(4) \qquad S =_{\mathrm{df}} \hat{x}\hat{y}(x\,N\,y\,.\,y\,N\,x).$$

Postulation of (3) then becomes unnecessary, for (3) is an abbreviation, according to (4), of a theorem which is demonstrable within pure logic.

A system having a single extralogical postulate of transitivity, or of symmetry, is of course very trivial. In practice one would be interested in a good many properties of Pt besides transitivity and its consequences, and hence would have adopted further postulates. Here, contrary to what we observed in the case of a single postulate, the shift to O will in general net no real saving; for, the desired properties of Pt other than transitivity remain to be supplied in an indirect and probably more complex way by appropriate postulation regarding O.

But suppose we write together in a single conjunction *all* the desired postulates regarding Pt, thus getting a single postulate adequate to all the properties of Pt which we may ever care to prove. What if we were able to eliminate this entire conjunctive postulate by shifting our primitive and appropriately defining Pt, just as we eliminated the transitivity postulate above? This would be surprising enough to challenge the whole notion of postulational economy.

We shall show that a wholesale elimination of this sort is in fact possible in a wide range of cases. Indeed, it will turn out that in order to be wholly eliminable in the described fashion a postulate set need fulfill little more than the requirement of consistency.

2. Conditions on the Definiens

What sort of definition, in general, will serve thus to eliminate a set of postulates? We may limit our attention to extralogical postulates, in interpreted systems presupposing logic. Only extralogical postulates are amenable to the kind of elimination suggested; for this consists in reducing the postulates via definitions to statements that are validated automatically by the logic presupposed.

For the present let us limit our attention further to the case of a system involving no extralogical primitives beyond a single constant term, say "d". This term is to be thought of as given some specific extralogical interpretation. Now if a definition of "d" in terms of a new primitive is to eliminate the postulates of the system, the definiens must be such that its substitution for "d" turns the postulates into logical truths. Let us use "$P(d)$" as an abbreviation for the conjunction of the postulates; and let us represent the definiens in question as "$f(a)$", where "a" is the new primitive and no other extralogical expression is involved. The requirement is, then, that "$P(f(a))$" be logically true; in other words, that "$(x)P(f(x))$"—which contains only logical signs—be true.

But the definiens must also meet a second requirement. No matter what interpretation may have been chosen for "d", under the restrictions imposed by the postulates, we must be able so to interpret "a" that the proposed definiens will provide the chosen interpretation for "d". For example, in the case of the system that had (1) as its only postulate, it would have been unsatisfactory to eliminate the postulate by defining Pt in terms of a new primitive relation K as

$$\hat{x}\hat{y}\,(\exists z)\,(\exists w)\,(x\,K\,z\,.\,y\,K\,w),$$

because we could not find any interpretation for "K" according to which this definiens would have the intended interpretation "part of". Indeed, we can be sure that there is no relation K satisfying this condition; for if there were, the part-whole relation would be symmetrical. Our second requirement, then, is that there be some interpretation of "a" such that $d = f(a)$; in short, it is required that $(\exists x)\,(d = f(x))$.

Thus definition of "d" as "$f(a)$" will reduce the postulates to logical truths, and still yield the intended interpretation of "d" (under some interpretation of "a"), if and only if

(5) $\qquad\qquad (x)P(f(x))\,.\,(\exists x)\,(d = f(x)).$

3. Existence of Logical Models

The contemplated elimination of "$P(d)$" in favor of a logical truth cannot of course be effected unless "$P(d)$" is in fact true; indeed, "$P(d)$" is a logical consequence of (5). But granted that $P(d)$, under what circumstances will there be a definiens "$f(a)$" meeting the conjoint requirement (5)? We shall show that there will be

327

such a definiens if and only if the postulate set has a logical model; i.e., if and only if there is a logical constant fulfilling the conditions that the postulates impose on the primitive.

Suppose there is such a constant, abbreviated say as "c"; so that "$P(c)$" is true. Now a definiens "$f(a)$" conforming to (5) is:

$$(\imath y)\,[P(a)\,.\,y = a\,.\,\mathsf{v}\,.\sim P(a)\,.\,y = c],$$

as is apparent from the following considerations. The expression corresponding to "$f(x)$" is now:

(6) $\qquad (\imath y)\,[P(x)\,.\,y = x\,.\,\mathsf{v}\,.\sim P(x)\,.\,y = c];$

and clearly the statement:

(7) $\qquad (x)\,[P(x)\,.\,f(x) = x\,.\,\mathsf{v}\,.\sim P(x)\,.\,f(x) = c]$

is true when "$f(x)$" is construed as (6). But (7) implies that

$$(x)\,[P(f(x))\,\mathsf{v}\,.\,f(x) = c],$$

which in turn implies that

$$(x)\,[P(f(x))\,\mathsf{v}\,.\,P(c) \supset P(f(x))]$$

and hence that

$$(x)P(f(x))$$

in view of our hypothesis "$P(c)$".

Again, since "$P(d)$" is by hypothesis true, it is obvious that

$$d = (\imath y)\,[P(d)\,.\,y = d\,.\,\mathsf{v}\,.\sim P(d)\,.\,y = c]$$

and hence that

$$(\exists x)\,(d = f(x))$$

where "$f(x)$" is construed as before.

We see therefore that there will be a definiens "$f(a)$" conforming to (5) whenever the postulate set has a logical model. Now it is easy to see conversely that the set will have a logical model whenever there is such a definiens; for the first part of (5) implies e.g. that $P(f(\Lambda))$ and hence that "$f(\Lambda)$" is a logical model of the postulates.

328

The choice of "Λ" here is of course arbitrary; any other logical constant, say "V" or "32", would have served as well. Our choice is indeed subject to certain restrictions so long as logic is thought of as requiring a theory of types; but these restrictions vanish when the theory of types is abandoned in favor of one or another of the alternative theories.[1]

4. The Case of Many Primitives

Suppose now that our postulate set "$P(d_1, \cdots, d_n)$" involves many primitive terms "d_1", $\cdots$, "d_n". Definitions of these in terms of new primitives "a_1", $\cdots$, "a_n" will be appropriate for the purpose of eliminating the postulates if and only if the respective definientia "$f_1(a_1, \cdots, a_n)$", $\cdots$, "$f_n(a_1, \cdots, a_n)$" are such that

$$(8) \quad (x_1) \cdots (x_n) P(f_1(x_1, \cdots, x_n), \cdots, f_n(x_1, \cdots, x_n)) . (\exists x_1)$$

$$\cdots (\exists x_n)(d_1 = f_1(x_1, \cdots, x_n) . \cdots . d_n = f_n(x_1, \cdots, x_n)),$$

as may be seen by reasoning analogous to that of §2.

Paralleling the case of one primitive, it is easy to show that there will be such definientia if and only if the postulate set has a logical model; i.e., if and only if there are logical constants, say "c_1", $\cdots$, "c_n", such that $P(c_1, \cdots, c_n)$. Suppose, first, that there are such constants. Then definientia "$f_1(a_1, \cdots, a_n)$", "$f_2(a_1, \cdots, a_n)$", etc. conforming to (8) are:

$$(\imath y)[P(a_1, \cdots, a_n) . y = a_1 . \mathbf{v} . \sim P(a_1, \cdots, a_n) . y = c_1],$$

$$(\imath y)[P(a_1, \cdots, a_n) . y = a_2 . \mathbf{v} . \sim P(a_1, \cdots, a_n) . y = c_2],$$

etc., as is apparent from the following considerations. The expressions corresponding to "$f_1(x_1, \cdots, x_n)$", "$f_2(x_1, \cdots, x_n)$", etc. are now:

$$(9) \quad (\imath y)[P(x_1, \cdots, x_n) . y = x_1 . \mathbf{v} . \sim P(x_1, \cdots, x_n) . y = c_1],$$

$$(10) \quad (\imath y)[P(x_1, \cdots, x_n) . y = x_2 . \mathbf{v} . \sim P(x_1, \cdots, x_n) . y = c_2],$$

etc.; and the statement:

---

1. For one such theory and citations of others see Quine, *Mathematical Logic* (New York: W. W. Norton, 1940), pp. 128–132, 155–160, 162–166.

(11) $(x_1) \cdots (x_n) [P(x_1, \cdots, x_n) \cdot f_1(x_1, \cdots, x_n) = x_1 \cdot f_2(x_1, \cdots,$
$x_n) = x_2 \cdot \cdots \cdot \mathsf{v} \cdot \sim P(x_1, \cdots, x_n) \cdot f_1(x_1, \cdots, x_n) = c_1 \cdot f_2(x_1,$

$$\cdots, x_n) = c_2 \cdot \cdots]$$

is true when "$f_1(x_1, \cdots, x_n)$", "$f_2(x_1, \cdots, x_n)$", etc. are construed
as (9), (10), etc. From (11), by reasoning analogous to that in §3,
we conclude that

$$(x_1) \cdots (x_n) P(f_1(x_1, \cdots, x_n), \cdots, f_n(x_1, \cdots, x_n)).$$

The other half of (8) can likewise be established by following the
analogy of §3. We see therefore that there will be definientia conforming to (8) whenever the postulate set has a logical model; and
it is easily shown conversely, again following the analogy of §3,
that the postulate set will have a logical model whenever there are
such definientia.

We have confined our consideration to postulates in which
the sole extralogical primitives are *terms;* i.e., signs capable
of occurring alongside "$=$" or "ϵ" or indeed wherever a free variable can occur. Our findings would not apply directly to a system
which involves e.g. a primitive functor "$\oplus$", admissible only in
contexts of the form "$x \oplus y$" and not separable as a term in its own
right. Actually this is no restriction, however, for extralogical
primitives other than terms are always readily avoidable. Instead
of "$x \oplus y$", e.g., we can write "$d^t(x;y)$" where the primitive term
"d" designates the relation of $x \oplus y$ to the ordered pair $x;y$.

5. Consequences

We have seen that we can reduce a set of extralogical postulates
to logical truths, by defining ideas identical with the erstwhile
primitives in terms of new primitives, if and only if the postulates
have a logical model. The variety of extralogical systems whose
postulates can be eliminated in this way is thus exceedingly wide.
This is especially apparent when we reflect that logical constants
of any degree of complexity may be used as models, and that a
constant is a model for any set of postulates that ascribes to a primitive a subclass of the properties of that constant.

Consider e.g. the calculus of individuals, which has the single primitive *discreteness* ($\rceil$) and the following three postulates:[2]

(12) $(w)(\exists x)(y)[y \rceil x \,.\, \equiv (z)(z \,\epsilon\, w \,.\, \supset \,.\, y \rceil z)]$,

(13) $(x)(y)[(w)(x \rceil w \,.\, \equiv \,.\, y \rceil w) \,.\, \sim (x \rceil x) \,.\, \supset \,.\, x = y]$,

(14) $(y)(z)\{(\exists x)[(w)(y \rceil w \,.\, \mathsf{v}\,.\, z \rceil w \colon \supset \,.$
$$x \rceil w) \,.\, \sim (w)(x \rceil w)] \equiv \sim (y \rceil z)\}.$$

The relation of class exclusion, $\hat{x}\hat{y}(x \subset \bar{y})$, is a logical model of these postulates. It must be borne in mind that the elimination of the three postulates does not proceed by defining $\rceil$ as $\hat{x}\hat{y}(x \subset \bar{y})$; such a definition would give " $\rceil$ " a meaning different from that originally intended. Discovery of a logical model assures us rather (by §3) that some definition can be found that will reproduce the original interpretation of " $\rceil$ " and still reduce the three postulates to logical truths. A definition to which the reasoning of §3 directly leads is:

$$\rceil =_{\mathrm{df}} (\imath z)[P(Sep) \,.\, z = Sep \,.\, \mathsf{v}\,.\, \sim P(Sep) \,.\, z = \hat{x}\hat{y}(x \subset \bar{y})]$$

where *"Sep"* ("separateness") is a new primitive synonymous with the original " $\rceil$ ", and *"P(Sep)"* is short for the conjunction of (12)–(14) with *"Sep"* put for " $\rceil$ ". Since *"P(Sep)"* is in fact true, this definition preserves the intended interpretation of " $\rceil$ "; but the definition makes (12)–(14) logically true independently of the truth of *"P(Sep)"*.

What postulate sets, now, cannot be eliminated by this procedure? Inconsistent sets, obviously; for they have no logical models. But there are also other postulate sets, presumably consistent, for which no logical model is known. One such set consists of the postulates *"d ε d"* and *"d ε 2"*; models are readily found for these respective postulates taken singly, viz. V and $\imath\Lambda \cup \imath$V, but no model is known for the pair. A still simpler set of the same kind

---

2. Cf. Leonard and Goodman, "The Calculus of Individuals and its Uses", *Journal of Symbolic Logic*, Vol. 5 (1940), pp. 48–49. The postulates of that paper are here rendered in unabbreviated form, and so recast as not to depend on the theory of types. On abandonment of the theory of types the range of *"x"*, *"y"*, etc. ceases to be limited to individuals; hence we find ourselves called upon to decide whether to construe *"x $\rceil$ y"* as vacuously true or as false when x and y are not both individuals. We here arbitrarily adopt the former alternative; thus the clause *"$\sim (x \rceil x)$"* in (13) and (14) stipulates that x is an individual.

consists of the single postulate "$d = \iota d$". In general, of course, the question whether a postulate set has a logical model will depend on details of the underlying logic. Logic might be constructed in so strong a fashion as to endow these bizarre examples with logical models, or in so weak a fashion as to deprive even more ordinary postulate sets of their models. Particularly weak logics aside, however, we have yet to find a postulate set that has a plausible extralogical interpretation but still lacks a logical model and thus resists elimination. In any case, a postulate set that can be proved consistent by the usual device of citing a logical (e.g., arithmetical) model is *ipso facto* eliminable in the described fashion.

Such elimination cannot be dismissed as trivial on the ground that postulates and definitions are somehow essentially the same. They differ formally in the obvious circumstance that we can dispense with the need for definitions, but not the need for postulates, simply by writing all statements of the system in terms of primitives. A general proof of the possibility of eliminating postulates in favor of definitions, far from being rendered unnecessary by the claim that the two are essentially alike, is precisely the kind of evidence that would be needed to substantiate such a claim.

The discovery that extralogical postulates are ordinarily eliminable challenges conventional notions of postulational economy as applied to extralogical systems. We are thus moved to seek a standard according to which the economy achieved by the present method can be distinguished as in some sense trivial—like the economy achieved by simply conjoining many postulates as one. We first observe that the present method of eliminating postulates leads to a system that is incomplete, in the sense that many statements involving the new primitive are neither demonstrable nor refutable. Hence we may be tempted to rule that postulational economy is significant only in complete systems; but this is unsatisfactory, because any extralogical system contains logic and is therefore necessarily incomplete in view of Gödel's theorem. A better solution is suggested by the concept of *categoricity*, or the related concept of *synthetic completeness*.[3] An extralogical system is synthetically complete if and only if it is as complete as the

---

3. The latter notion, under the name "completeness relative to logic", is due to Tarski. It is easier to formulate than the older concept of categoricity,

underlying logic; i.e., if and only if every statement of the system is demonstrable or refutable or demonstrably equivalent to a statement containing only logical signs. It would seem that economy of extralogical postulates is significant only in systems that are synthetically complete. This constitutes a considerable modification of old standards of postulational economy. Discrimination between real and apparent economy comes to depend upon proof of the synthetic completeness of the system in question. Not only is such a proof normally very difficult, but most of the useful extralogical calculi on record are in fact synthetically incomplete. Unless some quite different criterion in discovered, the extensive economies here shown to be possible will in practice seldom be distinguishable from those effected in any of the usual ways.

---

and is related to the latter as follows: systems that are categorical (with respect to a given logic) are synthetically complete, and synthetically complete systems possessed of logical models are categorical. These matters were set forth by Tarski at the Harvard Logic Club in January 1940, and discussed in a paper *On Completeness and Categoricity of Deductive Theories.* See also Lindenbaum and Tarski, *Über die Beschränktheit der Ausdrucksmittel deduktiver Theorien, Ergebnisse eines mathematischen Kolloquiums,* Heft 7 (1936), pp. 15–22, wherein "Nichtgabelbarkeit" answers to "synthetic completeness".

6

Safety, Strength, Simplicity

When the evidence leaves us with a choice among hypotheses of unequal strength, how is the choice to be made?

Caution would counsel us to choose the weakest, the hypothesis that asserts the least, since it is the least likely to fail us later. But the principle of maximum safety quickly reduces to absurdity; for it always dictates the choice of a hypothesis that does not go beyond the evidence at all.

The very opposite proposal has been advanced by Popper:[1] that the strongest hypothesis not falsified by the evidence should be preferred. But for every hypothesis strong enough to go beyond the evidence, there is an equally strong conflicting hypothesis based upon the same evidence. This is easily shown. Suppose our evidence tells us just that every examined A is a B, and suppose hypothesis H_1 affirms in addition that every (or even some one) other A is a B. Then hypothesis H_2, affirming that every examined A is a B and that every (or the particular one) other A is *not* a B, likewise conforms to the stated evidence. Hence strength is indifferent as between any projection and its opposite. And to exclude every hypothesis that conflicts with another equally strong one unviolated by the evidence would be, once more, to exclude every hypothesis that goes beyond the evidence at all.

Thus although both safety and strength are desirable features of a theory, they are by themselves incompetent criteria for choice. Another and controlling factor, simplicity, must be taken into account. Simplicity has sometimes been mistakenly identified with safety or with strength, but is readily shown to be distinct from both. Suppose we have examined many and widely distributed specimens of maple trees and found them all to be deciduous, and suppose this constitutes our entire evidence. Since we still will not have examined specimens from every small locality, our evidence

---

1. Karl R. Popper, *The Logic of Scientific Discovery* (New York: Basic Books, 1959), especially Chaps. VI and VII. Translated from the German by the author with the assistance of Julius Freed and Lan Freed.

may then leave us with a choice between the following two
hypotheses:

> (1) All maples, except perhaps those in Eagleville, are
> deciduous.

> (2) All maples are deciduous.

The second is clearly both the stronger and the simpler. We would
incorporate (2) in our theory, and retreat to (1) only if further
evidence indicated that (2) is false. Insertion of the *ad hoc* ex-
ceptive clause both weakens and complicates the hypothesis. Cases
like this, where the preferable hypothesis is the simpler and
stronger one, give plausibility to the view that strength is the measure of simplicity and is the cardinal principle of choice. But exactly comparable cases point to the opposite conclusion. The stated
evidence also leaves unfalsified the hypothesis:

> (3) All maples whatsoever, and all sassafras trees in
> Eagleville, are deciduous.

Now (3) is stronger than (2) but is less simple and acceptable. The
expansion made in (3) is as unwelcome as the exception made in
(1). Hypothesis (2), although it lies between (1) and (3) in safety
and strength, is simpler than and preferable to either.

This shows that neither safety nor strength is the measure of
simplicity, and that simplicity takes precedence over both as a factor in the choice of hypotheses. The delicate problem of balancing
safety and strength against each other is significant only as between hypotheses of equal simplicity.

If neither safety nor strength determines simplicity, what does?
Formulation of general standards for comparing the simplicity of
hypotheses is a difficult and neglected task. Here brevity is no reliable test; for since we can always, by a calculated selection of
vocabulary, translate any hypothesis into one of minimal length,
the simplicity of the vocabulary must also be appraised. I am inclined to think that the standards of simplicity for hypotheses
derive from our classificatory habits as disclosed in our language,
and that the relative entrenchment of predicates underlies our
judgment of relative simplicity; but spelling this out takes some

pains. Merely to reject unfamiliar predicates wholesale in favor of familiar ones would be to disallow the introduction of needed new terms into scientific language. Furthermore, we must ordinarily decide not merely which of two hypotheses is the simpler but which one makes for the simpler total theory. I have discussed these matters in *Fact, Fiction, and Forecast;*[2] and the criteria of projectibility I have outlined there in terms of entrenchment is perhaps essentially a simplicity criterion. But the whole matter wants more study. What is evident is that adequate canons of induction must incorporate criteria of simplicity that cannot be given solely in terms of strength or safety.

2. See especially Chapter IV of that book.

7

Science and Simplicity

Should science be simple? Or must science be complex as the world is complex? Is simplicity a necessity, a luxury, or a vice? And is degree of simplicity determinable by objective measure or only by personal prejudice?

Philipp Frank has said that without simplicity there is no science. If we add that likewise without science there is no simplicity, we are on the way to understanding a good deal about science and simplicity and the relationship between them.

The search for simplicity in science is sometimes questioned on the ground that the world may actually be complex. This betrays a curious perversion of ideas. Rather than the simplicity of science being limited by the simplicity of the world, the simplicity of the world is limited by the simplicity of science. I do not mean that the world is complex until we simplify it. It is neither simple nor complex except relative to—as organized under—a given system. The world has as many different degrees of complexity as it has different structures, and it has as many different structures as there are different true ways of describing it. Without science, or some other mode of organization, there is no simplicity or complexity. To suppose that a simple system must be false if the world is complex is to suppose that a simple system must be false if an alternative complex system is true. The world, indeed, is as simple as any true system, but it is also as complex as any true system. And it is as grammatical, as ungrammatical, as coherent, as incoherent, as any true system. These descriptions apply to the world only obliquely, through applying to discourse about the world. We need not shun syntax or coherence or simplicity for fear the world is ungrammatical or incoherent or complex.

Still, does simplicity matter? The standard counsel seems to be to aim at truth and hope for simplicity. The objective of science, the reasoning runs, is to achieve a true system, and any effort to make a true system simpler is merely for the sake of making it

337

prettier or more convenient. The injunction to seek truth regardless of simplicity has the self-righteous ring of a commandment not to put other gods before truth. Nevertheless, I submit that to seek a true system is to seek system as well as to seek truth. A mere collection of particular truths does not constitute science. Science is systematization, and systematization is simplification. If discovery of a way of dispensing with one of Peano's postulates or a way of defining one of three primitives of a system in terms of the other two does not seem momentous, that is only by comparison with the enormous systematization already effected through deriving vastly many theorems or terms from so meager a basis. Some economies are indeed minor, but complete disregard for economy would imply a willingness to take all terms and statements as primitive, to waive all definition and proof, and so to forgo all system. Without simplicity, there is no science.

But what is the measure of simplicity? Our confident judgments of comparative simplicity often conflict with one another; and we have ready at hand no very explicit or complete principles for resolving conflicts or filling gaps. Attempts at formulating a general criterion run so quickly into trouble that the problem is often dismissed as hopeless. Can we measure a property so multifarious, inconstant, and subjective? Before we give up, let's observe that the prospect of measuring physical size must once have looked equally dim for similar reasons. Size may mean total displacement or maximum diagonal or height and length and breadth, or any of many other quantities. It changes with time and circumstances, and our judgments of it vary with our physiology, prejudices, and point of view. Indeed, the case against the measurability of almost any property is overwhelming—until the property is measured. Consistency and objectivity are the products of measurement, not prerequisites for it.

To make a beginning, we may mark off a small but central part of the problem. Since systematization increases as the set of undefined ideas and unproved statements is reduced, what concerns us here is the simplicity of such a *basis* for a system. And since derivation of a system depends upon structural characteristics of the basis, what concerns us is formal or structural rather than psychological or semantic simplicity. For the moment, I shall put aside the question of the simplicity of sets of basic statements (that is, the question of axiomatic or postulational simplicity) to look first at the simplicity of sets of basic *terms*. Since the usual logical apparatus is common to all the systems under consideration, the question now before us is how to measure the structural simplicity of the basic *extralogical* vocabulary of a system.

One safe rule is that a basis is simpler than another if the first consists of some but not all the terms in the second. For example, if we succeed in deriving one of three primitive terms from the rest, we obviously effect a genuine saving. But so far we have no way of comparing the simplicity of two bases when each contains some term that the other does not. How can we broaden our rule to deal with such cases?

We might suppose that what counts is not merely whether one basis is included in another, but whether one is definable from the other; that a basis *A* is simpler than a basis *B* if *A* is definable from *B* but not *B* from *A*, and that two bases are equally simple if they are interdefinable. But this is plainly wrong. For since all the terms in any system are defined from the primitives, the set of all the terms would by this criterion be at least as simple as any narrower basis from which they can be defined. Thus we could never achieve any simpler basis for a system than by taking all of its terms as primitive and defining none of them. Obviously, then, the inverse of definitional yield is no measure of simplicity in any sense such that simplification of basis increases overall systematization. Yet many of the most sophisticated investigators of these problems have fallen victim to the error of taking definitional weakness for simplicity, of identifying power with complexity.

Let's try a different tack. Perhaps a basis properly included in another is simpler merely by virtue of containing fewer terms. Is the basis with more primitives always the more complex, then? Does simplicity always vary inversely with the number of terms in a basis? This popular and plausible notion quickly reduces to absurdity, for so long as all the terms in a basis have actual application, all can be combined into one. Consider, for example, the class-term or one-place predicate "conducts electricity", applying to certain materials, and the relation-term or two-place predicate "is denser than", relating certain materials to certain others. These can be compounded into the three-place predicate (with letters indicating the distinct blanks or predicate places) "x conducts electricity, and y is denser than z", and from this our original two predicates can be readily retrieved. But clearly no genuine simplification has been accomplished by this trick. If complexity were solely a matter of a number of primitives, maximum simplicity could always be attained by thus trivially combining into one all the terms to be introduced into the system. The mere counting of primitives ignores differences in their internal complexity.

The next likely suggestion is to count the total number of predicate places in a basis; so that a basis consisting of two one-place predicates, for example, would have a complexity of 2, while a basis consisting of one three-place predicate would have a complexity of 3. This is indeed an improvement, but it still will not do. For while we have a good reason for not considering a single predicate to be simpler than a set of several predicates having the same total number of places, we have no comparable reason for not considering the set to be simpler than the single predicate. We can always combine several applicable predicates into one without loss; we cannot always divide one applicable predicate into several without loss. For example, if we divide the two-place predicate "is a parent of" into the two one-place predicates "is a parent" and "has as a parent", we cannot retrieve the two-place predicate; for John may be a parent and William may have a parent without John's being a parent of William. The two-place predicate has some complexity that is missing in the set of two one-place predicates.

Perhaps we should stop grasping at surface hypotheses that promptly let us down, and look rather for an underlying principle governing some of our firmest judgments of simplicity. Obviously, we do not simplify a basis by adding more primitives or by putting in a predicate with more places for a predicate with fewer places. And, as we have seen, no genuine simplification is achieved by combining several predicates into one. What have all these cases in common? The fact, I suggest, that in all of them the replacement of one basis by another can be accomplished by a purely routine procedure. An elementary canon of simplicity seems to be that a basis A is no simpler than a basis B if every basis of the same kind as B can always be replaced by some basis of the same kind as A. This may seem pretty timid and negative, and it surely needs a good deal of clarification, but it embodies the fundamental postulate for a calculus of structural simplicity.

One obscurity lies in what constitutes a *kind* of basis in the purview of this rule. If we take "kind" very narrowly, no two bases are of the same kind; and it we take it very broadly, every two bases are of the same kind. But the relevant classification here is according to certain structural properties. Determining just *which* properties calls for that mixture of arbitrary stipulation with faithfulness to common practice that is always needed in setting up standards of measurement, but I cannot now attempt to explain the particular reasons for the choice made. The relevant structural kinds of basis are those defined by giving the number of predicates and the number of places in each, together with any or no information concerning three further properties. I shall describe these properties briefly, but understanding of such technical details is not altogether essential for understanding the general procedure.

The first of the properties is *reflexivity*. Since every number is at least as great as itself, the two-place predicate "is at least as great as" relates every number to itself and is said to be reflexive. On the other hand, since no number is greater than itself, the two-place predicate "is greater than" is irreflexive. The second of the properties in question is *symmetry*. Since every number differs from every number that differs from it, the two-place predicate "differs from" applies in both directions if it applies in either, and this predicate is said to be symmetric. On the other hand, "is greater than" never applies in more than one direction between two numbers, and is thus asymmetric. The final property, a strengthened version of the familiar property of transitivity, might be called "loose-jointedness" or *self-completeness*. If 3 and 5 are both primes, and also 7 and 11 are both primes, then 3 and 11 are both primes. The two-place predicate "x and y are both primes" is *self-complete* in that if it relates one number to a second, and also relates a third to a fourth, it likewise relates the first to the fourth. Most ordinary two-place predicates, like "is greater than", are not self-complete; for example, although 3 is greater than 2, and 5 is greater than 4, still 3 is not greater than 4. Predicates with more than two places can be partially reflexive, partially symmetric, partially self-complete in a bewildering variety of ways.

The relevant structural kinds vary in comprehensiveness depending upon how specifically the requirements in terms of these properties are stated, and some kinds will include others. For example, the class of bases consisting of a single two-place predicate is a relevant kind; so also is the subclass of bases consisting of a single two-place symmetric predicate; and so on. Thus a basis may belong to several different relevant kinds. The narrowest relevant kind a basis belongs to may be called its *minimal kind*.

The principle of routine replaceability that stands as the first postulate of our calculus of structural simplicity can now be more clearly formulated. When replacement of one basis by a second requires nothing more than ordinary logic and the information that the first basis is of a given minimal kind, every basis of the same minimal kind as the first can be replaced by some basis of the same minimal kind as the second. The replacement is purely routine, and no simplification is achieved.

I cannot now follow through the development of the rest of the calculus, which requires four supporting postulates and provision for all applicable and inapplicable one-place and many-place predicates of elements and of classes, but let me cite some sample results. The complexity-value of a basis consisting of a single three-place predicate turns out to run from 1 to 15, depending upon what the minimal kind for the predicate is, as determined by the structural properties. The complexity-value of a basis consisting of a single four-place predicate ranges, similarly, from 1 to 59. Maximum complexity increases very rapidly with each increase in the total number of predicate places; but where the total number of predicate places is held constant, maximum complexity *decreases* as the number of predicates increases. Whereas a basis consisting of one three-place predicate has a maximum complexity of 15, a basis consisting of three one-place predicates has a complexity of 3. Reflexivity tends to *increase* complexity: compare a maximum complexity of 15 for a reflexive three-place predicate with a maximum complexity of 5 for an irreflexive one. On the other hand, both symmetry and self-completeness tend to *reduce* complexity: a three-place predicate that is either symmetric or self-complete has a maximum complexity of 3. And a predicate that is both symmetric and self-complete always has a complexity of exactly 1, no matter how many places it may have. All this may suggest how much more than a mere count of predicates or predicate places must be considered in measuring the complexity of a basis.

When we turn to the set of unproved extralogical *statements* of a system, the problem of their simplicity looks much like the problem of the simplicity of the set of undefined extralogical terms. In the first place, we must clearly distinguish complexity from strength here, too; for since all the theorems of a system are derivable from the postulates, the set of all the statements of the system is no stronger than the set of postulates. Thus, if weakness were the measure of simplicity, we would achieve as simple a basis by merely postulating all the statements of the system as by deriving most of them from the others. In the second place, mere number of postulates is no measure of complexity, for all the postulates of any system can be reduced to one merely by conjoining them.

These comparisons may lead us to suspect that the clue to measuring simplicity of postulates, as of primitive terms, lies in a principle of replaceability. But this reasonable hope is frustrated by a paradoxical discovery. Virtually any set of extralogical postulates can be completely eliminated, by a purely routine procedure, without loss of deductive yield or increase in the complexity of the set of basic terms. As an illustration, suppose we have a system with the single primitive two-place predicate "intersects" and the single postulate of symmetry—that is, that everything intersects whatever intersects it. Now proceed as follows: instead of "intersects", take as primitive another word, say "cuts", for the same relation. Then introduce "intersects" into the system by the following definition: x intersects y if either x cuts y or y cuts x. From this definition, without any postulate, we can easily prove that "intersects" is symmetric. A general method has been found for so replacing postulates by definitions.

Should we, then, consider definitions to be postulates in determining the complexity of a postulate set? There are two troubles with this. First, definitions function in a system as devices for abbreviating theorems and can themselves be dropped without essential sacrifice of deductive yield. Second, we have seen earlier that our set of definitions inevitably becomes more intricate and comprehensive as we reduce the complexity of our set of undefined terms; hence we are working at cross purposes if we take the complexity of a set of definitions to be an indication of any complexity in the basis for a system.

As yet we have no satisfying answer to this puzzle, and no feasible way of measuring complexity of sets of postulates. But we are at much too early a stage in our investigation to despair of finding a better approach.

So far, I have been speaking of structural simplicity alone. I have said nothing of semantic or psychological simplicity. And I have treated simplicity as tantamount to systematization, and as complementary to, rather than as either contributing to or competing with, truth in science. But now I shall go much further. Simplicity, in at least some respect, is a test of truth.

If this seems simple-minded scientific treason, consider how we proceed in science. Suppose we are studying the relationship between the volume and pressure of a gas at constant temperature. We make many observations and plot them on a graph. We find that all the plotted points fall along a certain neat curve, and the function describing that curve is then incorporated in our theory and used for predicting further cases.

Notice, however, that no matter how many points we have plotted, infinitely many curves of different degrees of jaggedness or complexity pass through all these points. Any prediction whatever concerning an unobserved case could be made by using one or another of these curves. Our chosen curve has no more direct evidence in its favor than does any of the others. Simplicity of some sort governs the choice, and, without such a criterion, even the most comprehensive collection of data would stand neutral with respect to untested cases.

Take another example. Suppose a botanist finds that all the elm trees he examines, in many localities and under varying conditions, are deciduous. He may very well adopt the hypothesis that all elm trees are deciduous. He is unlikely to choose, instead, any of the countless other hypotheses that can claim exactly the same evidence. Among these, for example, if no trees in Smithtown happen to have been examined, are the following:

1. All elm trees everywhere, and also all pines in Smithtown, are deciduous.

2. All elm trees, except perhaps for those in Smithtown, are deciduous.

3. All other elm trees, but not those in Smithtown, are deciduous.

Moreover, any statement that combines the assertion that all the examined elm trees are deciduous with the ascription of any property whatsoever to unexamined things will belong on this list. The chosen hypothesis, "all elm trees are deciduous", is not the weakest; indeed, the conservative policy of choosing only the weakest hypothesis would prohibit going beyond the evidence at all. Nor is the chosen hypothesis the strongest; indeed, for any hypothesis that does venture beyond the evidence there is an alternative hypothesis that gives conflicting results for the unexamined cases. We take neither the safest nor the boldest course but the one that is in some sense or other the simplest.

Here and in the choice among curves, simplicity is used as a test of truth. That does not mean that we choose the simplest hypothesis even if it is controverted by the evidence, but rather that among hypotheses fitting the known cases we tend to choose the simplest hypotheses for judging the unknown cases. The simplicity involved here is surely not the structural simplicity I was talking about a few minutes ago, or a purely formal property at all. It has something to do not only with brevity or grammatical simplicity of statement but also with the familiarity of the language employed. The pragmatic factor of linguistic habit clearly plays a fundamental role in simplicity of this kind.

But what justification have we for so using simplicity as a test of truth? Can there be any ground for supposing that a statement has a better chance of being true merely because it is shorter and grammatically simpler and in familiar words or symbols? We are here in the middle of the notorious problem of justifying induction and we must be on guard; for that problem in some formulations turns out to be empty, and in others to be very different from what it seems on the surface. All I can say here is that some such test as simplicity is indispensable if we are to make predictions at all, and that it is justifiable in the sense and to the degree that science in general is justifiable.

If your scientific sensibilities have been shocked by the idea that simplicity is a test of truth, they are now in for an even heavier blow. For in science the consideration of simplicity must often override that of truth. We must not ignore the facts, but truth and simplicity often contend with one another, and truth cannot always win. Consider again, for example, the matter of fitting a curve to plots on a graph. Seldom does the chosen curve pass exactly through each of the points plotted; sometimes it may miss them all. Rather than choosing the simplest among the complex curves that fit the evidence, we choose among simple curves the one that comes nearest to fitting the evidence. Most of our scientific theories are neat approximations, less controlled than inspired by the evidence. Failing to transcend the detailed results of observation and experiment is as bad as playing fast and loose with them. Theory and fact have to be adjusted to each other. The able scientist develops a keen sense of when to yield to recalcitrant observations by modifying his theory and when to blame them on dirty test tubes and faulty instruments.

In review, then, I have argued that there is no science without simplicity—and no simplicity without something like science. I have discussed some measures of simplicity, and simplicity as a measure of systematization. And I have argued that simplicity not only functions as a test of truth but sometimes outweighs truth. What is important about simplicity, though, is not arguments for its importance, but painstaking analysis of it into component factors, study of how they function in relation to each other and to other factors, and development of means of measurement. Much of this work remains to be done, and in this essay I could not give any adequate idea of even the beginnings that have been made. I have tried only to attract your interest to a new and vital aspect of the science of science.

8

Uniformity and Simplicity

I am concerned neither with the history of a controversy nor with its effect upon the development of geology, but with what meaning, if any, the Principle of Uniformity and the issue over uniformitarianism have for the geologist today. Past prominence by no means implies present pertinence. Bruno and Galileo established modern cosmology by insisting that the earth moves; but whether the earth stands still or moves depends now merely upon what frame of reference we choose. If Hutton and Lyell put scientific geology on its feet by advocating the Principle of Uniformity, that of itself does not guarantee that the Principle has any validity or significance today.

We need only leaf through Dr. Albritton's fascinating bibliography[1] or look at the other papers in this symposium to discover that there is no uniformity at all concerning what the Principle of Uniformity is. Some writers regard it as an indispensable belief about the world. After all, the argument seems to run, the scientist can succeed only if nature plays fair; and therefore nature will play fair. Furthermore, playing fair is sometimes equated with being utterly docile; and the Principle of Uniformity is taken as denying any sudden or drastic change.

So interpreted, the Principle is plainly false. Volcanic eruptions, earthquakes, collisions in space, and atomic explosions have occurred and do still occur. The state of the earth in climate, ocean coverage, and countless other features varies widely from time to time. If the Principle of Uniformity is to be taken seriously, it cannot be identified with any such blatant lie as that nature remains always the same or moves only with dignity.

Sometimes we are told that the Principle affirms rather that whatever violent and sweeping changes may occur, they are always the result of underlying continuous and gradual processes.

1. C. C. Albritton, Jr., *The Fabric of Geology* (Stamford, Conn.: Freeman, Cooper, 1963), pp. 262–263.

But this version can be as readily discredited. The picture that physics gives us of the universe is of relative macrocosmic stability overlying violent and discontinuous microcosmic activity. The bland and sluggard boulder is a maelstrom of particles dashing madly hither and yon, colliding with each other, flickering into and out of existence. Nothing favors taking an exactly opposite view in geology. Uniformitarianism of this sort defies the findings and the whole tenor of modern science.

As a third try, the Principle of Uniformity is sometimes construed not as denying either the most radical changes or the most turbulent elementary processes but rather as affirming constancy of laws. Nature is assumed neither to run smoothly on the surface nor to grind slowly beneath but only to be governed by immutable laws; for what we rely upon in reconstructing the past and predicting the future is said to be merely that the natural laws in force today were in force yesterday and will be in force tomorrow. A danger here lines in a fanciful notion of these laws as potent agencies exerting actual control over the court of events. Whatever made the world and whatever makes it go, the scientist writes its laws. And whether or not nature behaves according to the law depends entirely upon whether we succeed in writing laws that describe its behavior. Once this is understood, the formula that laws now holding have held in the past and will hold in the future becomes either false or empty. Surely not *all* laws for any given period hold for other periods; we can always write special laws for a given stretch of time. On the other hand, the thesis that *some* laws hold for all time is an empty truism. No matter what happens, some laws will remain forever inviolate; for this is merely to say that some statements concerning the course of events will be true. The real question is *which* among the laws holding for the present hold also for the past and future.

Thus the Principle of Uniformity, construed as denying change or abrupt change in the course or the laws of nature can be rejected as false or futile. The uniformity required is not in nature's activities but in our account of them. Assumption concerning what we shall encounter gives way to prescription concerning how we are to proceed. The outlaw event must be looked upon as testifying not to a miraculous performance by nature but to an unsatisfactory

—or at least incomplete—one by the scientist. For while he will always be faced with recalcitrant facts, he must never accept any of them as ultimate exceptions to a unified theory. In this version, the Principle of Uniformity does not tell nature how to behave but tells us how to behave if we are to be scientific. This will, of course —and I think quite properly—make even Dr. Newell (p. 63, of this symposium) a prime example of a uniformitarian; for he insists upon using scientifically acceptable hypotheses both in arriving at the conclusion that many catastrophes must have occurred and in explaining their occurrence. Indeed, if I am correct, the residual issue between uniformitarianism and catastrophism comes down to the issue between naturalism and supernaturalism, or at least between naturalism and antinaturalism. It separates *geologists* from what we might call *geologians*. On this issue, the decision has surely already been taken; whether or not to be scientific in geology may once have been figuratively and literally a burning question, but I doubt if it keeps many of us awake nights now.

But being scientific involves more than refusal to accept any event as irredeemably lawless. It equally prohibits the lazy device of accommodating exceptions by incorporating special amendments in the laws. Science abhors the *ad hoc*. Being scientific requires projecting from the evidence to the unexamined cases by means of the smooth curve and the simple hypothesis. Perhaps the first step toward clarifying the Principle of the Uniformity of nature is to transform it into a principle of the simplicity of theory.

Consider an example. A primitive geophysicist investigates the tides. In all the cases he examines, successive ebb tides occur about 12 hours and 25 minutes apart. After many, varied, and careful observations he adopts the hypothesis that this also happens in all the cases not examined. How so? His evidence is equally in accord with the hypothesis that in all examined cases the interval is 12 hours and 25 minutes but in all other cases is 24 hours—and indeed equally in accord with any hypothesis that says the interval is 12 hours and 25 minutes in the examined cases and says anything whatever about the rest. Furthermore, by conforming to any of these hypotheses, nature would be obeying a fixed law. The hypothesis that the interval is about 12 hours and 25 minutes in all cases is chosen because it is somehow simplest; and without such a criterion, we could never select from among a welter of alternative, conflicting hypotheses, and so never succeed in going beyond the evidence at all.

Notice that the choice of hypothesis here cannot be attributed to knowledge of—or even conjecture concerning—the underlying mechanism. Our early scientist proceeded without knowing anything about the cause of tides or about the laws of gravitation. (Incidentally, even as late as the seventeenth century, Galileo accused Kepler of virtual astrology for suggesting the sun and moon had something to do with the tides.)[2] On the contrary, knowledge of the way the tides behave is a step toward discovery of the laws of gravitation. And 'the way the tides behave' is what our geophysicist decides in choosing among conflicting hypotheses that are consonant with his observations; his chosen hypothesis becomes one of the solid facts to be subsumed under a more comprehensive theory. Moreover, in arriving at the more general theory, he must again choose among conflicting hypotheses that fit the accepted facts; for the laws of gravitation are merely the simplest among indefinitely many alternative hypotheses (some of them grotesquely irregular) that survive confrontation with all the known facts. Sometimes, of course, already accepted background laws can be applied to effect a choice; but, if the choice in every case depended upon more general laws being already available, science could never get started. Often, as in our example, the choice must be made without reference to any such laws.

Again, if our geophysicist began with any naive assumption of uniformity in nature, he was soon disillusioned. Not only is the ocean always rising or falling, but the tides occur at different times on successive days; and even the interval between tides varies somewhat. The scientist demands little of nature but much of himself. Where there is change, he looks for constancy in the

2. Galileo, *Dialogue on the Great World Systems,* Salusbury, trans. (Chicago: University of Chicago Press, 1953), p. 469. ". . . among all the famous men who have philosophized upon this admirable effect of Nature, I wonder more at Kepler than at any of the rest, who, being of a free and penetrating intellect, has, for all that, given his ear and assent to the Moon's predominance over the water and to occult properties and such-like trifles."

rate of change; and failing that, for constancy in the rate of change of the rate of change. And where he finds no constancies, he settles for approximation. He copes with change not by a change in laws but by a law of change. Whatever the geologist finds happening, he devises formulas to fit, and chooses among these formulas by a principle of simplicity.

Now why this insistence upon simplicity? Must not the righteous scientist rather aim at truth and only hope for simplicity? Efforts to simplify a theory are often thought to be merely for the sake of elegance; but actually simplification is the soul of science. Science consists not of collecting particular truths but of relating, defining, demonstrating, organizing—in short, of systematizing. And to systematize is to simplify; an integrated system is achieved just to the extent that everything can be reduced to a minimal apparatus of underived terms and statements—that is, of undefined or primitive terms, and postulates or axioms. Science is the search for the simplest applicable theory.

Yet while the scientist must thus obviously choose the simplest among equivalent or mutually compatible theories, what are his grounds for choosing the simplest among nonequivalent theories that fit the evidence but conflict for unexamined cases? The simplest theory is not the most likely to be true just because the scientist hopes it will be true. Shall he then, after all, have to justify his choice by assuming that nature more often than not obeys the simplest among surviving alternative theories? If we understand that simplicity of theory is a matter of logical and syntactical structure, that it varies with the language used and is affected even by such pragmatic factors as familiarity of vocabulary, we can begin to appreciate how preposterous such an assumption would be. The attempt to defend it by arguing that nature usually has obeyed the simplest hypothesis and so probably always will is doubly doomed. In the first place, the argument begs the very question at issue—the validity of inferring what will happen from what has happened. And in the second place, the premiss is false: nature has by no means usually followed the simplest theory. We have been repeatedly forced, as in the case of the tides, to abandon a simpler in favor of a more complex hypothesis. Nature has, indeed, always obeyed the simplest—and also the most complex—among the theories it has not yet violated; but that hardly helps much. Nothing whatever can be said in support of the assumption that nature will usually follow the simpler theory; and about all anyone can justify by making so utterly unjustifiable an assumption is the suspicion that he is simple-minded.

Does this mean, then, that the practice of choosing the simplest surviving theory is quite indefensible? On the contrary, justification is virtually automatic once we admit that we are always faced with making a choice among hypotheses when there is no ground for supposing any of them more likely to be true than any of the rest. For if as scientists we seek simplicity, then obviously we try the simplest surviving theory first, and retreat from it only when it proves false. Not this course, but any other, requires explanation. If you want to go somewhere quickly, and several alternate routes are equally likely to be open, no one asks why you take the shortest. The simplest theory is to be chosen not because it is the most likely to be true but because it is scientifically the most rewarding among equally likely alternatives. We aim at simplicity and hope for truth.

I have had to skim very quickly over some complicated and subtle questions. We must not suppose that the principle of simplicity always calls for the choice, among alternative hypotheses, of the one that looks simplest. The injunction is rather to choose the hypothesis that makes for maximum simplicity in the over-all theory[3]—indeed, in the total fabric of science. Furthermore, accurate appraisal of comparative simplicity is often a difficult and delicate undertaking. Simplicity is multifaceted, and the analysis, interrelation, and measurement of its several factors is a study still in its earliest stages.[4] Full exposition of the principle and the grounds for it would have to take into account all these factors.

3. For example, the curve chosen among those fitting plotted points is often not the simplest (assuming we have adequate standards for the simplicity of curves) but rather the one most like curves accepted in similar contexts. The principle of simplicity operates here at a higher level in the criteria of "most like" and "similar".

4. For some beginnings, see VII,1 above and the publications cited therein. For the outlines of a formal calculus dealing with one aspect of the problem —measurement of the logical simplicity of basic scientific vocabularies— see SA III.

However, we are hardly called upon to go further into these matters now; for as questions of what constitutes being scientific they concern the geologist no more and no less than they concern the physicist or any other scientist. I will be charged here with forgetting that what raises special and acute problems for the geologist is that geology is a historical science and therefore basically different from a science like physics. But the difference has been grossly exaggerated.

We can dismiss at once the notion that geology is historical in the sense of dealing solely with the past. Tomorrow's earthquake no less than yesterday's belongs to the seismologist. And even where a science, such as paleontology, *is* confined to study of the past, this makes little difference; for the process of inference from examined to unexamined cases is the same whether it goes forward or backward in time. Postdiction and prediction alike consist of extrapolation from the evidence, and are governed by common principles.

What may seem more consequential is that geology is often a descriptive service, charged with determining and describing facts rather than with formulating theories, and that a principle for choosing theories does not necessarily apply in the finding of facts. But this contrast, too, is overdrawn. We do not merely find facts and make theories; we fit facts to theories as well as theories to facts. From accepted facts we proceed to covering theories, and we use these theories to decide further facts. Moreover, where fact and theory conflict, either may yield; accepted fact as well as accepted theory is subject to reconsideration and revision. Indeed, the very distinction between fact and theory is one of relative scope; a fact amounts to a small theory, a theory to a broad fact. And as we have seen in the case of the tides, what stands as a theory for one investigation or stage of investigation may become a fact for another. Science no more unearths absolutely stubborn facts than it reads off divine commandments. It makes the world as it makes theory; the two processes are one. The principle of simplicity, while it neither prescribes nor proscribes any possible fact or theory, operates in the determination of fact as in the formulation of theory. It plays the same role in descriptive as in theoretical science.

In conclusion, then, the Principle of Uniformity dissolves into a principle of simplicity that is not peculiar to geology but pervades all science and even daily life. And the geologist works under no uncommon handicaps and enjoys no special privileges merely because his work may be historical or descriptive. Thus he can now forget the obsolete controversy over uniformitarianism and cease defending himself for practicing what he fears may be not quite a science. He can more profitably turn his philosophical efforts to fundamental and far-reaching problems in the theory of classification, simplicity, measurement, and mapping. Geology has long since come of age.

Supplementary Readings for Chapter VII
secondary to references within text and footnotes

Bohnert, H. G., *The Interpretation of Theory* (Doctoral Dissertation, University of Pennsylvania, 1961).

Hempel, C. G., Review of a paper by Langord, *Journal of Symbolic Logic*, Vol. 7 (1942), p. 98.

———., *Aspects of Scientific Explanation*, New York: The Free Press, 1965, Chap. III, Sec. 8, "The Theoretician's Dilemma", pp. 173–226.

Langford, C. H., "Note on a Device of Quine and Goodman", *Journal of Symbolic Logic*, Vol. 6 (1941), pp. 154–155.

Lindenbaum, A., "Sur la Simplicité Formelle des Notions", in *Actes du Congrès International de Philosophie Scientifique*, Sorbonne, Paris, 1935, Vol. 7 *Logique*, Hermann, Paris, 1936.

Winnie, J., "The Implicit Definition of Theoretical Terms", *British Journal for the Philosophy of Science*, Vol. 18 (1967), pp. 223–229.

VIII

Induction

FOREWORD

The central piece in this chapter is the third chapter of *Fact, Fiction, and Forecast*. The first two papers foreshadowed it, and many others defend or explain points in it. That its main thrust here is negative—the disclosure of fundamental difficulties in the theory of induction—should not obscure the fact that the final chapter of *Fact, Fiction, and Forecast* and "An Improvement in the Theory of Projectibility" outline positive proposals for meeting these difficulties. But induction is a notoriously touchy subject, and the positive proposals are almost as widely resented as the paradoxes they are designed to resolve. Even people who calmly accept the fact that physical solidity rests upon particles in helter-skelter motion rebel at the suggestion that scientific procedure rests upon chance choices sanctified by habit. The characteristic response is either a denial of the problem or a search for a nobler solution.

Nevertheless, we may by now confidently conclude that no general distinction between projectible and non-projectible predicates can be drawn on syntactic or even on semantic grounds. Attempts to distinguish projectible predicates as purely qualitative, or non-projectible ones as time-dependent, for example, have plainly failed. Hilary Putnam,[1] in a paper on Carnap, likewise reaches the conclusion that any adequate definition of confirmation will require something more. Although Putnam does not refer to 'the new riddle' he seems to depend upon substantially the same point.

Many recent papers look for psychological grounds for our decisions as to what predicates or hypotheses to project. Were such an explanation found, it would not conflict with my treatment of

---

1. "Degree of Confirmation and Inductive Logic", *The Philosophy of Rudolf Carnap* (LaSalle, Illinois: Open Court, 1963), pp. 761–783.

projectibility in terms of entrenchment of predicates but would merely make the initial choices psychologically determinate rather than matters of chance. The difficulties of providing such a psychological explanation, though, are enormous; for any argument that the initial choices of projectible predicates are determined by some non-random operation of the mind requires showing that these predicates are distinguished by some common and independent characteristic that can be correlated with such an operation of the mind. The unavailability of any such characteristic (which would of itself provide a definition of projectibility) is just what gives rise to the riddle and turns our attention to chance and habit. Some further thoughts on the roles these may play in inductive processes, mechanical or human, are contained in "Inductive Translation".

The claim has now and again been made that the choice between equally supported conflicting hypotheses on grounds of projectibility is based not on comparative entrenchment but on past successes and failures. This cannot mean that H "All emeralds are green" is chosen over K "All emeralds are grue" because H has never failed us, for neither has K. And to hold merely that we choose H because we have projected it before and we stick to a hypothesis once chosen until it is violated or exhausted or indirectly discredited would simply rest projectibility on entrenchment. What is advocated, I think, is rather that K is rejected because kindred hypotheses have been violated in the past—where a kindred hypothesis is, for example, K_1 "All emeralds are grue$_1$" (i.e. "examined before 1900 A.D. and determined to be green, or not so examined and blue"). But by a parallel argument, we should choose K over H; for hypotheses kindred to H, such as H_1 "All emeralds are green$_1$" (i.e. "examined before 1900 A.D. and determined to be grue, or not so examined and bleen") have likewise been violated in the past. Thus this proposal comes to nothing. Accordingly, no appeal to survival of the fittest[2] will explain why H but not K is projected or projectible. They have been, and until 2000 A.D. will be, equally useful for survival; and while past choice of some hypotheses kindred to K would have been detrimental to survival, so would past choice of some hypotheses kindred to H.

2. *E.g.* as in W. V. Quine and J. S. Ullian, *The Web of Belief* (New York: Random House, 1970), pp. 57–58.

The new riddle of induction is sometimes carelessly said to arise from confirmation, by the same evidence, of two such conflicting hypotheses as "All emeralds are green" and "All emeralds are grue". Actually, evidence consists of statements, and the statements "emerald a is green", etc. that confirm the former hypothesis are not the same as the statements "emerald a is grue", etc. that confirm the latter. This, of course, does not dispose of the real riddle. A thing is grue if examined before 2000 A.D. and determined to be green, or is not so examined and is blue; hence at any earlier time, an examined thing is determined to be green if and only if it is determined to be grue, so that we have exactly equal and parallel evidence for the two conflicting hypotheses.

Occasionally "grue" is given some different interpretation. For example, in "Positionality and Pictures" and the paper it discusses, "grue" is taken to apply not to entire enduring entities but rather to green time-slices examined before 2000 A.D. and to blue time-slices not so examined. Basically the same riddle arises and the shift in interpretation may often go unnoticed. Contrary to a common misunderstanding, however, the interpretation of "grue" and "bleen" originally given in *FFF* (and in the above paragraph) does not require that a thing change from green to blue in order to remain grue, or from blue to green in order to remain bleen. "All emeralds are grue" may be true even though some emeralds are permanently green and the rest permanently blue.

My analogy between justification for rules of induction and justification for rules of deduction has been challenged by some writers[3] on the ground that for a deductive but not an inductive rule there is a positive test of validity: the rule must never lead from true premises to a false conclusion. This points to an obvious difference between deduction and induction but misses the point of my analogy. In testing a proposed rule of deduction, we examine in case after case whether it leads from premises we accept as true to conclusions we do not accept as true. When it does, we must choose between three alternatives: (1) rejecting the premises, (2) accepting the conclusion, (3) rejecting the rule. Although we want rules that always yield true conclusions from

---

3. *E.g.* J. Katz, *The Problem of Induction and its Solution* (Chicago: University of Chicago Press, 1962), pp. 46–49.

true premisses, we have no magic test for truth; the search for deductive rules is part of the search for truth. The process involves fitting our rules to the inferences we accept and our inferences to the rules. The comparison with induction is clear. An inductive rule must not lead from what we accept as the evidence to what we do not accept as a fair prediction. When a proposed rule does, we must choose between three alternatives: (1) rejecting the supposed evidence, (2) accepting the prediction as fair, (3) rejecting the rule. Just here is the significant analogy.

Coextensive predicates, I have said, have the same entrenchment. Isn't application of this principle in making an inductive choice circular, since deciding whether two predicates such as "ravens" and "blackbirds" are coextensive requires making a prior induction? The objection is entirely misguided on two counts. In the first place, it assumes that generalizations are accepted only on inductive grounds, whereas in fact they are accepted on a wide variety of good and bad grounds. In the second place, the objection misconstrues the problem of induction: how an entertained hypothesis must be related to the body of accepted statements in order to be considered confirmed. To say that coextensive predicates are equally entrenched is not to say that we must know what predicates are coextensive before making any inductive choices but to say how whatever judgments of coextensivity we do make are relevant to our inductive choices. That these judgments may be wrong does not distinguish them from any others.

Only a few of the points raised in the literature or in conversation have been dealt with here and in papers below and papers by Ullian,[4] Hullett and Schwartz,[5] Ackermann,[6] Foster,[7]

4. J. S. Ullian, "Luck, License, and Lingo", *Journal of Philosophy*, Vol. 58 (1961), pp. 731–738; and "More on 'Grue' and Grue", *Philosophical Review*, Vol. 70 (1961), pp. 386–389.

5. J. Hullett and R. Schwartz, "Grue: Some Remarks", *Journal of Philosophy*, Vol. 64 (1967), pp. 259–271.

6. R. Ackermann, "Howard Kahane's Entrenchment Theory", *Philosophy of Science*, Vol. 33 (1966), pp. 70–75; and "Conflict and Decision", same journal, Vol. 34 (1967), pp. 188–193.

7. Lawrence Foster, "Feyerabend's Solution to the Goodman Paradox", *British Journal for the Philosophy of Science*, Vol. 20 (1969), pp. 259–260; and "Differential and Projectible Predicates", *Critica*, Vol. 3 (1969), pp. 101–108.

Hanen,[8] and others; but I hope these examples may warn the reader to look very critically at other plausible objections and proposals encountered in the stream of commentary on *Fact, Fiction, and Forecast.*

On the positive side, appreciable progress has been made recently. In "The New Riddle of Induction", I dealt with the ravens paradox by observing that "R*a*.B*a*" supports "All ravens are black" but violates "All ravens are non-black" and so may be said to confirm the former as against the latter, while "R*a*.B*a*" supports "Nothing is a raven", which yields both "All ravens are black" and "All ravens are non-black". Israel Scheffler pointed out[9] that this amounts to recognizing a new relation of confirmation, with good intuitive credentials, that might be called *selective confirmation.*

Selective confirmation obviously does not meet the equivalence condition. Starting from this and from some of my remarks in "Comments", Marsha Hanen[10] has undertaken a thoroughgoing study of all proposed adequacy conditions for confirmation. The net result seems to be that all are dispensable and that our intuitive demands are otherwise met. Imposing the consequence condition, for example, leads to all sorts of trouble; and the underlying intuition is easily accommodated by noting that while evidence that confirms a hypothesis may fail to confirm a consequence, we are nevertheless required by a deductive rule to accept all consequences of every statement that we accept for any reason. Thus, if evidence leads us to accept a hypothesis, it leads us to accept all the consequences but not to regard the evidence as itself standing in the relation of confirmation to those consequences.

Incidentally, the situation was quite different for the definition of aboutness. The equivalence condition for aboutness neither gives rise to paradox, as in the case of confirmation, nor is so

8. Marsha Hanen, "Goodman, Wallace, and the Equivalence Condition", *Journal of Philosophy,* Vol. 64 (1967), pp. 271–280.

9. *The Anatomy of Inquiry* (New York: Knopf, 1967), Part III, pp. 286–291 especially.

10. *An Examination of Adequacy Conditions for Confirmation,* doctoral dissertation, Brandeis University, 1970.

readily dispensable. We can do without the consequence and even the equivalence condition for confirmation because confirmation is a guide to acceptance, and the principle of accepting equivalents and other consequences of statements we accept will suffice. That principle cannot, however, be made to do the work of an equivalence condition for aboutness; for since a statement and its negate are about the same things, what a statement is about is no guide to its acceptance.

The review of Reichenbach's book, though touching on many topics, is included here for its discussion of nomological statements. "Snowflakes and Wastebaskets" outlines briefly some salient ideas of C. I. Lewis, the teacher who most stimulated my thinking on induction and on many another philosophical problem.

1

A Query on Confirmation

Hempel, Carnap, Oppenheim, and Helmer[1] have recently made important contributions towards the precise definition of the concepts of confirmation and degree of confirmation. Yet they seem to me to leave untouched one basic problem that must be solved before we can say that the proposed definitions are intuitively adequate—even in an approximate sense and for very limited languages.

Induction might roughly be described as the projection of characteristics of the past into the future, or more generally of characteristics of one realm of objects into another. But exact expression of this vague principle is exceedingly difficult. Some of the contradictions that result from seemingly straightforward formulations of it were explained and overcome in Hempel's papers. Unfortunately, equally serious difficulties remain.

Suppose we had drawn a marble from a certain bowl on each of the ninety-nine days up to and including VE day, and each marble drawn was red. We would expect that the marble drawn on the following day would also be red. So far all is well. Our evidence may be expressed by the conjunction "$Ra_1 \cdot Ra_2 \cdot \ldots \cdot Ra_{99}$", which well confirms the prediction "Ra_{100}". But increase of credibility, projection, "confirmation" in any intuitive sense, does not occur in the case of every predicate under similar circumstances. Let "S" be the predicate "is drawn by VE day and is red, or is drawn later and is non-red". The evidence of the same drawings

1. In the following papers: C. G. Hempel, "A Purely Syntactical Definition of Confirmation", *Journal of Symbolic Logic*, Vol. 8 (1943), pp. 122–143; "Studies in the Logic of Confirmation", *Mind*, n.s., Vol. 54 (1945), pp. 1–26; Hempel and Paul Oppenheim, "A Definition of 'Degree of Confirmation'", *Philosophy of Science*, Vol. 12 (1945), pp. 98–115; Oppenheim and Olaf Helmer, "A Syntactical Definition of Probability and of Degree of Confirmation", *Journal of Symbolic Logic*, Vol. 10 (1945), pp. 25–60; Rudolf Carnap, "On Inductive Logic", *Philosophy of Science,* Vol. 12 (1945), pp. 72–97; and "The Two Concepts of Probability", *Philosophy and Phenomenological Research*, Vol. 5 (1945), pp. 513–532.

above assumed may be expressed by the conjunction "$Sa_1 \cdot Sa_2 \cdot$ . . . $\cdot Sa_{99}$". By the theories of confirmation in question this well confirms the prediction "Sa_{100}"; but actually we do not expect that the hundredth marble will be non-red. "Sa_{100}" gains no whit of credibility from the evidence offered.

It is clear that "S" and "R" cannot both be projected here, for that would mean that we expect that a_{100} will and will not be red. It is equally clear which predicate is actually projected and which is not. But how can the difference between projectible and non-projectible predicates be generally and rigorously defined?

That one predicate used in this example refers explicitly to temporal order is inessential. The same difficulty can be illustrated without the supposition of any order. Using the same letters as before, we need only suppose that the subscripts are merely for identification, having no ordinal significance, and that "S" means "is red and is not a_{100}, or is not red and is a_{100}".

The theories of confirmation in question require the primitive predicates to be logically independent.[2] This is perhaps a dubious stipulation since it places a logical requirement upon the informal, extrasystematic explanation of the predicates. Such doubts aside, the requirement would make it impossible for the predicates "R" and "S" to belong to the same system. Hence the conflicting confirmations would not occur in any one system. But this is of little help, since the system containing the predicate "S" alone is quite as admissible as the one containing "R" alone; and in the former system, as we have seen, "Sa_{100}" will be formally confirmed by the very evidence that intuitively disconfirms it. Carnap's concept of the "width" of a predicate does not bear on this point, since all atomic predicates are the same width.[3]

More complex examples illustrating various phases of the same general question can easily be invented. I give only one more, to show how the theory of degree of confirmation is affected.

2. Although this requirement is not explicitly stated in the articles cited, Hempel tells me that its necessity was recognized by all the authors concerned.

3. See page 84 of the first article by Carnap listed in footnote 1.

Suppose[4] that a certain unfamiliar machine tosses up one ball a minute and that every third one and only every third one is red. We observe ninety-six tosses. How much confidence does this lead us to place in the prediction that the next three tosses will produce a non-red ball, another non-red ball, and then a red ball? Plainly a good deal. But what degree of formal confirmation does the prediction derive from the observations according to the theories under consideration? The answer seems to be that this varies widely with the way the given evidence is described.

(i) If we let "a_1", "a_2", and so on represent in temporal order the individual tosses, our evidence may be expressed by

$$\text{``}-Ra_1 \cdot -Ra_2 \cdot Ra_3 \cdot -Ra_4 \cdot -Ra_5 \cdot Ra_6 \cdot \ldots \cdot -Ra_{94} \cdot -Ra_{95} \cdot Ra_{96}\text{''}.$$

This imparts to the prediction "$-Ra_{97} \cdot -Ra_{98} \cdot Ra_{99}$" the degree[5] of confirmation $\frac{2}{3} \cdot \frac{2}{3} \cdot \frac{1}{3}$, or $\frac{4}{27}$. This figure seems intuitively much too low.

(ii) If we let "b_1" stand for the discontinuous individual consisting of the first three tosses, "b_2" for the individual consisting of the next three tosses, and so on, and let "S" mean "consists of three temporally separated parts ('tosses') of which the earliest and second are non-red and the latest red", our evidence may be expressed by

$$\text{``}Sb_1 \cdot \ldots \cdot Sb_{32}\text{''}.$$

This gives to "Sb_{33}" the degree of confirmation 1. Yet "Sb_{33}" expresses the same thing as "$-Ra_{94} \cdot -Ra_{95} \cdot Ra_{96}$", and we have assumed the same observations. Hence we seem to get different degrees of confirmation for the same prediction on the basis of the same evidence.

4. The example in its present form is due to Hempel. He constructed it as the result of a conversation with Quine and the present writer concerning the problems here explained.

5. The degrees of confirmation given in this paper are computed according to the Hempel-Oppenheim theory. The values under Carnap's theory would differ somewhat, but not in a way that appreciably affects the general question under discussion.

Now it may be argued that in (i) we ignored the fact of temporal order in stating our evidence, and that it is thus not surprising that we get a lower degree of confirmation than when we take this fact into account, as in (ii). However, it would be fatal to accept the implied thesis that an intuitively satisfactory degree of confirmation will result only when all the observed facts are expresesd as evidence. Suppose the first ninety-six tosses exhibited a wholly irregular distribution of colors; the hypothesis that this distribution would be exactly repeated in the next ninety-six tosses would have the degree of confirmation 1. What is worse, if we are to express *all* the observed data in our statement of evidence, we shall have to include such particularized information—e.g., the unique date of each toss—that repetition in the future will be impossible.

Undoubtedly we do make predictions by projecting the patterns of the past into the future, but in selecting the patterns we project from among all those that the past exhibits, we use practical criteria that so far seem to have escaped discovery and formulation. The problem is not peculiar to the work of the authors I have named; so far as I am aware, no one has as yet offered any satisfactory solution. What we have in the paper cited is an ingenious and valuable logico-mathematical apparatus that we may apply to the sphere of projectible or confirmable predicates whenever we discover what a projectible or confirmable predicate is.

2

On Infirmities of Confirmation-Theory

Carnap's paper "On the Application of Inductive Logic"[1] sets forth certain assumptions on the basis of which he seeks to answer the question raised in my "Query on Confirmation".[2] Not much comment on these assumptions is necessary; the reader may decide for himself whether he finds them acceptable, as Carnap does, or quite unacceptable, as I do. The root assumption is that there are absolutely simple properties into which others may, and indeed for some purposes must, be analyzed. The nature of this simplicity is obscure to me, since the question whether or not a given property is analyzable seems to me quite as ambiguous as the question whether a given body is in motion. I regard "unanalyzability" as meaningful only with respect to sphere of reference and a method of analysis, while Carnap seems to regard it as having an absolute meaning.

By way of partial justification for the restrictions Carnap places upon the interpretation of the predicates admissible in his system, he argues that these restrictions are also necessary for deductive logic. The analogy does not seem to me well drawn. He says that in deductive logic, knowledge of such matters as the independence of predicates, etc., is necessary if we are to be able to determine whether or not a statement is analytic. But certainly we do not need such knowledge in order to carry out perfectly valid deductions; I can infer S_1 from $S_1 \cdot S_2$ quite safely without knowing anything about the independence of the predicates involved in these sentences. On the contrary, in the case of Carnap's system of inductive logic, I cannot safely make an inductive inference without such knowledge; I must have this knowledge before I can tell whether the computation of a degree of confirmation will be at all correct. The analogy Carnap seeks to draw would seem to me convincing only if he could show that the assumptions necessary to

1. *Philosophy and Phenomenological Research,* Vol. 8 (1947), pp. 133–148.

2. [VIII,1 above.]

guarantee the correctness of inductive inference (by his methods) are likewise necessary to guarantee the validity of deductive inference.

Furthermore, even supposing all predicates to have been classi- fied into purely qualitative, positional, and mixed, we are offered no evidence or argument in support of Carnap's conjecture that either the class of purely qualitative predicates is identical with the class of intuitively projectible predicates, or that such predi- cates as are intuitively projectible though not purely qualitative will also prove to be projectible by his definition. The first alter- native seems *prima facie* dubious since predicates like "solar", "arctic", and "Sung" appear to be intuitively projectible but not purely qualitative; the grounds for the second alternative are not evident.

In the last page or two of his article, Carnap seems almost to be claiming that no such question of intuitive adequacy any longer exists. He maintains that with his present restrictions on the in- terpretation of primitive predicates, his formal system of inductive logic provides a definition of projectibility; and he suggests there- fore that anyone who has queries about projectibility can find out the answers by studying his system, just as one can learn about right triangles by studying Euclid. The catch is, though, that the question whether the formal system is intuitively adequate is quite pertinent both to Euclid's system and to Carnap's. In fact, the only difference in the two cases is that I am better satisfied that the triangles to which the Pythagorean theorem applies are just those I know as right triangles than I am that those properties to which Carnap's formula in terms of c^* applies are just those that are intuitively projectible.

Concerning the principle of total evidence, a rather complex discussion has grown out of a subsidiary point that I apparently did not explain very well. The point was this: it might have been possible to claim that a criterion of projectibility is unnecessary be- cause the evidence need never contain any nonprojectible predi- cates. Examples show, however, that such predicates as those of order must be admitted into our evidence if we are to avoid counterintuitive results. If it is therefore required that order and all other properties be covered in our evidence-statement, then we shall have to have a criterion of projectibility in order to determine which are to be expected to attach to future cases; if no such distinction is made in our formal system, or in the rules for applying it, we shall reach the absurd conclusion that future cases will probably have all the properties common to past cases. (Incidentally, Carnap's example of an investigator who omits all cases unfavorable to the hypothesis being tested is not parallel to mine and does not bear on the same point; for in my example, no cases were omitted but only, quite consciously, some information about these cases.)

One further point concerning my examples having to do with order. I was in effect asking how the obviously relevant fact of order was to be taken into account by the theories in question, and pointing out that in trying to devise a method for doing this, we must face the fact that regular orders influence our expectations in a way that irregular ones do not. Thus if a method should give a high degree of confirmation for repetition of the pattern *red, red, not-red,* on the evidence that this pattern had repeatedly occurred, it would seem likely that this method would be in danger of giving a high degree of confirmation for the repetition of a wholly irregular pattern of, say, 96 tosses. In effect, if not technically, we would seem to be regarding each occurrence of a pattern as a confirming instance; hence in the irregular case we have the equivalent of one positive and no negative instances. I am not clear as to how Carnap's proposal would render regular order effective without rendering irregular order equally effective and thus leading to counterintuitive results. Carnap cannot say antecedently that regular order is relevant and irregular order isn't. This would mean just that the former but not the latter affects the c* computation, and would indeed, were it true, provide us with an interesting definition of degree of regularity. But I am afraid that if order is so to affect the computation as to give intuitive results when the order is regular, it will be difficult to avoid getting counterintuitive results when the order is irregular. It is worth noting, however, that this difficulty might be overcome by a definition of degree of confirmation for which the number of confirming cases is always important, since an irregular order is perhaps one that does not consist of repetitions of a smaller pattern.

But the consideration of the examples involving order are in any case quite secondary to my main point which is adequately illustrated by the other examples I gave. I regret that Carnap's method of dealing with it involves assumptions I cannot accept and that no other answer has been forthcoming. For until this problem is solved, we are seriously hampered in our efforts to solve certain other important problems.[3]

3. For example, see *FFF I.*

3

The New Riddle of Induction

1. The Old Problem of Induction

At the close of the preceding lecture, I said that today I should examine how matters stand with respect to the problem of induction. In a word, I think they stand ill. But the real difficulties that confront us today are not the traditional ones. What is commonly thought of as the Problem of Induction has been solved, or dissolved; and we face new problems that are not as yet very widely understood. To approach them, I shall have to run as quickly as possible over some very familiar ground.

The problem of the validity of judgments about future or unknown cases arises, as Hume pointed out, because such judgments are neither reports of experience nor logical consequences of it. Predictions, of course, pertain to what has not yet been observed. And they cannot be logically inferred from what has been observed; for what *has* happened imposes no logical restrictions on what *will* happen. Although Hume's dictum that there are no necessary connections of matters of fact has been challenged at times, it has withstood all attacks. Indeed, I should be inclined not merely to agree that there are no necessary connections of matters of fact, but to ask whether there are any necessary connections at all[1]—but that is another story.

Hume's answer to the question how predictions are related to past experience is refreshingly non-cosmic. When an event of one kind frequently follows upon an event of another kind in experience, a habit is formed that leads the mind, when confronted with a new event of the first kind, to pass to the idea of an event of the

---

1. Although this remark is merely an aside, perhaps I should explain for the sake of some unusually sheltered reader that the notion of a necessary connection of ideas, or of an absolutely analytic statement, is no longer sacrosanct. Some, like Quine and White, have forthrightly attacked the notion; others, like myself, have simply discarded it; and still others have begun to feel acutely uncomfortable about it.

second kind. The idea of necessary connection arises from the felt impulse of the mind in making this transition.

Now if we strip this account of all extraneous features, the central point is that to the question "Why one prediction rather than another?", Hume answers that the elect prediction is one that accords with a past regularity, because this regularity has established a habit. Thus among alternative statements about a future moment, one statement is distinguished by its consonance with habit and thus with regularities observed in the past. Prediction according to any other alternative is errant.

How satisfactory is this answer? The heaviest criticism has taken the righteous position that Hume's account at best pertains only to the source of predictions, not their legitimacy; that he sets forth the circumstances under which we make given predictions—and in this sense explains why we make them—but leaves untouched the question of our license for making them. To trace origins, runs the old complaint, is not to establish validity: the real question is not why a prediction is in fact made but how it can be justified. Since this seems to point to the awkward conclusion that the greatest of modern philosophers completely missed the point of his own problem, the idea has developed that he did not really take his solution very seriously, but regarded the main problem as unsolved and perhaps as insoluble. Thus we come to speak of 'Hume's problem' as though he propounded it as a question without answer.

All this seems to me quite wrong. I think Hume grasped the central question and considered his answer to be passably effective. And I think his answer is reasonable and relevant, even if it is not entirely satisfactory. I shall explain presently. At the moment, I merely want to record a protest against the prevalent notion that the problem of justifying induction, when it is so sharply dissociated from the problem of describing how induction takes place, can fairly be called Hume's problem.

I suppose that the problem of justifying induction has called forth as much fruitless discussion as has any halfway respectable problem of modern philosophy. The typical writer begins by insisting that some way of justifying predictions must be found, proceeds to argue that for this purpose we need some resounding universal law of the Uniformity of Nature, and then inquires how this universal principle itself can be justified. At this point, if he is tired, he concludes that the principle must be accepted as an indispensable assumption; or if he is energetic and ingenious, he goes on to devise some subtle justification for it. Such an invention, however, seldom satisfies anyone else; and the easier course of accepting an unsubstantiated and even dubious assumption much more sweeping than any actual predictions we make seems an odd and expensive way of justifying them.

2. Dissolution of the Old Problem

Understandably, then, more critical thinkers have suspected that there might be something awry with the problem we are trying to solve. Come to think of it, what precisely would constitute the justification we seek? If the problem is to explain how we know that certain predictions will turn out to be correct, the sufficient answer is that we don't know any such thing. If the problem is to *find* some way of distinguishing antecedently between true and false predictions, we are asking for prevision rather than for philosophical explanation. Nor does it help matters much to say that we are merely trying to show that or why certain predictions are *probable*. Often it is said that while we cannot tell in advance whether a prediction concerning a given throw of a die is true, we can decide whether the prediction is a probable one. But if this means determining how the prediction is related to actual frequency distributions of future throws of the die, surely there is no way of knowing or proving this in advance. On the other hand, if the judgment that the prediction is probable has nothing to do with subsequent occurrences, then the question remains in what sense a probable prediction is any better justified than an improbable one.

Now obviously the genuine problem cannot be one of attaining unattainable knowledge or of accounting for knowledge that we do not in fact have. A better understanding of our problem can be gained by looking for a moment at what is involved in justifying non-inductive inferences. How do we justify a *deduction*? Plainly, by showing that it conforms to the general rules of deductive inference. An argument that so conforms is justified or valid, even if its conclusion happens to be false. An argument that violates a rule is fallacious even if its conclusion happens to be true. To justify a deductive conclusion therefore requires no knowledge of the facts it pertains to. Moreover, when a deductive argument has been shown to conform to the rules of logical inference, we usually consider it justified without going on to ask what justifies the rules. Analogously, the basic task in justifying an inductive inference is to show that it conforms to the general rules of induction. Once we have recognized this, we have gone a long way towards clarifying our problem.

Yet, of course, the rules themselves must eventually be justified. The validity of a deduction depends not upon conformity to any purely arbitrary rules we may contrive, but upon conformity to valid rules. When we speak of *the* rules of inference we mean the valid rules—or better, *some* valid rules, since there may be alternative sets of equally valid rules. But how is the validity of rules to be determined? Here again we encounter philosophers who insist that the rules follow from some self-evident axiom, and others who try to show that the rules are grounded in the very nature of the human mind. I think the answer lies much nearer the surface. Principles of deductive inference are justified by their conformity with accepted deductive practice. Their validity depends upon accordance with the particular deductive inferences we actually make and sanction. If a rule yields inacceptable inferences, we drop it as invalid. Justification of general rules thus derives from judgments rejecting or accepting particular deductive inferences.

This looks flagrantly circular. I have said that deductive inferences are justified by their conformity to valid general rules, and that general rules are justified by their conformity to valid inferences. But this circle is a virtuous one. The point is that rules and particular inferences alike are justified by being brought into agreement with each other. *A rule is amended if it yields an inference we are unwilling to accept; an inference is rejected if it violates a rule we are unwilling to amend.* The process of justification is the delicate one of making mutual adjustments between rules and accepted inferences; and in the agreement achieved lies the only justification needed for either.

All this applies equally well to induction. An inductive inference, too, is justified by conformity to general rules. And a general rule by conformity to accepted inductive inferences. Predictions are justified if they conform to valid canons of induction; and the canons are valid if they accurately codify accepted inductive practice.

A result of such analysis is that we can stop plaguing ourselves with certain spurious questions about induction. We no longer demand an explanation for guarantees that we do not have, or seek keys to knowledge that we cannot obtain. It dawns upon us that the traditional smug insistence upon a hard-and-fast line between justifying induction and describing ordinary inductive practice distorts the problem. And we owe belated apologies to Hume. For in dealing with the question how normally accepted inductive judgments are made, he was in fact dealing with the question of inductive validity.[2] The validity of a prediction consisted for him in its arising from habit, and thus in its exemplifying some past regularity. His answer was incomplete and perhaps not entirely correct; but it was not beside the point. The problem of induction is not a problem of demonstration but a problem of defining the difference between valid and invalid predictions.

This clears the air but leaves a lot to be done. As principles of deductive inference, we have the familiar and highly developed laws of logic; but there are available no such precisely stated and well-recognized principles of inductive reference. Mill's canons hardly rank with Aristotle's rules of the syllogism, let alone with

2. A hasty reader might suppose that my insistence here upon identifying the problem of justification with a problem of description is out of keeping with my parenthetical insistence in the preceding lecture [*FFF II*] that the goal of philosophy is something quite different from the mere description of ordinary or scientific procedure. Let me repeat that the point urged there was that the organization of the explanatory account need not reflect the manner or order in which predicates are adopted in practice. It surely must describe practice, however, in the sense that the extensions of predicates as explicated must conform in certain ways to the extensions of the same predicates as applied in practice. Hume's account is a description in just this sense. For it is an attempt to set forth the circumstances under which those inductive judgments are made that are normally accepted as valid; and to do that is to state necessary and sufficient conditions for, and thus to define, valid induction. What I am maintaining above is that the problem of justifying induction is not something over and above the problem of describing or defining valid induction.

Principia Mathematica. Elaborate and valuable treatises on probability usually leave certain fundamental questions untouched.
Only in very recent years has there been any explicit and systematic work upon what I call the constructive task of confirmation
theory.

3. The Constructive Task of Confirmation Theory

The task of formulating rules that define the difference between
valid and invalid inductive inferences is much like the task of
defining any term with an established usage. If we set out to define
the term "tree", we try to compose out of already understood
words an expression that will apply to the familiar objects that
standard usage calls trees, and that will not apply to objects that
standard usage refuses to call trees. A proposal that plainly violates either condition is rejected; while a definition that meets
these tests may be adopted and used to decide cases that are not
already settled by actual usage. Thus the interplay we observed
between rules of induction and particular inductive inferences is
simply an instance of this characteristic dual adjustment between
definition and usage, whereby the usage informs the definition,
which in turn guides extension of the usage.

Of course this adjustment is a more complex matter than I
have indicated. Sometimes, in the interest of convenience or theoretical utility, we deliberately permit a definition to run counter
to clear mandates of common usage. When accept a definition of
"fish" that excludes whales. Similarly we may decide to deny
the term "valid induction" to some inductive inferences that are
commonly considered valid, or apply the term to others not usually
so considered. A definition may modify as well as extend ordinary
usage.[3]

Some pioneer work on the problem of defining confirmation or
valid induction has been done by Professor Hempel.[4] Let me re-

---

3. For a fuller discussion of definition in general see *SA I.* [See also IV,3
above.]

4. The basic article is "A Purely Syntactical Definition of Confirmation",
Journal of Symbolic Logic, Vol. 8 (1943), pp. 122–143. A much less technical
account is given in "Studies in the Logic of Confirmation", *Mind,* n.s., Vol. 54
(1945), pp. 1–26 and 97–121. Later work by Hempel and others on defining
degree of confirmation does not concern us here.

mind you briefly of a few of his results. Just as deductive logic is concerned primarily with a relation between statements—namely the consequence relation—that is independent of their truth or falsity, so inductive logic as Hempel conceives it is concerned primarily with a comparable relation of confirmation between statements. Thus the problem is to define the relation that obtains between any statement S_1 and another S_2 if and only if S_1 may properly be said to confirm S_2 in any degree.

With the question so stated, the first step seems obvious. Does not induction proceed in just the opposite direction from deduction? Surely some of the evidence-statements that inductively support a general hypothesis are consequences of it. Since the consequence relation is already well defined by deductive logic, will we not be on firm ground in saying that confirmation embraces the converse relation? The laws of deduction in reverse will then be among the laws of induction.

Let's see where this leads us. We naturally assume further that whatever confirms a given statement confirms also whatever follows from that statement.[5] But if we combine this assumption with our proposed principle, we get the embarrassing result that every statement confirms every other. Surprising as it may be that such innocent beginnings lead to such an intolerable conclusion, the proof is very easy. Start with any statement S_1. It is a consequence of, and so by our present criterion confirms, the conjunction of S_1 and any statement whatsoever—call it S_2. But the confirmed conjunction, $S_1 \cdot S_2$, of course has S_2 as a consequence. Thus every statement confirms all statements.

The fault lies in careless formulation of our first proposal. While some of the statements that confirm a general hypothesis are consequences of it, not all its consequences confirm it. This may not

---

5. I am not here asserting that this is an indispensable requirement upon a definition of confirmation. Since our commonsense assumptions taken in combination quickly lead us to absurd conclusions, some of these assumptions have to be dropped; and different theorists may make different decisions about which to drop and which to preserve. Hempel gives up the converse consequence condition, while Carnap, *Logical Foundations of Probability* (Chicago: University of Chicago Press, 1950), pp. 474–476, drops both the consequence condition and the converse consequence condition. Such differences of detail between different treatments of confirmation do not affect the central points I am making in this lecture.

be immediately evident; for indeed we do in some sense furnish support for a statement when we establish one of its consequences. We settle one of the questions about it. Consider the heterogeneous conjunction:

8497 is a prime number and the other side of the moon is flat and Elizabeth the First was crowned on a Tuesday.

To show that any one of the three component statements is true is to support the conjunction by reducing the net undetermined claim. But support[6] of this kind is not confirmation; for establishment of one component endows the whole statement with no credibility that is transmitted to other component statements. Confirmation of a hypothesis occurs only when an instance imparts to the hypothesis some credibility that is conveyed to other instances. Appraisal of hypothesis, indeed, is incidental to prediction, to the judgment of new cases on the basis of old ones.

Our formula thus needs tightening. This is readily accomplished, as Hempel points out, if we observe that a hypothesis is genuinely confirmed only by a statement that is an instance of it in the special sense of entailing not the hypothesis itself but its relativization or restriction to the class of entities mentioned by that statement. The relativization of a general hypothesis to a class results from restricting the range of its universal and existential quantifiers to the members of that class. Less technically, what the hypothesis says of all things the evidence statement says of one thing (or of one pair or other n-ad of things). This obviously covers the confirmation of the conductivity of all copper by the conductivity of a given piece; and it excludes confirmation of our heterogeneous conjunction by any of its components. And, when taken together with the principle that what confirms a statement confirms all its consequences, this criterion does not yield the untoward conclusion that every statement confirms every other.

New difficulties promptly appear from other directions, how-

6. Any hypothesis is 'supported' by its own positive instances; but support —or better, direct factual support—is only one factor in confirmation. This factor has been separately studied by John G. Kemeny and Paul Oppenheim in "Degree of Factual Support", *Philosophy of Science*, Vol. 19 (1952), pp. 307–324. As will appear presently, my concern is primarily with certain other important factors in confirmation, some of them quite generally neglected.

ever. One is the infamous paradox of the ravens. The statement
that a given object, say this piece of paper, is neither black nor a
raven confirms the hypothesis that all non-black things are non-
ravens. But this hypothesis is logically equivalent to the hypothesis
that all ravens are black. Hence we arrive at the unexpected conclusion that the statement that a given object is neither black nor
a raven confirms the hypothesis that all ravens are black. The
prospect of being able to investigate ornithological theories without going out in the rain is so attractive that we know there must
be a catch in it. The trouble this time, however, lies not in faulty
definition, but in tacit and illicit reference to evidence not stated
in our example. Taken by itself, the statement that the given object
is neither black nor a raven confirms the hypothesis that everything that is not a raven is not black as well as the hypothesis that
everything that is not black is not a raven. We tend to ignore the
former hypothesis because we know it to be false from abundant
other evidence—from all the familiar things that are not ravens
but are black. But we are required to assume that no such evidence is available. Under this circumstance, even a much stronger
hypothesis is also obviously confirmed: that nothing is either black
or a raven. In the light of this confirmation of the hypothesis that
there are no ravens, it is no longer surprising that under the artificial restrictions of the example, the hypothesis that all ravens
are black is also confirmed. And the prospects for indoor orni-
thology vanish when we notice that under these same conditions,
the contrary hypothesis that no ravens are black is equally well
confirmed.[7]

On the other hand, our definition does err in not forcing us to
take into account all the *stated* evidence. The unhappy results are
readily illustrated. If two compatible evidence statements confirm
two hypotheses, then naturally the conjunction of the evidence
statements should confirm the conjunction of the hypotheses.[8]

7. An able and thorough exposition of this paragraph is given by Israel
Scheffler in his *Anatomy of Inquiry* (New York: Knopf, 1963), pp. 286–291.

8. The status of the conjunction condition is much like that of the consequence condition—see Note 5. Although Carnap drops the conjunction condition also (p. 394), he adopts for different reasons the requirement we find
needed above: that the total available evidence must always be taken into
account (Carnap, pp. 211–213).

Suppose our evidence consists of the statements E_1 saying that a given thing b is black, and E_2 saying that a second thing c is not black. By our present definition, E_1 confirms the hypothesis that everything is black, and E_2 the hypothesis that everything is non-black. The conjunction of these perfectly compatible evidence statements will then confirm the self-contradictory hypothesis that everything is both black and non-black. Simple as this anomaly is, it requires drastic modification of our definition. What given evidence confirms is not what we arrive at by generalizing from separate items of it, but—roughly speaking—what we arrive at by generalizing from the total stated evidence. The central idea for an improved definition is that, within certain limitations, what is asserted to be true for the narrow universe of the evidence statements is confirmed for the whole universe of discourse. Thus if our evidence is E_1 and E_2, neither the hypothesis that all things are black nor the hypothesis that all things are non-black is confirmed; for neither is true for the evidence-universe consisting of b and c. Of course, much more careful formulation is needed, since some statements that are true of the evidence-universe—such as that there is only one black thing—are obviously not confirmed for the whole universe. These matters are taken care of by the studied formal definition that Hempel develops on this basis; but we cannot, and need not, go into further detail here.

No one supposes that the task of confirmation-theory has been completed. But the few steps I have reviewed—chosen partly for their bearing on what is to follow—show how things move along once the problem of definition displaces the problem of justification. Important and long-unnoticed questions are brought to light and answered; and we are encouraged to expect that the many remaining questions will in time yield to similar treatment.

But our satisfaction is shortlived. New and serious trouble begins to appear.

4. The New Riddle of Induction

Confirmation of a hypothesis by an instance depends rather heavily upon features of the hypothesis other than its syntactical form. That a given piece of copper conducts electricity increases the credibility of statements asserting that other pieces of copper conduct electricity, and thus confirms the hypothesis that all copper conducts electricity. But the fact that a given man now in this room is a third son does not increase the credibility of statements asserting that other men now in this room are third sons, and so does not confirm the hypothesis that all men now in this room are third sons. Yet in both cases our hypothesis is a generalization of the evidence statement. The difference is that in the former case the hypothesis is a *lawlike* statement; while in the latter case, the hypothesis is a merely contingent or accidental generality. Only a statement that is *lawlike*—regardless of its truth or falsity or its scientific importance—is capable of receiving confirmation from an instance of it; accidental statements are not. Plainly, then, we must look for a way of distinguishing lawlike from accidental statements.

So long as what seems to be needed is merely a way of excluding a few odd and unwanted cases that are inadvertently admitted by our definition of confirmation, the problem may not seem very hard or very pressing. We fully expect that minor defects will be found in our definition and that the necessary refinements will have to be worked out patiently one after another. But some further examples will show that our present difficulty is of a much graver kind.

Suppose that all emeralds examined before a certain time *t* are green.[9] At time *t*, then, our observations support the hypothesis that all emeralds are green; and this is in accord with our definition of confirmation. Our evidence statements assert that emerald *a* is green, that emerald *b* is green, and so on; and each confirms the general hypothesis that all emeralds are green. So far, so good.

Now let me introduce another predicate less familiar than "green". It is the predicate "grue" and it applies to all things examined before *t* just in case they are green but to other things just in case they are blue. Then at time *t* we have, for each evidence statement asserting that a given emerald is green, a parallel evidence statement asserting that the emerald is grue. And the

9. Although the example used is different, the argument to follow is substantially the same as that set forth in my note 'A Query on Confirmation' [VIII,1 above].

statements that emerald a is grue, that emerald b is grue, and so on, will each confirm the general hypothesis that all emeralds are grue. Thus according to our definition, the prediction that all emeralds subsequently examined will be green and the prediction that all will be grue are alike confirmed by evidence statements describing the same observations. But if an emerald subsequently examined is grue, it is blue and hence not green. Thus although we are well aware which of the two incompatible predictions is genuinely confirmed, they are equally well confirmed according to our present definition. Moreover, it is clear that if we simply choose an appropriate predicate, then on the basis of these same observations we shall have equal confirmation, by our definition, for any prediction whatever about other emeralds—or indeed about anything else.[10] As in our earlier example, only the predictions subsumed under lawlike hypotheses are genuinely confirmed; but we have no criterion as yet for determining lawlikeness. And now we see that without some such criterion, our definition not merely includes a few unwanted cases, but is so completely ineffectual that it virtually excludes nothing. We are left once again with the intolerable result that anything confirms anything. This difficulty cannot be set aside as an annoying detail to be taken care of in due course. It has to be met before our definition will work at all.

Nevertheless, the difficulty is often slighted because on the surface there seem to be easy ways of dealing with it. Sometimes, for example, the problem is thought to be much like the paradox of the ravens. We are here again, it is pointed out, making tacit and illegitimate use of information outside the stated evidence: the information, for example, that different samples of one material are usually alike in conductivity, and the information that different men in a lecture audience are usually not alike in the number

10. For instance, we shall have equal confirmation, by our present definition, for the prediction that roses subsequently examined will be blue. Let "emerose" apply just to emeralds examined before time t, and to roses examined later. Then all emeroses so far examined are grue, and this confirms the hypothesis that all emeroses are grue and hence the prediction that roses subsequently examined will be blue. The problem raised by such antecedents has been little noticed, but is no easier to meet than that raised by similarly perverse consequents.

of their older brothers. But while it is true that such information is being smuggled in, this does not by itself settle the matter as it settles the matter of the ravens. There the point was that when the smuggled information is forthrightly declared, its effect upon the confirmation of the hypothesis in question is immediately and properly registered by the definition we are using. On the other hand, if to our initial evidence we add statements concerning the conductivity of pieces of other materials or concerning the number of older brothers of members of other lecture audiences, this will not in the least affect the confirmation, according to our definition, of the hypothesis concerning copper or of that concerning this lecture audience. Since our definition is insensitive to the bearing upon hypotheses of evidence so related to them, even when the evidence is fully declared, the difficulty about accidental hypotheses cannot be explained away on the ground that such evidence is being surreptitiously taken into account.

A more promising suggestion is to explain the matter in terms of the effect of this other evidence not directly upon the hypothesis in question but *indirectly* through other hypotheses that *are* confirmed, according to our definition, by such evidence. Our information about other materials does by our definition confirm such hypotheses as that all pieces of iron conduct electricity, that no pieces of rubber do, and so on; and these hypotheses, the explanation runs, impart to the hypothesis that all pieces of copper conduct electricity (and also to the hypothesis that none do) the character of lawlikeness—that is, of amenability to confirmation by direct positive instances when found. On the other hand, our information about other lecture audiences *dis*confirms many hypotheses to the effect that all the men in one audience are third sons, or that none are; and this strips any character of lawlikeness from the hypothesis that all (or the hypothesis that none) of the men in *this* audience are third sons. But clearly if this course is to be followed, the circumstances under which hypotheses are thus related to one another will have to be precisely articulated.

The problem, then, is to define the relevant way in which such hypotheses must be alike. Evidence for the hypothesis that all iron conducts electricity enhances the lawlikeness of the hypothesis that all zirconium conducts electricity, but it does not similarly affect the hypothesis that all the objects on my desk conduct electricity. Wherein lies the difference? The first two hypotheses fall under the broader hypothesis—call it *"H"*—that every class of things of the same material is uniform in conductivity; the first and third fall only under some such hypothesis as—call it *"K"*— that every class of things that are either all of the same material or all on a desk is uniform in conductivity. Clearly the important difference here is that evidence for a statement affirming that one of the classes covered by *H* has the property in question increases the credibility of any statement affirming that another such class has this property; while nothing of the sort holds true with respect to *K*. But this is only to say that *H* is lawlike and *K* is not. We are faced anew with the very problem we are trying to solve: the problem of distinguishing between lawlike and accidental hypotheses.

The most popular way of attacking the problem takes its cue from the fact that accidental hypotheses seem typically to involve some spatial or temporal restriction, or reference to some particular individual. They seem to concern the people in some particular room, or the objects on some particular person's desk; while lawlike hypotheses characteristically concern all ravens or all pieces of copper whatsoever. Complete generality is thus very often supposed to be a sufficient condition of lawlikeness; but to define this complete generality is by no means easy. Merely to require that the hypothesis contain no term naming, describing, or indicating a particular thing or location will obviously not be enough. The troublesome hypothesis that all emeralds are grue contains no such term; and where such a term does occur, as in hypotheses about men in *this room,* it can be suppressed in favor of some predicate (short or long, new or old) that contains no such term but applies only to exactly the same things. One might think, then, of excluding not only hypotheses that actually contain terms for specific individuals but also all hypotheses that are equivalent to others that do contain such terms. But, as we have just seen, to exclude only hypotheses of which *all* equivalents contain such terms is to exclude nothing. On the other hand, to exclude all hypotheses that have *some* equivalent containing such a term is to exclude everything; for even the hypothesis

384

All grass is green

has as an equivalent

All grass in London or elsewhere is green.

The next step, therefore, has been to consider ruling out predicates of certain kinds. A syntactically universal hypothesis is lawlike, the proposal runs, if its predicates are 'purely qualitative' or 'non-positional'.[11] This will obviously accomplish nothing if a purely qualitative predicate is then conceived either as one that is equivalent to some expression free of terms for specific individuals, or as one that is equivalent to no expression that contains such a term; for this only raises again the difficulties just pointed out. The claim appears to be rather that at least in the case of a simple enough predicate we can readily determine by direct inspection of its meaning whether or not it is purely qualitative. But even aside from obscurities in the notion of 'the meaning' of a predicate, this claim seems to me wrong. I simply do not know how to tell whether a predicate is qualitative or positional, except perhaps by completely begging the question at issue and asking whether the predicate is 'well-behaved'—that is, whether simple syntactically universal hypotheses applying it are lawlike.

This statement will not go unprotested. "Consider", it will be argued, "the predicates 'blue' and 'green' and the predicate 'grue' introduced earlier, and also the predicate 'bleen' that applies to emeralds examined before time t just in case they are blue and to other emeralds just in case they are green. Surely it is clear", the argument runs, "that the first two are purely qualitative and the second two are not; for the meaning of each of the latter two plainly involves reference to a specific temporal position." To this I reply that indeed I do recognize the first two as well-behaved predicates admissible in lawlike hypotheses, and the second two as ill-behaved predicates. But the argument that the former but

11. Carnap took this course in his paper "On the Application of Inductive Logic", *Philosophy and Phenomenological Research*, Vol. 8 (1947), pp. 133–147, which is in part a reply to my "A Query on Confirmation" [VIII,1 above]. The discussion was continued in my note "On Infirmities of Confirmation Theory" [VIII,2 above], and in Carnap's "Reply to Nelson Goodman", *Philosophy and Phenomenological Research*, Vol. 8 (1947), pp. 461–462.

not the latter are purely qualitative seems to me quite unsound. True enough, if we start with "blue" and "green", then "grue" and "bleen" will be explained in terms of "blue" and "green" and a temporal term. But equally truly, if we start with "grue" and "bleen", then "blue" and "green" will be explained in terms of "grue" and "bleen" and a temporal term; "green", for example, applies to emeralds examined before time t just in case they are grue, and to other emeralds just in case they are bleen. Thus qualitativeness is an entirely relative matter and does not by itself establish any dichotomy of predicates. This relativity seems to be completely overlooked by those who contend that the qualitative character of a predicate is a criterion for its good behavior.

Of course, one may ask why we need worry about such unfamiliar predicates as "grue" or about accidental hypotheses in general, since we are unlikely to use them in making predictions. If our definition works for such hypotheses as are normally employed, isn't that all we need? In a sense, yes; but only in the sense that we need no definition, no theory of induction, and no philosophy of knowledge at all. We get along well enough without them in daily life and in scientific research. But if we seek a theory at all, we cannot excuse gross anomalies resulting from a proposed theory by pleading that we can avoid them in practice. The odd cases we have been considering are clinically pure cases that, though seldom encountered in practice, nevertheless display to best advantage the symptoms of a widespread and destructive malady.

We have so far neither any answer nor any promising clue to an answer to the question what distinguishes lawlike or confirmable hypotheses from accidental or non-confirmable ones; and what may at first have seemed a minor technical difficulty has taken on the stature of a major obstacle to the development of a satisfactory theory of confirmation. It is this problem that I call the new riddle of induction.

5. The Pervasive Problem of Projection

At the beginning of this lecture, I expressed the opinion that the problem of induction is still unsolved, but that the difficulties that face us today are not the old ones; and I have tried to outline the changes that have taken place. The problem of justifying induction has been displaced by the problem of defining confirmation, and our work upon this has left us with the residual problem of distinguishing between confirmable and non-confirmable hypotheses. One might say roughly that the first question was "Why does a positive instance of a hypothesis give any grounds for predicting further instances?"; that the newer question was "What is a positive instance of a hypothesis?"; and that the crucial remaining question is "What hypotheses are confirmed by their positive instances?"

The vast amount of effort expended on the problem of induction in modern times has thus altered our afflictions but hardly relieved them. The original difficulty about induction arose from the recognition that anything may follow upon anything. Then, in attempting to define confirmation in terms of the converse of the consequence relation, we found ourselves with the distressingly similar difficulty that our definition would make any statement confirm any other. And now, after modifying our definition drastically, we still get the old devastating result that any statement will confirm any statement. Until we find a way of exercising some control over the hypotheses to be admitted, our definition makes no distinction whatsoever between valid and invalid inductive inferences.

The real inadequacy of Hume's account lay not in his descriptive approach but in the imprecision of his description. Regularities in experience, according to him, give rise to habits of expectation; and thus it is predictions conforming to past regularities that are normal or valid. But Hume overlooks the fact that some regularities do and some do not establish such habits; that predictions based on some regularities are valid while predictions based on other regularities are not. Every word you have heard me say has occurred prior to the final sentence of this lecture; but that does not, I hope, create any expectation that every word you will hear me say will be prior to that sentence. Again, consider our case of emeralds. All those examined before time t are green; and this leads us to expect, and confirms the prediction, that the next one will be green. But also, all those examined are grue; and this does not lead us to expect, and does not confirm the prediction, that the next one will be grue. Regularity in greenness confirms the prediction of further cases; regularity in grueness does not. To say that valid predictions are those based on past regularities, without being able to say *which* regularities, is thus quite pointless. Regularities are where you find them, and you can find them anywhere. As we have seen, Hume's failure to recognize and deal with this problem has been shared even by his most recent successors.

As a result, what we have in current confirmation theory is a definition that is adequate for certain cases that so far can be described only as those for which it is adequate. The theory works where it works. A hypothesis is confirmed by statements related to it in the prescribed way provided it is so confirmed. This is a good deal like having a theory that tells us that the area of a plane figure is one-half the base times the altitude, without telling us for what figures this holds. We must somehow find a way of distinguishing lawlike hypotheses, to which our definition of confirmation applies, from accidental hypotheses, to which it does not.

Today I have been speaking solely of the problem of induction, but what has been said applies equally to the more general problem of projection. As pointed out earlier, the problem of prediction from past to future cases is but a narrower version of the problem of projecting from any set of cases to others. We saw that a whole cluster of troublesome problems concerning dispositions and possibility can be reduced to this problem of projection. That is why the new riddle of induction, which is more broadly the problem of distinguishing between projectible and nonprojectible hypotheses, is as important as it is exasperating.

Our failures teach us, I think, that lawlike or projectible hypotheses cannot be distinguished on any merely syntactical grounds or even on the ground that these hypotheses are somehow purely general in meaning. Our only hope lies in re-examining the problem once more and looking for some new approach. This will be my course in the final lecture.

4

An Improvement in the
Theory of Projectibility

with ROBERT SCHWARTZ and ISRAEL SCHEFFLER

Discovery of a long-overlooked discrepancy in *Fact, Fiction, and Forecast* has pointed the way to an important improvement in the theory of projection. The rules of unprojectibility can now be reduced to one, so that elementary projectibility can be defined in a simple and straightforward way.

On page 102 of the second edition of *FFF* the hypothesis:

All emerubies are green,

where the evidence consists of green emeralds and red rubies, all examined before *t*, is said to be eliminated according to the first rule as a result of conflict with the better entrenched:

All rubies are red.

Actually, the first rule reads as if it applied only where the *consequent*-predicates differ in entrenchment.

The trouble lies not in the statement on page 102, but in the formulation of the first rule. It was meant, as was often assumed later in the text, to cover all cases of genuine conflict between two hypotheses of unequal entrenchment, i.e., between hypotheses with equally well entrenched antecedent-predicates and unequally well entrenched consequent-predicates, or with equally well entrenched consequent-predicates and unequally well entrenched antecedent-predicates, or with both the antecedent- and consequent-predicates of one better entrenched than the corresponding predicates of the other. If we state the first rule correctly and modify it somewhat, no further rules are needed.

What decides between two hypotheses that conflict by ascribing incompatible predicates to some future cases? We may have to await more evidence. But if the choice always depended on that, no hypothesis could ever be projected; for, given any supported, unviolated, and unexhausted hypothesis, we can always concoct another such hypothesis that thus conflicts with it. Another consideration must be brought to bear: the relative entrenchment of the conflicting hypotheses.

Since only supported, unviolated, and unexhausted hypotheses are projectible, we may confine our attention to these for the present. Among such hypotheses, H overrides H' if the two conflict and if H is the better entrenched and conflicts with no still better entrenched hypothesis.[1] Our revised rule then reads:

A hypothesis is *projectible* if all conflicting hypotheses are overridden, *unprojectible* if overridden, and *nonprojectible* if in conflict with another hypothesis and neither is overridden.

In each of the following cases, the hypothesis in question is overridden and hence is unprojectible:

H_1 "All emeralds are grue", when all emeralds examined before t are found to be grue and hence green,[2] is overridden by "All emeralds are green."

H_2 "All emeralds are grund", when all emeralds examined before t are green, and all are also square, succumbs to "All emeralds are square."

H_3 "All emerubies are green", when all emeralds examined before t are green and all rubies examined before t are red, gives way to "All rubies are red."

H_4 "All emerubies are gred",[3] when all emeralds examined before

---

1. So stated, this covers only hierarchies of at most three supported, unviolated, unexhausted, and successively better entrenched and conflicting hypotheses. Hierarchies of more such hypotheses can be covered if necessary by making the definition more general so that a hypothesis is overridden if it is the bottom member of a hierarchy that cannot be extended upward and has an even number of members.

2. Specifications of the available evidence are often elliptical in this paper. In the present case, for example, we tacitly assume also that some emeralds have been examined before t, while some things other than emeralds may or may not have been found to be green or of some other color.

3. [Donald Davidson first introduced a case of this sort in "Emeroses by Other Names", *Journal of Philosophy*, Vol. 63 (1966), pp. 778–780.]

t are gred and hence green, is overridden by "All emerubies are green."

The evidence for H_1 carries with it, so to speak, the evidence for the overriding hypothesis; that is, whatever the evidence gathered before t, if H_1 is supported and unviolated, the cited conflicting hypothesis will also be supported, unviolated, and not overridden. The same cannot be said for the other cases; and we must consider the effect of different evidence. For example, if all emeralds examined before t are found to be green but either none has been examined for shape or some have been found to be square and others not square, then "All emeralds are square" is either unsupported or violated and so cannot override H_2. Here, however, H_2 conflicts with the equally well entrenched hypothesis "All emeralds are grare [green and examined before t, or not so examined and square]", so that both hypotheses are nonprojectible.[4] And, indeed, if we have found anything, say the Eiffel tower, to be of some shape other than round, say pointed, H_2 will conflict with some such hypothesis as "All Eifferalds are pointed."

Suppose, though, all emeralds examined before t have been both green and round. Now, since all such conflicting hypotheses as "All emeralds are grare" are overridden by "All emeralds are round", H_2 qualifies as projectible. Plainly, projection of H_2 is harmless where the evidence makes projectible two well entrenched hypotheses, "All emeralds are green" and "All emeralds are round", such that H_2 follows from their conjunction. This is *not* to say that consequences of projectible hypotheses are always projectible; for some such consequences are unsupported or exhausted. But a consequence of a projectible hypothesis meets two of the requirements for projectibility: it is unviolated, and all conflicting hypotheses are overridden. And thus H_2, since also supported and unexhausted by the evidence given, is projectible.

Still, are we content to say that H_2 is projectible in this case?

---

4. When some emeralds have been found to be square and others round, we can retreat from these two hypotheses to the weaker hypothesis "All emeralds are square or round", which does not conflict with them but is projectible whereas they are not. If statistical hypotheses are taken into account, H_2 may be *un*projectible, being overridden by some hypothesis concerning shape distribution among emeralds; but the treatment of statistical hypotheses is a complicated matter requiring redefinition of support, violation, conflict, and so on.

Lingering reluctance to do so arises, it seems, from confusing two senses of "projectible". In one sense, a hypothesis is projectible if support normally makes it credible. In another sense, a hypothesis is projectible only when the actual evidence supports and makes it credible.[5] In the first sense, "All emeralds are green" is projectible. In the second sense, it is not projectible when deprived, by evidence that violates or exhausts it or leaves it in conflict with hypotheses that are not overridden, of its normal capacity to derive credibility from support. On the other hand, "All emeralds are grund" is normally not projectible but may be relieved, by evidence that neither violates nor exhausts it but overrides all conflicting hypotheses, of its normal incapacity to derive credibility from support. In sum, just as a normally projectible hypothesis may lose projectibility under unfavorable evidence, so a hypothesis not normally projectible may gain projectibility under sufficiently favorable evidence.

If all emeralds examined before t have been green, H_3 is projectible only under weird circumstances: either (i) that all rubies examined have been green, so that H_3 follows from the projectible hypothesis "All emeralds are green" and "All rubies are green", or (ii) that nothing of any other color has been found, so that H_3 follows from the projectible "All things are green." If all sapphires examined are blue, H_3 will be nonprojectible because of conflict with the no-less-well entrenched hypothesis "All sapphirubies are blue." And if we have found anything, say the Eiffel tower, of some color other than green, say black, H_3 will conflict with some such hypothesis as "All Eifferubies are black."

Even H_4 becomes projectible when all emeralds examined before t are green and all rubies red; for the formerly overriding hypothesis "All emerubies are green" is now itself overridden by "All rubies are red." Again, while the hypothesis "All emerubies are grund" is not projectible if before t neither emeralds nor rubies

---

5. In a third sense, a hypothesis is projectible only if projectible in both these senses. Of the three senses, only the second is studied in *FFF* and this paper; and we are concerned only with whether or not a hypothesis is made credible to some degree, not with degrees of increase or decrease in credibility. Robert Schwartz is planning a further paper on some senses of projectibility.

have been examined for shape, or some emeralds or rubies found to be of other shapes than round, it is projectible if all examined emeralds are green and all examined rubies round.

The rules set forth in *Fact, Fiction, and Forecast* (*IV,4*) are thus to be replaced by a single one that makes no use of any 'variety of disagreement' between hypotheses other than incompatibility. Indeed, subject to the further considerations[6] under the heading "Comparative Projectibility" in that book, we now have the following definitions:

A hypothesis is *projectible* if and only if it is supported, unviolated, and unexhausted, and all such hypotheses that conflict with it are overridden.

A hypothesis is *unprojectible* if and only if it is unsupported or violated or exhausted or overridden.

A hypothesis is *nonprojectible* if it and a conflicting hypothesis are supported, unviolated, unexhausted, and not overridden.

6. With such modifications as may be made necessary by the present paper.

5

Inductive Translation

Among the many ways a computer may process messages are *deletion* and *supplementation*. The first occurs, for example, where a curve is scanned and the positions of some points on it reported. The second occurs where some points are fed in and a curve or other points on it produced, whether by interpolation or extrapolation. Deletion is often, but not always or exclusively, involved in translation from analog into digital messages, and supplementation in translation from digital into analog messages. Some important functions of symbols are illustrated in the process of supplementation.

Consider machines designed to receive two or more points and supply others. A crude machine might simply select[1] each point by spinning a wheel or casting dice. The choices cannot be said to be based in any way upon the data; the available evidence is utterly ignored. At the opposite extreme, a machine might be so constructed as to handle straight lines only. Any two points will then determine a line and thereby all points to be interpolated and extrapolated. Far from being ignored, the data dictate all remaining points by dictating the choice of line. If the first machine was little more than a roulette wheel, the second is a simple calculator like an adding machine.

Now consider a computer capable of handling curves of various types. When the data are compatible with several of these curves, how shall the machine decide? Even if it now resorts to wheel-spinning or dice-throwing, it still differs radically from our first machine; for this one, like the second, chooses among curves rather than points and rejects curves incompatible with the evidence. If a linear order of preference among curves is given and the machine is instructed to choose the remaining curve highest on that scale,

---

1. "Selects", "chooses", "decides", etc., in the present context do not imply any deliberation but mean only "gives one among alternative responses". On computers with a random element, see A. M. Turing, "Computing Machinery and Intelligence", *Mind,* Vol. 59 (1950), pp. 443–460.

chance will not enter at all. Or such a scale may be used merely
to weight the odds so that the choice, though made by wheel or
dice, will not be purely random. Yet in all these cases, the machine
operates independently of what has gone before except for canceling out curves that conflict with the data.[2]

A more sophisticated machine might make more use of the past.
Let us suppose data have been fed to a machine, a choice of curve
made, additional data supplied, a new choice made accordingly,
and so on. The several choices may be regarded as steps in dealing
with a single problem having as its cumulative data all those supplied from start to finish. Now the registers are cleared, data again
are supplied, and the machine begins work on a new problem. Our
present machine may, whenever it thus faces a new problem, look
back to its encounters with earlier problems. After eliminating
curves incompatible with the present data, it may find earlier
problems with sets of data that properly include the present set,
and proceed to cancel out every curve that conflicts with any of
these more inclusive sets. It thus takes into account not only the
immediate evidence, but evidence in past related cases.

Nevertheless, if the machine can handle enough curves, eliminations on the basis of present and past data will always leave a wide
choice of alternatives—so wide, indeed, that no prediction concerning remaining points is excluded.[3] No matter for how many
values of x the value of y is given, still for every remaining value

2. My treatment throughout this section attempts only a simple schematic
analysis of the process of supplementation. Variations and elaborations of all
sorts may occur. The task may be to choose not one curve but a group of
curves; e.g., if the ordinate at only one or a few abscissas is wanted, differences among curves that coincide at these abscissas can be ignored. Or, rather
than canceling out curves not fitting the data, the machine may be asked
to find among curves meeting some standard of smoothness the curve that
comes nearest to fitting the data—though it miss some or even all points.
Again, the response called for may not be to select or reject curves but to
rate them according to relative probability. Also, the ways of taking cog-
nizance of experience on past problems may be complicated and subtle.
And where a scale of preference is involved it may be based upon simplicity
of one sort or another, or upon more or different factors; and it may be fixed
or variable. Finally, "points" and "curves" may be read more generally as
"instances" and "hypotheses". None of this occludes the central issues above
discussed.

3. Cf. *FFF*, pp. 72–81.

m of x and every value n of y, at least one of the curves compatible with the data will pass through m,n. And this will hold true for any more comprehensive sets of data for past problems. Thus the less circumscribed the machine, the more often it must either consult a mandatory fixed scale of preference or resort to chance procedures. The erudite machine has to be either pigheaded or henheaded.

Both faults are corrected in a machine that can acquire habits. Appropriate inertia is required for maximum profit from experience. Suppose a machine to be so designed that in making any choice after its first, it consults not only the data for the present and for past related problems but also the record of its own past choices. Among the curves remaining after deletions on the basis of all data, it selects or at least favors the one used most often before. And it sticks to a curve once chosen until forced to change by new data. Habit, in effect, establishes or modifies a preferential weighting; and a unique choice often results.

What I have been speaking of as 'the curves a machine can handle' constitute the inventory of responses it can make. No distinction has been drawn between those curves the machine has initially at its command and those, if any, that it can invent. A machine that can initially respond with straight lines only may be able, when fed three noncollinear points, to invent some new curve to accommodate these data. But this machine is as well described as one that, among all the curves it can handle, always chooses a straight line until forced by the data to make a different choice. The question what curves are 'there at the start' and what curves the machine 'generates' is thus displaced by the question what curves the machine can handle at all and how it chooses among them.

All these machines perform a task of supplementation, some by sheer guess, some by pure calculation, some by a mixture of the two. Some take no, some minimal, and some very extensive and complex account of the evidence. Those that take account of the evidence operate with curves that relate the given points to the rest. Some such machines can handle very few curves, some many, and some all possible curves in their universes. Certain machines, when confronted with open alternatives after all eliminations on the basis of the evidence, always make a unique choice by applying a preferential scale. Others, lacking such a fully automatic procedure, must sometimes resort to chance. Among these, some do and some do not take account of their past choices, in effect forming habits that perpetuate as far as possible chance decisions once made.

Questions concerning the nature of induction thrust themselves forward here.[4] Does supplementation become induction when account is taken of the evidence? Or not unless the evidence sometimes leaves open alternatives, so that a decision must be made by other means? Or only if for some such decisions a chance procedure is used? Giving an answer is perhaps less important than noting the several significant lines of demarcation. Again, what are the characteristics of the induction performed by human beings? Obviously, we can take account of the evidence in subtle and sophisticated ways. Obviously, also, we can handle any possible curve (or hypothesis). And on the whole we tend to persist in a choice so long as the evidence permits. But are we provided with a completely decisive preferential ordering among these curves, or must we sometimes resort to chance?

Our brief look at some ways of accomplishing message supplementation thus leads directly to the heart of active current controversy in epistemology. More to the immediate point of our present inquiry, though, is the disclosure of certain special features of the functioning of symbols not only in overt induction but also in such kindred processes as category detection and pattern perception: first, that evidence takes effect only through application of a general symbol (label or term or hypothesis) having an extension that properly includes the data; second, that the alternatives are primarily such general symbols, divergent in extension, rather than isolated particulars; and third, that pertinent time-and-trouble-saving habits can develop only through use of such symbols. Perhaps, indeed, these are earmarks of cognitive behavior in general.

---

4. Cf. Marvin Minsky, "Steps toward Artificial Intelligence", in *Computers and Thought,* ed. E. A. Feigenbaum and J. Feldman (New York: McGraw-Hill, 1963), pp. 448–449. This article originally appeared in the special computer issue of the *Proceedings of the Institute of Radio Engineers,* 1961.

6

Replies to Comments on
Fact, Fiction, and Forecast

(a) Reply to an Adverse Ally

John Cooley has recently published a long study[1] of my book
Fact, Fiction, and Forecast.[2] His critical comment begins with an
argument designed to show that the problem of cotenability results from failure to take into account the temporal relationships
involved in the ordinary 'causal framework'.[3] He thinks it is impossible to cite an instance of the problem of cotenability where a
causal time-sequence is not explicitly involved. But consider a
bolt *b*, which at time *t* is black and iron. The normal counterfactual:

(i) If the temperature of *b* had been 650° at time *t*, then *b* would
have been red at *t*

is established by taking as our statement *S* of relevant conditions
the sentence "*b* was iron at *t*", perhaps conjoined with some other
clauses. However, the unacceptable counterfactual:

(ii) If the temperature of *b* had been 650° at *t*, then *b* would not
have been iron at *t*

will also be admitted if we take as S_1 the statement "*b* was black
at *t*", perhaps conjoined with other clauses. S_1 here is logically and
physically compatible with the antecedent of (ii) and with both the
consequent and the negate of the consequent. To attempt to ex-

1. *Journal of Philosophy*, Vol. 54 (1957), pp. 293–311.

2. First edition, 1955.

3. A similar point has been urged by William Parry in his "Reëxamina-
tion of the Problem of Counterfactual Conditionals", *Journal of Philosophy*,
Vol. 54 (1957), pp. 85–94. In my reply, "Parry on Counterfactuals", Vol. 54
(1957), pp. 442–445, I have shown why the remedy he proposes is ineffective.

clude S_1 on the ground that it would not be true if the antecedent were true is to employ a counterfactual and so to beg the question.[4] Hence what I have called the problem of cotenability arises here in a case where only a single moment is mentioned throughout; and no restriction upon the temporal references admissible in supporting laws and statements of relevant conditions will let in (i) and exclude (ii).

However, perhaps Cooley's main point here is that the way to deal with the problem of cotenability is not to modify the specifications for relevant conditions, but rather to find a different analysis of counterfactuals that will take pertinent historical features of a situation into account. If so, then—as Cooley observes —the treatment of counterfactuals suggested late (p. 118 [p. 120, 2nd ed.]) in my book has this in its favor; for such historical facts may often need to be considered in determining which one among several conflicting counterfactuals outweighs the others.

Next, Professor Cooley charges me with a vacillation in policy. I have argued against Carnap that non-positionality is no criterion of projectibility, since the projectible predicate "green" is as positional relative to the nonprojectible predicate "grue" as "grue" is relative to "green". Cooley asks why I should advance this argument when I am quite willing to accept other relative distinctions in other contexts. But I surely do not mean to foreswear all use of relative distinctions. My point is simply that non-positionality is not concomitant with projectibility.

In discussing the problem of dispositions, I described it roughly as the problem of defining predicates for enduring characteristics of things in terms of predicates for what actually happens. I remarked in a footnote that definition of dispositional predicates in terms of predicates for microcosmic structures does not solve the problem of dispositions thus conceived, since these predicates for structures are themselves dispositional in the sense explained. Cooley says this leads him to feel that the definitions required

---

4. Perhaps it should be remarked that the problems of cotenability and lawlikeness, as they relate to the problem of counterfactuals, have this in common: they are problems of distinguishing between statements that will, and statements that will not, withstand the assumption that the antecedent of the counterfactual is true.

by my statement of the problem are impossible; but he apparently means only that the very broad and loose dispositional terms of ordinary usage may not be definable in the required way—that we may have to be satisfied with definitions of narrower or more specialized dispositional predicates. This seems to me no more than an application of the truism that in defining terms of any kind belonging to ordinary language, we usually have first to do a good deal of trimming and patching, refining and dividing—and often end with several definitions for more specific terms.

Although he admits that nothing turns upon whether "projectible" is a true disposition term, Cooley takes some pains to show that it is not. His argument is that a normal disposition term applies at least wherever the projected manifest predicate applies. This, for reasons explicitly stated in my book,[5] seems to me mistaken. Consider the predicate "fragile". Not all things that break are fragile; a thing that breaks is fragile if the blow was light. Similarly, not all predicates that are projected are projectible; a projected predicate is projectible if certain other requirements are met. And if the manifest predicate in question in the case of "fragile" is held rather to be "breaks easily", then the manifest predicate in question in the case of "projectible" will be something like "is projected properly".

The treatment of the problem of projectibility in my book has two phases: the first describes means for eliminating many definitely nonprojectible hypotheses; the second outlines methods for comparing the projectibility of the remaining hypotheses. I remarked that it might be worthwhile to investigate the possibility of omitting the first phase entirely and dealing with the whole matter in terms of comparative projectibility. Cooley likes this idea and seeks to develop it. But whereas the procedure I envisaged begins by assigning initial projectibility-indices to hypotheses on the basis of the relative entrenchment of the predicates involved, Cooley wants to dispense with the initial indices altogether and so obviate the need for reference to entrenchment. If

5. See p. 55, and footnote 18 on pp. 61 and 62. [Footnote 18 is on p. 56 in the second edition.] For an interesting sidelight on the matter see Morton White, "Value and Obligation in Dewey and Lewis", *Philosophical Review*, Vol. 58 (1949), pp. 321–329.

we confine ourselves to hypotheses that are supported, un-violated, and unexhausted, then he thinks all will go well without any initial indices. But actually this will not work at all. Consider, for example, the hypothesis:

H_1: All diamonds are very hard

and the hypothesis:

H_2: Everything that is either a diamond examined before 2000 A.D. or a live mushroom examined thereafter is very hard.

How are we to account for the patent difference in projectibility between these two? If no initial differences are to be recognized, this difference must be explained as acquired from overhypotheses. But for each overhypothesis of H_1, say:

O_1: Every geological species of stone is of about uniform hardness,

there is a parallel overhypothesis of H_2, say:

O_2: Every class that is either a geological species of stone or is the class of diamonds examined before 2000 A.D. and live mushrooms examined thereafter is of about uniform hardness,

that is similarly well supported, unviolated, and unexhausted. We know, of course, that in fact O_2 is virtually nonprojectible and so does not actually endow H_2 with any projectibility; but if we recognize no initial differences in projectibility, and try to explain the difference in projectibility between O_1 and O_2 by means of overhypotheses of these in turn, we are plainly getting nowhere. In short, *unless some initial differences of projectibility are admitted, no differences will result from the relation of hypotheses to their overhypotheses.*

In a paragraph that introduces the critical part of his review, Professor Cooley gives the impression that he disagrees with most of the "basic assumptions" of my book. But this is not borne out by the criticisms he advances. They are, as we have seen above, mainly of two kinds: arguments concerning such minor matters as whether "projectible" is a genuine disposition-term; and earnest efforts to modify my theory in ways that he thinks will improve it. The final third of his review consists in an attempt to work out tentative suggestions of mine, and a defense of my conception of the problem of counterfactuals against the views of other writers. This professedly adverse critic often reads more like an ally.

(b) *Positionality and Pictures*

Luckily we need not bother with the artistic *dramatis personae*, the talk of extrasensory perception, or the other embellishments of the paper by Stephen Barker and Peter Achinstein.[1] The only serious question is whether the authors succeed in defining the distinction between positional and non-positional predicates. In substance, the formulation they propose is this: a single picture or representation can be given for all instances of application of a non-positional predicate, while at least two different representations are needed to cover all instances of application of a positional predicate. For example, a single present patch of green paint will represent the color of all green things irrespective of their dates; but two present patches will be needed to represent all grue things: a green one for cases up to time *t* and a blue one for cases thereafter.

The limitations upon what can represent what are far from obvious. We often see black-and-white diagrams in which different colors are represented by different shadings: say green by cross-hatching, blue by dotting, and so forth. Plainly symbols like these can equally well be used for grue. Vertical shading, say, for what is green up to time *t* or blue thereafter is as legitimate a representation of grue as the other symbols are of green and blue. Presumably Barker and Achinstein will reject such diagramming as not the natural representation they have in mind. Just what, then, constitutes representation within their meaning? To stipulate that a color must be represented by a sample of it will not do; for a present patch of paint that is a sample of green is also a sample of grue. And if we deny that grue is a single color we are in effect merely saying that grue is positional, and so begging the question. Does representation perhaps require, then, that the color of an object be represented by another object that is indiscrim-

---

1. I am indebted to the authors for showing me their manuscript before publication.

inable from, or matches, the first in color? This will not work either; for then a patch of green paint, since it matches very few green things, cannot represent the color of all green things.[2]

At this point Barker and Achinstein may say that while precise definition of what they mean by representation is difficult, all they have in mind is ordinary, everyday, realistic representation, and that this notion is clear enough without definition. They are saying, then, that so long as only accustomed modes of representation— only common and familiar representational devices—are used, a non-positional predicate is one such that there is a single time-indifferent representation for all its instances of application. But if one is willing to put the matter thus, relying upon restriction to a familiar representational vocabulary, representation need not be brought in at all. "Grue" can be classed as positional on the ground that in terms of ordinary, familiar language, no one term describes the color of all grue objects; two different ordinary words, "green" and "blue", are needed. This, however, depends entirely upon "green" and "blue" rather than "grue" happening to belong to ordinary language; that is, it depends entirely upon the facts of habit or entrenchment. In resting their definition of positionality upon a restriction to the most accustomed means of representation, Barker and Achinstein are making much the same appeal to entrenchment but in a more roundabout and covert way. They are not offering a new alternative.

Furthermore, the line between natural and artificial representation can hardly be so drawn as to support the use these authors want to make of it. This becomes glaringly apparent in the final paragraphs of their paper. As a time-indifferent representation for "conducts electricity", they suggest a picture showing a battery connected by wires to an ammeter with its pointer indicating a flow of current. That this is clearly a representation for "conducts electricity" rather than for "is a closed circuit" or "is a live bat-

---

2. "Grue" might be classed as positional on the ground that its instances of application before t cannot match those after t in color, while this does not hold for "green". Noam Chomsky pointed this out to me a couple of years ago, but did not publish it because it is too *ad hoc* to be of much interest. Other clearly non-projectible color predicates that are not positional by this criterion are easily constructed; and the criterion is inapplicable where, as in the case of "conducts electricity", matching is irrelevant. Barker and Achinstein, in correspondence, reject this possible formulation of their proposal.

tery" or "is an operating meter", or the like, is highly implausible. Even aside from that, unless the word "ammeter" or some equivalent expression is included in the picture, by what means is the meter pictured shown to be an ammeter rather than a thermometer or a meter registering the remaining hours of life in the battery or the loss of current in transmission? But if verbal inscriptions are admissible in a picture, we can construct a representation for "condulates electricity" simply by labelling the pictured meter "b-meter" for an easily made instrument whose pointer rests elsewhere than at zero up to time t when a current passes through and thereafter when no current passes through (or we can replace "b-meter" by the description in familiar terms just given). Any claim that this is a less natural or admissible representation for "condulates electricity" than the original picture is for "conducts electricity" would be rather absurd. Perhaps with enough ingenuity an unambiguous representation of an ammeter could be achieved without use of a word or even of dial figures; but such ingenuity would hardly falter at representing a b-meter without use of words or figures, especially after one had been produced.

Accordingly, it seems to me that the authors succeed neither in defining positionality nor in showing that anything in *Fact, Fiction, and Forecast* needs modification.

(c) Faulty Formalization

Professor R. M. Martin, in an appendix to his *Toward a Systematic Pragmatics*,[1] has tried to formalize the treatment of projectibility in my *Fact, Fiction, and Forecast*. He quotes (page 96) from my text (page 90 [p. 87, 2nd ed.]): "A hypothesis will be said to be *actually projected* when it is adopted after some of its instances have been examined and determined to be true, and before the rest have been examined." He then writes: "To say that a sentence a 'is examined and determined to be true' at time t we take to mean merely that a is accepted at t. (No reference to the semantical truth-concept here seems needed. Nor do we need a separate primitive for 'examined').” Actually this policy makes nonsense of his formalization.

His definition of "actually projected", if we somewhat simplify

1. Amsterdam, 1959.

the temporal clauses to stress the main point, amounts to this: A hypothesis "$(x)(Px)$" is actually projected when it is accepted while some instance "Pb" is accepted and some other instance is not accepted. Looking back to Martin's treatment of "accept", we find (page 44, TC9) that every sentence that is not accepted is rejected (in one of two senses of rejection that he defines). Thus actual projection would require accepting a hypothesis while accepting some of its instances and rejecting others. Obviously, projection as I have described it has nothing to do with such inconsistent behavior.

There is further trouble. A hypothesis is actually projected only when it has some positive instances, no negative instances, and some undetermined instances. Martin defines an instance as positive if it is accepted, negative if its negate is accepted, and undetermined if it is neither positive nor negative. Since a statement not accepted is for him rejected, using these definitions will give the following remarkable result: A hypothesis is actually projected only when it and some of its instances are accepted, the negates of none of its instances are accepted, *and some instance and its negate are both rejected.*

The specific anomalies so far pointed out could be corrected by allowing for a class of statements that are neither accepted nor rejected. But the root of the trouble lies much deeper. Projection does not consist in accepting a hypothesis while accepting some but not others of its instances. Projection consists rather in accepting a hypothesis and therefore presumably all its instances when only some of these have been examined and all so examined have been determined to be true. Projection is not less-than-complete acceptance but acceptance on the basis of less-than-complete evidence. In dealing with projection, some such notions as "examine" and "determine to be true" are needed along with "accept".

(d) Three Replies[*]

The three papers following are neither the first nor the last to appear concerning my book and articles on induction, but they

* To the following papers, all in the *Journal of Philosophy,* Vol. 63 (1966): R. C. Jeffrey, "Goodman's Query", pp. 281–288; Judith Jarvis Thomson, "Grue", pp. 289–309; J. R. Wallace, "Goodman, Logic, and Induction", pp. 310–328.

represent an impressive amount of work by three serious philosophers with widely differing approaches. We need no longer
listen to the charge that the new riddle of induction, or the problem of projectibility, is merely sophistical—a charge cherished only
by those philistines who regard a color film of a physicist working in his laboratory as the ultimate truth about science. And
no one who understands the problem hopes any longer for a purely
syntactical solution. Responsible discussion thus usually concerns
itself with critical (as in Mr. Wallace's paper) or constructive
study of my admittedly rough and tentative formulation of a
solution, or (as in Mrs. Thomson's paper) with the search for a
better and somehow more essential solution to supplant or supplement mine, or (as in Mr. Jeffrey's paper) with relating my work
to other work on confirmation. I feel that such discussion, whether
right or wrong, can help us to see more clearly and deeply into
the nature of inductive inference.

Since these papers come to me not long before press time, and
since more detailed discussions of at least two of them are in prospect,[1] I shall comment only briefly and on a few salient points.

All three papers make some reference to an objection or question attributed to Donald Davidson: Doesn't my treatment err by
ruling out as unprojectible such perfectly acceptable statements as:

> H_1 All emerubies are gred

(where an emeruby is an emerald examined before t or a ruby not
so examined, and anything is gred if it is a green thing examined
before t or a red thing not so examined)? Let us remember that
truth of a statement by no means implies projectibility. If our
evidence here consists entirely of emeralds examined before t and
found to be green, then H_1 is clearly unprojectible, and is properly
eliminated (in two steps) by our rules. If our evidence consists
entirely of rubies examined before t and found to be red, then,
since such rubies are not emerubies, the hypothesis is entirely unsupported. If our evidence consists of emeralds examined before

---

1. A discussion of Mr. Wallace's paper by Marsha Hanen and of Mrs.
Thomson's paper by Robert Schwartz and James Hullett should appear soon.
[See footnotes 5 and 8 of the Foreword to this chapter.] I am heavily indebted
to all three for help in preparing the above remarks.

t and found to be green and rubies examined before t and found to be red, then both the following are projectible:

H_2 All emeralds are green
H_3 All rubies are red.

Now of course H_1 is true if H_2 and H_3 are; but this is not to say that H_1 is projectible if H_2 and H_3 are. Obviously, many consequences of projectible hypotheses are not themselves projectible. In summary, however true H_1 may be, it is unprojectible in that positive instances do not in general increase its credibility; emeralds found before t to be green do not confirm H_1.

In the second edition of *Fact, Fiction, and Forecast*, I wrote (p. 96n.): "Elimination of a hypothesis by means of any principle is of course always overruled where that hypothesis follows from some hypothesis that entirely escapes elimination." 'Elimination' of a hypothesis consists in refusing to accept it as true. When the elimination is on grounds of relative unprojectibility, the overruling in question here amounts to canceling that refusal, not to classifying the hypothesis as lawlike. Although the hypothesis may now be legitimately accepted, and may be supported, unviolated, and unexhausted, it is not therefore projectible in the sense of being lawlike. Some confusion might be prevented by using "lawlike" rather than "projectible" in such contexts.

Mr. Jeffrey drives home the point I urged in my earlier articles: that the various Hempel and Carnap definitions of confirmation work only to the extent that we apply them to or build in just the right predicates and that these treatments provide no general criterion of what the right predicates are. While Carnap is content to leave the selection to particular extrasystematic decisions, I consider a theory of confirmation deficient unless it incorporates a general formulation of the distinction between the right (or projectible) predicates and the wrong ones. To rest with particular extrasystematic judgments here is to raise the question why we seek a systematic treatment of confirmation at all rather than resting with judgments of the validity of each particular inductive inference.

In saying that projectibility depends not merely upon syntax but upon meaning, Mr. Jeffrey is not claiming that projectibility

can be defined in terms of some general semantic property of predicates but is saying only that judgment of the projectibility of a
particular predicate requires knowing the interpretation as well
as the spelling of the predicate. Once we have chosen a con-
firmation-function that assigns degrees of projectibility in accord
with our particular judgments—that is, once we have built in the
right degree of projectibility for each predicate—then we may
attempt to retrieve by definition within the system the distinction
between projectible and nonprojectible predicates that has been
put there. A surpising result of Mr. Jeffrey's paper is how difficult this seemingly trivial task proves to be. He finds that the
semantic definition he first proposes makes "grue" projectible,
and he has therefore to provide a more complex pragmatic definition. A theory of meaning that goes beyond the theory of reference is required here; and all this is directed not toward any
general definition of projectibility but only toward retrieving a
distinction already built ad hoc into a given system.

Mrs. Thomson seeks a definition of projectibility in terms of
the notoriously obscure notion of observability. "Green" is an
observation-predicate while "grue" is not, she says, because we
can tell whether a thing is green but not whether it is grue by
simply looking at it in a good light. This, to say the least, does
not submit to easy generalization. An object is not spherical if it
looks spherical in good light, or even from a good angle, but rather
if it looks round from all angles. To arrive at any good general
definition of the class of observation-predicates would be exceedingly difficult.

In the second place, judging from what seem to be reasonably
clear cases, the line between observation-predicates and others
does not coincide with the line between projectible and nonprojectible predicates. "Conducts electricity" and many other
predicates more remote from unaided momentary inspection are
plainly projectible. Thus, even given an adequate definition of
observability, definition of projectibility in terms of it would be
at best a hard task.

In the third place, I am not quite sure just what Mrs. Thomson
is claiming. Is she saying merely that English-speaking people
normally do not apply the predicate "grue"—or apply it incorrectly

—after simply examining a thing in good light? That is a sheer truism. Or is she saying that no human being can so apply "grue"? And if so, is she claiming that no human being in fact can do this or that no human being possibly could? In the former case, she would be saying little more than that the way humans behave must be due to some characteristic they happen to have— and this again is an empty truism. The stronger claim, that no human being could be otherwise, is (in the absence of any argument as to the limitations implied by "human") utterly groundless in view of the fact that we can readily construct a machine that will apply "grue" correctly upon being shown an object in a good light.[2]

Finally, even if Mrs. Thomson could give a general and acceptable definition of observability, could define projectibility in terms of this, and could show that these distinctions are rooted in some essential features of the human organism—and these would be three very large orders indeed—nothing here would be incompatible with a definition of projectibility in terms of entrenchment; rather we would have a psychological explanation of the facts of entrenchment. But I cannot see that Mrs. Thomson's patient and earnest effort makes any real progress in this direction.

Mr. Wallace charges that my treatment of projectibility transgresses the boundaries of 'quantificational logic'. At first sight, this carries the ominous intimation that I, of all people, have been caught trafficking with intensions, modalities, non-truth-functional connectives, and referential opacity. But as we read on we find that my sin amounts to refusing to consider equivalent hypotheses identical. To this, I confess eagerly. For me a hypothesis is a statement, and an equivalent hypothesis may be a different statement. Whether in the context of inductive or deductive logic, a statement and its contrapositive, for example, are equivalent but not identical.

Once this is recognized, and it seems plain enough in my writing, all the difficulties so painstakingly detailed by Mr. Wallace evaporate. In the primary sense of confirmation, whatever confirms a hypothesis confirms every equivalent hypothesis; but

---

2. Compare the description of a 'b-meter' in my "Positionality and Pictures" [VIII,6,b above].

equivalent hypotheses may nevertheless differ in many other respects: in their antecedents and their consequents, in their positive and negative instances, in their evidence classes and projective classes, etc. etc. Sometimes, as is the case of a hypothesis and its contrapositive, they may have different contraries; and this leads to an interesting and pertinent secondary version of confirmation such that what so ('selectivity') confirms a hypothesis does not always so confirm an equivalent hypothesis.[3]

Along the way, Mr. Wallace raises an incidental point that calls for some clarification. He argues that to deny that "grue emerald" is as well entrenched as "emerald" is to deny that the two are coextensive and, hence, to decide without evidence that "All emeralds are grue emeralds" is false. But comparisons of entrenchment, in my treatment of projectibility, are always relative to the occurrence of the two predicates in parallel positions in a pair of hypotheses, and are conditional in character. Consider parallel hypotheses of the following sort:

> All soandso's are emeralds.
> All soandso's are grue emeralds.

If these conflict, then the consequent-predicates are not coextensive and the first is obviously much better entrenched than the second. If the hypotheses do not conflict, we need not choose between them. Extensional divergence of the two predicates is not asserted categorically; rather we say that unless the two are coextensive, the first is the much better entrenched.

Let me repeat in closing that I by no means suppose that my brief and almost impromptu remarks do full justice to any of these thoughtful papers.

(e) Two More Replies*

Mr. Davidson asks for a reason against accepting the hypothesis:

> H_1 All emeroses are gred

---

* To the following papers, both in the *Journal of Philosophy,* Vol. 63 (1966): Donald Davidson, "Emeroses by Other Names", pp. 778–780; and J. R. Wallace, "Lawlikeness = Truth", pp. 780–781.

3. See Israel Scheffler's *The Anatomy of Inquiry* (New York: Alfred A. Knopf, 1963), pp. 287–289.

as lawlike. The reason is the same as the reason against accepting

H_2 All emeralds are grue

as lawlike: that positive instances do not in general confirm the hypothesis. An emerald found before t to be grue does not increase our belief that emeralds examined after t will be grue. Likewise, an emerose found before t to be gred does not increase our belief that emeroses examined after t will be gred. In contrast, emeralds found before t to be green *do* increase our belief that emeralds found after t will be green.

Mr. Davidson seems to want a reason, in terms of the syntactic or semantic character of the predicates involved, why this is so; but no such reason has ever been found. Just this raises the crucial problem of projectibility and leads to my attack upon it in terms of entrenchment.

That H_1 seems true while H_2 seems false is quite irrelevant. In accepting H_1 we make tacit use of evidence that all roses are red, which, together with evidence that all emeralds are green, confirms the hypothesis

H_3 All emeralds are green and all roses are red,

which has H_1 as a consequence.

Mr. Davidson suggests that lawlikeness depends upon some relation between the predicates of a hypothesis. Even if we agree—as I do not—that H_1 is lawlike, how would we characterize the significant relationship that obtains between "emerose" and "gred", and also between "emerald" and "green", but not between "emerald" and "grue"? Equality of entrenchment is hardly enough; but attempting any syntactic or semantic characterization of the relationship would seem at least as futile as attempting any such characterization of the projectibility of separate predicates.

Mr. Wallace ingeniously produces a statement that is true if and only if lawlike. This does not, as he seems to think, have any dire consequences for my theory of projection. The lawlikeness in question here is a fixed property like truth; and to know that a given hypothesis is true if and only if lawlike does not help us decide whether or not it is true and lawlike, or whether to project it at a given time in favor of a competing hypothesis. Although the hypothesis

H_4 All emeralds are grue emeralds

may be true if and only if lawlike, whether it is to be projected at a given moment depends upon whether it survives competition with other hypotheses, such as

H_5 All emeralds are green emeralds.

H_4 and H_5 compete if we assume that some emerald is either a green emerald or a grue emerald but not both. The entrenchment of 'grue emerald' is judged now to be much less than that of 'green emerald'; and H_4 is accordingly rejected. Our judgment may, of course, be wrong. If the two predicates are in fact coextensive, then they are equally well entrenched. But our mistake under these circumstances carries small penalty; for in this case H_4 and H_5 are equivalent. Hence, though H_4 is rejected, an equivalent is accepted—and subsequent discovery of this equivalence will reinstate H_4.

7

Review of Reichenbach's
Elements of Symbolic Logic

Hans Reichenbach, *Elements of Symbolic Logic* (New York: Macmillan, 1947), pp. ix, 444.

This book offers a clear and competent exposition of the essentials of modern logic, together with a provocative discussion of several often neglected but highly relevant problems. Sometimes, however, what is at best a suggestion concerning a still unsolved problem is presented as an adequate solution.

Throughout the book the usual sentential operations are regarded as having two different meanings, depending upon the context. Conjunction, disjunction, etc., may be either purely truth-functional or more powerfully "connective". The sign " ⊃ " may stand for adjunctive (i.e., material) implication, or for some stronger logical or nonlogical relationship between antecedent and and consequent. This does not mean that Hans Reichenbach is an avowed intensionalist; for he regards sentences containing connective operations as "improper object sentences" requiring eventual metalinguistic translation, and he writes in his Preface: "To prove that a satisfactory solution can be attained without abandoning the principles of what has been called an extensional logic constitutes one of the major objectives of the book."

Unfortunately, the book does not achieve this objective. The idea of grouping together all statements compounded by means of connective operations, whether or not the connection is logical or nonlogical, is good; but the elaborate attempt to define such "nomological statements" is unsuccessful. A nomological statement is defined as a statement that (1) can be proved or at least 'practically' proved to be true, (2) is an 'all' statement, (3) is fully exhaustive, i.e., nonvacuous in a strong and complex sense, and (4) is universal in the sense that no argument is an individual-term, and that the statement 'cannot be written' in a form in which

413

an argument is an individual-term. No criteria are given by which to tell whether a given extralogical statement satisfies the first requirement, and it is precisely here that the most difficult aspect of the question lies. Reichenbach dismisses the matter as belonging to inductive logic and therefore outside the scope of his book; but inductive logic has not so far provided any satisfactory answer to the question how to distinguish between confirmable and nonconfirmable statements. As for the requirement of universality, it is either much too strong or much too weak. The statement (i) "(x) (if x is a region of the surface of the Earth, then x is sometimes in the light of the Sun)" has as a counterpart the statement, (ii) "(x) (if x is a region of terrestrial surface, then x is sometimes sunlit)". If (ii) is nonuniversal because it "can be written" as (i), then virtually all apparently universal sentences will be ruled out on a similar score. On the other hand, if (ii) does qualify as universal, it is pointless to exclude sentences like (i), since theoretically their content can always be expressed in sentences like (ii). In general, the requirements Reichenbach sets up for nomological statements will be effective only if one places substantial and perhaps question-begging restrictions on the kinds of predicates that may be used.

Mr. Reichenbach, as an extensionalist and physicalist, declares that only physical entities have actual existence. He frankly admits, however, that he is unable as yet to solve the very difficult problem of developing a logic that is consistent with the claim that properties have only fictitious existence. He makes no such apologies for his unnecessary acceptance, as basic physical entities, of what he calls 'situations'. A situation, he says, is what is denoted by a sentence; and the sentence may split the situation into a thing and a property of the thing, or an event and a property of the event. Thus situations are for him not things nor properties nor even events. The reviewer cannot understand what these "situations" are, cannot conceive how they can be regarded as physical existents, and cannot reconcile acceptance of these pseudo entities with the general philosophical theses Reichenbach sets forth.

In the section on fictitious existence, there is a more technical defect. The sentence "x_i perceives a dog" (whether or not a dog is actually present) is interpreted to mean "There exists immediately for x_i an entity y such that y is a dog and x_i perceives y." The entity y is a fictitious 'immediate thing' (i.e., an image), and the existential quantifier is explictly extended to include such fictitious entities in its range. But surely it is false to say that this immediate perception y *is a dog*. Adequate translation along these lines would seem to require modification of the predicates used as well as modification of the range of the quantifier. The same difficulty appears in other examples given in this section.

On the other hand, the discussion of the nature of logical truth is very sound. Avoiding the excesses of both extreme conventionalism and careless empiricism, Mr. Reichenbach makes the point that statements about the reliability of logical formulas are empirical; e.g., that while a logical formula may be a tautology, the statement that it is a tautology is itself "not a tautology but an empirical statement".

In the section on 'token-reflexive words' such as "here" and "I" and the tensed forms of verbs, Reichenbach goes considerably beyond Russell's remarks on 'ego-centric particulars'. The reviewer, as a result of his own study of the problem, feels that Reichenbach's treatment is still incomplete and faulty in some respects. Nevertheless, the approach is essentially correct, and there is probably no equally adequate discussion of the matter in print.

On the whole, the book deserves study by those who are concerned with some of the most pressing questions of present-day logical philosophy. That fact alone accounts for some of its merits and some of its defects as a textbook.

8

Snowflakes and Wastebaskets

In earlier days, the order of the world lay awaiting discovery by inspection or revelation. And the durability of order, once found, depended upon the trustworthiness of nature or the goodness of God. Subjectivism inevitably intruded upon this innocent view; and Kant relegates the cosmos and its order to an inaccessible realm and an inconsequential status. Any attempt even to conceive of the real order, let alone observe it, ends in antinomy and confusion. Order is to be found only in our experience, and is innate in us rather than inherent in what comes to us. Order results from the processing of raw material by the knower; and can be discovered by determining what forms and categories the understanding, by its very nature, must impose. The order in experience, like order in the world beyond, depends upon its maker; but the maker of the order of experience is the human mind. And the guarantee of continuance of this order lies in the inability of the mind to operate in any other way, or with any other forms or categories.

Lewis goes as far beyond Kant as Kant goes beyond his predecessors. I remember that Lewis used to say to his class: "Anyone who really succeeds in deducing the categories will make a lasting name for himself." Then, after pausing long enough for each student to resolve to make that his life work for at least the next two weeks, Lewis would destroy all dreams by saying ". . . but it can't be done."

And the reason why it can't be done is that the categories are not uniquely determined by the nature of the understanding, are not articulations of the fixed way the mind does and must work, are not innate and ineradicable ideas. Categorial schemata are rather tools the knower uses in coping with what comes to him. He invents them, alters them, chooses among alternatives, rejects, and replaces or reinstates them. They serve, rather than constrain, him.

This memorial paper for C. I. Lewis was written to honor some of his important ideas. Discussion of any points of disagreement between us seemed inappropriate in this context.

416

Thus not only have we seen the center of order pass from the cosmos to the cognitive faculty and on into categorial schemata; but we have travelled the whole way from objective absolutism through subjective absolutism into conceptual relativism. The mind is free. Coercion is confined within the compass of a chosen categorial scheme. The impossibility of a square circle does not derive from the mind's incapacity to conceive of a square circle; rather, the inconceivability of a square circle derives from the incompatibility of the concept of a square with that of a circle.

Lewis was not, of course, the founder of pragmatism. But on the basis of his crystallized version of it, he treats the stubborn problems of the status and assurance of order with unprecedented brilliance.

How can we be sure that what comes to us will be amenable to the ordering we have invented? In much the same way, Lewis answers, that I can be sure my filing system—miserable as it is—will accommodate all my correspondence. A poet once had a filing system consisting of four folders severally marked: "Unpaid Bills", "Rejection Slips", "Love Letters", and "Miscellaneous". It had a place for everything he could possibly receive. Some years later, when one of his poems was accepted, he made a minor improvement by re-marking the miscellaneous folder "Acceptances", and dumping the rest of its contents into the wastebasket. But this was only for convenience. The wastebasket now became an integral part of his filing system. And the point is that so long as a filing system contains a "miscellaneous" folder or a wastebasket, we shall never be at a loss. No demon can frustrate us by producing something that won't fit anywhere. That whatever we encounter will fit our scheme depends upon no assumption about what we shall encounter but only upon reasonable care in devising our scheme—especially by providing a wastebasket.

But what can such an arbitrary sorting accomplish? A good deal, says Lewis. It guarantees limited variety, insures against unending novelty. If we sort everything into n jointly exhaustive categories, then we can be sure of some repetition as soon as we have more than n items to sort. Whatever the demon may deal us, some properties will recur. What is more, sequences will soon have to be repeated. Not only does any string of 0's and 1's that consists of three or more characters contain at least two 0's or two

1's, but also as the string grows, couples, triples, and longer sequences will be repeated.

Moreover, by adjusting our categories, we can change the probability of recurrences as we like. A sorting system consisting of a single compartment—the solitary wastebasket—will achieve maximum dependability by sacrificing all discrimination. Increasing differentiation reduces reliability. Lewis is fond of the example of snowflakes. The demon really does us dirt here, seeming never to give us two snowflakes of the same shape. But we are not downhearted; we simply retreat to a broader scheme of classification— say into geometrical and nongeometrical shapes—and find a remarkable uniformity among snowflakes. We are in constant tension between the need for safety and the need for specificity; and we can strike a balance wherever it suits our purposes. All the justification needed for induction is assurance that the probability of our predictions is greater than zero; and this depends not upon what a benign deity or a malevolent devil may do, but upon our free choice.

What neither the demon nor we can achieve, though, even with the worst will in the world, is utter chaos. Some of Lewis's most memorable passages argue the impossibility of chaos. Nature does not lie beyond experience but is organized within experience. Reality must be regular because reality is distinguished by the very fact that it conforms to the requirements of the non-wastebasket compartments of our categorical schemes. After many a geometric snowflake, one that turns up in the form of a portrait of Napoleon is likely to be rejected as no real snowflake. To be real, relative to any context, is to exhibit certain prescribed uniformities. If the prescription is too exacting, reality may be meagre or even null, but it cannot be disorderly. Without law, there is nothing—that is, there are *no things;* for things are what obey laws. To suppose that nature can be completely chaotic is self-contradictory.

But chaos is impossible even if there are no things—even if none of our experience meets the requirements for reality. Chaos is absolutely inconceivable, not from any infirmity of the mind, but because the concepts of chaos and conceivability are incompatible. To conceive or even to describe is to impose a conceptual scheme, hence to organize and order. And what is organized and ordered is not chaotic.

Thus no assumption whatever is needed as insurance against chaos either in nature or in experience.

Although Lewis insists throughout upon a sharp distinction between analytic and synthetic judgments, I suspect that his theory of probability and induction actually depends very little upon this now highly controversial matter. That the probability of recurrences varies with the schemata we apply, and that chaos conceived is no chaos at all, seem to me true and pertinent principles, whether or not we regard them as following from the meanings of the terms involved. But it remains a question whether there is an evident and absolute distinction between what we have been referring to as 'what comes to us' and the schemata we apply.

Lewis's treatment of these problems will perhaps suggest the importance of his general position. If we use categorical schemes to make the world, the study of these schemes becomes a primary concern of philosophy. Wistful speculation concerning forever inaccessible realms of being or consciousness gives way to investigations in logic, to the analysis of concepts, to the examination of the nature, varieties, and functions of symbolic systems and media. Only upon some such view can I see how such diverse activities as, for example, systematic construction, ordinary-language study, and structural linguistics can all contribute directly to the philosophic endeavor. Not the least of the heritage Lewis leaves to philosophers is the invitation to a variety of fascinating and rewarding work that will occupy many of them for a long time to come.

Supplementary Readings for Chapter VIII
secondary to references within text and footnotes

Carnap, R., *The Continuum of Inductive Methods*, Chicago: University of Chicago Press, 1952.

———., "Replies and Systematic Expositions", Nos. 25–31, in *The Philosophy of Rudolf Carnap* (P. A. Schilpp, ed.), LaSalle, Ill.: Open Court, 1963.

Hullett, J. N., "Discussion on a Simple-Minded Solution", *Philosophy of Science*, Vol. 37 (1970), pp. 452–454.

Hume, D., *A Treatise of Human Nature* (L. A. Selby-Bigge, ed.), Oxford: The Clarendon Press, 1928, Book I, Part III.

Lewis, C. I., *Mind and the World Order*, New York: Scribner, 1929, Chap. XI.

Smokler, H., "Goodman's Paradox and the Problem of Rules of Acceptance", *American Philosophical Quarterly*, Vol. 3 (1966), pp. 71–76.

Stegmüller, W., Review of *Fact, Fiction, and Forecast*, *Kantstudien*, Vol. 50 (1958–1959), pp. 363–390.

Vickers, J. M., "Characteristics of Projectible Predicates", *Journal of Philosophy*, Vol. 64 (1967), pp. 280–286.

IX

Likeness

FOREWORD

The calculus of quality-orders, or system of scaling, developed in *SA* has over the years attracted the attention of a number of mathematicians and psychologists. Yet because it is framed in the language of a special philosophical system, it has remained rather inaccessible to most nonphilosophers. Some psychologists have complained of the difficulty of following it through, some have misinterpreted it and raised mistaken objections, and some have been unaware of its anticipation of their own work.

"Order from Indifference" may perhaps make the outlines of the matching-calculus more readily available and understandable. In this paper of some fifteen years ago, here expanded and brought up to date, I have tried to free the exposition from the peculiar philosophical features and the technical terminology of the more comprehensive system outlined in *SA*. The advantages and disadvantages of the 'algebraic' and the 'probabilistic' matching-calculi and of other systems, are also discussed, with no presumption that any one system is exclusively right or even decisively best. And I have added as a postscript my hitherto unpublished reply to Luce and Galanter.

The matching-calculus as a graph-theoretical system has some independent mathematical interest. Several mathematicians have participated in its development; and whatever slight contribution I may have made to mathematics lies here. But for anything more than the most elementary glimpse of the mathematics of the calculus, the reader will have to go back to *SA* and to the mathematical papers mentioned in the footnotes.

At first glance "Order from Indifference", which proposes a way of measuring similarity, might seem either to refute or to be undermined by the relativism of "Seven Strictures on Similarity". But "Seven Strictures" argues not that there is no way of ordering qualities but that there are many ways; and "Order from Indifference" is concerned not with *the* way of ordering qualities but with one way. Among the many ways, none is peculiarly and exclusively validated by our highly unstable ordinary judgments of similarity. Of course we may, as elsewhere in measurement (e.g., see VII,1 above), adopt one or another system as standard; and acuity of discrimination may offer a firmer basis than does estimation of comparative likeness. As we have seen earlier (III, 1), though, discrimination is far from constant, varying notably with interest, information, and practice.

If different quality-orderings result from different systems, and if the judgments called for by any of these methods change readily with circumstance, we may well wonder about talk of 'innate quality-spaces'. Which of the several orderings is supposed to be innate? And what does the attribution of innateness mean? We make, rather unreliably, judgments of all the kinds called for by the several methods. Which judgments come first, and whether what comes first is built in or learned or hit upon at random, seem rather fragile questions.

1

Order from Indifference

1. Basis

Psychologists have based systems of sensory scaling—or quality ordering and measuring—on data of many different kinds. For example, a subject may be asked to judge which of two grays is the lighter, or whether two colors are more alike than two others, or to say when a difference is first noticed when a light is gradually intensified, or to turn a knob until the sound produced is half as loud as a given one. In the system outlined in the present paper,[1] the subject is asked simply whether the presented qualities *match* —that is, whether he can tell them apart.

The relation of matching is dyadic, symmetric, reflexive, non-transitive, and non-quantitative. It differs in one or more of these respects from each of the basic relations of the other systems mentioned.

For the purpose in hand, matching has some notable advantages, especially in simplicity, generality, and neutrality. In the first place, matching is simpler, everything considered, than any of the other relations mentioned; and simplicity, as I have argued elsewhere,[2] is not merely a matter of elegance but is of the essence of science. Structurally, matching has a complexity-value of 2 on my scale—less than any of the other relations except just-noticeable difference. Moreover, the subject is required only to compare elements, not intervals, and to judge only difference as such, not the direction or amount of difference. In the second place, matching is a ubiquitous relation, unlike louder-than, which obtains between sounds but not literally among colors, or brighter-than, which obtains among colors but not literally among odors. Matching obtains

1. The system summarized here is that of *SA;* and the reader is referred to Chaps. IX and X of that book for much fuller explanation and additional material. The present version of this paper has been revised in accordance with the Second Edition of *SA,* and "Postscript" (Section 7) has been added.

2. See VIII,1 above and *SA III,3.*

between colors, between sounds, between odors—indeed between qualities of every kind. In the third place, matching is neutral, implying nothing concerning the dimensionality or other features of the order under investigation. In this it contrasts with just-noticeable difference, which calls for judgment of the first difference within an already accepted ordering.

Matching has its drawbacks, too. Vast quantities of matching judgments have to be gathered and processed in investigating any quality-order; and while the processing can nowadays be expedited by computer, the gathering tries the patience of experimenter and subject. Again, significant results can be obtained only with extreme delicacy in the control of stimuli and of conditions of observation; and sensory acuity is enough to challenge the most sensitive available means of measurement and control. Still, these obstacles have not blocked some rather extensive experimental investigation on the basis of matching judgments. Furthermore, the difficulties arise less from the choice of matching as a basis than from the facts of matching, which any adequate system of scaling must somehow take into account.

2. Bridge

But how do we go on from here? A reflexive, symmetric, non-transitive relation of matching or apparent indifference is an unpromising basis for constructing an order. Some bridge is needed from this relation to an ordering relation like betweenness. Certain simple cases offer a clue: a quality that matches two non-matching qualities lies between them, and a quality between two matching qualities matches both. Perhaps the underlying principle here is that matching qualities are always to be placed nearer together than non-matching qualities; but the full strength of this principle will not be needed until we go beyond the problem of order to the problem of measure. Until then a weaker consequence will do: that no interval between non-matching qualities lies within an interval between matching qualities.[3] Neither the stronger nor the weaker

3. This weaker rule was stated, and its use explained, in *A Study of Qualities* (pp. 434ff.). Publication of it ten years later in the first edition of

principle, however, stands as a postulate or definition of the system but rather as a rule guiding the formulation of definitions. The problem now is to develop, with the guidance of the weaker rule, a comprehensive calculus of quality-order.

I have been taking the qualities exhibited by two stimuli under given conditions to be matching or non-matching according to the subject's single response. If the same stimuli are presented more than once under the same conditions, with some positive and some negative matching-responses, some arbitrary rule is adopted that counts qualities as matching if they are judged to match a stated percentage (say 51 percent) of the time. The system is thus categorical in its foundation and algebraic or graph-theoretic in its construction.

A quite different way of developing order from matching-data has been more often used by psychologists. It consists in reading directly from percentage of positive matching-responses to nearness of the qualities in question; the distance between qualities is the less the more often they are judged to match. The attractions of this approach are evident. To measure likeness of qualities by relative infrequency of discrimination is intuitively plausible. Available statistical information is put to work. Order and measure are derived immediately and simultaneously from the data; and the results are supposedly stable—i.e. such that the placing of qualities in relation to each other remains unaffected by the introduction of other qualities.[4] But these advantages must not be overrated. Most pairs of qualities, after all, either never match or always match; and since frequency of matching is no guide to relative likeness either among pairs with a matching frequency of 0 or among pairs with a matching frequency of 1, the problem of developing a comprehensive order from the cases established by the initial principle is neither avoided nor obviously simplified. Again, making order depend entirely upon measure is not an

---

SA antedated by five years its adoption by Luce as the fundamental postulate of his theory of 'semiorders'. See his "Semiorders and a Theory of Utility-Discrimination", *Econometrica*, Vol. 24 (1956), pp. 178–191, especially axioms S3 and S4 and the discussion of them on pp. 181–182.

4. But this is a false lure; see 7 below.

unquestionable virtue. And the cherished stability of positioning risks anomaly; for if by the measure proposed x and z should turn out to be farther apart than the sum of the distance between x and y and the distance between y and z, no order of any dimensionality would accommodate these results (see also 7 below).

The categorical or graph-theoretical approach, which is the subject of the present paper, has in its favor the treatment of quality-order independently from measure, a flexibility that readily accommodates new qualities and relationships, and the intrinsic mathematical interest of the graph-theoretical problems involved and their treatment. But no claim of superiority is implied. Each system has its peculiar merits. Comparison of results obtained by applying the two systems to the same subject-matter might be illuminating. Furthermore, the two systems might supplement one another. The graph-theoretical method may be more effective in crowded neighborhoods, where qualities, many of them matching each other, are closely clustered, while the statistical method may reach across gaps that would otherwise destroy connexity—i.e., where some two qualities are not joined by any chain of links between qualities that match simply (or more often than not) but are joined by a chain of links between qualities that match with a frequency greater than 0.

3. Order

The relationship between (non-transitive) matching and (transitive) identity must be made clear at the start. To mistake one for the other would be to identify black and white, which are joined by a chain of matching-links. Qualities that match may be distinguishable through the fact that one matches some quality the other does not. Qualities x and y are identical if and only if they match all the same qualities.

To order qualities we must be able to determine when two of them are immediately adjacent or next to each other. The special variety of nextness in question here I shall call *besideness*. Two qualities will not be beside each other if there is anything between them. Accordingly, two qualities must match to be beside each other; for if they do not match but belong to the same array they must be joined by a chain of matching-links, so that some other quality will be between the two.

In the simplest case, where y matches two non-matching qualities x and z, the order is clearly $x,y,z;$ that is, y is between x and z. If only the three qualities are involved, y is also beside both x and z. But if there are two or more qualities matching, and hence lying between, x and z, how are the intermediate qualities to be placed in relation to each other? A general definition of besideness must be developed in conformity with our guiding rule.

Looking again at a case of the simplest sort, with only three qualities and with b matching the non-matching qualities a and c, let us compare the lists of qualities matching each:

a	matches	a b
b	matches	a b c
c	matches	b c.

Noting that here, where b is between a and c, (i) all qualities that match both a and c, match b; and (ii) that the qualities matching both a and c are fewer than those matching both a and b, and fewer than those matching both b and c, we might hope that one or the other of these principles would serve to define the more general relation of betweenness that we need for defining besideness.

Unfortunately, neither one works. Consider the case of five qualities, with matching relationships as follows:

a	a	b	c		
b	a	b	c	d	
c	a	b	c	d	e
d		b	c	d	e
e			c	d	e

While the proper ordering of these in accordance with the guiding rule is the alphabetical one, we see that (i) although c is not between a and b, all qualities that match both a and b also match c, and (ii) although b is between a and c, no more qualities match both a and b than match both a and c. Both proposed definitions thus break down near the ends of very simple linear arrays.

Oddly enough, we do better to attend not to qualities that match both of two others but to qualities that match only one of the two.

That a and c lie on opposite sides of b in the case just considered is reflected in the fact that the number of qualities matching a or c but not both is greater than the number matching a or b but not both and greater than the number matching b or c but not both. And here, indeed, is the principle we need.

Since, as we have seen, qualities are beside each other if and only if they match and nothing lies between them, the only betweenness relation required for defining besideness is that obtaining among three matching qualities. This subrelation of betweenness, which I shall call *betwixtness,* may be defined quite generally in the way just suggested. To condense the definition, I shall write "$x/y/z$" for "y is betwixt x and z", "$x\dagger y$" for "the class of qualities matching x or y but not both", and "G" for "has a cardinal number greater than". Thus the definition runs:

$$x/y/z =_{df} \mathrm{M}x,y \cdot \mathrm{M}y,z \cdot \mathrm{M}x,z \cdot x\dagger z \text{ G } x\dagger y \cdot x\dagger z \text{ G } y\dagger z.$$

Then since two matching qualities with none betwixt them are beside each other, besideness is defined as follows:

$$\mathrm{B}\, x,y =_{df} \mathrm{M}x,y \cdot x \neq y \cdot (z)\, (\sim x/z/y).$$

These definitions are provably adequate;[5] that is, in linear arrays conforming to the guiding rule, betwixtness so defined coincides with normal betweenness among matching qualities, and besideness with normal nextness. Furthermore, we can define the class of linear arrays in terms of besideness. An array is linear if (i) for some two qualities (the end points), there is only one beside each, and (ii) for all other qualities (the interior points), there are two beside each. The general definition of betweenness in linear arrays can then be given as follows: y is between x and z if y is identical with neither but lies in the shortest chain of besideness-linked qualities that contains both x and z.

4. Irregularity

So far, the examples considered have all been regular linear arrays; that is, linear arrays such that the M-span—or number of besideness-steps from a quality to the nearest non-matching one in

---

5. For the proof, see *SA X,3* "Justification of the Definition of Betwixtness".

either direction—is constant throughout. However, our definitions work equally well for irregular arrays. In the following example

$$
\begin{array}{ll}
a & a\ b \\
b & a\ b\ c\ d \\
c & \quad b\ c\ d \\
d & \quad b\ c\ d\ e \\
e & \qquad\quad d\ e\ f \\
f & \qquad\qquad e\ f,
\end{array}
$$

the order established is

$$a\ b\ c\ d\ e\ f,$$

and the M-span varies; for the number of besideness steps from a to the nearest non-matching quality c is 2, while the number from b to the nearest non-matching quality e is 3.

A remarkable feature of such irregular arrays is that if we define just-noticeable difference in the obvious way, so that the first element (in either direction) that does not match x is just-noticeably different from x, then just-noticeable difference unexpectedly turns out to be non-symmetric. For example, the first quality to the right of b that does not match b is e, but the first quality to the left of e that does not match e is c. Thus although e is just-noticeably different from b, still c rather than b is just-noticeably different from e. At first glance, this paradox might be blamed on careless formulation of the definition of just-noticeable difference; but we soon discover that we get unwelcome results no matter how we frame our definition. Suppose we make c and e just-noticeably different, and also b and e; then to the left of e lie two qualities, one further than the other from e, such that both will be called just-noticeably different from e. Suppose, then, we make b and e just-noticeably different, but not c and e; then not the first but the second quality to the left of e that does not match it will be called just-noticeably different from e. If, finally, we make c and e just-noticeably different but not b and e, then although there are to the right of b many qualities that do not match b, none is just-noticeably different from b. Thus, whichever choice we make, just-noticeable difference here behaves in an intuitively objectionable way.

This trouble, far from being an accident of our particular example, is characteristic of all irregular linear arrays. Such arrays satisfy our weaker rule (that no span between non-matching qualities is enclosed within a span between matching qualities) but not our stronger rule (that the span between any two matching qualities is less than the span between any two non-matching qualities). In the example above, for instance, the two matching qualities b and d are as many besideness-steps apart as are the two non-matching qualities a and c. The order of such arrays is uniquely and irrevocably determined by the weaker rule, but the question arises whether adjustments in spacing can be made to map such arrays in conformity with the stronger rule, not only to remove the anomalies concerning just-noticeable difference but also to reconcile two different measures.

5. Measure

The number of besideness-steps from a quality to the nearest non-matching quality varies in an irregular array. Can we, without disturbing the mandatory order, so space the qualities in such an array as to achieve a constant M-span and symmetric just-noticeable difference?

The indicated course is to spread the array over a more extended map, strategically leaving certain positions vacant, so that when all steps between positions (occupied or vacant) are counted as besideness-steps, the number of besideness-steps between nearest non-matching qualities will be constant throughout the array. In the example above, two vacant positions must be left: one between a and b, the other between d and e. Each vacant position is in effect treated as a dummy quality matching other qualities, with the following result:

a	$a\ v_1\ b$
v_1	$a\ v_1\ b\ c$
b	$a\ v_1\ b\ c\ d$
c	$v_1\ b\ c\ d\ v_2$
d	$b\ c\ d\ v_2\ e$
v_2	$c\ d\ v_2\ e\ f$
e	$d\ v_2\ e\ f$
f	$v_2\ e\ f.$

Now just-noticeable difference is the symmetric relation between nearest (occupied or vacant) non-matching positions; and the number of besideness-steps between such positions is everywhere the same. The array has a uniform M-span and satisfies the stronger rule.[6]

Successful interpolation of required vacant positions by trial-and-error sometimes becomes so difficult that one may well wonder whether it can always be accomplished. N. J. Fine and R. Harrop have shown that and how every irregular linear array can be thus regularized.[7] The theory of linear arrays is thus complete: given any M-connected set of qualities orderable under the weaker rule as a linear array, we can from the matching-relationships alone, construct the order and regularize the array.

6. Non-linear Arrays

Before considering how our definitions work in non-linear arrays, we need some terminology for classifying them. We may take them as mapped by graphs, with the nodes standing for qualities and the edges for nextness-links. Only the topological—not the geometrical—properties of these graphs are to be taken into account.

Simple closed linear arrays are *polygons;* and polygons may be called *triangular, square* (although "quadrilateral" would be more appropriate), etc. according as they have three, four, etc. nodes and edges. A branching array, containing no polygons is a *tree.* An array that consists of polygons joined at their edges is called a *network;* and an array that consists of polygons joined at their vertices but containing no circuit of polygons, I call a *chandelier.* When all the polygons in a network or chandelier are

---

6. In "Proof of a Conjecture of Goodman", *Journal of Symbolic Logic*, Vol. 19 (1954), pp. 41–44, N. J. Fine has demonstrated the equivalence, for all linear arrays, of the following four properties: uniformity of M-span, symmetry of just-noticeable difference, satisfaction of the stronger rule, and having no two qualities beside each other such that either matches more than one quality the other does not.

7. In "Uniformization of Linear Arrays", *Journal of Symbolic Logic*, Vol. 22 (1957), pp. 130–140.

triangular, quadrilateral, etc., the array may be called a *triangular-cell, square-cell,* etc. *network* or *chandelier.*[8]

I shall call a graph *homogeneous* if it is not only node-homogeneous but also next-pair homogeneous; that is, such that for each two next-pairs x,y and w,z there is a one-one mapping of the graph onto itself that maps w onto x and maps z onto y and preserves nextness. Homogeneity is thus defined without reference to M-span and is independent of regularity. Obviously, only closed or infinite arrays can be homogeneous. Although in sensory scaling we are concerned only with finite arrays, the study of infinite homogeneous arrays throws light on some properties of finite arrays.

How far is our definition of besideness adequate for constructing non-linear arrays? It works more often than we might expect;[9] but it breaks down—fails to coincide with nextness—in an interesting way in square-cell networks. Consider the example in Figure 1, with a uniform M-span of 4. Here not only y but also z turns out to be beside x, although z is not next to x but two steps away. The remedy is to interate our definitional procedure. We first define "$x\backslash y\backslash z$" (or "$y$ is twixt x and z") by writing "B" for "M" in the full expansion of our definiens for betwixtness. Then we define "Fx,y" (for "x flanks y") by writing "B" for "M" and writing "$\sim x\backslash y\backslash z$" for "$\sim x/y/z$" in the

---

8. All discussion of dimensionality has been omitted above. By the usual mathematical definition of dimensionality, all graphs are zero-dimensional. Classification of graphs by some other definition of dimensionality inevitably conflicts in some way with inconsistent ordinary usage. One way is this: an array is at least n-dimensional if it contains some $n + 1$ nodes such that each two of these are next to each other. By this standard, a triangular-cell array will be two-dimensional, while a square-cell network—often thought of as typically two-dimensional—will be one-dimensional. For another treatment of dimensionality, see *SA,* p. 342.

9. In Figure 1, y will be betwixt the qualities next to it on the same horizontal line. By certain other formulae that might work for linear arrays, y would not turn out to be betwixt these two qualities; for instance, in linear arrays one of three different matching qualities is betwixt the other two if and only if it matches every quality that matches both of them, and matches no quality that does not match at least one of them. But in Figure 1, there are qualities matching y (e.g. the one four steps directly above y) that match neither of the qualities next to y on the same horizontal line. Accordingly, this formula was rejected for defining betwixtness. It has been adopted for linear arrays by Restle in "A Metric and an Ordering on Sets", *Psychometrika,* Vol. 24 (1959), p. 210.

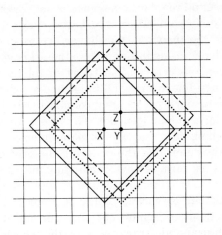

FIGURE 1

The diamond-shaped boundaries enclose
nodes for all qualities matching x (solid
line), y (dotted line), and z (broken
line).

definiens for besideness. In the case under discussion (Figure 1),
flanking obtains between x and y but not between x and z. Thus
here and everywhere else in this array, if we assume that it is
homogeneous (continuing on infinitely), flanking coincides with
nextness; and our definition succeeds in drawing the delicate distinction between qualities that are on a side and those that are
on opposite corners of a square cell in such a network.

Flanking also works much more generally; it coincides with
nextness in all linear arrays and all polygons, in all regular homogeneous trees, in all regular homogeneous triangular-cell networks
where c (the constant number of cells having a common vertex)
is not more than 6, and in all regular homogeneous square-cell
networks where c is not more than 4. A slightly modified definition
of nextness will work not only for all these but also for all regular
homogeneous chandeliers.[10] These proven results can perhaps be

10. I have proved the first three of these theorems, Pownall the last three.
For details of all these proofs, see Malcolm W. Pownall's *An Investigation of
a Conjecture of Goodman*, doctoral thesis, Department of Mathematics, University of Pennsylvania, January 1960.

433

extended to cover all regular homogeneous networks of triangular, square, or any other single type of cell, whatever c may be.

Nevertheless, the theory of non-linear arrays is nowhere near complete. We have no definition of nextness known to work for regular homogeneous arrays of all types, or for irregular or non-homogeneous non-linear arrays. In particular, difficulties even arise near the boundaries of segments of non-linear arrays that are as wholes regular and homogeneous. Thus we cannot as yet, given a body of matching-data that cannot be accommodated by linear mapping, always determine the ordering directly and uniquely. Rather we must try various ways of mapping the qualities in question, with a view to maximizing regularity while minimizing complexity and number of vacant positions. Regrettable as this is, many other methods of scaling not only depend almost entirely upon some such trial-and-error procedure, but consider only a few among the many possible types of array. For example, triangular-cell networks, despite their peculiar importance, are almost always completely ignored.

7. Postscript: Non-fatal Non-flaw

In a chapter on "Discrimination" in *Handbook of Mathematical Psychology*,[11] Luce and Galanter argue (p. 239) that the categorical matching-system outlined above "has a fatal flaw" since this system ". . . does not define an invariant distance measure." Thus there may be arrays that are non-linear by Goodman's definition which have subsets that are linear." I enthusiastically plead guilty to this charge, since any theory for which non-linear arrays contain no linear subsets convicts itself of absurdity.

To illustrate their complaint, the authors plot a linear path with many turns in a square-cell network. They cannot suppose that my system does not properly determine the linear order of elements along the path. What horrifies them is that if these are the only elements given, the linear ordering will not reveal the shape of the graph as embedded in the full network—will not show, for

11. Volume I (edited by Luce, Bush, and Galanter), New York, 1963, pp. 237–240.

example, that the two end-elements of the path are nearer together in that network than either is to some interior elements of
the path. They suppose that use of the statistical method will establish this directly and finally.

Now in the first place, Luce and Galanter give no hint as to why
they consider this feature 'fatal'. Insofar as the statistical method
does thus give greater stability and so avoid the inconvenience of
adjusting distances when new elements are introduced, this may
be counted as one disadvantage of the categorical method, to be
balanced against such advantages as the independence of order
from measure, and the flexibility that insures against anomaly
(see 2 above).

Moreover, the statistical method itself cannot be taken, without
paralyzing its effectiveness, to fix uniquely and finally the shape of
an array comprising a few elements from a larger array. Suppose
b is determined to be halfway between a and c, so that we have i
of Figure 2.

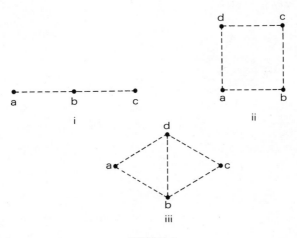

FIGURE 2

Then a new element d is found to be halfway between a and c,
and such that a and c are both halfway between b and d; now
we have ii of Figure 2, with distance measured not across the
background but along shortest paths. If instead of d we have e,
determined to be halfway between a and c, and as near to b as to

a and c, then we have iii of Figure 2. In other words, if several elements halfway between two others are to be accommodated, determination that y is halfway between x and z must be taken only as placing y on the plane perpendicular to the line from x to z. Initial placing of y within that plane is subject to adjustment in accordance with further restrictions imposed by relationships to and among new elements as they are introduced. Any firmer fixity would be fatal.

Incidentally, a later passage (p. 240, lines 5–7) raises serious doubt that Luce and Galanter understand that the weaker mapping rule is the only principle I appeal to for ordering the elements of a linear array.

2

Seven Strictures on Similarity

Similarity, I submit, is insidious. And if the association here with invidious comparison is itself invidious, so much the better. Similarity, ever ready to solve philosophical problems and overcome obstacles, is a pretender, an impostor, a quack. It has, indeed, its place and its uses, but is more often found where it does not belong, professing powers it does not possess.

The strictures I shall lay against similarity are none of them new, but only recently have I come to realize how often I have encountered this false friend and had to undo his work.

First Stricture: Similarity does not make the difference between representations and descriptions, distinguish any symbols as peculiarly 'iconic', or account for the grading of pictures as more or less realistic or naturalistic.[1]

The conviction that resemblance is the necessary and sufficient condition for representation is so deeply ingrained that the evident and conclusive arguments to the contrary are seldom considered. Yet obviously one dime is not a picture of another, a girl is not a representation of her twin sister, one printing of a word is not a picture of another printing of it from the same type, and two photographs of the same scene, even from the same negative, are not pictures of each other.

All that this proves, of course, is that resemblance alone is not enough for representation. But where reference has been established—where a symbol does refer to some object—is not similarity then a sufficient condition for the symbol's being a representation? Plainly *no.* Consider a page of print that begins with "the final seven words on this page" and ends with the same seven words repeated. The first of these seven-word inscriptions surely refers to the second, and is as much like it as can be, yet is no more a picture of it than is any printing of a word a picture of another printing.

Still, once pictures are somehow distinguished from other de-

1. See further, *LA I.*

437

notative symbols—and this must be by some other means than similarity—does not comparative naturalism or realism among pictures depend upon their degree of resemblance to what they represent? Not even this can be maintained. For pictures of goblins and unicorns are quite easily graded as more or less realistic or naturalistic or fantastic, though this cannot depend upon degree of resemblance to goblins and unicorns.

The most we can say is that among pictures that represent actual objects, degree of realism correlates to some extent with degree of similarity of picture to object. But we must beware of supposing that similarity constitutes any firm, invariant criterion of realism; for similarity is relative, variable, culture-dependent. And even where, within a single culture, judgments of realism and of resemblance tend to coincide, we cannot safely conclude that the judgments of realism follow upon the judgments of resemblance. Just the reverse may be at least equally true: that we judge the resemblance greater where, as a result of our familiarity with the manner of representation, we judge the realism greater.

Second Stricture: Similarity does not pick out inscriptions that are 'tokens of a common type', or replicas of each other.[2]

Only our addiction to similarity deludes us into accepting similarity as the basis for grouping inscriptions into the several letters, words, and so forth. The idea that inscriptions of the same letter are more alike than inscriptions of different letters evaporates in the glare of such counterexamples as those in Figure 1. One might argue that what counts is not degree of similarity

$$a \qquad d \qquad A$$

$$m \qquad w \qquad M$$

FIGURE 1

but rather similarity in a certain respect. In what respect, then, must inscriptions be alike to be replicas of one another? Some who should know better have supposed that the several inscriptions of the same letter are topologically equivalent, but to show how wrong this is we need only note that the first inscription in

2. See further *SA,* pp. 360–364, and *LA,* pp. 131–141.

Figure 2 is not topologically equivalent to the second, and that the second mark in Figure 3 is topologically equivalent not to the first but to the third.

$$a \qquad\qquad a$$

FIGURE 2

$$B \qquad B \qquad O$$

FIGURE 3

We have terrible trouble trying to say how two inscriptions must be alike to be replicas of one another—how an inscription must resemble other inscriptions of the letter a to be itself an a. I suspect that the best we can do is to say that all inscriptions that are a's must be alike in being a's. That has the solid ring of assured truth, but is hardly electrifying. Moreover, notice that to say that all a's are alike in being a's amounts simply to saying that all a's are a's. The words "alike in being" add nothing; similarity becomes entirely superfluous.

Third Stricture: Similarity does not provide the grounds for accounting two occurrences performances of the same work, or repetitions of the same behavior or experiment.[3]

In other words, what I have said about replicas of inscriptions applies also to events. Two performances of the same work may be very different. Repetitions of the same behavior, such as hitting a tennis ball against a barn door, may involve widely varying sequences of motions. And if we experiment twice, do the differences between the two occasions make them different experiments or only different instances of the same experiment? The answer, as Sir James Thomson stresses, is always relative to a theory[4]—we cannot repeat an experiment and look for a covering theory; we must have at least a partial theory before we know whether we have a repetition of the experiment. Two performances

3. See further, *LA IV.*

4. See "Some Thoughts on Scientific Method" in *Boston Studies in the Philosophy of Science,* Vol. II, ed. R. S. Cohen and Marx W. Wartofsky (New York, 1965), p. 85.

are of the same symphony if and only if, however unlike they may be, they comply with the same score. And whether two actions are instances of the same behavior depends upon how we take them; a response to the command, "Do that again", may well be the question: "Do what again? Swat another fly or move choreographically the same way?"

In each of these cases, the grouping of occurrences under a work or an experiment or an activity depends not upon a high degree of similarity but upon the possession of certain characteristics. In the case of performances of a Beethoven symphony, the score determines what those requisite characteristics are; in the case of repetitions of an experiment, the constitutive characteristics must be sought in the theory or hypothesis being tested; in the case of ordinary actions, the principle of classification varies with our purposes and interests.

Fourth Stricture: Similarity does not explain metaphor or metaphorical truth.[5]

Saying that certain sounds are soft is sometimes interpreted as saying in effect that these sounds are like soft materials. Metaphor is thus construed as elliptical simile, and metaphorical truths as elliptical literal truths. But to proclaim that certain tones are soft because they are like soft materials, or blue because they are like blue colors, explains nothing. Anything is in some way like anything else; any sounds whatever are like soft materials or blue colors in one way or another. What particular similarity does our metaphor affirm? More generally, what resemblance must the objects a term metaphorically applies to bear to the objects it literally applies to?

I do not think we can answer this question much better than we can answer the question what resemblance the objects a term literally applies to must bear to each other. In both cases, a reversal in order of explanation might be appropriate: the fact that a term applies, literally or metaphorically, to certain objects may itself constitute rather than arise from a particular similarity among those objects. Metaphorical use may serve to explain the similarity better than—or at least as well as—the similarity explains the metaphor.

5. See further *LA*, pp. 68–80.

Fifth Stricture: Similarity does not account for our predictive, or more generally, our inductive practice.[6]

That the future will be like the past is often regarded as highly dubious—an assumption necessary for science and for life but probably false, and capable of justification only with the greatest difficulty if at all. I am glad to be able to offer you something positive here. All these doubts and worries are needless. I can assure you confidently that the future will be like the past. I do not know whether you find this comforting or depressing. But before you decide on celebration or suicide, I must add that while I am sure the future will be like the past, I am not sure in just what way it will be like the past. No matter what happens, the future will be in some way like the past.

Let me illustrate. Suppose in investigating the relationship of two variables—say pressure and volume, or temperature and conductivity—for a given material, we obtain the data plotted as un-labelled dots in Figure 4. Where shall we expect the next point to be? Perhaps at a, since a is like all preceding points in falling on the same straight line. But b is like all earlier points in falling on the same curve (the broken line—and many others), and in fact *every* value of y where $x = k$ will be like all earlier points in falling on some—and indeed many a—same curve.

Thus our predictions cannot be based upon the bald principle that the future will be like the past. The question is *how* what is predicted is like what has already been found. Along which, among countless lines of similarity, do our predictions run? I suspect that rather than similarity providing any guidelines for inductive practice, inductive practice may provide the basis for some canons of similarity.[7]

Sixth Stricture: Similarity between particulars does not suffice to define qualities.[8]

Many a good philosopher has supposed that, given particulars and a relation of likeness that obtains between two particulars if

---

6. See further, *FFF*, pp. 72–81, and *LA*, pp. 164–170.

7. See *FFF*, pp. 121–122.

8. See further *SA*, pp. 145–149.

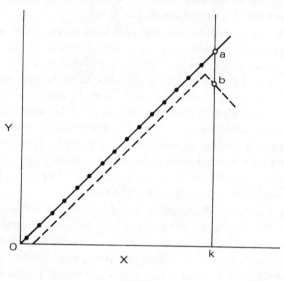

FIGURE 4

and only if they share at least one among certain qualities, he
can readily define such qualities and so avoid admitting them as
additional undefined entities. If several particulars are all alike,
the reasoning runs, they will all share some one quality or other;
and qualities can thus be identified with the most comprehensive
classes of particulars that are all alike.

The flaw here went unnoticed for a long time, simply for lack
of logical scrutiny. Just how do we go from likeness between
two particulars to likeness among several? Several particulars are
all alike, we are tempted to say, if and only if each two of them
are alike. But this will not work. Each two among three or more
particulars may be alike (that is, have a quality in common)
without all of them having any quality in common. Suppose, for
example, we have three discs, the first one half red and half blue,
the second one half blue and half yellow, and the third one half
yellow and half red:

rb   by   yr

1   2   3

Each two of the three discs have a color in common, but there is no color common to all three. Dyadic likeness between particulars will not serve to define those classes of particulars that have a common quality throughout.

Seventh Stricture: Similarity cannot be equated with, or measured in terms of, possession of common characteristics.

This is a rather more general stricture, underlying some of the earlier ones.

When, in general, are two things similar? The first response is likely to be: "When they have at least one property in common." But since every two things have some property[9] in common, this will make similarity a universal and hence useless relation. That a given two things are similar will hardly be notable news if there are no two things that are not similar.

Are two things similar, then, only if they have all their properties in common? This will not work either; for of course no two things have all their properties in common. Similarity so interpreted will be an empty and hence useless relation. That a given two things are similar in this sense would be notable news indeed, but false.

By now we may be ready to settle for a comparative rather than a categorical formula. Shall we say that two things a and b are more alike than two others c and d if a and b have more properties in common than do c and d? If that has a more scientific sound and seems safer, it is unfortunately no better; for any two things have exactly as many properties in common as any other two. If there are just three things in the universe, then any two of them belong together in exactly two classes and have exactly two properties in common: the property of belonging to the class consisting of the two things, and the property of belonging to the class consisting of all three things. If the universe is larger, the number of shared properties will be larger but will still be the same for every two elements. Where the number of things in the universe is n, each two things have in common exactly 2^{n-2} properties out of the total of $2^n - 1$ properties; each thing has 2^{n-2}

9. Of course as a nominalist, I take all talk of properties as slang for more careful formulations in terms of predicates.

properties that the other does not, and there are $2^{n-2} - 1$ properties that neither has. If the universe is infinite, all these figures become infinite and equal.

I have, indeed, been counting only first-order extensional properties. Inclusion of higher-order properties will change the arithmetic but not the argument. The inevitable suggestion that we must consider intensional properties seems to me especially fruitless here, for identifying and distinguishing intensional properties is a notoriously slippery matter, and the idea of measuring similarity or anything else in terms of number of intensional properties need hardly be taken seriously.

More to the point would be counting not all shared properties but rather only *important* properties—or better, considering not the count but the overall importance of the shared properties. Then a and b are more alike than c and d if the cumulative importance of the properties shared by a and b is greater than that of the properties shared by c and d. But importance is a highly volatile matter, varying with every shift of context and interest, and quite incapable of supporting the fixed distinctions that philosophers so often seek to rest upon it.

Here, then, are seven counts in an indictment against similarity. What follows? First, we must recognize that similarity is relative and variable, as undependable as indispensable. Clear enough when closely confined by context and circumstance in ordinary discourse, it is hopelessly ambiguous when torn loose. In this, similarity is much like motion. Where a frame of reference is tacitly or explicitly established, all is well; but apart from a frame of reference, to say that something moves is as incomplete as to say that something is to the left of. We have to say what a thing is to the left of, what it moves in relation to, and in what respects two things are similar.

Yet similarity, unlike motion, cannot be salvaged merely by recognizing its relativity. When to the statement that a thing moves we add a specification of the frame of reference, we remove an ambiguity and complete our initial statement. But when to the statement that two things are similar we add a specification of the property they have in common, we again remove an ambiguity; but rather than supplementing our initial statement, we render it superfluous. For, as we have already seen, to say that two things are similar in having a specified property in common is to say nothing more than that they have that property in common. Similarity is not definitionally eliminated here; we have neither a definiens serving as an appropriate replacement for every occurrence of "is similar to" nor a definitional schema that will provide an appropriate replacement for each occurrence. Rather we must search for the appropriate replacement in each case; and "is similar to" functions as little more than a blank to be filled.

Furthermore, comparative judgments of similarity often require not merely selection of relevant properties but a weighting of their relative importance, and variation in both relevance and importance can be rapid and enormous. Consider baggage at an airport check-in station. The spectator may notice shape, size, color, material, and even make of luggage; the pilot is more concerned with weight, and the passenger with destination and ownership. Which pieces of baggage are more alike than others depends not only upon what properties they share, but upon who makes the comparison, and when. Or suppose we have three glasses, the first two filled with colorless liquid, the third with a bright red liquid. I might be likely to say the first two are more like each other than either is like the third. But it happens that the first glass is filled with water and the third with water colored by a drop of vegetable dye, while the second is filled with hydrochloric acid—and I am thirsty. Circumstances alter similarities.

But have I overlooked the residual and most significant kind of similarity—similarity between qualities as measured by nearness of their positions in an ordering? We are no longer speaking of concrete things, with their countless properties, but of qualities like hues or pitches, which are ordinarily treated as unidimensional. Is not such similarity free of variations resulting from different selections and weightings of relevant properties? Surely, pitches are the more alike as they differ by fewer vibrations per second. But are they? Or is middle C more like high C than like middle D? The question is argument enough. Similarity of so-called simple qualities can be measured by nearness of their positions in an ordering, but they may be ordered, with good reason, in many different ways.

What, then, shall we say of the orderings of sensory qualities as mapped by psychophysicists on the basis of paired comparisons, fractionations, matching, and so forth? If many such methods yield closely congruent maps, relative nearness of position on such a map amounts to similarity under the general conditions and in the general context of the laboratory experiments, and has good title to be taken as a standard measure of similarity among the qualities in question. But can we test the validity of the methods used by examining how well similarity so measured agrees with ordinary judgments of likeness? I think there is no satisfactory way of stabilizing ordinary, as against laboratory, conditions and context to obtain judgments of sensory similarity that are qualified to stand as criteria for appraising the laboratory results. The laboratory results create rather than reflect a measure of sensory similarity. Like most systems of measurement, they tend to govern ordinary judgments at least as much as to be governed by them. And we have seen that the relative weighting of the different qualities of objects is so variable that even reliable measures of similarity for qualities of each kind will give no constant measure of overall similarity for the objects themselves.

Relativity, even volatility, is not a fatal fault. Physics does not stop talking of motion merely because motion is not absolute. But similarity, as we have seen, is a much more slippery matter. As it occurs in philosophy, similarity tends under analysis either to vanish entirely or to require for its explanation just what it purports to explain.

You may feel deprived, depressed, or even angry at losing one more handy tool from the philosopher's dwindling kit. But the rejection of similarity is not, as in the case of classes, rejection of some logical hanky-panky on grounds of philosophical distaste, nor, as in the case of intensions, modalities, analyticity, and synonymy, the rejection of some philosophical tomfoolery on grounds of utter obscurity. If statements of similarity, like counterfactual conditionals and four-letter words, cannot be trusted in the philosopher's study, they are still serviceable in the streets.

Supplementary Readings for Chapter IX
secondary to references within text and footnotes

Coombs, C. H., "A Method for the Study of Interstimulus Similarity", *Psychometrika*, Vol. 19 (1954), pp. 183–194.

———, *A Theory of Data*, New York: Wiley, 1964.

Galanter, E., "An Axiomatic and Experimental Study of Sensory Order and Measure", *Psychological Review*, Vol. 63 (1956), pp. 16–28.

Gulliksen, H., "Paired Comparisons and the Logic of Measurement", *Phychological Review*, Vol. 53 (1946), pp. 199–213.

Luce, R. D. and Edwards, W., "The Derivation of Subjective Scales from Just Noticeable Differences", *Psychological Review*, Vol. 65 (1958), pp. 222–237.

Shepard R., "Stimulus and Response Generalization: Tests of a Model Relating Generalization to Distance in Psychological Space", *Journal of Experimental Psychology*, Vol. 6 (1958), pp. 509–523.

———, "The Analysis of Proximities: Multidimensional Scaling with an Unknown Distance Function", I. *Psychometrika*, Vol. 27 (1962), pp. 125–140; II. *Psychometrika*, Vol. 27 (1962), pp. 219–246.

———, "Attention and the Metric Structure of the Stimulus Space", *Journal of Mathematical Psychology*, Vol. 1 (1964), pp. 54–87.

———, "Circularity in Judgments of Relative Pitch", *Journal of the Acoustical Society of America*, Vol. 36 (1964), pp. 2346–2353.

Stevens, S. S., "The Psychophysics of Sensory Function", *American Scientist*, Vol. 48 (1960), pp. 226–253.

X

Puzzle

FOREWORD

My first publication in logic and philosophy, though it appeared anonymously, has been by far the most popular and widely circulated of all my writings. In 1931, a sudden wave of interest in logical and mathematical puzzles was recognized or generated by a Boston newspaper. At the crest of the wave, a 'daily brain-teaser' appeared in boldface type, double column, often on the front page, of the *Boston Post*.

Some years before, an enlightened king—in an abortive Dunsany-inspired attempt of mine at writing a high school play —had faced the problem of convincing his people that he was not divine. He argued that he proved his claim by merely asserting it; for if he were divine, he would be truthful and so unable to say he was not divine.

Recalling this, I used the principle of his argument as the basis for concocting a brain-teaser of my own, and sent it to the *Boston Post* where it was published, with some editorial alteration, on the front page of the issue of June 8, 1931. My solution, with full explanation, was published the following day, on page 15.

Before long, the puzzle in one version or another, began to come back to me from varied directions. In an article in *Esquire*, J. C. Furnas remarked that by identifying nobles with truth-tellers, the unknown inventor of this problem 'betrayed his bourgeois ideology'. Bourgeois I am, but more convinced of the mendacity of hunters than of the veracity of nobles. And I suppose I could claim I was using "noble" here as an epithet rather than as a title.

Rudolf Carnap, when I first met him at Quine's house in 1936, gave us a version of the puzzle he had recently heard from one of

449

the Polish logicians at a meeting in Warsaw. Shortly afterward, I heard that it had reached Japan.

Meantime, it appeared in various domestic contexts, such as in an advertisement for engineers by an electronics firm. Sometimes carelessness in formulation resulted in an insoluble puzzle. The problem as I stated it depended upon the second speaker having uttered two separate sentences rather than the single sentence conjoining them; for the falsity of the conjunction does not imply the falsity of the components severally. The two components together indeed imply and are implied by their conjunction, but the assiduous liar has to be more careful in asserting the components separately than in asserting the conjunction; for in the former case but not the latter, he must make sure that each of the component statements is false if he is not to risk telling a truth.

Some years later, I heard an interesting variation of this puzzle. The country is the same, its population divided into inveterate liars and unexceptionable truth-tellers. A stranger approaching a fork in the road wants to ascertain from a native, who may be either a liar or a truth-teller, which way leads to the capital. How can he ask one question, to be answered "yes" or "no", so that the answer will tell him which way to go? The solution given was the question, "If I were to ask you if the right-hand road goes to the capital, would you say 'yes'?"

Having some scruples about counterfactuals, I wondered whether there is a truth-functional solution to this problem—a non-subjunctive, non-contrary-to-fact question the traveller can use—and indeed there is.

The Truth-tellers and the Liars

All the men of a certain country are either nobles or hunters, and no one is both a noble and a hunter. The male inhabitants are so nearly alike that it is difficult to tell them apart, but there is one difference: nobles never lie, and hunters never tell the truth.

Three of the men meet one day and Ahmed, the first, says something. He says either, "I am a noble", or "I am a hunter." (We don't know yet which he said.)

Ali, the second man, heard what Ahmed said, and in reply to a query, answered, "Ahmed said, 'I am a hunter'." Then Ali went on to say, "Azab is a hunter."

Azab was the third man. He said, "Ahmed is a noble."

Now the problem is, which is each? How do you know?

Sources and Acknowledgments

I. Philosophy

1. "The Revision of Philosophy", *American Philosophers at Work* (Sidney Hook, ed.), New York: Criterion Books, 1956, pp. 75–92, with the permission of the Open Court Publishing Co., La Salle, Illinois, and S. G. Phillips, Inc., New York.

2. "The Way the World Is", *Review of Metaphysics*, Vol. 14 (1960), pp. 48–56, with the permission of the editors.

3. "Some Reflections on the Theory of Systems", *Philosophy and Phenomenological Research*, Vol. 9 (1949), pp. 620–626, with the permission of the editors.

4. "Review of Urmson's *Philosophical Analysis*", *Mind*, Vol. 67 (1958), pp. 107–109, with the permission of the editors.

5. "Descartes as Philosopher", a talk delivered to the Cartesian Research Bureau, Boston, March 31, 1946.

6. "Definition and Dogma", *Pennsylvania Literary Review*, Vol. 6 (1956), pp. 9–14. A talk given at the Philomathean Society of the University in 1951.

II. Origins

1. "Sense and Certainty", *Philosophical Review*, Vol. 61 (1952), pp. 160–167, with the permission of the editors. Part of a symposium, "The Experiential Element in Knowledge", with C. I. Lewis and Hans Reichenbach, at the meeting of the American Philosophical Association at Bryn Mawr College, December 29, 1951.

2. "The Epistemological Argument", *Synthese*, Vol. 17 (1967), pp. 23–28, with the permission of the editors and D. Reidel Publishing Co., Dordrecht, Holland. Part of a symposium, "Modern Contributions to the Theory of Innate Ideas", with Hilary Putnam and Noam Chomsky, at the joint meeting of the Association for the

Philosophy of Science and the Boston Colloquium on the Philosophy of Science, Boston, December 29, 1964.

3. "The Emperor's New Ideas", *Language and Philosophy* (Sidney Hook, ed.), pp. 138–142. Reprinted by permission of New York University Press, © 1969 by New York University. Part of a symposium, "Language and Philosophy", at the New York University Institute of Philosophy, April 12 and 13, 1968.

4. "Review of Armstrong's *Berkeley's Theory of Vision*", *Philosophy and Phenomenological Research*, Vol. 23 (1962), pp. 284–285, reprinted with the permission of the editors.

III. Art

1. "Art and Authenticity", Chap. III, *Languages of Art*. An earlier version was the Alfred North Whitehead Lecture at Harvard University in April, 1962.

2. "Art and Inquiry" (Presidential Address, American Philosophical Association, Eastern Division, New York, 1967), *Proceedings and Addresses of The American Philosophical Association*, Vol. 41 (1968), pp. 5–19.

3. "Merit as Means", *Art and Philosophy* (Sidney Hook, ed.), pp. 56–57. Reprinted by permission of New York University Press, © 1966 by New York University. Part of a Symposium, "Art and Philosophy", at the New York University Institute of Philosophy, October 23 and 24, 1964.

4. "Some Notes on *Languages of Art*", *Journal of Philosophy*, Vol. 67 (1970), pp. 563–573, reprinted with the permission of the editors. Part of a symposium on *Languages of Art* at the meeting of the American Philosophical Association in New York, December 29, 1969.

5. Further Notes
   (a) "Reply to Morris Weitz", a talk delivered in a symposium on *Languages of Art* at the meeting of the American Society for Aesthetics at the University of Virginia, October 1969. Not previously published.

(b) "Reply to Joseph Margolis", from the same symposium. Not previously published.

(c) "A Circle Squared", not previously published.

(d) "Reply to Matthew Lipman", *Man and World* (1971, forthcoming), with the permission of the editors.

(e) "Reply to Rudolph Arnheim", a letter to the editor printed under the title "Misinterpretation", *Science*, Vol. 164 (20 June 1969), p. 1343, copyright 1969 by the American Association for the Advancement of Science; reprinted with permission of the editors.

6. "Review of Gombrich's *Art and Illusion*", *Journal of Philosophy*, Vol. 57 (1960), pp. 595–599, with the permission of the editors.

IV. Individuals

1. "A World of Individuals", *The Problem of Universals*, Notre Dame, Indiana: University of Notre Dame Press, 1956, pp. 13–31, reprinted with the permission of the University of Notre Dame Press. Part of the Aquinas symposium, "The Problem of Universals", with Alonzo Church and I. M. Bochenski, at Notre Dame University, March 9 and 10, 1956.

2. "Steps Toward a Constructive Nominalism" (with W. V. Quine), *Journal of Symbolic Logic*, Vol. 12 (1947), pp. 105–122, reprinted with the permission of Professor Quine and the editors.

3. "A Revision in the *Structure of Appearance*", *Journal of Philosophy*, Vol. 66 (1969), pp. 383–385, with the permission of the editors.

V. Meaning

1. "Talk of Time" consists of Secs. 2 and 3 of Chap. XI of *The Structure of Appearance*.

2. "On Likeness of Meaning", *Analysis*, Vol. 10 (1949), pp. 1–7, with the permission of the editors.

3. "On Some Differences about Meaning", *Analysis,* Vol. 13 (1953), pp. 90–96, with the permission of the editors.

4. "On a Pseudo-test of Translation", *Philosophical Studies,* Vol. 6 (1952), pp. 81–82.

VI. Relevance

1. "About", *Mind,* Vol. 70 (1961), pp. 1–24, with the permission of the editors.

2. " 'About' Mistaken", *Mind,* Vol. 74 (1965), p. 248, with the permission of the editors.

VII. Simplicity

1. "The Test of Simplicity", *Science,* Vol. 128 (31 October 1958), pp. 1064–1069, copyright 1958 by the American Association for the Advancement of Science; reprinted with the permission of the editors.

2. "Recent Developments in the Theory of Simplicity", *Philosophy and Phenomenological Research,* Vol. 19 (1959), pp. 429–446, with the permission of the editors.

3. "Condensation versus Simplification", *Theoria,* Vol. 27 (1961), pp. 47–48, with the permission of the editors.

4. "Review of Craig's 'Replacement of Auxiliary Expressions' ", *Journal of Symbolic Logic,* Vol. 22 (1957), pp. 317–318, with the permission of the editors.

5. "Elimination of Extralogical Postulates" (with W. V. Quine), *Journal of Symbolic Logic,* Vol. 5 (1940), pp. 104–109, with the permission of Professor Quine and the editors.

6. "Safety, Strength, Simplicity", *Philosophy of Science,* Vol. 28 (1961), pp. 150–151.

7. "Science and Simplicity", number 16, *Voice of America* Philosophy of Science series of talks, 1963.

8. "Uniformity and Simplicity", *Geological Society of American Special Paper 89* (1967), pp. 93–99, with the permission of the

editor. Part of the 75th Anniversary Symposium of the Society, "Uniformity and Simplicity", New York, November 1963.

VIII. Induction

1. "A Query on Confirmation", *Journal of Philosophy*, Vol. 43 (1946), pp. 383–385, with the permission of the editors.

2. "On Infirmities of Confirmation-Theory", *Philosophy and Phenomenological Research,* Vol. 8 (1947), pp. 149–151, with the permission of the editors.

3. "The New Riddle of Induction", Chap. II of *Fact, Fiction, and Forecast.*

4. "An Improvement in the Theory of Projectibility" (with Robert Schwartz and Israel Scheffler), *Journal of Philosophy,* Vol. 67 (1970), pp. 605–608, with the permission of the co-authors and the editors.

5. "Inductive Translation" is Sec. 9 of Chap. IV of *Languages of Art.*

6. "Replies to Comments on *Fact, Fiction, and Forecast*".

   (a) "Reply to an Adverse Ally", *Journal of Philosophy*, Vol. 54 (1957), pp. 531–533, with the permission of the editors.

   (b) "Positionality and Pictures", *Philosophical Review,* Vol. 69 (1960), pp. 523–525, with the permission of the editors.

   (c) "Faulty Formalization", *Journal of Philosophy,* Vol. 50 (1963), pp. 578–579, with the permission of the editors.

   (d) "Three Replies", consisting of "Foreword" and "Comments", *Journal of Philosophy,* Vol. 63 (1966), pp. 63, 328–331; reprinted with the permission of the editors.

   (e) "Two More Replies" was published as "Two Replies", *Journal of Philosophy,* Vol. 64 (1967), pp. 286–287; reprinted with the permission of the editors.

7. "Review of Reichenbach's *Elements of Symbolic Logic*", *Philosophical Review,* Vol. 58 (1948), pp. 100–102, with the permission of the editors.

8. "Snowflakes and Wastebaskets", a talk given at a memorial meeting for C. I. Lewis at Harvard University, April 23, 1964; not previously published.

IX. Likeness

1. "Order from Indifference", a revised version, with 7 (Postscript) added, of a talk given to the Psychology Colloquium of the University of Pennsylvania, probably in the middle 1950s, though I have no record of the date. Not previously published.

2. "Seven Strictures on Similarity", from *Experience and Theory* (Lawrence Foster and J. W. Swanson, eds.), Boston: University of Massachusetts Press (1970). Reprinted with the permission of the University of Massachusetts Press and the editors; copyright 1970 by the University of Massachusetts Press.

X. Puzzle

"The Truth-Tellers and the Liars", first published anonymously in the *Boston Post*, June 8, 1931, p. 1, cols. 1 and 2. My solution with explanation was published in the same paper, June 9, 1931, p. 15, cols. 6 and 7.

Name Index

459